D0317678

Education Limited

TITLES OF RELATED INTEREST

Resistance through rituals: youth subcultures in post-war Britain
CCCS (eds)

Culture, media, language: working papers in cultural studies
edited by Stuart Hall *et al*.

The Empire strikes back: race and racism in 70s Britain

Working class culture: studies in history and theory
edited by John Clarke *et al*.

Off Centre: feminism and cultural studies
edited by J Stacey, S Franklin and C Lury

Education Limited

Schooling, training and the New Right in England since 1979

Education Group II
Department of Cultural Studies
University of Birmingham

London
UNWIN HYMAN
Boston Sydney Wellington

Published by the Academic Division of
Unwin Hyman Ltd
15/17 Broadwick Street, London W1V 1FP, UK

Unwin Hyman Inc.,
955 Massachusetts Avenue, Cambridge, Mass. 02139, USA

Allen & Unwin (Australia) Ltd,
8 Napier Street, North Sydney, NSW 2060, Australia

Allen & Unwin (New Zealand) Ltd in association with the
Port Nicholson Press Ltd,
Compusales Building, 75 Ghuznee Street, Wellington 1, New Zealand

First published in 1991

British Library Cataloguing in Publication Data

Education limited : schooling, training and the New Right in
    England since 1979.
    1. England. Education. Reform, history – Political aspects
    I. Education Group II   II. University of Birmingham
    Department of Cultural Studies
    379.42

    ISBN 0-04-445312-4
    ISBN 0-04-445312-2 pbk

Library of Congress Cataloging-in-Publication Data

Education limited : schooling, training and the New Right in England
    since 1979 / Education Group II. Department of Cultural Studies,
    University of Birmingham.
        p.   cm.
    Includes bibliographical references and index.
    ISBN 0-04-445312-4. – ISBN 0-04-445313-2 (pbk.)
    1. Education and state – Great Britain – History.   2. Politics and
education – Great Britain – History.   3. Educational sociology – Great
Britain.   4. Education, Secondary – Great Britain – History.
I. University of Birmingham.   Dept. of Cultural Studies.   Education
Group II.
LC93.G7E373   1990
379.41 – dc20   90-39783
                                                                CIP

Typeset in 10/12 Bembo by CentraCet, Cambridge and printed in Great Britain by
The University Press, Cambridge

Contents

Part Three: *Alternatives: Public education and a new professionalism*

Preface

After more than a decade of furious debate over educational policies and ideas, major institutional changes are being imposed. Under the 1988 Education Act, the powers and procedures of local education authorities (LEAs) are being reordered. Balances between 'partners' (the Department of Education and Science [DES], LEAs, teachers) tilt powerfully towards the state. New types of school are artificially implanted (invented? restored?) by 'philanthropic' alliances, where there is little desire for them. In existing institutions we face layer after layer of imposed tasks, novel drudgeries and imperative demands to account for ourselves. Whatever the outcome of the first election of the 1990s, the 1988 Act and the National Curriculum have set many conditions for the new phase, rather as the 1944 Act constrained the postwar reforms, though in a different direction. The 1944 Act could be turned into a charter for 'universal' public provision and local experimentation; the 1988 Act, though complex and ambiguous as we shall see, sets the scene for split provision and central curriculum control. If 1944 was informed by a heavily qualified universalism, 1988 is animated by the spirit of Education Ltd, Education-as-a-Business-Corporation: commercial in outlook, hierarchical in organization, 'limited' in liberality or extent – unless you pay for more. Even if 1992 brings in a Labour government, it will still be difficult, even if desirable, to restore public education to its pre-1979 state.

So those of us who believe in 'Education un-Limited' have to work *under* or *in* these new conditions, as well as *against* them. Freeing public education from the limits of its new ERA will involve a difficult, tangled kind of a struggle, with many traps and pitfalls: that of adopting Conservative aims along with the slogans; that of attempting to restore the recent past; that of believing that an alternative already waits in the wings, adequate without more rehearsals.

But there are important resources too. Hidden or misrecognized in the noisy rise of the New Right and the rather inglorious retreats of British social democracy have been other stories, especially the genesis of critical and reconstructive educational theories and practices. These have been closely connected with the politics of gender and race, with the new social movements of the 1960s to 1980s, and with changing class formations and experiences. At a more popular level increasing cultural diversity and fusion have created the possibility of new orientations to identity, culture and education. Already influencing LEA and school policies in partial ways – through equal opportunities, multiculturalism, anti-racism and special education, for example – these tendencies have often been checked by the viciousness and limited polemical accuracy of right-wing and governmental responses. The failure of the liberal educational 'mainstream', many administrators and teachers, and sections of the political left to recognize the significance of these tendencies has been just as disabling.

Yet the New Politics and its critical theories are, we believe, the basis (but not the finished form) of the anti-Thatcherite alternative. Neither socialist nor labourist traditions are adequate, without major transformations, to found our social and educational alternatives. Modern movements – especially around gender, race and ethnicity, sexuality, age and 'ability/disability' – show that simple (usually class) models of domination or power are not adequate political guides any more. Their straightforward binary oppositions – class versus class – do not fit the social complexities. This is not to deny the continuing importance of class divisions in something like the old Marxist sense, though class divisions that are continually recomposed. Similarly, the notion that modern societies are uniform in terms of social identity and culture (or that somehow they ought to be) can no longer (if it ever could) be the basis of an adequate education policy and practice. The idea of a 'common culture' whether in its Conservative nationalist forms or as a democratic socialist objective does not take enough account of cultural heterogeneity and cosmopolitanism, in a society which draws its cultural traditions from across the globe. Existing professional practices and loyalties have likewise to be reformed. Making public education really popular, deserving of widely based support across an extremely diverse and deeply divided people, involves a lot more than restoration. Were it possible, this would only restore Education Limited or Unpopular in its older and more familiar forms.

Many of the educational changes of the last ten years, including the 1988 Act, can be traced to the impact of 'Thatcherism' or (as we generally prefer it) 'The New Right', a political tendency we later take pains to define. A critique of New Right education is one way of developing alternatives, but critique itself often gets stuck in a kind of critical appreciation of Thatcherite *achievements*. It is more important today, and much easier as the project wavers, to analyse its *limits*: how New Right educational policies, for example, stay within the traditional horizons of the English political and cultural elite: 'the peculiarities of the English'. The New Right has shaped our modern dilemmas to a surprising degree, but it has also been shaped by histories and structures which its theorists give little credence to. The New Right faces contradictions it cannot grasp, let alone solve. There are corresponding opportunities for the oppositions.

These arguments – the formative power of New Right ideas and policies, but also their limits and contradictions; the rise of new social movements and critical theories as sources of alternatives; the underlying historical trend towards a more heterogeneous and culturally diverse society; the process of the recomposition of classes, especially around public institutions; the importance of policies which grasp the educational implications of cultural difference and power (e.g. equal opportunities and anti-racism); the impossibility of restoration; the importance of expanding public education and strengthening it, but also of reworking professional and educational practices – are our leading themes. Our first title for this book was *Education Still Possible*. We hope this optimism comes through under the new one too.

In Part One, we engage with the New Right as an educational tendency: philosophically as a movement of ideas; practically as policy and strategy. On a narrow front, as a strategy which seeks to out-manoeuvre opponents and put together alliances, we argue it has been rather successful. More broadly, in relation to the history and structural problems of English society and education, we argue it fails. This evaluation of New Right education – as theory, as politics, as policy, and as a 'modernizing' solution – is the concern of the first three chapters of the book. Chapter 1 places the New Right project in the context of a longer comparative history of educational peculiarities in England. Chapter 2, necessarily the longest in the book, is a detailed explanatory history of New Right policy. Chapter 3 analyses New Right theory from the point of view of a (male, white) professional influenced by the New Politics of the 1970s. It constructs a critical dialogue between neo-liberalism and neo-conservatism on one side and modern critical theories on the other.

New Right education (as represented by the Black Papers, the voucher lobby, or the Hillgate Group) has not monopolized education debate. Movements for educational modernization, far from attacking the progressivism of the 1960s and 1970s, claim to extend it. These modernizing impulses, best represented in the educational programmes of the late-lamented Manpower Services Commission (MSC), cannot simply be identified with Thatcherism, though they have, on occasion, been politically connected to it. Is educational modernization of this kind our best bet as an 'alternative' then? How does it relate to the social politics of the 1970s and 1980s and the continuing concern with social inequalities and power? These issues are explored in Chapter 4 and the questions posed more fully in the introduction to Part One.

In Part Two, we shift our focus to educational agents and their choices. What has it been like teaching, studying, or parenting under the new conditions, under 'choices that are not your own' (Leon Rosselson, 'I Didn't Mean It', Fuse Records, 1988)? How are teachers, students, parents and others making sense of recent changes and what new possibilities are arising from their responses? An exploration of the experiences of some students and trainees, some teachers and parents adds an 'ethnographic' dimension to the book. We stress the themes of agency and of choice because agency has often been neglected in left accounts of education, and because 'choice' is a key notion for the New Right. How is 'choice' actually manifested in day-to-day educational practice? How real is it? If choice is circumscribed, how none the less do people exercise real agency, in important if conditional ways, making their own world?

Since everyday situations are so specific, we proceed, in Part Two, by case study. We have tried to cover as many educational sites or stages as possible, but our own experiences are necessarily limited, in ways we explore below. The case studies include the transition from secondary school to the Youth Training Scheme (YTS) (Chapter 5); the experience of YTS, primarily from the point of view of 'trainees' (Chapter 6), the interaction of student experiences and curriculum categories in further education (FE) (Chapter 7), the choices before teachers in a progressive secondary school (chapter 8), and the dilemmas of working-class parents and middle-class teachers enabled temporarily to exercise a rather fuller set of choices than those envisaged under the 1988 Act (Chapter 9).

It is hard in local and 'ethnographic' work, which grapples with the rush and muddle of everyday life, to come out with clear guidelines or a unified programme of reform. Each writer in this section was asked to point to the practical implications of his findings. We pull out some common themes and findings in the introductions to Parts Two and Three. Some of the arguments are taken up in Chapter 10.

Since New Right policies do not solve the main problems, but create difficulties of their own, Part Three focuses on alternative structures and practices. We believe that alternatives are actually emerging all the time, in scattered, piecemeal, often mutually opposed ways. On the one hand alternatives are arising from the best elements, or the worst problems, in our everyday practice: here a teacher organizing students to invent and act out a drama on the subject of racism in and around the school; there a committee or working party wrestling with equal opportunities and the school curriculum. On these occasions, we badly need to link with others who are attempting similar tasks and in this a more explicit theoretical framework is often helpful. (This is a different model of educational change from the usual one in which innovations flow 'downwards' from educational theorists, academic locations and 'educationists'). But sometimes, and this goes for 'theorists' especially, we need to turn theoretical arguments into practical results – having, as they say, the courage of our convictions. At a theoretical level there has, in the 1970s and 1980s, been an extraordinary explosion of critical theory and innovative research (the latter too seldom fully accomplished perhaps) especially on questions of culture, social relations, knowledge and identity. Yet its full implications for daily practice in education have only just begun to be explored.

The difficulty of bridging the gap between 'theory' and 'practice' is illustrated in our own volume, especially in the relations of Parts One and Two. Even in our own group, there was a tendency to polarize on these lines. For these reasons we hope that all our chapters will be read as part of the search for alternatives, not just the three rather particular essays with which we end our book. Chapter 10 is an essay on redefining educational professionalism. Chapter 11 argues for expanding public education. Chapter 12 takes the form of reflections on personal educational practice. Part Three as a whole engages with the three essential areas of reform: changes in educational organization and structure; changes in professional and educational practices and outlooks; and changes of a personal kind.

A word about our aims in relation to the contexts of readership. We are especially keen to be read by teachers, lecturers, public professionals and students – while recognizing discrepancies of interest and language. We also want to contribute to the emergence, among these groups and others, of alternatives to New Right solutions. When alternatives not to the government's liking do emerge, ferocious public campaigns are launched. Some run the gamut of Conservative crusades: spotted by some local Conservative moralist, misrecognized in the press, stigmatized by the minister, dealt with in some new regulation. The opening up of questions of sexually based identity in the schools, a crucial issue for everyone, is one example; the counter-strikes against anti-racism are another. In a similar way, those patterns of unfairness, organized around class differences which have been recognized since the 1930s, are marginalized by the new emphases on training and vocationalism. Though the publishing of books seems frail in the face of all this cultural power, and is certainly limited in terms of audience, it may none the less play a part in developing alternative definitions and practices. As academic authors we acquire some limited access to the public domain. We can attempt to install criteria of social recognition different from those of Conservative campaigns. As Thatcherite hegemony cracks and splinters, such minor subversions accumulate. Anyway, we hope our project gives back some positive recognitions to the dispersed forces of the post-Thatcher future and gives heart to colleagues and allies.

Education Groups, with changing memberships, have met regularly in the Centre for Contemporary Cultural Studies/Department of Cultural Studies since the late 1970s. It is therefore a bit of a cheek to describe ourselves as Education Group II. We probably should be Education Group VIII or IX, but this would mystify bibliographers even more. Nor is it possible to acknowledge all contributions to the decade's conversations. Yet some of our essays, perhaps the whole project, bear marks of, say, Education Group

III when the focus was on 'training', 'youth' and FE, or VI when we were puzzling over earlier 'Josephite' forms of New Right policy. We do offer thanks to all those who have contributed to the long discussions. The larger context here is a tradition or 'school' of work, cultural studies at Birmingham, which has taken education, Thatcherism, ethnographies of schooling and youth, and issues of culture and power among its chief concerns. In particular this book is in dialogue with the work of the first Education Group, which published *Unpopular Education* in 1980.

In some ways our relation to this book is simple. *Unpopular Education* was mainly about the limits of Labour or social-democratic educational traditions; the rise of the New Right was a kind of historical rebuke to that tradition. *Education Limited* concerns the ten years from 1979 to 1989 and focuses on the New Right. With the exception of a brief section in Chapter 11, we pay little attention to Labour. For this reason, if no other, we might insist the books be read as a pair!

Of course, the relation is more complicated than this; this book makes some explicit criticisms of *Unpopular Education* (see especially pp. 31–4 below) and several implicit ones (e.g. *Unpopular Education*'s lack of ethnography and neglect of 'local' conditions generally). We cannot claim to have solved the problem of how to relate large-scale and small-scale studies, but at least we work at the different levels: international comparisons, national policies, local conditions and microscopic dilemmas! In the end, however, the continuities with *Unpopular Education* are probably more important than the differences. The first book ended with the search for a 'new popular politics of education', and here we are again, ten years later, a different group (with one common member only) but a similar agenda. Some of the parameters of a popular alternative have become clearer in the meantime. But the main continuity may lie in the cultural studies approach. Although this is a book about education, it is heavily influenced by all the modern debates about social difference, cultural diversity and power which are the hallmark of the cultural studies tradition, and its most vital political connection.

Some features of our collective authorship, though obvious to careful readers, need stressing at the outset. We are an all-male, all-white group, employed in schools, colleges, polytechnics and universities. We can fairly claim to be practitioners not theorists only, but our practices are particular of course. All of us are teachers (rather than educational managers); all have recent experience of higher education and research if only through the group. Typically, as men, we are involved in the education of older age groups, where professional prestige also, unfairly, tends to accrue. We cover in our recent employment histories, secondary schools (three members), further education colleges (two members), youth-work training and teacher education (one member), and polytechnic and university teaching (three members). We are all active, in one way or in several, in the politics of schools and/or colleges – as fathers, for instance, or governors, or members of college or school working-parties. Typically, however, we have little direct knowledge of primary education, adult education, or special education, and this is reflected in serious absences in this volume.

There are more complex and subtle ways in which our identities have influenced our writing. We are all relatively well-established professionals (anyway by the time this volume was completed!). This predisposes us to take an insider's view of education. It undoubtedly underpins some of our hostility to the populism, or anti-professionalism, of New Right policy. This is one reason why we have spent a lot of energy in trying to be critical of the limits of our professional identities, but also, in the face of Conservative denigration, to rescue some positives too. In this we have often been aided by many other aspects of our lives or 'backgrounds'.

We also have a particular relation to feminism and anti-racism, two key sources of alternatives. This relation is, in some ways, an external or abstract one. It easily slips into romanticism or neglect. We do not have the *same* relation to struggles around gender or race as we would if we were women and or if we were black. Our lives do not force on us the same daily consciousness of injustice, and, where we have acquired some 'consciousness', we have considerable interests in forgetting! When we admit to the importance of the issues and try to act on them, we know our responses look hesitant and will (always) be judged inadequate. There is no way that we can avoid having egg on our faces. We do not say this to excuse or to exclude ourselves. We are necessarily involved in all these forms of power and in more or less active *relationships* with 'women's politics' and struggles around ethnicity and race. Challenges and insights from these points of view have changed, are changing, how we understand our lives, ourselves, our relations to others, and our professional practices.

The form of this book sits uneasily between a text produced as if by a single author and an edited series of essays. It is more than just a collection. The project took its present form about five years ago, though members have joined and left the group since. Meeting once a fortnight or so, on an evening after 'work', it would be surprising if we had not learned from each other, developed a common position, shared a vocabulary. Book and chapter outlines were discussed and first, second and even further drafts appraised by the group as a whole. The fact that some of us have written two or even three articles owes more to time and opportunity for research and writing than anything else. On the other hand, the book resembles a collection in that we have not removed all hints of difference and expect that some remain. We hope we have already introduced, in this preface, some main points of convergence. These are re-stated, as the book proceeds, in the introduction to each of the three parts. It may be useful to refer back to the preface and the part introductions at later stages in the reading. We have tried to make each chapter reasonably self-contained, however, since we realize that selection will be a common way of reading.

We would like to thank Claire L'Enfant, now at Routledge, and Sarah Roberts-West, her successor at Unwin Hyman, for easing the transfer to our new publisher; and Rajinder Bhogal and Ann Lane for helping with communications, which have latterly spanned six cities in two continents. A special thank-you also to Madeleine Arnot whose reader's report on the first version of our text was extraordinarily thorough and full of valuable critical insights. We have tried to respond to her comments, though we recognize often inadequately. Thanks also to Paul Johnson for compiling the index. As for the typing, it was done by ourselves, on machines of varying levels of technical sophistication (manual, electric and electronic) and variable compatibility. This appearance of 'autonomy', technical 'mastery' and general Thatcherite 'freedom' is totally illusory, however, because of the people and the personal and social relationships on whom we each depend.

Education Group II:
James Avis,
Phil Carspecken,
Peter Clason,
Andy Green,
Bob Hollands,
Richard Johnson,
Dan McEwan,
Andrew Vickers

Department of Cultural Studies,
University of Birmingham,
January 1990

Part One
New Right Education
History, evaluation, critique

Introduction to Part One
New Right education: history, evaluation, critique

Our main aim in Part One is to throw light on the ideas and practices of the New Right: more specifically, on educational Thatcherism, or was it 'Bakerism'? – a not inconsiderable difference sometimes. This involves a detailed history of policy, including the genesis of ideas and aims, and the curious, devious dramas of their implementation.

There are difficult issues of approach here. Until very recently, it was possible to be so impressed by Thatcherism's *successes* that its *limits* were not seriously sought. This goes for loyalist accounts of course (e.g. Graham and Clarke, 1986; Green, 1987), but for some critical versions too (e.g. Hall and Jacques, 1983; Hall, 1988). There have been good reasons for critical appreciation of Thatcherism on the left. It has been vital to gauge its strengths and to incite the left to match them; critical to insist on the cultural dimensions of struggle, in which the right has excelled since the mid-1970s. For much of the 1980s, however, a sense of Thatcherism as limited, contradictory, transient and vulnerable was lost and in this the search for alternatives was not well served. This is why, in this volume, we stress evaluation and critique. Just as the New Right arose out of arguments against what it calls socialism, so the new political movement will be formed in a critical or dialectical relation to the right. Appraisal has to be more profound and more appreciative of strengths than most anti-Thatcherite polemic has been. But we need also to seek the limits. Does Thatcherism work? Does it produce socially desirable outcomes? What are its weaknesses compared with the critical alternatives that are beginning to form up? How can this engagement be sharpened?

There are two main ways of developing a critique. We can track back from immediate ideas and events and view them in broader contexts. What do the years of New Right dominance look like in the context of a longer history and the recurrent features it reveals? How far have New Right contributions conformed to English peculiarities? How far have they transcended them? How does English education compare with that of other First World countries?

The second approach is to analyse New Right ideas and policies more in their own terms. Are the ideas themselves coherent or are they, as has often been argued, fundamentally contradictory? In particular can 'neo-liberal' faith in the market be squared with 'neo-conservative' belief in the strong state and a unified national culture? How does this contradiction show up in the policies? Do ideas match practices, or do the obstinate realities of social forces divert and distort impossible ideals? Are the ideals desirable anyway? This approach requires close attention to New Right theory and to the way policies are inflected by historical conditions and by opposition.

Chapter 1, Andy Green's 'The peculiarities of English education', adopts the first critical strategy, viewing New Right education historically and comparatively. It is important that this essay is about England, not about Scotland and Wales, where structural and cultural patterns have been different. The reading of New Right policy with which the essay ends, necessary in order to make the connections between past and present, is provisional, filled out in Chapter 2 especially.

The second chapter develops our first sketch in more detail. Like Chapter 1, Chapter 2 is in dialogue with *Unpopular Education*. In the first few pages of the piece the differences are stated explicitly. In general 'A new road to serfdom' is an attempt to combine the analysis of political and ideological struggles and conditions ('the history of hegemony') in the manner of *Unpopular Education* and *Policing the Crisis* with a close-up but still critical account of the derivation and course of policy, more characteristic of a political history. The chapter ends with a detailed assessment of the 1988 Education Act, drawing on the social theories of the 1970s, to account for its main contradictions.

As the title implies, 'My New Right education' (Chapter 3) extends the definition of education well beyond the work of colleges and schools. At issue, really, is an assessment of the New Right as an ideological move-ment, in relation to some of the resources of opposition. This argument links the three main themes: the 'anti-social ideas' of the New Right; the relation between Thatcherite politics and the public professionals (teachers and others); and the centrality of the new social movements and their critical theories to the political dynamics of the 1980s. Both 'the New Politics' and the public professions are viewed as key antagonists of Thatcherism, as important as Labour and older formations of the left as sources of alternatives. These themes are focused through an autobiograph-ical lens, a way of writing that owes much to the new movements too.

Chapter 4 develops the question of 'alternatives' further. In Chapter 2 Richard Johnson argues that the New Right's hostility to progressivism gave a predominantly traditional twist to its curriculum politics. In Chapter 4, James Avis looks at 'the strange fate' of progressivism in the meantime.

Our choice of further education and training here is certainly related to the competencies of our group, but has value for our argument too. The Manpower Services commission (MSC) and the Further Education Unit (FEU) were among the main agencies through which 'the new vocationalism' or 'the training paradigm' were disseminated in the 1970s and 1980s, a theme first picked up in *Unpopular Education*. In this approach progressivist themes were fused with those of 'training', 'skills', 'employability' and 'enterprise'. Ways of thinking about the curriculum, first generated in those sectors nearest to employment (FE and the training schemes), were canvassed as models for the whole education system. New versions of progressivism emerged, based on further not primary education (the classic location of progressivism), and with a different ideological character. For a while, in the 1970s, it looked as though the new paradigm would become dominant. Some of us were predicting this as late as 1985. In fact, the struggle between modernizing the curriculum in 'enterprising ways' and restoring 'the grammar school' has been an extraordinarily extended one – a key contradiction on the right. The delayed dominance of the grammar school models, reinforced by the National Curriculum, however, has opened the way for claims that the new fusion of vocationalism and progressivism is an appropriate curriculum politics for the left. Chapter 4 is written as a warning against this strategy.

1

The peculiarities of English education

Andy Green

British education, and more specifically education in England and Wales, is widely regarded to be in a state of crisis. This situation was first diagnosed, and some would say created, in the early 1970s with a campaign against 'progressive' education inspired by right-wing politicians and ideologues and effectively raised into a public issue by the press. It was taken up by Callaghan's Labour government in the so-called 'Great Debate' which conceded ground to the popular belief that school standards and discipline were deteriorating and that education was failing to respond to the needs of industry (see Chapter 3). Since then the older progressive ideals of comprehensive education have been subject to sustained attack from various quarters, education budgets have been slashed and repeated efforts have been made by Conservative governments to transform the whole basis of English education. Governments, right-wing pressure groups and quasi-government agencies like the Manpower Services Commission (MSC) have repeatedly argued that our education system is failing, not least in comparison with its overseas counterparts, in its allegedly poor performance in preparing children for the modern world of technology.

This crisis, graphically manifested in deteriorating school buildings, low teacher morale, the breakdown of policy consensus, and the real problems of pupil disenchantment and consequent early school leaving, has been variously analysed by educationists of the left and of the right. The right has blamed it on the teacher-led progressive policies of the 1960s and early 1970s in particular and more generally has seen it as a demonstration of the inadequacy of the statist social–democratic policies which have underpinned the welfare state as a whole in the postwar era. The left has tended to see it as part of a more widespread crisis in education which has affected all western countries. The egalitarian ideals of the 1960s had been shown to be unrealizable within capitalist societies structured by class, racial and gender inequalities. Sociologists like Bowles and Gintis in America, Boudon and Bourdieu in France and Bernstein and Halsey in England had effectively demonstrated how little progressive educational policies could transform basic inequalities in society, and in so doing contributed in no small part to the crisis of confidence in socialist educational policies. If the limits of educational progress in western nations in the 1970s were generally understood within this pessimistic framework, the further deterioration of education in England has been attributed to financial retrenchment and the divisive policies pursued by Thatcherism. Socialist debate has thus revolved around the inherent problems facing egalitarian educational policies in all capitalist countries and in particular in periods like our own when a right-wing government rules with such strong parliamentary majorities. Little attention has thus been given to the historically specific problems of English education.

This chapter will not seek to dispute the real limits to egalitarian education reform in capitalist countries, although these are perhaps some-what more relative than many would believe. However, it will seek to show that specific historical conditions in England have left a legacy of peculiarly deep and wide-ranging educational problems which are not shared to the same degree by all western countries. Education in England is, and has long been, backward in a number of ways, compared with its US and continental counterparts. The origins of these problems do not lie specifically in the social-democratic policies of the postwar period as the neo-liberals of the New Right would argue. Rather they go much further back into the nineteenth century when a national education first emerged under the particular conditions of the British liberal state. The defining characteristic of nineteenth-century education in England was the tradition of voluntarism which was the only form of national education allowable under the liberal state. This singular education ideology has continued in a modified form into the modern period and has continued to undermine efforts to create a viable system of public education to this day.

English education in the nineteenth century was uniformly backward by comparison with other leading continental and American states. Contemporary reformers were well aware of this fact and made frequent reference to our comparative disadvantages. From the declaration of Henry Brougham's Select Committee of 1818 'that England is the worst educated country in Europe', to Balfour's assertion in 1902 that 'England is behind all continental rivals in education', the verdict was monotonously and almost unanimously the same (Hansard, 28 June 1820, c.49; Maclure, 1986, p.125).

England was exceptionally slow to develop a national system of elementary schools. By the mid-century when Holland, Switzerland, the German and northern US states had achieved more or less universal enrolment in elementary schools, England and Wales still had barely over half the age group in attendance. Secondary education was slow to reform itself and technical schooling was almost non-existent. England had no public education system until 1870 and free and compulsory elementary schooling was not fully implemented until the next century. A unified central authority for education was not created until 1899, almost a century after France and Germany had created theirs. State secondary schooling was not instituted until 1902, exactly 100 years after Napoleon had created the *lycées* in France and almost as long since the USA and the German states created public secondary schools.

The origins of national education systems in continental Europe lay in the mercantilist and state-building policies of the absolutist monarchs of the eighteenth century. Maria Theresa in Austria and Frederick the Great in Prussia first introduced state funding for schools and legislation on attendance to create an education system which would furnish the military and bureaucracy with trained recruits and school the masses in acceptable beliefs. During and immediately after the revolutionary era national education systems were consolidated through state action in Germany, France and elsewhere as part of the intensely nationalistic drive to promote national development and as an integral element in the process of consolidating the bourgeois state. Development occurred differently in the North American states which had no history of absolutism and which, like England, sought to avoid the strong central state. Public education in the USA developed in a more decentralized and 'democratic' manner, owing much to the populist rhetoric of American capitalism, but it was equally influenced by a nationalistic drive towards development, and by the mid-century most northern states had their own education systems in accordance with the federal structure of government (Kaestle, 1983).

Alone amongst the major European powers England delayed creating a national education system throughout the century. The protracted conflict over educational development has often been put down to religious divisions: the Anglican Church was unwilling to allow anyone but itself to control education and Dissent would not support state intervention in education if this meant consolidating the control of the church. Underlying this real problem, however, were more profound structural obstacles to educational advance. In the early decades of the century aristocratic and gentry opposition to popular education, which it was feared would put the masses above their station in life, provided a serious obstacle in a country where the landed class still controlled the political apparatus. A rather weak bourgeois hegemony within the state apparatus, which persisted even after the reforms of the 1830s, continued to provide an impediment to the realization of middle-class aims in education. Britain's early and successful industrialization also paradoxically had a negative effect on educational development. First, it removed that most powerful incentive for educational development which had fired the continental reformers, that is, the desire to catch up economically. Secondly, it encouraged an enormously complacent view of technical education. Since Britain had achieved an industrial revolution through the technical accomplishments of largely self-taught engineers, it was wrongly concluded that further economic development had no need of anything but the old empirical and *ad hoc* methods of scientific and technical learning. Thirdly, it created an enormous thirst for child labour in industry which forced working-class parents to allow their children to forfeit education to provide an additional wage and which set the manufacturing class against the extension of working-class education.

However, dwarfing all other reasons for England's slow advance in education, was the effect of the dominant liberal *laissez-faire* ideology. Political economy taught that the individual pursuit of self-interest in the market was the most legitimate way to promote the common good, and that intervention by the state should be limited to the defence of the realm, the protection of private property and the maintenance of law and order. The liberal ideas of Adam Smith actually had their origins in the nature of the state in the eighteenth century. It was the victory of decentralized gentry rule after the settlement of 1688 which laid the basis of the distinctive liberal forms of the British capitalist state. Jealous of their independence, the capitalist gentry had effectively limited the powers of the state in the name of market liberalism. By the early nineteenth century the ideology of economic individualism and the minimal state was deeply pervasive not only amongst the gentry but also within the middle class for whom it was a crusading creed. Even amongst the working class, hostility to state action, where the state was not under democratic control, was intense. Britain thus never developed the Jacobin tradition of reform through the command state, or what Marx and Gramsci referred to as the 'universalizing' bourgeois state. Successful early industrial development occurring 'organically' without state intervention and within a liberal order merely entrenched the belief in the benevolence of economic individualism. By the mid-century, as Eric Hobsbawm has remarked (1969), Britain had come about as close to a pure *laissez-faire* order as any capitalist country has ever done.

Educational reform could thus occur only within the framework of the liberal state. To the majority of the middle class this meant that state intervention in education was an affront to freedom and liberal values and created an unnecessary tax burden on the 'creators of wealth'. The only group to argue strongly for the state to intervene in developing a national education system were the Benthamite utilitarians and they did so only with the greatest equivocation. Like the political economists whom he followed, Bentham was essentially an individualist. Society to him was a mere 'fiction' just as to today's modern neo-liberals 'society does not exist'. State intervention in education could only be justified as an exception to liberal principles, since, although it was generally believed that the free market would spontaneously achieve the common good, this could only occur if individuals recognized their own best interests in political economy, and this self-evidently the working class would not always do. State elementary education to Bentham and other middle-class reformers was thus a means to teach the working class the merits of bourgeois ideology.

However, the Benthamites failed to create an effective alliance around the campaign for national education. Their arguments were contradictory and they could advocate state intervention only in the most negative and limiting terms. They lacked the revolutionary tradition which advocated education as a 'human right' and a means of democratic advance, and what they offered the working class was so blatantly a vehicle for their own instrumental class aims that it never achieved the support that middle-class campaigns received, for instance, in the United States. The result was an impasse in state educational reform that lasted until the late 1860s.

In accordance with the liberal tradition education thus developed less through state action than through private and philanthropic initiatives, a uniquely English form of development commonly known as voluntarism. The mainspring of popular education became the voluntary societies, first the nonconformist British and Foreign Schools Society and soon afterwards the Anglican National Society. These institutions, which were in fact loose confederations of local groups, pioneered the monitorial schools, the first form of mass education in England. Secondary education was also organized according to the voluntary principle. The old public schools and grammar schools existed by virtue of ancient endowments and the conditions attached to them but were effectively controlled by the local gentry. When the middle class sought to provide education in accordance with their own needs they did not turn to the state but rather substituted their own private schools in place of the inadequate traditional institutions.

By the middle of the century England thus still had no national system of education and such state interventions as had occurred took exceptionally weak and permissive forms. Alone amongst European nations England had no statutory framework governing school attendance, the licensing of schools and teachers and the nature of the curriculum. Less than a third of educational expenditures came from the state, and the Education Department, which had been set up to administer these, had very limited powers bearing no comparison with the unified central educational bureaucracies in continental Europe (West, 1975, p.41). The apparatus of school inspection was relatively slender and had insufficient authority to affect the conduct of education much. The first attempt to co-ordinate the curriculum on a national basis was not made until Robert Lowe introduced his infamous 'payment by results' system but this was more a form of accountancy than an attempt to promote good educational practice.

The lack of a central authority in education, which many considered to be its chief deficiency, had numerous consequences. Not only did it mean that the existing voluntary systems lacked co-ordination between their various parts, but also that educational services that could not occur through voluntary initiative simply did not exist. Teacher training developed late and then according to a typically English system of apprenticeship which lacked the rigour and spread of the continental 'normal schools'. The status of teachers remained extraordinarily low even by contemporary standards. Whereas France and Germany had developed a national examination system in the Napoleonic era with the *baccalauréat* and *Abitur* certificates operating as a means of ensuring 'meritocratic' selection for public office, England had no equivalent system and entry to the civil service was not placed on a fully competitive footing until 1870, if then. There were no national exams until the emergence of the Oxford and Cambridge 'local examinations' in the 1860s and, as their name suggests, it was some time before these gained a genuinely national status. Lastly, perhaps most serious, England did not develop the trade schools and polytechnics which were another typical product of state intervention on the continent and which became such a powerful instrument in later economic development. Technical education remained dependent instead on the empirical and rule-of-thumb methods of the workshop and the apprenticeship, and when the state did intervene to improve technical training, as it did with its evening class programmes, it left the system intact with the consequence that technical education remained normatively part-time, anti-theoretical, low status and entirely marginalized from mainstream education.

An effective campaign for national education was finally launched in the 1860s as the dangers of an undereducated work-force became increasingly apparent. Superior continental education was acknowledged to be a factor behind Britain's diminishing industrial lead, and with the inevitable extension of the franchise the middle class became increasingly keen, as Lowe put it, 'to compel our future masters to learn their letters'. Coincidently, the increasing contradictions between 'letting alone' and necessary social reform undermined the credibility of pure *laissez-faire* doctrines and hostility to state intervention was waning. The result of these various forces was the Education Act of 1870 which is rightly seen as the beginnings of state education in England and Wales. However, the Act was never more than a compromise with the old voluntary system. It instituted neither free, universal nor compulsory elementary education and although it brought in the board schools which did 'fill up the gaps in the voluntary system' as its architect, Forster, had intended, it left the voluntary sector as the dominant force in the system (Murphy, 1972, p. 39). Secondary schools remained almost entirely independent of public control and were not brought into any connection with the elementary schools which provided the sole means of education for the working class.

The education system which emerged by the last decades of the century was characterized above all by its extreme class segmentation and its singular lack of systematic co-ordination. Secondary schools had remained fiercely independent and although the Taunton Inquiry had recommended that they be inspected by the state, the influence of the prestigious Headmasters' Conference on the Tory establishment had been sufficient for Disraeli to abolish the commissioners whose responsibility it had been and replace them by a toothless charity commission, thus ensuring their continuing autonomy as schools for the ruling class. Technical education was supervised by yet another government department which had little connection with the Education Department responsible for elementary schools and thus there were three separate state authorities for education. The state of administration in this still quasi-voluntary system was, according to the comparative historian Margaret Archer, little short of chaotic, and England had less integration in its educational provision than any other European country (Archer, 1979).

The Acts of 1899 and 1902 finally instigated a unified educational administration in the state sector and brought the first state secondary schools. However, the deeply unpopular Conservative legislation was framed in such a way as to maintain maximum autonomy for the powerful independent interests in education, and to preserve the most rigid class barriers between educational sectors. The voluntary societies were given rate support for their elementary schools in exchange for local authority representation on their governing bodies. By 1902 the voluntary schools still outnumbered the state elementary schools by more than two to one and this measure ensured their predominance for some years to come (Archer, 1979, p. 14). Independent secondary schools, though subject to state inspection, were also allowed to maintain maximum autonomy. Balfour's Act also ensured the continuing division between working-class elementary and middle-class secondary schooling. By limiting the local authority schools to a maximum age of 15 years it effectively killed off the popular higher grade schools through which progressive education boards had provided a surrogate form of secondary education for the working class. The new state grammar schools included only a limited number of scholarships to assist working-class families with fees and under Robert Morant the curriculum was cast in an 'academic' mould, along public school lines, thus emphasizing the barriers to working-class entry. Elementary education for the working class was still in no way articulated with the secondary sector, which continued to be conceived as a middle-class preserve.

What had characterized the English liberal tradition in education throughout the nineteenth century had been the singular absence of any strong and concerted state action to bring about wholesale reforms in education. The want of this had delayed the achievement of universal mass schooling for half a century after other comparable states and had prolonged the existence of an archaic structure of classical secondary schooling for just as long.

When a national system was finally introduced, it retained many of the distinctive features of the voluntary tradition. Powerful local interests were preserved at the expense of a more integrated public system, and so lacking in coherence was the whole that many have wondered whether it deserved the title of system at all. The Bryce Commission had celebrated the English educational tradition for its 'freedom, variety and elasticity' (Maclure, 1986, p. 147) but frequently in practice elasticity had meant *ad hoc* and unplanned development; variety had meant class differentiation; and freedom had meant the unchecked licence of the powerful to provide education solely in their own interests. A more accurate characterization of the English tradition was later made by R. H. Tawney (1931, p. 142): 'the hereditary curse of English education', he wrote, 'has been its organization along the lines of social class.'

If the nineteenth century represented a period of almost uniform educational backwardness in England relative to other major states, the comparative situation in this century has been considerably more complex. The patterns of education in all western industrial nations have tended in some degree towards convergence. The principle of a universal public system of education, free at the point of delivery and supported from taxation, has been increasingly adopted as the primary form of provision at all levels. Systematic teacher training and certification have been generalized, and in most countries all schools, whether public or private, are subject to state inspection. National examination systems have been developed, organized either by the state or by independent bodies recognized by the state.

The major issue in education throughout the century has been the democratization of schooling and the question of equality of opportunity for all students within each level of the school system. At different periods the frontier of educational development has thus shifted from elementary schools to secondary schools and now to tertiary education as struggles have been fought to make each of these a universal entitlement. Progress in this respect has often been slow and, as numerous postwar studies have shown, increasing access to education at different levels has not necessarily had much impact on equality of educational outcomes (Halsey, Heath and Ridge, 1980). More often it has simply amounted to shifting the goalposts so that, as one sector becomes universal, privileged groups simply increase their monopoly of the higher levels.

In most obvious respects English educational development has been more or less in line with developments in other western countries. In secondary education the United States has been in advance of other countries: first, in the provision of free secondary schooling and, second, in its levels of enrolment in that sector. By 1910 it already had 68 per cent of its 15-year-olds in high school and by 1950 the same proportion of 17-year-olds were in school. This compared with 31 per cent in Japan, 17 per cent in France and 10 per cent in England and Wales (Benn and Simon, 1972, p. 29; Lipset and Bendix, 1967, p. 94). However, most European countries have developed at a broadly similar rate. France adopted free secondary schooling in 1933, abolished it during the Vichy regime, and reintroduced it again after the Liberation. England and Wales and most other European countries adopted the same after the war. By the late 1950s enrolment rates in English secondary schools were similar to those in France and higher than in Germany (Ringer, 1979, p. 222). Comprehensive secondary education was adopted in Japan after the war, and became national policy in Sweden in 1962, in France in 1963 and in England in 1965. Full conversion to comprehensive lower secondary schooling in the state sector was completed in Sweden by 1969, in France by the early 1970s, and more or less in England by the late 1970s. By 1986, 90 per cent of local authority pupils in England were in non-selective schools (Chitty, 1987). Other countries like Germany, Austria and Switzerland are still only beginning to go comprehensive.

In certain other respects, however, the pattern of English education has remained exceptional. Three features stand out particularly by international comparisons. Technical education and training have remained markedly underdeveloped and undervalued. Successive governments since the last war have been aware of this, but it has proved to be a remarkably intractable problem and one that the present government has still arguably failed to rectify. Private schools have remained uniquely powerful and independent; a factor that no government has seriously tried to alter and which continues to mark out the English education system as one of the most elitist in the western world. Lastly, state education has developed in ways which are notably unsystematic and fragmented by comparison with equivalent continental systems. This last consideration is perhaps the most difficult to pin down or quantify but is probably the key to the other two. The origins of all these peculiarities can be traced back to the voluntary forms of nineteenth-century education, and demonstrate the persistence of the liberal legacy into the era of the welfare state.

The public schools are the most notorious of Britain's old institutional anachronisms and the most out of place in a modern, supposedly democratic society. They are probably the feature of our education which most baffles foreign observers. Even the name is incomprehensible to most people, apparently saying the exact opposite of what it actually means. To the majority of our own citizens they are hardly more intelligible. Television documentaries still find it necessary to present their strange rituals to audiences rather as they would life on another planet. E. M. Forster's laconic characterization still applies today – 'these extraordinary institutions', he wrote, 'are local' (Warner, 1945, p. 7). They are local not only to one country but also to one class within it. They are, in short, 'another country' in their own land.

The independent public schools have maintained a level of autonomy and prestige in England throughout the century that has no parallel anywhere else in the world. Whilst subject to nominal state inspection, they have managed to evade further regulation at every crucial stage in educational legislation throughout the century. The 1944 Butler Act left them intact and unaffected and comprehensive reform occurred as if they did not exist. They have now been exempt from all the proposals for national curricula and testing in the 1988 Education Act. In various ways their position has actually been enhanced, sometimes quite deliberately by Conservative governments. They have been accorded charity status which reduces their costs by exempting them from taxation; they can employ teachers trained at the expense of the state whilst making no financial contribution to this; their enrolments are increased by the numerous categories of military and state officials whose children can attend at the public expense, and, more recently, they have benefited in a similar fashion from the Assisted Places Scheme. Enrolments in independent secondary schools are currently on the increase with about 7 per cent of the age group now attending.

All western nations have retained some private secondary schools but England's are unique. In other countries the private schools exist in the main to satisfy minority and mainly religious groups. Where they are the preserve of social elites they provide an education which is socially exclusive but not necessarily academically superior to the state upper secondary schools. In England, however, a uniquely prestigious and influential private sector exists whose main purpose is to provide an intensive education for the children of the upper middle class which gives far better access to positions of influence, power and affluence than do other schools. The effects of this have not only been to provide the privileged with greater educational opportunities but also to damage the state sector. Not only do they siphon off a certain amount of talent from the state schools, but they also ensure the continued existence of a ruling class that has no direct personal interest in maintaining a good state system. As R. H. Tawney once remarked, state education has been largely run, for over a century, by people who have little real interest in it, and who would not dream of sending their children to its schools (Bishop, 1971, p. vii). The difference with other countries is profound. In Sweden, Japan and the USA the social and political elites are educated largely within the comprehensive state sector. Even in the more elitist systems of France and Germany, the ruling elites are mostly educated within the state sector and thus have an investment in it. England is exceptional in having an entirely segregated system of education for the elite within the private sector.

The corollary of a uniquely independent private sector has been a relatively weak commitment to a collective or public provision. The notion of education as a 'right' and a 'civic virtue', a matter for which there is a collective public responsibility, has been traditionally weak in a country noted for its individualist and *laissez-faire* culture. Although the idea of corporate or public responsibility has been considerably strengthened in the era of the welfare state, and has been central to the politics of social democracy, there has continued to be a sense in which the concept of the 'public realm' has been attenuated and impoverished by the power of an antecedent liberal philosophy which puts the individual above the community and opposes the use of the state as a developmental force.

Weak commitment to a collective form of provision has led to a loosely integrated structure of state schooling. Indeed, there is a sense in which England has never quite created a public system, and certainly not one which could win widespread confidence. Voluntary and church schools were never disbanded and still represent some 30 per cent of all secondary schools. Private examination bodies have never been replaced by a national apparatus, and no uniform system of public secondary schooling has ever been adopted. Efforts to impose national models on institutions have been strongly resisted and those kinds of rationalizations and standardized practices which are normally associated with the idea of a public education system have often not occurred. While permissive legislation allowed the multiplication of numerous types of secondary school within the comprehensive system, the absence of any legislation in the area has encouraged the growth of an extraordinarily diverse and fragmented structure of post-16 institutions. Uniquely amongst European states Britain did not implement a national core curriculum for secondary schools when these were restructured along comprehensive lines. The final adoption of a 'national curriculum' in the 1988 Act still exempts the private schools and its emphasis on curriculum differentiation arguably disqualifies it from the term 'national'.

This lack of systematic integration in English schooling not only creates a certain amount of confusion and inefficiency but, more importantly, has meant that despite the creation of a comprehensive structure in education there are so many distinctions and inequalities between different types of school, curriculum and examination that no normative social expectations of educational achievement for all children of different ages have taken root. This has no doubt encouraged the high rates of early school-leaving for which England has been historically renowned. State schools have remained in a way unpopular institutions. Attitudes towards them still reflect that complex of paternalism, deference and working-class defensiveness that was the product of a nineteenth-century education provided by the ruling class for the social and political control of the masses.

The state education system in England and Wales has been traditionally characterized as one based on 'decentralized control'. This can be a most misleading term but the official definition of it by the Department of Education and Science (DES) is 'A national service locally administered'

(Simon, 1988, p. 150). Official documents and typical commentaries on the post-1944 education system have frequently stressed the idea of 'partnership'. Educational control is said to be shared between the government, local education authorities (LEAs), school governing bodies and the teaching profession. If this notion has constituted part of the official ideology of the English tradition, it has also been close to the hearts of the teaching unions. The idea of decentralized control is closely related to the belief in teacher expertise and autonomy which constitutes the key motif of the ideology of teacher professionalism. Shirley Williams well summed up the traditional belief in remarks made in a speech in 1976. 'Among the splendours of the English system', she said, 'are its flexibility, its imagination, and the freedom of the teacher in the classroom' (Chitty, 1987, p. 21).

More concretely, decentralization is generally taken to refer to the tradition whereby the day-to-day running of schools and the implementation of national policies are delegated to the local authorities who in turn pass responsibility for curriculum and other matters to school heads. The DES, which spends only about 15 per cent of public funds for education, has been responsible for the broad allocation of resources, for the supply and training of teachers, and for issuing periodic guidance on curriculum matters. It has had no authority over determining pupil-teacher ratios, class sizes, or class contact hours for teachers; it has not had powers to distribute teachers between schools or to determine levels of capitation and, until the new Education Act, has had no powers as yet to enforce a national curriculum or any particular curriculum policies. Local education authorities have controlled expenditure on and the employment of teachers, in-service training, the closing and opening of schools (subject to ministerial approval) and the allocation of pupils between schools (Lauglo and Mclean, 1985, pp. 119–21). Headteachers in schools have generally been responsible for the design and delivery of the curriculum. The tradition of decentralized control has also meant that legislation and central directives on education have frequently been permissive rather than prescriptive. When the DES issued its circular 10/65 on comprehensive education it requested LEAs to draw up plans for comprehensive secondary schooling rather than instructing them to implement a particular plan. For all these reasons it is often said that English education is subject to less central control than is the case in most other European countries. This will probably still be the case even after the implementation of the 'centralizing' measures in the new Education Act.

The advantages of a decentralized system are said to be that it promotes flexibility and teacher initiative, allows more creative and imaginative curriculum development at the school level, and ensures that schools are responsive to local needs and the different cultural and employment conditions that prevail in particular localities. It has been defended not only from what might still be called the liberal tradition in education but also generally by socialists. Jackson Hall, for instance, has recently defended it on the grounds, first, that education is a major instrument of social control and should not therefore be 'the creature of the central state', and, secondly, that 'progress in education comes not from the centre but from the periphery' (Hall, 1985, pp. 4–7). Brian Simon has also argued that 'it is the local authorities, not central government, that have been responsible for most new initiatives that have been developed historically within the education system' (Simon, 1988, p. 145). He cites the early local initiatives in comprehensive schooling, the local development of the community schooling movement in Cambridgeshire in the 1930s and the more recent development of new forms of profile assessment. One might also note the development of integrated subject-teaching schemes and anti-racist teaching materials which occurred first at the local level.

The idea of decentralization is clearly central to all the dominant ideological traditions in English education. If its historical origins are partly the legacy of nineteenth-century liberalism, its main themes have in this century been comprehensively reworked within the dominant social-democratic ideologies of education and it has supporters in various camps. It is popular within the teaching profession because it is widely believed that a decentralized system gives more autonomy to teachers, leaving them free to make the crucial decision about what is taught in schools and how. It is generally supported by advocates of child-centred and 'progressive' pedagogy since the latter puts great stress on the treatment of learners as autonomous individuals and only a system which allows freedom to teachers in the classroom is believed to have the flexibility to allow teachers to practise these methods of teaching effectively. It is also supported by advocates of community education who see it as enabling greater community participation.

The arguments for a decentralized system appear very sound and more or less unimpeachable from a socialist perspective. However, closer examination, particularly in the light of the experience of some more 'centralized' continental systems, casts some doubt on these arguments. The notion that local control is inherently more democratic is not sustainable at a general level. Local control can mean control in the hands of either local authorities or teachers, or, in some versions, parents. Local authority control is not necessarily any more democratic than central government control. Administration in their hands does not inevitably involve any greater popular participation than is the case in more centralized systems. A degree of autonomy for teachers is clearly important if they are to do their job effectively and the representatives of the teaching profession, as those responsible for putting policy into practice, must certainly have an important say in policy-making. Nevertheless, teachers do have their own, often contradictory and sectional interests, and the notion of control by the experts is a Fabian doctrine with fairly questionable democratic credentials. Direct popular control by parents at the local level has never yet existed and there is certainly no sound theory upon which to judge its viability. Parents have shown no great willingness to become involved in the running of schools except in exceptional circumstances and there is a clear danger that giving parents more control over individual school policy will only allow unrepresentative groups of (usually middle-class) parents to dominate decision-making. A Gallop opinion poll commissioned by the *Daily Telegraph* in October 1987 showed that only 19 per cent of those questioned called for parents to wield greater influence (Simon, 1988, p. 34). At the present time the call for greater parental control is no more than the populist rhetoric of a Conservative government determined to return education to the market-place.

The defence of local control will inevitably become a priority for socialists when central government consists of a right-wing party with enormous majorities. However, tactical responses of this sort should not be mistaken for a general theory or a long-term strategic programme. In the long run there is little evidence that decentralized control of the sort we are used to is any more likely to produce a democratic education system. It certainly has not in practice meant that schools are free to determine their own policies nor has it encouraged high levels of popular participation. Resource allocation is determined to a large extent by central government, which has greatly restricted what individual areas can do and if this was not the case, and if LEA funding was raised entirely from local rates, there would be intolerable financial inequalities between different regions. Curriculum design may have been in the hands of LEAs and school heads but their hands have been tied in practice by the syllabuses set by the examination boards which are, of course, not democratically accountable at all. As Patricia Broadfoot has pointed out (Lauglo and Mclean, 1985, p. 106), decentralized control has not necessarily meant weak control. 'The assumption', she writes, 'that decentralized systems necessarily allow more grass-roots autonomy is increasingly ill-founded.'

Examination of educational reform in some continental systems also suggests that determined state action can be a necessary precondition for effective educational reform. In France socialists have long been aware that the central state can be an important counterbalance to local particularism and the dominance and rapacity of local oligarchies and elites. Central control can also counteract the inequalities that arise from regional and cultural differences. Such measures have increasingly caught the attention of comparative analysts in recent years. Garrique writes (quoted Broadfoot, 1985, p. 107):

> it is possible to wonder, today, whether a certain degree of centralization is not required for the efficient running of an education system and the

nature of their objectives. At a time when we are rightly asking ourselves in France about the advantages of a greater degree of freedom and thus a greater degree of decentralization, other countries with different traditions look with interest towards a more centralized model better adapted to the achievement of equality in education.

The best example of the use of determined central government action to create greater equality within an education system, however, is probably that of Sweden.

Sweden has long been seen as an international pace-setter in progressive and egalitarian educational reform. It was the first western European country to adopt a fully comprehensive system in lower secondary education and also the first to create a fully comprehensive 16–19 system. A government report in 1948 first proposed a comprehensive secondary system. A unified basic school, the *Grundskolan*, was proposed to take children up until 16, which would be divided into 7–10, 10–13 and 13–16 stages. There would be no tracking of pupils, mixed ability and child-centred teaching approaches would be adopted and there would be no terminal examinations. During the 1950s there was widespread experimentation in implementing the 'unity school' in various areas, the most celebrated example being Stockholm's experiment in running traditional and pilot schemes parallel in the north and south of the city. In no other country, writes Marklund (Boucher, 1982, p. 22), 'have reforms in education been preceded by such thoroughgoing preparatory work as in Sweden'. The *Grundskolan* was officially introduced by the Act of 1962, and by 1969, several years before any other European country, the comprehensive system was fully in place.

A similar process preceded the institution of comprehensive education in the 16–19 sector. A committee was established in 1960 to look into post-16 education and after widespread research and consultation involving teaching unions, parents' groups, academics and so on, the *Gymnasieskola* was introduced in 1971. This created for the first time a new form of upper secondary schooling which integrated all previous academic and vocational schools within one basic unit. Twenty-three different lines of study, each incorporating arts, science and technical subjects in differing proportions, were introduced, entry into which was non-selective except in a few particularly popular vocational areas. By 1980, 206 out of 278 local authorities had 340 *Gymnasieskola* between them and the provision of grants for students encouraged high levels of participation. The great achievement of the system has been to create an integrated provision that includes all subjects and all paths of vocational preparation with at least a degree of parity of prestige. Assessment through continuous evaluation and credit accumulation and the availability of through-routes for students in all lines of study into higher education has helped to facilitate this. The participation of up to 80 per cent of 16–18-year-olds in the *Gymnasieskola* witnesses to the success of the reforms.

These reforms, however, have been achieved only with considerable central direction. As Jon Lauglo puts it (Lauglo and Mclean, 1985, p. 129):

> strong concentration of authority at the centre – in the central administration directly responsible to the national political authorities – has been a necessary precondition for the reform of the school structure.

A political will on the part of government was necessary to overcome the opposition of conservatively minded academic secondary teachers who resented the equality of status for vocational and acadmic study. Central direction and planning were necessary to create a uniform and integrated structure which is arguably one of the reasons for the effectiveness of the system. Detailed national guidelines on the curriculum, which are a marked feature of the Swedish system, could also be defended on the grounds that only a balanced compulsory core curriculum in the lower secondary school could ensure that each child had an equal opportunity, since it would counteract the external cultural and class determinations which frequently assign children to different and unequal tracks in more libertarian systems.

Strong central direction to reform did not, however, signify an undemocratic process. As Marklund has written (Boucher, 1982, p. 60): 'the reforms . . . would not have been possible without a fairly firm central direction . . . [but this] should not be confused with authoritarian direction.' In fact what distinguishes the whole process was precisely the very high degree of consultation, experimentation and sustained research by the various partners to the process. This consensual process of egalitarian reforms was only possible, of course, because of the polical situation in Sweden where a social-democratic party with deep popular roots had been in power for some forty unbroken years until 1976.

Comparing this process of Swedish reform with the equivalent process of comprehensive reform in England after 1965, some of the problems of the decentralized system are immediately apparent. The permissive nature of central direction had three obvious consequences. First, the switch to comprehensive systems occurred relatively slowly since many Conservative local authorities did not wish to comply with the process. Thus by 1972, seven years after the comprehensive policy had been adopted centrally, only 41 per cent of children between 11 and 16 years were in comprehensive schools. Subsequently the figure has increased to some 90 per cent, despite Tory legislation which removes the compulsion on local authorities to go comprehensive (brought in by Labour in 1976), but the transition period has still been remarkably slow. Secondly, since local authorities have been entitled to devise their own systems of comprehensive schools, there have been an enormous number of different models adopted. Some have adopted all-through comprehensives, some have promoted the middle-school system, some have adopted the community-school model. Equally, in terms of internal school structures, some authorities have retained streaming, some have opted for setting in different subjects, and some have employed mixed-ability teachers in all subjects. Thirdly, the adoption of a comprehensive structure for secondary schools has not been accompanied by any agreed policy on curriculum and assessment. We have seen that in Sweden the creation of a comprehensive structure was accompanied by related reforms in curriculum and evaluation. The same has been true of France where the adoption of the comprehensive lower secondary *collège d'enseignement secondaire* in 1963 was matched by related national curriculum reforms and by changes to the examination system. In England there has been no national core curriculum such as might have given coherence to the objectives of comprehensive education and helped to ensure that all children did actually have a similar experience of learning in different schools. Equally there has been no thoroughgoing concomitant reform of the examination system. Over 300 private examination boards have continued to provide a chaotic array of different forms of certification that have ensured the survival of clearly distinct educational tracks, which make a mockery of the comprehensive principle.

There are good reasons for avoiding the more monolithic aspects of a centralized system such as that in France. Local authority control over the delivery of education provides an important counterbalance to central powers, and this is especially necessary when the central government is bent on forcing through the most reactionary reforms in education against the wishes of large sections of those involved in education. There are merits in having a broadly defined national curriculum, but it is essential to allow individual schools to have some control over the implementation of that curriculum, not least so that it provides a check against the use of education by the state as a means of promoting a particular ideology. Certainly most socialists in England would rightly recoil at the idea of state-vetted textbooks which is common in more centralized systems.

However, there are also drawbacks in the English model of decentralization. Creative curriculum innovation has undoubtedly occurred but without any mechanism for it this has not been generalized to all areas nor has it had the kind of consistent public advocacy from the political arena to gain the support of parents. As Margaret Archer has pointed out (1979), the advantage of continuous local innovation in a decentralized system can be outweighed by the difficulty of making innovation universal and by the speed with which it may be reversed. Most significantly, the enormous local variety that has been tolerated by 'permissive' legislation has deprived the system of the kind of uniformity which would seem to be an essential element of the comprehensive principle if that is to have anything to do with equality of opportunity.

We now have a national system of education in England and Wales which we did not have for the greater part of the nineteenth century, although the continued existence of powerful independent schools somewhat qualifies its national status. However, the relative lack of co-ordinated planning, and consequently of coherence and rationality in the system, still, though to a lesser degree, manifests the legacy of the ninteenth-century voluntarist tradition. The variegated and fissiparous nature of the system is still seen as a hallmark of its flexibility and dynamism and yet it is the very lack of uniformity which is one of the greatest barriers to greater educational equality. As the French sociologist, Raymond Boudon, has cogently argued (1974), in societies structured by class and other inequalities, the greater the variety of different routes through the education system, the more the 'branching-off' points, the greater the likelihood that differential class expectations, engendered from outside the education system, will structure student choices, even in a situation of ostensible equality of access, so that educational opportunities will be structured along class, race and gender lines. In educationally progressive countries the central state has been used to create more standardized educational structures which promote more uniform educational expectations of students. This may be one way to counter the external social pressures towards inequality which will always bear on education systems in capitalist countries. It is certainly not a perfect answer but the liberal tradition of education in England has none and this has produced what is almost certainly one of the most inegalitarian systems of education amongst major states in the western world.

If the decentralized system is one of the most obvious legacies of the nineteenth century in contemporary English education, the neglect of scientific and technical education has been another. We traced earlier the effects of the English 'empirical tradition' of employer/workshop-based technical training and the absence of the typical continental system of state-sponsored trade schools. The development of technical education in this century has, despite the arrival of the technical college, largely failed to break out of this mould. The basis of technical training has continued to be the industry-based apprenticeship system, and the college and, to an extent, the polytechnic have only been an extension of this. Post-school technical education has continued to be normatively part-time, exceptionally narrow and 'practical' in its emphases, and almost entirely marginalized from mainstream general education. The continued dominance of the City and Guilds qualification system, which has had no connections with General Certificate of Education (GCE) qualifications and has provided no routes into higher education, has maintained the segregation of technical from academic education, and has continued to underline the lower status that has traditionally been accorded to technique as against academic knowledge. This has not only denigrated technique but has greatly impoverished 'liberal education', perpetuating that mutual unintelligibility between the 'two cultures' of art and technology for which Britain has been so renowned. Symptomatically, when attempts have been made to break this mould and to introduce full-time technical education, as in the case of the technical secondary schools in the 1940s, the project has been stillborn. The technical schools never gained 'parity of prestige' and were consequently not popular.

The development of youth training programmes in the 1970s has been the only other concerted effort to improve technical training since the war, but they have done little more than reproduce all the old problems. The Youth Opportunities Programme (YOP), the Youth Training Scheme (YTS) and now Employment Training, have all sought to provide vocational training based on the workplace and supplemented by part-time education. In this they have been entirely consistent with the English tradition. However, they have failed more miserably than all previous attempts and are certainly a poor substitute for the apprenticeship system for all its faults. The reasons for this are quite clear. First, in creating an employer-led scheme in accordance with market principles, its advocates have ignored the clear lesson of history that British industry will not properly finance training programmes beyond its immediate and individual requirements. Employer investment in training has always been low in this country and since the Conservatives abolished the industrial training boards which made compulsory levies on employers, investment has dropped even further. Youth training has thus not been taken on with much enthusiasm by employers. The second reason for their failure has been that the way they have been set up has done nothing to counteract the low status that has traditionally been attached to technical education. In fact far from it; it has actually reinforced the worst stereotypes. The reason for this is that the schemes have never attempted to provide a proper technical education, even up to craft level. They have been much more concerned with inculcating work discipline, lowering wage expectations and providing a social skills training instrumentally designed to control social attitudes. The fact that these schemes have offered few recognized qualifications, have been clearly separated from mainstream general education, and have provided no passports either to further study or even into work for many of their 'graduates', only reinforces the point. It is scarcely surprising that many young people regard them as little more than 'cheap labour' (see Chapters 5 and 6 below). With the recent announcement that training will now be run by local training and enterprise councils (TECs), consisting predominantly of local employers, the tradition of employer-led training has been fully reinstated and will no doubt be subject to the familiar historical problems of employer self-interest and short-term calculation.

Post-compulsory education as a whole represents the area of greatest

Table 1.1   *Percentage of boys and girls in full-time education and training at 18 in EEC countries, 1981–3*

		boys	girls
Denmark	82/3	65.7	61.9
Netherlands	82/3	56.3	48.6
Italy	82/3	49.6	51.1
Belgium	82/3	44.7	47.1
France	82/3	38.8	50.1
Germany	81/2	28.1	33.7
Ireland	82/3	27.2	37.1
UK	82/3	17.8	16.8

Source: Eurostats (1985), Table 5

weakness in English education. It appears to be a point where the most damaging of England's historical peculiarities in education have converged to create unprecedented problems. Its technical provision still suffers from long-term historical problems; its low participation rates are the fruits of a tradition of early school-leaving which dates back to the Industrial Revolution and its structure and organization exhibit all the historical characteristics of irrationality and incoherence multiplied to a new power.

England and Wales have the lowest rates of retention in post-compulsory full-time education of any major country in Europe. In 1985–6, according to the DES's usually generous figures, there were only 30 per cent of the age group staying in full-time education, at school or college, until 18. In the previous year only 2 per cent of 18-year-olds were still in school and the figure had dropped since the beginning of the decade (*Social Trends*, 1987, p. 60). Currently, 72 per cent of US children graduate from high school at 18; 94 per cent of Japanese children remain in school until 18 and a similar number continue in Sweden's *Gymnasieskola* until that age (O'Connor, 1988). The main reason for this extraordinarily low rate of participation amongst English 16–18-year-olds is the unpopularity of sixth forms. Whilst retention in upper secondary education is the norm in most European countries, in England staying on after 16 is still the exception rather than the rule. The EEC authorities generally do not include youth training in Britain as full-time education and their comparative data show just how far behind Britain is in this.

One inevitable consequence of this is the relatively small proportion of school-leavers attaining the recognized qualifications which provide a passport to further training and better employment. Only 10.3 per cent of British children in 1985 gained five or more GCE 'O' levels at grades A–C. Conversely, 11.7 per cent gained neither GCE or CSE grades at any level (Simon, 1988, p. 30). At the higher level, in 1984–5 only 18 per cent in Britain got 'A' levels and only 14 per cent the two or three normally required for entry into higher education (*Social Trends*, 1987, p. 62).

Currently around 20 per cent get an 'A' level. By comparison over 70 per cent gain the high school diploma in Japan and the USA and 33 per cent gain the *baccalauréat* in France. The Monory reforms in France aim to increase this figure to 60 per cent by the year 2000 (O'Connor, 1988).

The story in higher education is much the same. In the United States 48 per cent enrol in college and 24 per cent get a bachelor's degree. Japan has 37.6 per cent enrolling in higher education where the vast majority graduate. France has 28 per cent of the age group entering university and Germany 19.5 per cent. Britain has only 14 per cent of the traditional age group in higher education and less than 10 per cent in university. Rates of mature student entry are also comparatively low.

If post-compulsory education in England is a disaster area the reasons are not hard to find. No government has yet produced a comprehensive policy for its development. Instead there has been a series of *ad hoc* developments in one area, youth training, which were largely motivated by political panic at growing youth unemployment and were scarcely inspired by educational or even genuine skills training considerations. Developments in this area have not been co-ordinated with other educational initiatives for the age group and predictably have been organized by an agency not connected with the educational structure. Even the Manpower Services Commission (MSC), its pioneers, has tacitly admitted in its 1984 report, *Competence and Competition*, that vocational training is greatly inferior to what exists in other countries. The result of all these unco-ordinated developments is a system, if that is the right word, of post-compulsory provision that is at best unintegrated and irrational and at worst chaotic. Currently, provision for 16-year-olds is spread between school sixth forms, traditional and new, sixth form centres, sixth form colleges, colleges of further education, community colleges, tertiary colleges, and youth training schemes run by employers consortia, private agencies and local authorities. Various other services including the Youth Service, the Probation and After-Care Service, and adult education institutes also offer remedial literacy and numeracy and social and life skills training.

Examinations and certificates on offer reflect the same diversity and lack of co-ordination. Young people can take the traditional academic subjects at 'A' level, and now 'AS' level, or they can take City and Guilds examinations in craft subjects, Business and Technical Education Council (BTEC) examinations in business and technology, the Certificate of Pre-Vocational Education (CPVE) at the vocational preparation level, or be issued with a multiplicity of school and college devised certificates and profiles which have no national validity whatever. It is not at all easy to combine these various options, and with the exception of the GCE and BTEC qualifications they have not been designed to provide through-routes to any further qualification. The effect of this has not only been to confine those involved to multiple and often terminal non-complementary tracks but to create such confusion amongst students that they have no idea which they should choose and where they can go with it.

Lack of any uniform or coherent structure of provision has been accompanied by lack of any clear normative goals for the age group. Such is the history of class division in English education that there has never been a social expectation of much educational achievement for working-class students beyond the level of basic education, especially if they happen to be black. This is why most children have left school at the first legal opportunity. The existence of an examination system that disqualifies the majority from the beginning has entrenched the syndrome of low expectations for the majority. The creation of youth training schemes based on the workplace has only confirmed the popular belief that further education is inappropriate for the majority. The lack of an integrated structure of provision not only makes the choice to stay on more confused but is evidence of a policy vacuum which promotes a very clear message that there is no normative expectation of educational achievement for the majority beyond 16.

The educational initiatives of the Thatcher era have been presented as an attempt to reform the education system from top to bottom, and they certainly do represent the most thoroughgoing changes in the postwar era. However, rather than breaking the pattern of past educational traditions they will in fact reproduce them at a new level. The principle that underlines all the changes of the last ten years is that of the educational market. Even those measures which appear to be increasing central state control in education are in fact a means to the same end. As with nineteenth-century political economy, they have found it necessary to strengthen central control to create the conditions for a free market in education.

Broadly speaking four trends have been apparent in educational legislation over the period of the Thatcher administration; these can be defined respectively as privatization, centralization, vocationalism and differentiation. The long-term goal of privatization was clearly signalled in Sir Keith Joseph's plans for educational vouchers. These were thought unworkable at the time and have been temporarily shelved, but other measures have been indicative of this trend. These include the delivery of youth training through private agencies, plans for privately financed community technology colleges, the support given to private schools through the Assisted Places Scheme, and legislation allowing charges for school 'extras'. The tendency towards the greater centralization of power has been exemplified in the work of the MSC, in the abolition of bodies incorporating teacher representation, such as the Schools Council and the Burnham Committee, in the imposition of new conditions of service on teachers, and in selective central funding of favoured government projects such as the Technical and Vocational Education Initiative (TVEI). The greater emphasis on vocational education for certain sections of the population has been evident in the

MSC programmes, the TVEI and vocational preparation courses. Greater differentiation in education was one of the objectives behind the introduction of assisted places and the unsuccessful attempt to reintroduce grammar schools, and has been one of the overall effects of the drive towards vocational education for working-class youth. We now have what is effectively a tripartite tertiary system, with middle-class children largely following the old GCE professional route and others forming part of the middle tier of technical and business training, or the lower tier of vocational preparation for semi- and unskilled work.

The 1988 Education Act not only takes all this one step further but creates a statutory framework which will allow much more far-reaching changes later. The key measures, as many have pointed out, are those for 'opting out', 'open enrolment' and 'financial derogation' to school heads. They are basically, as Brian Simon points out (1987, p. 15), enabling measures for a full-scale privatization programme which the government has considered it expedient not to attempt in one go. Open enrolment will allow flexibility in school intakes thus encouraging 'good' schools to prosper and unpopular schools to dwindle. This it is hoped will introduce market competition into education. Giving greater financial responsibilities to school heads is intended to introduce a business ethic into school management and thus again prepare the way for privatization. Finally, and most importantly, the provision to allow a bare majority of parents in a school to choose to opt out of local authority control and become 'independent state schools' is a direct move in the direction of privatization. These schools will initially be under the direct control of the DES but will no doubt later become selective and finally independent.

Plans for higher and further education also reflect the desire to return education to the market-place. The new funding councils for the universities and polytechnics are required to have a majority of industrial representatives and plans to fund the universities on a contract basis are another way of introducing market competition into the system. Similarly the colleges are now to be controlled in all essential matters by new governing bodies composed mainly of local industrial interests and they are being encouraged to seek private funding for 'self-financing' courses.

At first sight the other measures in the Education Act appear to contradict this market philosophy. We are now to have a national curriculum, national targets in core subjects to be specified by central curriculum councils, and a programme of national testing of all children in the state sector at the ages of 7, 11, 14 and 16. Can it be that after 150 years of educational liberalism we are now moving towards a monolithic Napoleonic model of centralized educational control? Or even towards a progressive rationalization under the benevolent direction of the central state? The answer to this is surely no on both counts. The new powers that have been adopted at the centre are certainly motivated by a political desire to undermine the Labour-controlled local authorities and in that sense may be seen as centralist. But their long-term aim is not to transfer the powers of the local state to the centre but rather to remove them altogether and replace them by market forces. The National Curriculum and testing should be seen as necessary concessions in the pursuit of this long-term aim. The government has to be seen to be doing something about educational standards since that is what it claims to offer the consumer. The National Curriculum is the means by which it claims to be doing this. The curriculum's main value lies not so much in encouraging given levels of achievement in a range of subjects, but rather, as Clyde Chitty has suggested (1988, p. 46), in providing the framework within which national testing can operate and it is the testing procedure which will provide the consumer quality tags on schools which will encourage free market forces to operate. Further, with the prospect of privatizing large chunks of education the government has to have some way of controlling what the free market throws up. It is rather like the recent proposals for television. The networks are to be opened up to a multitude of private initiatives through cable and so on but since this may also encourage some undesirable programming which will offend the moral and 'family' values of Thatcherism, a state watch-dog committee must be appointed to control the worst excesses. Likewise we are to have a free market in education, with an attractive range of 'choices' for the consumer but, lest this gets out of hand, quality control will be provided by the government. John Stuart Mill proposed the same solution a hundred years ago: private schooling but with examinations controlled by the state.

That these new centralizing measures have nothing to do with the kind of rationalization and egalitarian reform that have been promoted vigorously by central governments in countries like Sweden should be immediately apparent. The National Curriculum has been drawn up with virtually no consultation with the teaching profession or anyone else for that matter. It has not attempted to embody and generalize the 'good practice' of the last decades, but has all the hallmarks of being put together almost overnight without any coherent overall philosophy behind it. It is not really 'national' at all since the private schools are not included, and it is clearly not designed to provide a set of normative expectations for all children since it is in no way articulated with the programmes that will be followed in private schools, in city technical colleges (CTCs), or on youth training programmes. Nor is it apparently to be accompanied by any rational reform of the examination system. The government has just summarily dismissed the very moderate proposals of the Higginson Inquiry for a broadening of 'A' levels which one might have thought to be otherwise in line with its desire to increase scientific and technical awareness amongst the nation's youth. As far as the structure of the future education system is concerned the current measures will only increase its segmentation and incoherence. There are no plans for a unitary tertiary provision and the likelihood is that the provision for opting out will scupper tentative moves being made in that direction. Instead of a more uniform and egalitarian education system we will have one that is increasingly divided along class lines.

The Education Act of 1988 is thus best represented as a kind of conservative modernization programme. It is attempting to shake up the education system and to make it more 'efficient' and more 'responsive' to the modern technological world. In this sense it may be called modernizing. However, its chosen means are atavistic and backward-looking. Rather than create a modernized public education system as, for instance, in Sweden, it is reactivating the voluntary traditions of the nineteenth century in new ways. Its object is to create a market education provision on the principles of nineteenth-century liberal political economy. The last major nation to create a national education system will thus be the first to abolish it. As then, in the new educational market 'freedom' and 'choice' will be for those who can afford them and 'diversity' will be a polite word for multiple educational apartheid. Whether in fifteen years' time the present government will have made England again the 'worst educated country in Europe' remains to be seen.

2

A new road to serfdom? A critical history of the 1988 Act

Richard Johnson

The 1988 Education Act did not derive, straightforwardly, from New Right theories. A multitude of practicalities intervened: political divisions, administrative dilemmas, strong opposition. It took twenty years of campaigning, ten years of government and three election victories to develop a practice adequate to New Right purposes at all. I have tried to do justice to the complexity of this history – still unfinished, of course. I want to show that even those who seize historic advantages cannot do as they please. The limits arise from their thinking and from the historical conditions under which they act. There was no smoothly working all-powerful conspiracy here, rather an awkward uneven drama: on one side a story of crusading zeal and high expectations, frustration and political vulnerability, recovery, compromise and victory of a sort; on the other, resistance, stopping power and a kind of defeat, but also a certain conservatism – a failure to produce alternatives.[1]

First, I will identify some conditions which affected all policies. Then I will trace the run of events from the formation of the New Right to the passing of the Act. Finally, I will offer a reading of the measure.

This chapter should be read in association with Chapter 3 which deals more fully with theories, alternatives and the role of public professionals in the struggle.

Assets from the past: some historical conditions for New Right successes

What were the broad historical conditions, then, that made the New Right attack possible, successful even?

This question was the subject of *Unpopular Education* (CCCS, 1981) written by an earlier Education Group. Our emphasis in 1980 was on the failures of centre-left or 'social-democratic' politics. 'Unpopular education', we argued, was the product of unpopular politics. Crucial was Labour's failure to be a really educative movement, creating the knowledges to sustain its politics. For Labour, unlike earlier radical movements, education was less an activity requiring its leadership, more an institution to be managed. At best it sought more open access to the institutions – hence the postwar drives to comprehensive schooling and expanding higher education. Questions about the content of education and about popular control of the system were dropped from the political agenda – until the right revived them. Because the party did not represent popular interests adequately, the postwar reform programme was dominated by educational interests themselves – teachers, educationists and more broadly the public professions. This alliance was not as narrow as the New Right was to suggest, but its vulnerabilities were real. Consequently, New Right politics bit deep. 'Realistic' and morally conservative parents were allied with business interests against 'irresponsible' teachers and educationists. In the context of economic decline, Conservative campaigning transformed the educational agenda and pulled Labour on to the same ground.

Two criticisms of *Unpopular Education* are relevant here. We underestimated the generative role of the new social movements, not least for the New Right itself. In 1980, feminism, anti-racism and neo-Marxism seemed 'post-Thatcherite' in some sense, waiting in the wings, capable of forming an alternative without further transformations. Was this most subtle of marginalizations linked to our difficulty in developing alternatives in 1980? I have tried to correct this in Chapter 3.

The second criticism is carried in Andy Green's chapter (Chapter 1) and his broader project (Green, 1988; Green, 1990). Our explanation of the New Right's opportunities overemphasized Labour's limits. These were actually part of a larger pattern: 'the peculiarities of English education'. From its late beginnings, public education was weakly developed in England, sapped by private and voluntary provision, fragmented, exclusionary and lacking popular support. Postwar politics did not transcend these limits, but it did not create them either. New Right successes rest on a longer-term pattern, itself related to Britain's historical place in the world system and a particular history of the formation and struggle of social groups (Johnson, 1989).

I believe there is a further layer of determinations here. Today's reverses may be a symptom of the limits of *state schooling*, understood as one particular way of organizing educational processes in society. Separated, institutionalized, 'mass' educational provision may be less appropriate today than at any time since its late nineteenth-century origins. This will sound dangerously similar to the New Right case (which blames the *state* character of the institution) but not all such arguments have a rightwards tendency.

Before the New Right critique began to bite, sociologists, ethnographers and historians were discussing the limits of public education. We argued that it contributed to maintaining unequal social relations. The problems lay in the interactions of an unequal society and an educational system which institutionalized particular orientations to knowledge and presented them as objective or neutral (e.g. Young, 1971; Katz, 1971; Althusser, 1971; Illich, 1973; Bernstein, 1975; Bowles and Gintis, 1976; Bourdieu and Passeron, 1977; Willis, 1977). State education was not the source of inequalities, but it reproduced or legitimated them. These arguments were put first in relation to class; later in relation to gender and race (e.g. Deem, 1978; MacDonald, 1977; MacDonald, 1981; Stone, 1980; Connell *et al.*, 1982). These educational studies are examples of the general assessment of 'welfare' discussed in Chapter 3.

The timing is important here. The New Right interrupted these criticisms. Henceforth any criticism of schooling seemed to play into enemy hands. Pessimism and a tendency to functional explanation also seemed to disqualify the work itself. I now think that the problem was rather that we lacked the courage of our convictions: we failed to consider alternative educational arrangements more consistent with our analysis. Disorganized in this way, we lost an historical initiative.

The strongest versions of these arguments took account of resistances to unpopular education, the practical criticisms of users. They explored cultural defences against educational exclusion or against the devaluation of popular knowledges (e.g. Willis, 1977; McRobbie, 1978; Humphries, 1981; Johnson, 1988; Connell *et al.*, 1982). Such defences – 'resistances' we called them – are not necessarily transformative. In England they have often been part of an anti-educational, culturally conservative pattern (Johnson, 1988; Johnson 1989). As our own chapters show, these patterns persist, but also change. Bob Hollands's account of the 'lad' and 'lass' cultures, James Avis's of 'instrumentalism' and 'vocationalism', Phil Carspecken's of parental attitudes to assessment; and the rather general finding of resistance to schooling because it is 'childish' are examples of continuities. Bob's 'enterprisers', 'politicos' and 'survivors' may be newer.

The main consequence of the interplay of structure and resistance is that the working-class school-age population fails to benefit proportionately from schooling. A large section rejects what schooling stands for culturally. Merely formal access will not break this resistance; attempts to extend the logics of comprehensive provision will never suffice. This is because resistance is not to formal exclusion only: it arises from the actual encounter with the cultural character of the school, especially with the social orientations to knowledge which are incorporated in curriculum categories and the more general features of knowledge in school.

We can now reformulate the arguments of *Unpopular Education*. At the deepest level, the New Right's opportunities arose from the limits of state schooling as a historically specific form of education. The fundamental problems, however, do not derive from the state or public (as opposed to private or commercial) nature of provision. They arise from the ways in which knowledges are institutionalized in schools in relation to social inequality and cultural difference.

Overlaying and exacerbating this pattern are particular English features. English education has been particularly exclusive in class and perhaps in gender terms. It has reproduced 'colonial' patterns around race and ethnicity too. Educational peculiarities have helped to produce larger cultural formations: deep popular suspicion, for example, of 'intellectuals' of all kinds. The New Right works with the grain of these peculiarities, happy to preserve their conservatism: with the preference for 'common sense' over 'theory', for example, or for cashable assets ('skills') over the transformation of self and others by learning. These cultural affinities made it hard to raise a defence.

So this was the ground on which the major political forces strove to wrest advantages. Critical here were the blind spots in the postwar movements for educational reform, and in left strategies more generally. As the terms of struggle over education narrowed, many discontents were unheard. They were stoked up, even, by officious innovations, and offered to the other side. The other side, in innovations of its own, was quick to seize on them.

Phase 1: Forming the New Right educational tendency 1969–79

'New Right educational tendency' is a clumsy title for a complex formation. From the late 1960s, different right-wing groupings developed around educational issues. Their membership was not narrowly 'political' to begin with, nor limited to committed neo-liberals. Disillusioned academics and teachers were a major component. By the general election of 1979 these groups had formed quite a tight network, with a distinctive educational politics, influential inside the Conservative Party and making the running outside.

One focus was neo-liberal theory, in which public education was seen as a prime target. The state should compel attendance, supply some finance and maintain standards, but it should not, on the whole, provide education directly. For Friedrich von Hayek, who adopted Friedman's plan of vouchers, governments' educational functions could be redistributed:

> It would undoubtedly be possible to leave the organisation and management of education entirely to private efforts, with the government providing merely the basic finance and ensuring a minimum standard

for all schools where the vouchers would be spent. (Hayek, 1960, p. 381; Hayek and his ideas are discussed more fully in Chapter 3.)

For the Friedmans, public education amounts to an expropriation:

> In schooling, the parents and child are the consumers, the teacher and school administrator the producers. Centralization in schooling has meant larger size units, a reduction in the ability of consumers to choose, and an increase in the power of the producers. Teachers, administrators, and union officials are no different from the rest of us . . . However, their interests as teachers, as administrators, as union officials are different from their interests as parents and from the interests of the parents whose children they teach. Their interests may be served by greater centralisation and bureaucratisation even if the interests of the parents are not. (Friedman and Friedman, 1980, p. 191)

The Friedmans' analysis, pursued since the mid-1950s, remains the typical neo-liberal argument; their solution, the 'Friedman voucher' (Bosanquet, 1983, p. 171) is the first-choice mechanism of change. Taken up by British writers (Peacock and Wiseman, 1964; West, 1965) and the Institute of Economic Affairs (IEA) in the 1960s (e.g. Harris and Seldon, 1963), it was pursued politically by the pressure group Friends of the Education Voucher Experiment in Representative Regions (FEVER) founded in 1974. Voucher schemes were an early manifestation of the New Right, though not all voucher plans have this political character.

As Nick Bosanquet has noted, vouchers have not, to date, proved their worth by catching on (1983, p. 170). They retain their fascination, however, as a method of moving from non-fee-paying public education to a market where consumer pressure and price can operate 'freely'. The movement can be phased in according to the growth of demand (e.g. the various versions discussed in Seldon, 1986). The key shift is in the financial role of the central state. The state stops financing local authorities and/or curtails their power to raise finance. Instead it pays an earmarked educational subsidy to parents for an amount up to the full cost. Parents then learn to be consumers in an educational market, purchasing education from competing suppliers. In this way the monopoly of the state system is broken, private education enhanced and the way paved for education to be wholly private.

Voucher schemes come, appropriately, in many varieties, more or less disruptive of existing provision. We might compare Friedman's zeal in a popular text of 1980 with the modesty of Professors Peacock and Wiseman, writing for British readerships in the mid-1960s. Friedman is clear that vouchers are 'a partial solution', a route to full commercialization. Most parents (except 5–10 per cent of 'hardship' cases) will eventually pay full-cost fees and most schools will be provided entrepreneurially, not through public agencies (Friedman and Friedman, 1980, p. 196). Peacock and Wiseman's slender pamphlet of the mid-1960s risked only minimum disturbance. Vouchers will be introduced first for higher education, along with loans and there will be payments to encourage later school-leaving. The voucher levels will be high enough to cover the full educational costs of lower income groups. Schools will not be financed by taxation, but could be run by local authorities as 'self-financing municipal enterprises'. In a long footnote, the authors disavow any intention to damage local education authorities (LEAs) (Peacock and Wiseman, 1964, p. 65, note 1; and compare Peacock's 'half-way house' of 1982, discussed in Seldon, 1986, pp. 47–8).

The problem remains how to take the first step in a politically acceptable way. Vouchers do disrupt existing provision and are meant to, whatever the gradualist disguise. The ideological dimensions, noted in Chapter 3, are critical here: the acceptability of privatization depends of discrediting the existing system. Similarly governments may *make* the existing system unviable, easing the way to alternatives. Even with some of these conditions met, the introduction of vouchers is difficult, as the story will show.

'Voucher' became a battle-cry on right and left; but the elements that make up a 'voucher scheme' do not have to be introduced at one go. 'Schemes' bind together bundles of strategies, with a common logic, but potentially separable. It is possible to enhance choice, for example, without introducing vouchers: by supplying comparable information about schools, by 'open enrolment', by increased access to private education, by powers of 'exit' from public education ('opting out' by individuals or schools) and by reinstating direct-grant schools and promoting new semi-private institutions. There are also strategies for weakening or privatizing public education: cutting LEA finance; introducing payments; reducing the value of schooling as part of the 'social wage' (e.g. cutting free milk, school meals and transport); privatizing services like cleaning; introducing management criteria; delegating financial powers; allowing differential payments to teachers; etc. Neo-liberals have become more effective as they have abandoned the dogmatic letter of the voucher scheme in favour of this array of free-market strategies.

The New Right tendency was never reducible to the movement for vouchers. There were a number of campaigns. Networks were built and arguments sharpened in a series of public interventions through the 1970s. The Black Papers (1969–77) were an important focus. Early contributors denied they knew each other and disavowed political labels (e.g. Cox and Dyson, 1970, pp. 154, 157–8), but the papers connected up campaigns, drew in activists, and forged a political identity. Campaigns included the 'independent' University of Buckingham; criticism of progressive examinations like CSE Mode III, the 16+ and, later, the General Certificate of Secondary Education (GCSE) (Whitty, 1985, pp. 120–46); opposition to the 1975 Act on comprehensive reorganization and to the abolition of direct grant status; the campaign for the Assisted Places Scheme (Salter and Tapper, 1985); and the *causes célèbres* of William Tyndale school and the Polytechnic of North London (Cox, Jacka and Marks, 1975).

It is not clear how and when the educational campaigns linked up with the New Right networks more generally (the best account to date is in Salter and Tapper, 1985). More hidden than the public debates were the associated reorientations within the leadership of the Conservative Party itself, from 'Heathism' to 'Thatcherism', from 'wet' to 'dry'. One reason why 'Thatcherism' remains appropriate, despite the personalization, is that Thatcher herself and Sir Keith Joseph were early neo-liberal converts and played key roles in the reorientation. Through their Centre of Policy Studies (CPS) and their choices of advisers, they tapped into the networks already assiduously created by the organizing intellectuals of neo-liberalism.

This work began shortly before Thatcher became party leader in 1975. Especially important were the networks around the IEA, the best organized and most productive of the think-tanks and the focus for voucherism. In putting together an anti-Heath network of advisers, Thatcher and Joseph must have also looked to the groups already forming around the educational campaigns, especially the Black Papers, the National Council for Educational Standards, the Conservative Philosophy Group (including Roger Scruton), the Buckinghamites, and the groups canvassing for the Assisted Places Scheme.

There were signs of connections between the neo-liberals and the educational campaigners quite early, and connections between both and the New Right in the party by the mid-1970s. Ralph Harris (later Lord Harris) of the IEA was a Black Paper author. The IEA housed the National Council of Educational Standards and was an organizing base for the Buckingham campaign. Caroline (later Baroness) Cox became chairwoman of the education committee of the CPS; Max Beloff, principal of Buckingham, was chairperson of a party advisory group on policy in the early 1980s; Carlisle's personal adviser as shadow minister and secretary of state was the neo-liberal Stuart Sexton. The interconnections were personified by the leading activist of this phase, Dr Rhodes Boyson, who was a Black Paper editor, associated with the neo-liberals as early as 1967 (Seldon, 1986, p. 13), and active in Conservative Party educational policy-making by the mid-1970s. His summary text of 1975, *The Crisis in Education*, synthesized the tendencies: the Friedmanite stress on 'freedom' (citing the IEA's surveys of parental opinion); the Black Paper emphasis on excellence and standards:

It would seem obvious that a free society would move to more, not less, parental choice of school with advancing standards of living . . . The best way to obtain this choice would certainly not be by further enforcement of comprehensive schooling but by helping parents to buy the education they want by replacing state provision with a reverse income tax or the education voucher . . . It is possible that a combination of enforced minimum standards tested by HMIs combined with the voucher and parental choice would be best for British education . . . Enforced minimum standards would guarantee these basic standards while the campaign for excellence in schools to win parental choice would lift them higher. (Boyson, 1975, pp. 148 and 149)

By the mid-1970s a distinctive position had been forged around the themes of parental choice and educational standards, and connections made with Conservative politics. The themes proved to be durable, informing Conservative policy right through to the 1988 Act. They offered a framework for educational discontent, especially in reaction to Labour's abolition of direct-grant status and enforcement of comprehensive reorganization.

The educational tendency leaned towards one pole of the New Right repertoire – towards neo-conservatism. Neo-liberal aims were more implied than argued; 'parental choice' could be read as code for vouchers, for it implied a market. Yet, though Conservatives voted in favour of voucher experiments in the Commons in 1976, official policy only went as far as 'The Charter for Parents' Rights' eventually embodied in the Education Act of 1980. In the rhetoric, the case for the market took second place to attacks on educational disorder, the neo-liberal themes subordinated to the neo-conservative.

There are several possible explanations. The radical implications of neo-liberal doctrine for social institutions including the National Health Service could not be publicly spoken in the 1970s. This remained a problem until a transitional plan, more acceptable than vouchers, was devised. What mattered in the 1970s was effective campaigning in opposition, discrediting existing policies and disorganizing Labour support. It also seems that more Conservatives (old and new) were involved in educational campaigns than in other issues. The rhetoric was often authoritarian:

We shall not improve the quality of education in this country until we return to a sense of purpose, continuity and authority in our general attitude to life and society. (Boyson, 1975, p. 137)

The implications for curricula, methods of teaching and discipline were firmly traditional too. There were obvious, self-defining 'subjects' with 'basic' knowledges and standards. In a passage which anticipates later developments strikingly, but is sanguine to a fault, Boyson wrote:

> It is not difficult to draw up a basic curriculum occupying some 60–80 per cent of teaching time in the infant, primary and secondary schools. All that would be necessary is the stipulation of standards in numeracy and basic literacy, geographical, historical and scientific knowlege to be attained at various ages by the average child. Achievement could then be monitored by nationally set and marked examinations, or by HMIs. (ibid., p. 141)

It is important to see the educational movement which Boyson led in something like its own terms. 'Standards' meant the intelligible, dependable grammar school offerings of the past, complete with mental and moral disciplines, blazers, badges, corporal punishment and loyalty to the school. Such values were threatened by comprehensives and by progressive teachers who deserted the traditional curriculum for interdisciplinary schemes and 'indoctrination'. 'Standards' was a slogan invested with desire for an imaginary past, with anger and disappointment.

This side of the New Right appealed to all who clung to singular or absolute moral values in the face of cultural relativities: the 'personal politics' and the 'permissiveness', the dissolution of the nation, the multiplication of cultures, the recognition of actual variety in speech and language. While I revelled in the relativity, and joined the Centre for Contemporary Cultural Studies to study it, my businessman father, turned Anglican clergyman, was deeply disturbed by 'the times'. Everything, he felt, was getting worse. The New Right keyed into this conservative moral common sense which resisted all the postwar changes, including the recomposition of working-class life and culture. Moral conservatism was counterposed to the liberalism and 'new politics' of many young state professionals. There was a class dynamic here, or several: aspirant working class versus professional, but also provincial business versus metropolitan intellectual. The bitterness of change was sharpened if you felt that reliable routes of advance were being closed to 'bright children of the working class', including your own. The Black Paper of 1977 ended with questions about 'values', including

> Is it natural or unnatural for teachers and parents to tell children what to do? . . . In a society dominated by pop culture do children need more, or less direction by concerned adults? . . . How much Marxist indoctrination is taking place in schools, colleges, polytechnics and universities? . . . Should a teacher treat children as individuals in their own right instead of seeing them (and himself or herself) as a product of class struggle? (Cox and Boyson, 1977, p. 127)

The empirical basis of these anxieties was often dubious, but (if a class analysis can be risked!) comprehensivization did not markedly improve class chances yet threatened routes to a selective education. The strategy of social mobility through educational competition may have become more chancy, dependent on the accidents of neighbourhood and the cultural rough-and-tumble of a local school. It was harder to win a selective 'place' through 'merit'. New Right ideas may have found a popular grounding in the concern that schooling should give practical, tangible, vocationally useful skills and that education should employ forms of discipline (including sexual and 'moral' values) more in conformity with home and neighbourhood.

This educational movement was – is – contradictory. There is something paradoxical about yoking all that loss and nostalgia to the unpredictability of the market, in replacing loss by sheer flux. There were (and remain) contradictions around the curriculum values of the movement. It was significant for the future that the New Right so closely associated itself with traditional academic subjects and stood against interdisciplinarity, 'relevance', and educational progressivism generally. If Black Paperites had made their own appropriation of progressivism instead of parodying and harrying it so, the subsequent story would have been very different. It is by no means clear, to this day, that a subject-based curriculum is the best educational solution for a movement linked, in other ways, to a modernizing capitalism.

Certainly more modern measures can be used for 'standards'. Education can be judged against the requirements of a modern economy. 'Standards' can mean 'employability'; the curriculum can be rejigged to foreground 'enterprise'. Disciplines can be dissolved into 'skills', or into new cross-disciplinary combinations. This new paradigm, associated with the Manpower Services Commission (MSC), 'training' and the 'new vocationalism' had also taken a political form by the mid-1970s (Chapter 4 below; CCCS, 1981). There were some convergences with Black paper perspectives: on the accountability of teachers, the concern with basic skills, and the anxiety about anti-industrial attitudes and left-wing teachers. But a modernizing emphasis was more likely to be found among industrialists, MSC officials, or even Labour politicians than Conservatives or Black Paperites. In retrospect this tension should not surprise: it was another replay of Raymond Williams's opposition between 'the old humanists' and the 'industrial trainers' (Williams, 1965). This tension was to remain generative for the whole project (Whitty, 1985, pp. 113–19, 140–6).

Another tension was around degrees of central control. From a 'pure' neo-liberal perspective it was pointless to dismantle LEA bureaucracy to replace it by the Department of Education and Science (DES). From a 'dirty' neo-liberal (see Chapter 3) or neo-conservative stance centralization might be useful to modernize the educational system from above or to purge it of 'progressivism'. Before 1979, this conflict was rarely posed because no precise plan was needed. The slogans of parental choice and educational standards allowed a broad appeal, gathering up many sources of dissatisfaction. Once in office, though, the tensions were unavoidable.

Penalties of power: an administrative tradition revised

What difficulties lay in wait for the New Right in the event of electoral success? What difference would it make being in power?

Educational administration rested on the premiss of a public service, financed by central and local taxes. The statutory duty of the Secretary of State for Education – 'to promote the education of the people of England and Wales and the progressive development of institutions devoted to that purpose' (quoted Kogan, 1971, p. 26) – meant promoting LEA provision. But what if the secretary of state was committed to neo-liberal principles? Could you dismantle the state system? Could 'progressive development' be backwards? Was privatization a form of 'promotion'? This was unexplored territory.

The administrative system was often seen as 'a partnership' of central government, local authorities and teachers' unions (Salter and Tapper, 1981, pp. 40–2 and pp. 88–91). According to Maurice Kogan, writing in 1971:

> The range and level but not the style and quality, of local authorities' activities are . . . largely prescribed by central government. Yet local authorities are reckoned to be free bodies, relating as much to local electors' wishes as to national policy. There is however no necessary conflict between local authorities' freedom and the DES's strong control functions . . . American visitors admire, and now try to imitate, this combination of a strong national role and local freedom. (Kogan, 1971, p. 27)

But what if LEA freedom was a power to be curtailed? What if 'the range and level' of their activities were excessive? What if 'style and quality' were precisely the problem? Could 'partnership' survive? Conventional accounts likewise stress the advisory and consultative bodies, semi-autonomous and representative of the partners (Kogan, 1978, pp. 134–7). The Schools Council, founded in 1963, embodied a level of autonomy for teachers, both from the DES and the politicians (Tapper and Salter, 1981, ch. 8). Neo-liberals were concerned instead with the 'autonomy' of parents. The market was a way of making teachers accountable. Head-on clashes were inevitable.

This was only part of the administrative legacy, however. Already

Kogan's researches suggested changes due to the breakdown of the postwar consensus in the 1960s and early 1970s. Power was shifting between 'the partners' (whose roles were never equal anyway). More recent studies (especially Tapper and Salter, 1978; Salter and Tapper, 1981; Salter and Tapper, 1985) are more emphatic. If Conservatives would face difficulties from long-term features, would recent history aid them?

It is often argued (see Chapter 1 above) that decentralization is (or was) a feature of educational administration. There has certainly been a tradition of local involvement, from the nineteenth-century liberal bourgeoisie to Labour local authorities. In the postwar period, however, local control worked in favour of the educational professionals. The teacher public has been crucial, but there are levels of control within the educational interest, which make democratic claims even less plausible. The more powerful layers are composed not of teachers but of equally professional professionals who manage the system.

In January 1988 I attended the North of England Education Conference which is held in a different northern city each January. I was struck by the occupations on the attendance list: county education officers and directors of education, chairpersons and members of local education committees, inspectors and advisers at local and national levels, heads and deputies of colleges and schools, representatives of the teacher trade unions and voluntary associations (usually their national officers), officials from the MSC, a few professors of education and a scatter of other academics like me. It was an overwhelmingly masculine gathering, though Labour and northern.

According to Salter and Tapper, the permanent officials at such gatherings strengthened their hold on local educational policy in the 1960s and 1970s at the cost of the representative members. There was an 'encapsulation of the policy-making process within the ranks of the professionals' (1981, p. 99). This process had implications for New Right reform. Divorced from local interests, lines of corporate management might offer means for 'rationalizations' and construct interests eager to grasp at any new well-funded programme. The erosion of representation weakened LEAs as vehicles for popular wishes especially on vexed issues like school choice, school closures and local reorganizations. LEAs were more vulnerable to attack in the 1980s than the long history of local power might suggest.

In any case, decentralization was never the whole story. Local discretions were balanced by reserve powers at the centre. Ministers seeking power could connect with a tradition of exasperated administrative intervention. The first Thatcher government converged with such a trend when it took office. From the early 1960s the policy-making ambitions of the DES had been increasing. In the mid-1970s, the DES was redrawing the terms of 'partnership' to its own advantage, using ideologies of modernization and accountability. Threatened by the growth of the MSC, it 'harness[ed] the economic pressures for educational change in a way that suited its aspirations' (Salter and Tapper, 1981, p. 224). In their latest study Salter and Tapper move closer to *Unpopular Education*: 'the impact on the political agenda of the New Right's educational campaign should not be underestimated' (Salter and Tapper, 1985, p. 213). Since I readily accept their original argument, the problem of the relation between the two processes – the New Right's politics and 'the Department's bureaucratic dynamic' – can now be squarely posed.

Salter and Tapper stress the 'happy marriage of the Conservative Party's educational ideology and the Department's centralizing instincts (ibid., p. 229), citing moves to control LEAs, teachers and the curriculum up to 1984. Later developments reinforce this argument. Yet this is to omit the free-market strand in New Right thinking. From this viewpoint the 'internalization' of policy-making in the DES is another example of the state dominating the market. The DES, on its side, has reasons to oppose neo-liberal plans. So there was room for conflict here. At the same time, the government needed administrative means and expert advice. Some tactical convergence with bureaucracy was likely some of the time. We should keep all these possibilities in mind when returning to the narrative.

Certainly administrative practices were changing rapidly after 1975. The cuts, the department's Yellow Book, Callaghan's Ruskin speech of 1976, and the MSC heralded major changes in 'partnership'. The involvement of both major parties in these changes masked the leading role of the New Right. Turn-taking in making cuts (first Heath's government in 1973, then Labour in 1975), Labour's role in setting cash limits and promoting business criticisms hid the deeper polarizations of the period. The 'old moles' of social change still worked beneath the surface. They included Marx's dialectic of labour and capital, with the new Conservatism preparing to avenge Heath's humiliations. More complex class struggles were also being prepared. What price partnership or even bureaucratic ambitions in such a gathering of forces?

Phase 2: Promises, promises: the 1979 election and after

There was much studied moderacy in the Conservative campaign of 1979, especially in relation to welfare institutions.[2] As Peregrine Worsthorne put it:

> The message that the Tories must get across in the next two weeks is that they are the true conservers of social democracy, rescuing it from its own pitfalls. They are seeking not a new Jerusalem but safer paths to the same old shrine. (*Sunday Telegraph*, 15 April 1979)

According to Mrs Thatcher, 'Mr Callaghan has tried to frighten you with a picture of Conservatives "tearing everything up by the roots". But we are a party of the roots of tradition' (election broadcast, 2 April 1979). History and tradition were much invoked. The campaign's radicalism lay in what Worsthorne called Mrs Thatcher's 'Jacobinical' elements: in the new populist appeals and her speeches about 'the bulging socialist state and its insatiable appetites' and the bogey of 'Marxist socialism' (*Daily Telegraph*, 17 April 1979). Education was treated in much the same way. Mark Carlisle was described, reassuringly, as a 'tall, florid, utterly straight-forward lawyer from the North of England' (*Sunday Times*, 6 May 1979). Mrs Thatcher took pains to allay 'scares' (which proved justified) about putting up the price of school meals (*Daily Telegraph*, 24 April 1979). At the same time, Boyson and the popular Conservative dailies stressed the need to discipline the educators. His credo was typical: 'I believe in parents,' he said (in an interview with the *Times Educational Supplement*). 'What we have done is to decentralize power. That's something that needs doing if society is to survive' (*TES*, 16 November 1979). His co-editor, Cox, hoped the government would support the Black Paper counter-revolution for 'traditional standards' and scotch the Gramsci-influenced left-wing plans for the schools (*Daily Telegraph*, 20 April 1979).

The Conservative press was offered chances to attack teachers, linking education to the core theme of anti-unionism during the election itself. Sore from insults from politicians, media and DES, the teachers found their salary negotiations suspended for the election. The unions declared against Conservative Party policy and started industrial action. Conservative glee, union conferences and the warnings of headteachers about 'disruption' kept the issue in the headlines. Here were the teachers, supposed to be 'representatives of what is best in society, inculcating moral values through their hard work, their reliability' (Cox, *Daily Telegraph*, 20 April 1979) going slow again. As 'disruption' continued up to polling day, the *Telegraph* declared 'on any rational calculation, the teachers are ripe for resistance by the Government', and made connections with 'teaching's declining standards' (7 May 1979). Mrs Thatcher used her first speech after the election to attack the teachers' unions (*Sunday Times*, 13 May 1979). The election was a key round in the new politics of education: in a manoeuvre learned in opposition but indispensable in office, the government bypassed professionals by appealing to their clients. The significance of this was lost on teachers it seemed: according to the *TES*'s own poll, 59 per cent of primary teachers and 45 per cent of secondary teachers contributed to the Conservatives' 43-seat majority of the fifth of May (*TES*, 28 November 1979).

Education policy was quite prominent in the campaign. 'Improved Education' was one of the 'Six Steps' to put the 'Great' back into Britain, foregrounded in Conservative pamphlets. Yet the manifesto promises and Carlisle's speeches were modest in practice: more parental say on governing bodies, blanket testing in basic subjects at 8, 11 and 14, the publication of examination results of particular schools, repeal of the 1976 Education Act (enforcing comprehensives) and the introduction of the Assisted Places Scheme (making LEA money available for places at private schools). Carlisle's fullest proposals added a General Teaching Council (GTC), better teacher training, the retention of 'A' levels, a 16+ exam to replace CSE and 'O' level, and the rationalization of examining boards. The additional proposals seem unconnected with New Right agitations, the GTC apart. Some were consistent with ongoing DES plans (e.g. rationalization of examining boards); others were take-ups of long-standing educationists' initiatives (the 16+, opposed by the New Right, went back to a Schools Council recommendation of 1975). Retention of 'A' levels (against the Schools Council's 'N' and 'F' levels) was an indication of the strength of the 'old humanist' elements in the Conservative repertoire. There was little trace of 'modernization', unless testing was intended to satisfy employers as well as parents. There was even post-election speculation on the fate of the MSC, with Carlisle promising an early review (*Guardian*, 15 May 1979). The New Right core of the programme amounted to the modest moves towards 'choice' and 'voice', the Assisted Places Scheme, and the unformed but potentially radical proposals for testing.

Perhaps later divisions were not yet posed, as the party adjusted to office. Carlisle, no Thatcherite, presented himself as even-handed between public and private sectors (*Daily Telegraph*, 8 October 1980). He was more likely to support 'wets' in Conservative LEAs than line up with Boyson, his parliamentary undersecretary. A main focus of later divisions – vouchers – was absent from the manifesto, though Carlisle said he would 'welcome an experiment in the voucher system of education' and be 'very interested to see the results', a reference to poposals from John Barnes, chairman of Kent Education Committee, important in the FEVER/IEA network (*Daily Telegraph*, 27 April 1979). After the election Carlisle met with Barnes, Arthur Seldon (IEA), Marjorie Seldon (FEVER) and neo-liberal academics and was vaguely discouraging, stressing the cost which would have to be found by Kent (*TES*, 28 November 1979; Seldon, 1986, p. 14).

The gap in planning for the future was bridged, typically, by restoring the past. This matched the stress on tradition and the heavy rhetorical reworking of 1945 which had been a feature of Conservative rhetoric since the trade union actions of January and February.[3] The keynotes were to identify with 'our long history', to promise 'a clean break with the recent past' and 'to offer a new beginning' (Mrs Thatcher, Solihull speech, 24 March 1979). In education this meant promising a return to grammar schools, standards and tradition, and breaking cleanly from 1960s and 1970s developments. The manifesto declared 'Labour's destruction of good schools will be halted' but some Conservatives, especially Boyson, promised more: a return to selection, for example (*Daily Telegraph*, 21 April 1979).

How had these promises fared by May 1981? Some speedily passed into law in the first two Education Bills of the period. The 1975 Act was repealed (Education Bill I). Assisted places, changes in school government, the extension of choice and information within the LEA system, were through by April 1980 (Education Bill II).

Yet even these measures met with difficulties. To facilitate cuts, Education Bill I made milk, meals and free transport non-mandatory on LEAs. The transport clause caused disaffection among Conservative MPs, was defeated in the Lords and had to be dropped. It was an early rallying-point for supporters of Conservative LEAs, a source of resistance to more radical policies. If the Assisted Places Scheme was meant to become an avenue for 'able children from our poorest homes' (Boyson), it was a failure. It narrowly escaped being blocked on financial grounds, but was subject to successive cuts (Salter and Tapper, 1985). Many places, initially, went to children already in the private sector; as late as 2 September 1981 it was reported that places were not being filled. Later assessments showed participation was low among manual worker and 'inner city' families, and high among middle-class children with single parents or modest income – hardly the reinstatement of the scholarship child. The numbers, about 1.00 per cent of schoolgoers, were tiny (Fitz, Edwards and Whitty, 1986; Griggs 1988). Though some grammar schools were reprieved, the move towards comprehensives was not reversed. Labour's victories in the local elections of May 1980 dampened hopes of restoration. Similarly, the shift to parent power proved timorous, falling behind proposals of the Taylor Report. The Bill did not increase the powers of school governors, despite the search for accountability. The measures were an uneasy compromise between different conceptions, with no distinctive Conservative rationale (Whitehead and Aggleton, 1986). This emerged later in the 1984 Green paper, the 1985 White paper 'Better Schools', and the 1986 Act.

Other promises got lost in professional manoeuvres: blanket testing for example, in the Core Curriculum labyrinth. A possible focus of testing, the Assessment of Performance Unit (APU), ran into difficult technical issues and disappointed even as an information gatherer (Salter and Tapper, 1981, p. 234). Curriculum politics was dominated by a three- or four-sided conflict between DES, Her Majesty's Inspectorate (HMI) and Schools Council versions, with interventions from the MSC. The distinctive Conservative approach – testable 'basics' – disappeared without much trace, though it may have influenced the DES (Chitty, 1988; Maw, 1988). Conventional commitment to consultation posed real limits: the partners failed to agree, so progress was slow. There were continuing signs of DES attempts to centralize, most decisively in higher education, but the government, with no plans for systematic centralization, may even have checked the DES. As the *TES* said of Carlisle: 'he presided decorously over the

process by which rash promises to reform the school curriculum were
wound down' (*TES*, 18 September 1981).

Carlisle's problem was that he stood at the centre of a policy-making
juggernaut producing proposals with which he had to deal whether they
fitted the government's agenda or not. The government initially planned
to abolish 25 quangos, but it was not until after 1981 that obstreperous
bodies like the Schools Council and the Advisory Council for Continuing
and Adult Education (ACACE) were dispatched. Issues embarrassing to
the right included special education, 16+ examinations, the campaign
against caning, and the McFarlane Report on sixth form education.
Warnock's special education proposals were implemented, scandalously,
on the cheap in 1981, and the Centre for Information and Advice on
Educational Disadvantage was closed. GCSE was opposed by traditionalists
and havered over by ministers right up to 1984. The campaign by the
Society of Teachers Opposed to Physical Punishment (STOPP) produced
adverse judgments before the European Court of Human Rights. The
appointment of the Rampton Commission on the Education of Ethnic
Minorities in 1979, on a Select Committee recommendation, was not
reassuring. As the commission got under way, with black and Asian
parents organizing, more cross-currents complicated the creed of 'basics'
and 'parent power'. Even religion, a New Right 'basic', was implicated
here. The government had not yet found a way to use the educational
aspects of race to advantage.

So New Right activists, Mrs Thatcher included, might well have felt
frustration by late 1981. In September 1981 she replaced Carlisle with her
friend and mentor, Sir Keith Joseph, also giving Boyson greater prominence, hoping, no doubt, for more decision. For the educational public,
however, the main reality of these years was not promises, false or
redeemed, but cuts. Cuts in educational expenditure began in the early
1970s but the dilemmas around them are best understood in relation to the
next phase, the Conservative crisis of 1981–3.

Phase 3: The crisis of negativity 1981–3

Conservative dilemmas, latent under Carlisle, manifest under Joseph, arose
in part from historical conditions. It was hard to reconcile the main impulse
of New Right policy (towards the market) with the legacies of public
education, including the ideology of partnership, the power of LEAs, the
autonomies of professionals. But the New Right also had its own internal
ambiguities: to modernize or preserve traditional subjects; to centralize
or trust in the market? Joseph's ministry was an agonized search for
answers.

His own dilemma was how to be a New Right Minister of Education.

22222222

To act conventionally in this role, to defend and extend the existing system, was against his principles; to act as a true Thatcherite was to alienate his partners. This would have mattered less if a viable alternative had emerged and Joseph, like Baker, had been prepared to enforce it. But no such plan existed and Joseph himself was a reluctant centralizer. Yet he could not simply evade the issues as Carlisle had done. As central ideologist of the New Right, he had to face the contradiction or deny his own identity. His dilemmas were dramatic and personal, but also structural, dilemmas for the whole Tendency.

Problems were deepened by two political choices which, though compelling, proved reversible. First, there was the general commitment to cutting government expenditure. This was central to the strategy of economic recovery, a top priority. As the 1979 White Paper on Public Expenditure put it, 'Public Expenditure is at the heart of our current difficulties' (quoted Gamble, 1988, p. 101). Public education was a major spender, so cuts were obvious, 'common sense'. Yet the strategy had important consequences. It dominated policies for the public sector, hindering the development of more subtle solutions. Reductions were hard to achieve without more far-reaching changes (ibid., p. 122; David, 1988, pp. 28–54); yet they created an impression of maximum damage and minimum care. They precipitated conflicts – with local government, trade unions and professionals – that might have been handled more effectively on other occasions. They often required legislation, taking up parliamentary time. The resulting confrontations acquired their own momentum. By 1982, if not earlier, attacks on local authorities had become a leading edge of Conservative politics. Heseltine's call to war at the 1982 Conservative Conference coupled local authorities, the left and the professions, in a regular conspiracy:

> It is the professional Left which now confronts us – Left-Wing councils employing hard-left officials; hard-left councils employing Left-Wing councillors of neighbouring councils; Left-Wing Councils employing Labour candidates in the paid voluntary sector. (*Daily Mail*, 8 October 1982)

This struggle absorbed time and energy. Cuts, news of cuts, administration of cuts, campaigns against cuts, reports on the results of cuts, justifications for cuts, dominated the education scene. Cuts created forms of local left resistance which the government had then to counter. This forced it into its most obviously autocratic and self-interested actions, especially the abolition of the Great London Council (GLC) and the Inner London Education Authority (ILEA). Cuts deepened the rift between the government and teachers.

Despite the anti-professionalism, there was room for different tactics.

Teachers were not preponderantly anti-Conservative in 1979; less negative tactics might have won acquiescence. Cuts alienated the government's supporters: Conservative local authorities, lobbies around free transport and rural schools, middle-class parental interests around student grants. For teachers, administrators, pupils and parents ordinary educational tasks became more difficult to accomplish. Adjusting to the last set of deteriorations became a way of life. Unsurprisingly, teacher organizations and LEAs moved to near-unanimous opposition. There was even dissent from HMI. Already late in 1979 the *TES*, taking the voice of 'the service', regretted the policies of 'cutting the money and curbing the local authorities', and nothing more.

The second choice was unwillingness to centralize. Centralization did occur, dramatically in higher education, but often unsystematically. The pattern was consistent with contradictory impulses, perhaps with continued pursuit of centralization by the DES, but some ministerial reluctance? Joseph was a fairly consistent anti-centralizer, especially on curriculum matters. Perhaps he hoped that vouchers, recurrently considered in these years, would replace administration by regulation through the market. I do not think it was recognized, at first, that a shift in New Right directions required new powers at the centre, including targeted expenditure increases. Cutting the service might encourage some parents to go private, but this was not enough. Cuts on their own made the government vulnerable to accusations of not caring about education at all. Although the need to centralize could have been derived from Hayekian principles, it took time to learn in practice. The spur may not have been principles at all, but growing political unpopularity.

This analysis makes sense of Joseph's style. His curriculum policies, for instance, were ultimately consensual, even though he campaigned hard for his own versions. In this domain, if not in others, he tended to retain what remained of partnership. There was no speedy authoritative solution to the twin issues of testing and the core curriculum during his ministry: rather the usual succession of consultative documents, LEA responses, partial and competing codifications. The tendency was towards 'a framework', but very slowly. The culmination was Joseph's own *Better Schools*, distinctively his own, but an exemplary document, not a compulsory code. As Jane Maw has argued, the real shift came later with the National Curriculum (Maw, 1988). For Joseph's early years, *TES*'s judgement seems true:

> an ideologist of *laissez-faire* . . . profoundly sceptical about central government intervention and its limited capacity to bring about improvement . . . a reluctant dragon . . . who is constantly being forced back, against his will, to his responsibilities under the Education Acts. (*TES*, 24 June 1983)

It is important to distinguish between systematic centralization and *ad hoc* intervention. As campaigners, Joseph and Boyson were always intervening. They worked intervention into their ministerial roles – a kind of opposition from 'above' to the educational interest. They campaigned continually: Boyson on peace studies, sex education, religious and moral education, discipline in school and home, the evils of comprehensives, and the virtues of caning and traditional teaching; Joseph on the teaching of history, economics, profit and free enterprise, left-wing polytechnic and open university courses, tenure in universities, 'inefficient teachers', and the so-called social sciences. These campaigns were authoritarian in the most obvious ways, intimidating, bullying, discriminatory. They kept the educational climate shifting rightwards. They fitted ill with the insistence that education should not be political, or that 'indoctrination' should be banned! Double standards spread cynicism, and confirmed the arguments of left activists: education was 'political' anyway.

Unlike bureaucratic centralization, the interventions were highly personalized. Boyson was said to be making a collection of sex education manuals; Sir Keith let it be known he was scrutinizing Open University units. Attempts to regularize this kind of thing may have been resisted by officials. Perhaps it was a carry-over from the Black Paper years. More symptomatically, was campaigning a sign of weakness and frustration, in the main activities of ministers? What could not be enforced in detail, could be scotched in single instances. What could not be achieved politically, might be prepared for ideologically. Ideological range-riding reached a peak at the time of greatest political frustrations, from 1981 to 1983. Boyson's removal after the 1983 election led to significant reductions.

Underneath all the activity, the dilemmas deepened. Relations with teacher unions worsened through sustained warfare to eventual deadlock. A new layer of Conservative strategies towards professionals surfaced: perhaps the professions themselves could be reformed? Presented as ways of rewarding excellence or weeding out incompetence, the exercise was fundamentally about control. Restructuring schemes rewarded the teacher as manager, not the teacher as teacher (Lawn and Ozga, 1988, p. 326). The moves to restructure college and university teaching, including the abolition of tenure for the latter, were part of a similar movement, a kind of de-professionalization, accompanied by moves to casualization, managerial hierarchies, more 'appraisal' and lessening autonomy. Later policies were foreshadowed, yet note how little was achieved by Joseph here. Was this because the necessary powers were unpalatable?

Negativity was inevitable in a contracting situation, especially the unpopular school closures, deeply embarrassing for the authors of the Parents' Charters of 1975 and 1980. Battles over nursery provision, parental choice and appeals against LEAs, skirmishes with non-teaching school staff, anxieties over school discipline and violence, were endemic with, as yet, no solutions.

At the same time, more positive proposals kept coming from elsewhere. Initiative lay not with the government or the New Right, but with campaigning groups, LEAs, political opponents and even in Europe. The government was forced to block and spoil. Tertiary reorganization was one area where Labour-led innovation threatened to succeed. The caning debate went from bad to worse: the campaigning of STOPP, adverse rulings in Europe, bluster from Boyson, an abortive attempt to legislate on a parental right-of-refusal basis (1985), finally votes for abolition in Lords and Commons (1986). The discussion of multiculturalism and anti-racism was even more troubling. They presented central challenges to the whole New Right programme especially the strengthening of Christianity, maintenance of traditional subjects, the monocultural national curriculum. No wonder attacking multiculturalism and anti-racism became a priority, once a language and a pretext had been found.

There were two exceptions to this dismal pattern, examples of selective spending. In April 1981, the Prime Minister launched a scheme for micro-computers in all secondary schools, subsequently extended to primary schools. In charge was Kenneth Baker, in his second educational assignment. His first was as chairman of a 'secret' committee (with Stuart Sexton) to consider the abolition of the ILEA in 1979 (*TES*, 21 December 1979). In November 1982 it was again the Prime Minister who launched the Technical and Vocational Educational Initiative (TVEI), a joint government-MSC venture, said to be 'the brain-child' of Lord Young (then of the MSC), Joseph and Norman Tebbit, with Mrs Thatcher also deeply interested (Low, 1988, pp. 220–3; Chitty, 1988, p. 44). This was implemented, briskly and from the centre, using the MSC machinery. Both schemes used earmarked money to redirect educational energies in modernizing directions, and made bids to win teachers to new ways of being professional and 'progressive' (see Chapter 4). LEAs and school managers were offered money and kudos. For once, traditionalism was dislodged by an MSC-led coup. For a while it seemed as though the MSC was to be the preferred agency. One faction within the government saw it as the enterprise-led alternative to the DES, its organization of training, especially the use of private training agencies, a model for privatizing education more generally. Significantly, however, this version of government policy was not sustained. The main consequence of the MSC moment may well have been to deepen divisions between government and DES, and stimulate a DES fight-back.

In Joseph's early years, however, cuts and campaigning dominated, combining damage with provocation. Through the medium of the HMI annual reports, the damage was highly visible. The non-conservative press started to cover the effects of education cuts closely, especially the *Daily*

Mirror which ran a dramatic occasional series complete with pictures of closed or run-down schools. This forced the government to be more negative still. Joseph developed a distinctive line of argument about resources: the reported deteriorations were not to do with resources at all, but could be solved by better management training, appraisal and reward to teachers. Though continually repeated, this argument failed to convince anyone in contact with schools. It was clear that basic educational resources (like books) were in short supply, and that the morale of teachers was rapidly sinking. Soon there were sufficient indexes to prove the point: vacant posts (especially in poorer areas and among headteachers), high leaving rates, and low recruitment figures. Yet teachers continued to be battered by all kinds of accusations from ministers and the Conservative media. A major 'disruption' was predictable as early as 1982.

A second strategy was to censor critical voices. There was much discussion of the independence of HMI and the necessity of annual reviews, including accusations of censorship – and their denial. Doubts about the wisdom of annual reviews were inconsistent with the new policy of publishing reports on individual schools. Perhaps this is why some level of independence was preserved, despite important changes in personnel. More successfully the government managed to stem the flood of expert policy-making by abolishing most bodies with a mind of their own. The Schools Council ('too political') and the Advisory Council for Adults and Continuing Education were the most awkward customers. Consultation was replaced by government-dominated bodies: the National Advisory Body (NAB) for the colleges, a series of central curriculum and examination bodies for the schools.

Negativity came to a crisis towards the end of 1981, but was not resolved before the election of 1983 or even after. The Conservative Party Conference of October 1981 was a low point. Conservatives involved in local government and 'wet' critics were anxious about cuts. The Government was reckoned to be unpopular on education, alienating educationists yet failing to satisfy supporters. Cuts, according to Sir William van Straubenzee, now 'threatened the bone' of the service. Joseph gave a strangled speech in reply. Forced into a tangled distinction between apparent and 'real' resources, he stressed the importance of standards, but also the avoidance of centralization. No wonder he announced how intellectually attracted he was to vouchers (*The Times*, 14 October 1981)! When Mrs Thatcher attempted to still anxieties, as she had in the previous year's 'the lady's not for turning' speech, she had little new to offer. Education remained one of her main preoccupations, as well it might. The party's bankruptcy adds credence to the argument that the Falklands/Malvinas war was critical in covering over vulnerabilities in the whole Thatcherite project towards the end of the first term.

Phase 4: The trouble with vouchers: the New Right divided, 1981–3

In this phase Conservative difficulties deepened, apparently around vouchers, more fundamentally around the contradictions analysed earlier. The voucher debates heightened divisions among the now rather dishevelled 'partners', especially Joseph and the DES, but also in Conservative ranks. This phase may be dated from late 1981 to just after the 1983 election.

Vouchers were seriously considered between October 1981 and early summer 1983. Joseph took the lead after his October 1981 declaration of interest. The contents of this speech – insisting on choice, standards and the avoidance of centralization – and its context – the nadir of the party's fortunes in the first term – suggest a certain desperation. In November Joseph invited the voucher lobbies to comment on a DES document specifying difficulties in detail. The officials' comments were technical but discouraging. The revolutionary inplications of vouchers were well understood: they threatened 'a very far reaching change, raising many issues' (DES, December 1981). Could they be reconciled with rational planning and the duty of ensuring a decent education to all? The document ended by posing the question of the LEA role: would vouchers be compatible with 'individual LEA management of the educational service in its area'? Clearly the DES was opposed to vouchers because they would block its moves towards a 'national' system (see also *The Times*, 6 April 1983).

Voucher advocates complained about DES obstruction: IEA writers cited 'bureaucratic self-interest', 'producer power' and Salter and Tapper's 'ambitious bureaucracy' (Seldon, 1986, p. 65). At about this time (*TES*, 19 November 1982) it was announced that TVEI would be under MSC not DES. Relations between ministers and DES cannot have been cordial! Vouchers deepened the split. What price *any* reform, with such disarray at the centre?

The second consequence was disagreement among Conservatives. Late in 1982, with the party still bathed in a South Atlantic glory, divisions emerged more sharply. Before the general election, attempts were made to break the policy deadlocks. Some of the energy came from the frustrated activist at 10 Downing Street, but DES officials were also considering voucher schemes in July 1982. Was this to head off more radical versions? The main line was pursued by Joseph and his 'outside-right adviser' Oliver Letwin (*TES*, 12 November 1982). The outcome was Joseph's 'Two Part' scheme of late 1982: vouchers for private schools to replace the disappointing assisted places and moves towards open enrolement in LEAs with financial help from the centre (*TES*, 5 November 1982). A grant/loan scheme for higher education (HE) was also canvassed. Joseph reported in February 1983 on discussions with LEAs to launch pilot schemes. This or a successor scheme was put to the Cabinet via its 'Family Policy Group' early in 1983. It had the support of Sir Geoffrey Howe and Ferdinand Mount, whose book *The Subversive Family* had been published the year before (*TES*, 5 April 1983; David, 1986, p. 154). Joseph's plan was, however, rejected. The *TES* reported that private schools did not like the scheme, while the LEA aspect was weakened by the resignation of John Barnes as chairman of the Kent Education Committee, the favoured place and person for experiments (*TES*, 8 April 1983).

Joseph's own initiative failed to satisfy anyone, even the Cabinet. Heath attacked it as 'crack-pot' in the *Daily Mirror*. Professor Beloff, who chaired a party policy group, made his own position clear at the 1982 conference: central government should accept more responsibility because the LEAs were defying demands for higher standards and for more choice. This was the obvious alternative to vouchers, prioritizing standards not choice, using central control not the market. Beloff's group contained education 'wets' like Van Straubenzee (chairman of the Backbenchers' Education Committee) and Malcolm Thornton (former chairman of the Association of Metropolitan Authorities). With Beloff, an ex-Black Paperite, opposing the neo-liberals, even the New Right was split. Joseph too was losing neo-liberal support, especially after the IEA's protesting professors (including Friedman, Peacock and Wiseman) earned not even a reply from minister or DES (Seldon, 1986, p. 15).

Conflicts came to a head as the June 1983 election approached. It was widely expected that vouchers and loans would figure in the manifesto. As late as 3 April 1983, ministers and officials were reported to be considering these matters. Just when agreement on something new was most needed, the divisions erupted noisily. The Beloff report was leaked to *The Times* which printed it in full. It unambiguously rejected vouchers and loans; instead the money could be used to rescue rural schools.

> The great majority of the group do not believe that the voucher scheme is the best method for increasing parental choice and so improving standards, since its cost at a time of stretched resources would be hard to justify to a highly sceptical public. (*The Times*, 5 April 1983)

The report affirmed the dual system of state and private schools, with a strong emphasis on standards, controlling teachers, and centralization. It proposed an extension of assisted places, measures to increase competition between state schools, including the publication of HMI reports and examination results, and a rather far-fetched plan for competitive prizes for schools: the 'Queen's Awards for Schools'. It recommended increased central powers to counter LEA resistance to the 1980 Act. Generally traditional on the curriculum, it argued that courses on 'the industrial and commercial substructure' could 'usefully replace' the sociology of education in teacher education! 'O' levels should be retained, and national graded tests adopted. There should be a General Teaching Council, bypassing the unions, and strong LEA intervention on discipline matters. Ethnic minorities should receive no special treatment, since this would set them apart from fellow citizens, but religious (i.e. Christian) education (with rights of withdrawal) should be strengthened. Neglect of religion went along with general inattention to morals, to proper standards of speech, behaviour and appearance, and to duties to the community. Attitudes of a minority of teachers left much to be desired.

The report was a Black Paper without the populism. The authoritarian, centralizing, neo-Conservative side was in dominance. Though authoritative political sources declared the Beloff report irrelevant to the manifesto (*The Times*, 6 April 1983) it blew away chances of agreement in time for the election itself. So the party entered the election in disarray, split three or four ways: LEA Tories, ideological 'wets', neo-liberal voucherites, and Black-Paper traditionalists. Ministers were sandwiched in between, also somewhat divided, and in tension with officials. The confusion was evident in Conservative 'Briefing Notes' (issued for candidates) during the election. A first edition seemed to promise vouchers; this had to be explained away as 'a missing word'. Nor did the new version inspire: 'the Conservative Party is not committed to this, or any other particular method of increasing parental choice'. The manifesto took more from Beloff than from FEVER: the stress was on improved teacher training and parental information. As the *TES* put it, 'shorn' of earlier promises, it 'contains nothing of startling interest' (*TES*, 20 May 1983); there was only TVEI to boast about. Consequently positive education plans were little stressed. Victory depended heavily on Labour's overall vulnerability. With little to point to as Conservative achievements, the *Daily Mail*, key campaigner since Black Paper days, relied instead on scare stories from Labour ILEA (e.g. *Daily Mail*, 12 May 1983)

Phase 5: Divisions recomposed: Joseph's later policies, June 1983–May 1986

The rejection of vouchers set conditions for the next phase in policy. According to Mrs Thatcher, 'We have had a look at it. We simply cannot operate it.· The administrative consequences would be colossal' (quoted *TES*, 24 June 1983). Three months later Joseph told Conference that 'the voucher, at least in the foreseeable future, is dead' (Seldon, 1986, p. xii). Yet it was only the *letter* of the voucher that died: as an ideal it did not disappear, nor were its *implications* dropped, nor were all ministers equally sceptical. Abandonment, however, forced Joseph to develop policies of his own; and it switched neo-liberal energies from voucher schemes *to looking at ways of achieving the same goals by other means*. Internal differences were redrawn. Joseph now allied with DES and some educationists against his erstwhile comrades. Neo-liberals and traditionalists came together again around policies of their own. By 1986 the two lines were in direct rivalry. In this section I consider Joseph's policies; in the next I return to the New Right.

For Joseph the voucher issue was settled: he spoke against readoption in June 1984, August 1985, and during a second pre-election flurry in March/ April 1986. The decision was partly personal. Vouchers had been found wanting; but his official position was important too. The nub of his case against vouchers rehearsed DES arguments: vouchers were inconsistent 'with the requirements that schooling should be available to all without charge, compulsory and of an acceptable standard' (quoted Seldon, 1986, p. 67). In other words there was an absolute contradiction between the principles of the existing system and the tendency of vouchers. This escape route closed, Joseph sought to resolve the contradictions by exploring their other side: he became a reforming secretary of state. After the election, he and his ministers – Bob Dunn (MP for Dartford, in charge of schools) and Peter Brooke (MP for the City, in charge of HE) set to work as 'a slim-line team' to plan policy for the next five years. Was this an attempt to chart a ministerial direction, free from think-tanks and party squabbles? If so, it implied greater dependence on DES expertise. The dropping of Boyson, who linked the right's campaigns and the government, pointed in the same direction. Leaks suggested early plans for tighter central direction, selective financial expansion, distinctive curriculum policies, and a stress on teacher management and efficiency (*TES*, 17 and 24 June 1983).

The new departures were not so new. They resumed DES policy in the mid-1970s and echoed the Young–Tebbit stress on the MSC and TVEI. The strategy was to modernize from above, to extend 'the new vocation-alism' or 'the training paradigm'. Curriculum emphases, first developed in relation to training (especially YTS), were then applied to FE, and finally to 5–16 schooling and beyond. Joseph's version differed from Young's in one respect: its chosen instruments. Young looked to the MSC and the Private Training Agencies (a model for privatization); Joseph revived the co-operation of DES, LEAs and teachers, with relationships between them duly reformed. DES and LEAs were to be more directive, but the policy presupposed continuing the public service and the rhetoric of partnership. Joseph re-emerged as a 'public educator' with a bias towards industrial training (Williams, 1965). The most consolidated expression of his policy was *Better Schools* (March 1985). Its most dramatic statement was a speech at the North of England Education Conference in the same year. This won 'remarkable bi-partisan support' (Morris and Griggs, 1988, p. 21), presum-ably from the assembled managers. The objects of all this management (teachers) were not, as usual, consulted.

Better Schools departed from the familiar New Right lines in several ways.

Parental choice was de-emphasized. Only modest increases in parental representation on governing bodies were envisaged (DES, 1985, chs 7 and 9); local devolution plans were noted, but not pursued. It was argued that there were many social interests in education. Education was a 'national' issue, a 'public service', 'an investment in the nation's future' (ibid., p. 1). Government's task was to 'mediate and where necessary reconcile the needs and wishes of all those outside the system' (p. 4). The definitions of the 1944 Act were much cited (e.g. ibid., pp. 4, 11–12 and 59). Apart from governing bodies, there was no need for new law (ibid., p. 63). Reform was needed to 'raise standards'. Standards were not judged, however, by past excellence, but by 'the demands of the modern world' (ibid., p. 1). Indeed, the stress of *Better Schools* was less on *higher* standards than on *different* ones:

> It is vital that schools should always remember that preparation for working life is one of their principal functions. The economic stresses of our time and the pressures of international competition make it more necessary than ever before that Britain's work-force should possess the skills and attitudes, and display the understanding, the enterprise and adaptability that the pervasive impact of technological advance will increasingly demand. This applies equally to those who will be employed by others and to the many who may expect . . . to be self-employed. The balance within the curriculum and the emphasis in teaching it now need to alter accordingly. (ibid., p. 1)

This rejigging of knowledge – 'a broad, balanced, differentiated and relevant curriculum' – was an attempt to redefine the core values of the curriculum. Overtly political flourishes – the attack on peace studies on the grounds that war should be studied too (ibid., p. 24), the insistence on removing 'clutter' (p. 18), the silence on social matters but volubility on economic ones, 'notably the operation of market forces' (p. 23) – were the most naked aspects of this ambition. *Better Schools* tried to forge the missing link – a distinctive New Right curriculum, appropriate to the capitalist context. Main features were the consolidation of religion and morality, the foregrounding of science and technology, the privileging of 'the nature and values of British society' (ibid., p. 20), and the reiteration of MSC keywords: 'relevance', 'enterprise', 'adaptability'.

Joseph abandoned the nostalgic polemics of the Black Papers. He actually praised achievements since 1944, eschewed attacks on comprehensives and adopted educationists' policies like GCSE, TVEI, CPVE, 'AS' levels, and records of attainment. He even praised true teacher 'professionalism'. There were failings to be sure, but nothing that better management, training, appraisal could not put right. No fundamental structural change was necessary. The sting in the tail was well sheathed: 'a significant number of teachers are performing at a standard below that required to achieve the objectives now proposed for the schools' (ibid., p. 50): hence the demands for reorganizing the profession, not accountability to parents only but restructuring and appraisal from 'above'. Unsurprisingly, educational managers were the most enthusiastic supporters of the new Sir Keith. After all, he adopted their language and point of view. Several senior education officers and ex-civil servants had already spoken in favour of centralization. Yet the new moves did not become the basis of a larger alliance. Two crucial groups opposed them: the educational New Right and the teachers. Together they ensured that even after this mid-term rally, Joseph's epic ministry ended in disappointment.

Joseph alienated neo-liberals by rejecting vouchers, allying with the DES and trying reform rather than privatization. He alienated traditionalists by agreeing to educational reforms redolent of the 1970s. The 16+ (GCSE) was consistently criticized by the Centre for Policy Studies (e.g. March 1984, July 1985); the new 'AS' levels, even with their 'merit' grade, were attacked by the government's own advisers (November 1984). Multicultural and anti-racist education was another flashpoint. By the mid-1980s the New Right had spotted anti-racist policies as a suitable case for campaigning. Struggles over the final report of the Swann Committee, the adoption of anti-racist policies by Labour LEAs and the emergence of 'martyrs' in the anti-anti-racist cause, like the Bradford headmaster Ray Honeyford, provided political focuses. New Right campaigning revived from 1984 to 1987, with a plethora of think-tank reports and papers from *ad hoc* campaigning groups, with overlapping membership (Cox and Scruton, 1984; Adam Smith Institute, 1984; Flew, 1987; Scruton, Ellis-Jones and O'Keefe, 1985; Seldon, 1986; Palmer, 1986; No Turning Back Group of MPs, 1986; Hillgate Group, 1986; Hillgate Group 1987; Sexton 1987). Aside from the inevitable return of vouchers and other routes to the market, issues included discipline, sex education, religious education, and 'political indoctrination' in schools. Anti-racism was central in all this, raising critical curriculum issues and providing ways of attacking ILEA and other LEAs (Troyna, 1985).[4]

In his new role Joseph was poorly placed to exploit this militancy. The constraints of his office were illustrated in relation to multicultural education. His rejection of much of the Swann Report did not endear him to anti-racist campaigners, but *Better Schools* was more liberal than the anti-anti-racist lobby. It accepted that 'ethnic diversity' required help under Section 11, adding a new support grant of £1 million. It also had implications for the curriculum as a whole (pp. 61–2). Only in a speech delivered on the very day of his resignation, did Joseph align himself more firmly with the right:

> It would be unnecessary . . . and I believe wrong, to turn our education system upside down to accommodate ethnic variety, or to jettison those

many features and practices which reflect what is best in our society and its institutions. This position offers a spurious justification for prejudice – for the self-indulgent bias of those who in any case want to subvert our fundamental values and institutions. (*Daily Mail* 22 May 1986)

Schools should 'acknowledge' minority cultures, but 'transmit British culture, enriched as it has been by so many traditions'. The primary responsibilities for reproducing minority cultures lay with homes and communities. Presumably the process of national enrichment should stop in 1986!

So in office, Joseph alienated his own 'side'. But he also alienated teachers. He offered little relief in the daily struggle to make ends meet in the schools or at home. The teachers' action of 1985–6 expressed a ten-year accumulation of grievances sharpened by novel burdens and threats: pay, conditions of service, the intensification of labour, cuts, the threat to professional autonomies, the sense of being undervalued as a profession and as a service (Ball, 1988). A solution on the salary issue was repeatedly blocked by Joseph's insistence on the new conditions of service.

Again, his 'parting shots' were significant. On the day of his resignation, the HMI Annual Report on the conditions of schools appeared. The remedies were there, Joseph insisted: training, deployment, management and leadership (*Guardian*, 22 May 1986; and cf. *Mail* and *Mirror*). This final exchange showed his failure to resolve the key contradictions. Underneath the strenuous policy-making, the crisis of negativity persisted. With no alternatives in place, he could still be blamed for the run-down of the service. Centralization similarly remained an unresolved dilemma. Still wedded to free-market ideals, he took power unwillingly, preferring a more consensual model of change. The most important lesson of 1982–6 was that reform, even on neo-liberal lines, required decisive central control. It was a lesson that was to be well learned.

Phase 6: Conservative factions and the pool of ideas, 1985–6

Joseph's last year saw an intensive, polarized debate within the party. This created a pool of ideas on which the authors of the 1987 manifesto and the 1988 Act could draw.

Joseph was not allowed his independence for long. The Prime Minister intervened again in education, determined, no doubt, to avoid the chaos of 1983. In July 1985 she let it be known on television that 'I would like to bring back what are called direct grant schools. We are', she said, 'looking at that.' She also resuscitated the voucher:

I'm very disappointed that we were not able to do the voucher scheme and I sometimes think that I must have another go because there are a number of parents who come and say well look we would like to spend more of our money on educating our children, but there isn't the possibility. It's either all private or all state. (*TES*, 19 July 1985)

This bombshell was dropped four months after the 'settlement' of *Better Schools*, and a year after Joseph's last requiem for vouchers. There was speculation that he was about to be sacked (e.g. *TES* leader, 2 August 1985): this was wishful thinking, but the bombshell impacted in two directions.

First, after non-committal DES responses, the 'direct grant' plan was confirmed by Joseph, as his own initiative: 'The DES has, at my request been exploring the possibility of a limited experiment with the restoration of direct grant schools' (*TES*, 2 August 1985). Thereafter Joseph and Patten, his under secretary of state, pushed this idea as an alternative to vouchers. 'Crown schools' had some features of the CTCs and of 'opting out': they could be primary or secondary, set up by parents or charitable trusts, to receive per capita grants from the DES, and to charge fees (*TES*, 2 August 1985). A 1986 version prepared by Patten and a senior schools official at the DES was submitted to the Cabinet Home Affairs Committee under Joseph's name. It envisaged fifty such schools in 'inner city' locations (*TES*, 4 April 1986). According to Biddy Passmore's knowledgeable reports and leaks from LEA Conservatives, crown schools were pursued in opposition to vouchers (Passmore in *TES*, 4 April 1986; Demitri Argyropoulou in *TES*, 1 March 1986).

Secondly, Mrs Thatcher's statement heartened voucherites and stimulated think-tank activity, including Seldon's history of March 1986, *The Riddle of the Vouchers*. His most striking claim, in the circumstances, was that vouchers would have prevented the teachers' action, by undermining union power. They should be introduced in stages. A more influential focus was Bob Dunn, the other under secretary of state. He argued for direct-grant schools, but criticized Joseph's reliance on management rather than the market. In inner neo-liberal circles (an 'International Symposium of the Open Society' no less) he sketched an ideal destination: a system of independent schools, accountable to parents, free to run their own affairs and budgets. This might be achieved by diverse routes and in 'gentle evolutionary steps' (*TES*, 2 August 1985). The speech is the earliest example I found of flexible strategic thinking on the neo-liberal right. Dunn did not advocate vouchers in stages merely, as Seldon did, but took the *logic* of the voucher (the education market) and suggested there were many ways to achieve it.

Dunn was a committed neo-liberal. He worked with Oliver Letwin, one-time education adviser to Joseph and to the Prime Minister, and with Stuart Sexton, linchpin of the Assisted Places Scheme, and now Dunn's own adviser (*TES*, 5 March 1986). Sexton was in the Education Unit of the IEA (Demaine, 1988, p. 264, note 4). His work showed the same attention to detail as Dunn's speeches (Sexton, 1987; *Guardian*, 11 June 1987). The *TES* ascribed to this trio a version of the Direct Grant Scheme which foregrounded opting out. Were they central in working up a more practicable neo-liberal strategy for government?

Instead of splitting, as Beloff and the neo-liberals did in 1983, the New Right factions now unified. Arguments for the traditional curriculum and for choice were combined. The Hillgate Group, traditionalist to the point of self-parody, advocated Latin and Greek, European languages over Asian, 'hard' subjects over 'soft', and dismissed multiculturalism in favour of 'the traditional values of Western societies'. But the group was also anti-state and pro-market, causing a stir by attacking HMI: 'as likely as any other section of the educational establishment to be subverted by bureaucratic self-interest and fashionable ideology' (Hillgate Group, 1986; Hillgate Group, 1987; *Guardian*, 30 December 1986). The tendency was remarkably tightly knit with membership overlaps between the IEA, its Institute of Social Affairs, the Education Committee of the CPS, the Adam Smith Institute's Omega group on education and the Hillgate Group.

The voucher bundle untied, a cascade of ideas fell out. Schemes for 'gentle evolutionary steps' proliferated: new types of central funding ('direct grant'), opting out, financial delegation, strengthening of parental involvement, open enrolment, model or magnet schools. The broad strategy was common property to sensible new-rightists by the end of 1986. The tracing of more precise origins of Act or manifesto is more tricky. Think-tanks are not only about inventing policies; they may make policies *already devised* more feasible by speaking the unspeakable. More important, probably, was the hidden work of ministers and advisers, interest groups and officials.

By March 1986, the limits of Joseph's management were clear; he had decided to resign by Christmas 1985. Polarization now deepened. Right-wing parliamentarians tacked their favourite amendments (sex education and 'indoctrination') on to the Parent Governors Bill (introduced in October 1985). Joseph and Patten faced hostile meetings. To Teresa Gorman's insistence that voucher schemes were 'easy', Joseph snapped: 'It is not very simple. I assure you.' He had responsibility for every child, and 'You need very long and very complex legislation' (*TES*, 7 March 1986). Patten, quizzed by backbenchers demanding total privatization, insisted that there could be no market in education since schooling was compulsory and the parent could not be allowed to accept a shoddy service (*TES*, 21 March 1986). Such debates may have been educative. Mrs Thatcher, pro-voucher in February, was cautious in March: vouchers were 'a very, very long-term thing' (*TES*, 4 April 1986). Had she grasped the Dunn–Sexton–Letwin point? By April, the press had coined a phrase to describe the other, Joseph–Patten side, 'the new Butlerism' (*TES*, 4 April 1986). Their toughness was important in clarifying ideas too.

A final complexity was the influence of LEA Conservatives. According to an ex-chairman of the Conservative National Advisory Committee on Education, there was a party majority for Joseph's policies as the only way to improve all of the schools. An alliance of militants stood in the way: the ILEA and the National Union of Teachers (NUT) on one side; 'the loopy far right to a few senior ministers' on the other. 'Moderates' formed the Conservative Education Association in 1987. (*Guardian*, 31 March 1987), but established groups like the Conservative-dominated Association of County Councils (ACC) were more effective sources of pressure. Nor was stopping power the only local influence: Kent's experiments in open enrolment (see *TES*, 24 June 1983) and Cambridgeshire's introduction of financial delegation in January 1986 were the most significant experiments.

Phase 7: 'I love it when a plan comes together': the B(aker) team and the Education Act

Baker replaced Joseph in May 1986. Significantly the new team included Dunn, balanced by George Walden, a traditionalist on curriculum matters. Events now moved so rapidly that some new policies must have been in place before the change-over. Was Baker appointed to see them through, primarily for his political skills?

It was reported in May that Joseph had left Baker a draft submission for £1,000 million of extra spending. This proposal was activated in June. Baker also demanded tightened control, through the DES, over LEA spending. Extensions were anounced to TVEI. The moral that reform costs money was quickly grasped. In October, just six months after his appointment, Baker launched his city technical colleges, close relatives to crown schools. In this speech he also hinted at a Bill. Even his platitudes suggested larger ambitions: 'We must lift our eyes to the more distant horizon. We must plan for a better future for our young people' (*Guardian*, 8 October 1986). In November 1986, the English committee (later Kingman Report) was appointed. In January, Baker hinted at a national curriculum using continental comparisons to attack 'our maverick education system' (*Guardian*, 10 January 1987). The election approached to a crescendo of educational initiatives: March saw the delegation of powers and budgets to schools; a week later Mrs Thatcher confirmed a major Bill; in April a White Paper set out new arrangements for higher education and the National Curriculum appeared; early May saw open enrolment and the 'contract' system for higher education.

Education was a more significant issue for politicians, journalists and voters in 1987 than it had been in 1979 or 1983 (for voters see Ivor Crewe, *Guardian*, 15 June 1988). The Conservative manifesto anticipated the Education Reform Bill. Baker's moves to abolish teachers' negotiating rights, his pre-emptive solution to Joseph's stalemate, ensured that 1987, like 1979, was accompanied by teachers' action. The initiatives met some checks: mid-campaign differences between Baker and Thatcher exposed neo-liberal ambitions. The Prime Minister broke rudely into Baker's careful presentation of policy; her anticipations of selection and fee-paying had hastily to be explained away. Critics put Thatcher and the think-tank reports together and came up, not unreasonably, with a conspiracy for complete privatization. Sexton's pamphlet (March 1987) was especially indicative of what was 'really intended' (e.g. Sara Boseley in *Guardian*, 11 June and Jack Demaine's follow-up in the letters page).

When the government won on 11th June 1987, it was clear that a major measure was imminent. Three months later the *Daily Mail* jubilantly declared: 'Nothing Will Stop Us Now' (15 September 1987). Analysis of the vote suggested increased Conservative support among working-class voters and the business middle class, but losses among professionals, college-goers, and the public sector salariat. As Ivor Crewe put it, 'Mrs Thatcher's personal preference for businessmen over bureaucrats and profit-makers over professors is, it appears, fully reciprocated' (*Guardian*, 15 June 1987).

The parliamentary passage of the Education Act of July 1988 was less formative of the measure than its longer-term genesis. The critical and hidden story of 1986–8 is how Baker, Dunn and their advisers found a politically acceptable course among the Conservative factions. As a public measure, the Bill was modified very little. 'Consultation' with the educational interests was insultingly perfunctory and unproductive (Haviland, 1988; Simon, 1988). Among opponents, excessive faith was placed on magical interventions by their Lordships. In practice, the Bill was forced through by the parliamentary majority against the wishes of unions, teachers, educationists, organized parent groups and most LEA politicians, but with some complicity from Labour and its spokesman, Jack Straw. Parliamentary pressures firmed up the religious requirements, blunted attacks on 'academic freedom', secured outright abolition of ILEA, gained some space for teachers in the 'delivery' of the curriculum, and made it more difficult for minorities to hijack opting out (*Independent*, 28 July 1988, and *Guardian*, 17 August 1988). Government apart, the main beneficiaries of changes were the established Church and the university vice-chancellors.

It is tempting to close our tale by ascribing responsibility to individuals: 'the Baker Act', 'the Joseph Era', 'Mrs Thatcher's Coup', 'Rhodes Boyson's Great Adventure'? I prefer to exercise some modest authorial power by refusing to see these people as heroes! They seem to me to personify dilemmas or solutions, much larger than themselves. Carlisle was the defending lawyer for a system which was accused but not yet sentenced. His reassurances masked an absence of ideas, the evasion of contradictions. Boyson's campaigning role was unmatched by solidity in office. He embodied the New Right's more vindictive energies, but also its imaginary, romantic side, its nostalgia, odd in so 'practical' a man. In Joseph, Conservative contradictions found perfect expression. He was the anti-centralizing interventionist, the enterprising traditionalist, the public-service free-marketeer. His constant, verbal reiteration of principles and mad-cap activism, showed that the contradictions could no longer be contained. His frustration was intolerable. To ascribe the Act, the solution, to Baker is convenient but misleading: so much was learned before he came to office. His contribution was to achieve the possible. Yet there was something about his round appearance, complacency and ambition that told the world a 'settlement' had been found, sufficient for his purpose.

The 1988 Act as political strategy I: unifying the Thatcherite alliance

The 1988 Act was a major political success. It reproduced and reunified an alliance, dominated by the New Right. It offered ways for this alliance to expand. It disorganized the oppositions, professional and political. It broke through many constraints. Yet just as New Right theory lacked structural understanding, so its policy lacked historical range. It did not provide means to solve socio-educational problems in the long run. In the following sections, I consider the short-term strengths of the Act and its longer-term weaknesses.

It is revealing to relate the Act to our analysis of factions and contradictions. The New Right alliance was reunified by harmonizing the programmes of neo-liberals, neo-Conservatives and traditionalists, and even of Conservative modernizers and LEA Tories. The act was a set of compromises. Some programmes, however, were written in more strongly than others. Nor did the different factions reach a *final* settlement. So the Act must be read dynamically, for different *possibilities*. Though it rewrote the rules, it could not determine the outcomes. Its political character was mixed. The question is what mixture precisely, what *balance* of possibilities was inscribed there?

There is no question that it is a neo-liberal measure in three important respects. First, it creates an alternative network of schools, more consistent with neo-liberal principles. Opted-out schools, city technical colleges and an expanding private sector provide alternatives to the LEA system into which parents may 'exit' individually or as a body around a school. CTCs and some opted-out schools will be champions to ride against the local comprehensives. After decent delays, the secretary of state will manipulate the balance of advantages in favour of the opted-out sector, extending the logic of public-sector cuts. Already, deteriorating conditions in LEA schools, or adverse publicity, induce the better-off to go private. Soon, when complaints are made about public schooling, fanfares for the new sector will be played. All schools will be told to go and do likewise, whether they can or not.

Second, the public system is being restructured to adapt it to market pressures and a possible future of vouchers. Important here are the devolution of budgets and management to governing bodies and open enrolment. To complaints that these measures frustrate LEA attempts to plan, the honest neo-liberal answer is that this is the intention: introduce competition into the heart of the LEA system and you displace or discipline bureaucratic decisions. School closures, for example, should follow parental preferences, not dictate them. The logic of this is that LEA powers should be limited, and that they should compete with other agencies as providers of services to schools. The extended logic is that LEAs should cease to exist.

A third feature of these measures is that they promise to recruit parents to the theory and practice of 'choice'. Alliances can now be made with parents fighting school closures, demanding special provision on religious grounds, or wanting a return to clear marks of educational advantage within the public sector. Political liabilities (e.g. unpopularity over closures; uncertainties around sex education) are turned to advantage (opting out; giving powers to school governors). Mrs Thatcher sees the Act as equivalent to the sale of council houses:

> Just as we gained political support in the last election from people who had acquired their own homes and shares . . . we shall secure still further our political base in 1991–92 – by giving people a real say in education and housing, (Quoted in *The Independent*, 17 July 1987)

So one plausible reading of the Act is that it is a thorough going neo-liberal measure, introducing a free market by stealth (Johnson, 1988; Demaine, 1988; Simon, 1988). It certainly establishes some of the conditions for vouchers and loans, which are merely deferred. Baker himself often uses neo-liberal language to describe his policies:

> Education can no longer be led by the producers – the academic theorists, the administrators, and even the teachers' union . . . Education must be shaped by the users – by what is good for the individual child and what hopes are held by the parent, (Speech to the Conservative Party Conference, quoted in the *Guardian*, 8 October 1986)

> The Bill will lay important obligations on central government, on local authorities and on governing bodies. But it will be for the parents to judge performance – not the producers but the consumers. In the 18th century Adam Smith warned us that 'the interest of the producer ought

to be attended to only in so far as it may be necessary for promoting that of the consumer. (Speech to the North of England Education Conference, 6 January 1988; mimeo)

As we have seen, there was certainly a neo-liberal strategy – 'gentle evolutionary steps' – corresponding to this reading of the Act. Yet to see the Act as neo-liberalism in practice ignores its others aspects and involves too conspiratorial a view of policy-making. It overlooks divisions in Conservative politics and contradictions in the Act. One sign of this complexity is neo-liberal opposition to some aspects of the Act. The Institute of Economic Affairs, for example, was sceptical of the National Curriculum:

> Attempts by Government and by Parliament to impose a curriculum, no matter how 'generally agreed' they think it to be, are a poor second best in terms of quality, flexibility and responsiveness to needs than allowing the market to decide and setting the system free to respond to the overwhelming demand for higher standards. (Haviland, 1988, p. 28; and cf. pp. 156–8)

In another twist in his career, Lord Joseph moved an amendment to make the National Curriculum advisory only. The curriculum 'is the very opposite of the freedom, spontaneity, and decentralisation this Government has made its watchword for all its policies' (Joseph, quoted in the *Guardian*, 4 May 1988). On a different tack, the CPS supported opting out as an escape from the horrors of 'peace studies', 'gay and lesbian lessons' and 'hostility to Britain and its culture'; but it did wish that the new sector could become 'even more like independent schools'. It should not be subject to the National Curriculum and be permitted to be selective (Haviland, 1988, pp. 105–8). Neo-liberals refused to claim the curriculum as their own; it owed its genesis to other impulses.

The second feature of the Act was the tendency to centralization. It introduced an unparalleled degree of central direction into curriculum matters. It continued the erosion of LEA powers in relation to schools, colleges and polytechnics. It abolished the major rival to the central state, ILEA. It completed the long-standing moves away from consultative and representative bodies and towards managing agencies like the new Schools Examination and Assessment Council (SEAC) and the National Curriculum Council (NCC). It was accompanied by Baker's assumption of power over salaries and conditions. In short, the 1988 Act and its associated policies destroyed the conventions about 'partnership', subordinated LEAs to the DES, and restructured professional relationships. Many of these features were anticipated by Joseph and the DES. Under Baker, however, centralization was pursued with a new vigour, bringing 'order' into 'chaos':

Our 'maverick education system' was a muddle that defied description. Hardly anyone in it could be sure where responsibility lay . . . In my view the country is entitled to an education system which not only works well but is also intelligible and shows clearly where responsibility and accountability lie. (Speech to the North of England Education Conference, quoted in the *Guardian*, 6 January 1987)

We have already considered the pressures that led government to adopt this 'continental' stance, especially the lesson of the Joseph years that structural reform was impossible without taking power. LEAs and the professions had to be weakened first, a prospect that appealed for other political reasons. Further pressures to centralize must have come from the DES. Without inside knowledge, it is hard to say how far the Act was the product of the department, how far of the politicians and their advisers. Perhaps both the DES and Baker accepted the political inevitability of moves towards 'choice', while opposing the full logic of a neo-liberal restructuring. The DES remained committed to a public system though with less local autonomy; Baker, one might surmise, was concerned to harmonize the Conservative factions, taking some policies from each.

It is helpful to define 'centralizing' more tightly. Baker's way of handling this question has been to insist that the Act is 'devolutionary' not centralizing:

> I would ask those who have comments to make about the Bill not to misrepresent its nature and purpose. It is about enhancing the life chances of young people. It is about the devolution of authority and responsibility. It is about competition, choice and freedom . . . It is about quality and standards . . . It is not about enhancing central control . . . So far as *financial delegation* is concerned, the purpose of the legislation is to ensure that responsibility is shifted – not from local authorities to the centre – but from local authorities to the individual colleges and schools. It is thus a devolutionary not a centralising measure. (Speech to the North of England Education Conference, 6 January 1988; mimeo)

This manoeuvre is clever, but does not convince. In a long view, the English system has seen a balance of local and national powers. A succession of local elites have assumed local educational control. Latterly, professionals have dominated. The Act weakens the power of this local establishment and in this sense centralizes: it reverses a whole historical pattern (Johnson, 1988).

The strengthening of the powers of school and college governors is connected to this shift in several ways. First, it is one way LEAs are weakened. They do not lose particular powers only. The integrity of their districts as units of planning is threatened, especially by opting out. But secondly, the devolution of powers cannot be said to offset this loss of local competence. Individual schools are differently placed in relation to the DES than a massive organization like ILEA. An individual school can hardly be said to counterbalance a national state. It cannot even claim to speak for a whole locality or arbitrate competing local needs. So the effect of the 'devolutionary' erosion of LEA competence is to reduce local power overall, especially as a counterbalance to the centre.

Of course, it is hard to predict the future: there are three possibilities. The most probable is that oversight will be assumed by the centre. Already many functions in relation to opted-out schools and colleges have passed to the DES. As fresh problems arise in the localities, the power to arbitrate between local groupings may pass to HMI and the DES, adding to the already burgeoning powers of the minister. Against this, central officials may realize that they cannot do without LEAS, because impossible burdens will accrue to themselves. After all, the first local authorities (the school boards) were invented to relieve the centre from direct control of thousands of 'voluntary' schools (Johnson, 1988, p. 116). We might expect an increasingly explicit struggle over the extent and shape of LEA powers in the next few years, with neo-liberals pressing for further erosion and with LEAs and maybe the DES opposing the trend.

Another possibility is that as problems arise between schools and colleges co-operation will be established between their governing bodies. Inter-school negotiation could modify the harmful effects of competition. If this were to happen, devolution might become real, with the growth of new intermediate powers in education (groupings of schools or colleges) with a more democratic base than the old LEA. This is something for genuine democrats to aim for, but a long way from the purposes of the Act, in any of its versions.

The preferred model of inter-school relations is competitive. A main point of the National Curriculum, testing and the publishing of aggregate results, is to introduce choice, competition, market relations. If schools start to co-operate, this erodes 'consumer sovereignty'. Groups of schools would be behaving like 'monopolies', exercising producer power again. New Right theory would find this behaviour hard to grasp. As a local strategy it is promising; but if it becomes at all popular, we might expect further intervention to try to stop it happening.

This speculation allows us to identify the difference between democratic devolution and the neo-liberal model. The former aims to *extend* politics and revivify democratic practice by devising ways of negotiating the interests involved; the latter seeks to *contain* politics by reducing it to an economics – to 'choice' and 'consumption'. Voting to opt out is the expression of consumer choice not political will. A few parents may acquire another economic function: that of management. No means for handling genuine conflicts of interests are provided – appeal to higher authorities apart. Voting and 'management' are technical matters, expressing and satisfying wants. There is little room for negotiating wants in the first place. It is the market that decides.

Under the old system the LEAs were a focus of communal interest wider than those of one school. Their structures were inadequately democratic and were professionalized. The same has been true of wider national debates about educational and social goals. But the Act displaces these forms of expert participation, without putting more democratic means in their place. It may therefore increase bureaucracy and coercion. My argument about the Act's 'devolutions' parallels Andy Green's about its centralizations (Chapter 1). The Act is flawed as a centralizing measure because it offers complication, diversity and inequality rather than standardization, intelligibility and fairness. It fails as a 'devolutionary' measure because it enhances rather than checks central control. In fact, both categories – 'centralization' and 'devolution' – are inadequate descriptions of the measure.

If the National Curriculum alienated neo-liberals, it drew support from traditionalist and neo-Conservatives. Baker frequently justified it in terms of the long debate about the core curriculum: 'this historic reform represents the culmination of over ten years of debate' (speech on the Consultative Document on the National Curriculum, quoted in the *Guardian*, 25 July 1987). Actually it represented ten or more years of frustration in the Conservative Party. As in this 'debate' so in the Act, traditional views of the curriculum predominated. Many commentators have stressed its endorsement of traditional subject boundaries, neglect of interdisciplinarity, insistence on 'objective' forms of testing, and general closures on experimentation (Simon, 1988; Lawton and Chitty, 1988; Haviland, 1988). It has been argued, persuasively, that it owes little to previous versions, even *Better Schools* (Maw in Lawton and Chitty, 1988, pp. 56–63). Appropriately nostalgic, it resembles nothing more than the grammar school curriculum of 1902 (Aldrich, 1988 in Lawton and Chitty, pp. 22–3)!

The makers of the Act passed over attempts to rejig the curriculum according to MSC or FEU ideas; it disappointed the modernizers. They had to make do with minor concessions, especially the inclusion of science and technology in the compulsory core. Disappointment is clear from responses to the Consultative Document on the National Curriculum (July 1987). They welcomed the assumption of control, but regretted the choice of curriculum. The Royal Society of Arts supported a national curriculum 'as the entitlement of all pupils', but noted that 'the consultation paper offers no philosophical or other justification for the list of foundation subjects proposed (or even for a subject-based approach)'. It stressed how 'much recent experience, including that of TVEI, shows the value of an integrated approach rather than a single subject approach' (Haviland, 1988,

p. 14). The Confederation of British industries (CBI) reaffirmed its commitment to 'cross-curricular themes that relate to life after school and the world of work in particular' (ibid., p. 29). The MSC urged the government to take account of TVEI and 'cross-curricular schemes'. The FEU noted the gap between the National Curriculum and the latest innovations in FE: 'testing competence on multi-disciplinary tasks, an emphasis on the integration of learning, individualized learning programmes and personal effectiveness as a curriculum objective in its own right' (ibid., p. 58). The School Curriculum Development Committee (itself to be replaced by the National Curriculum Council) summed it up nicely:

> the specification of the national curriculum is in terms of *traditional subjects* . . . By contrast there has been recognition in recent years that traditional subjects alone are not an adequate vehicle for conveying the knowledge, concepts, skills and attitudes required by pupils in the last years of the twentieth century and the early years of the twenty-first (ibid., p. 54).

The Consultative Document developed no curriculum philosophy of its own. It referred to *Better Schools* and an alleged consensus over educational aims (Consultative Document, p. 2). Baker himself, while commenting copiously on curriculum matters from history to Shakespeare, from grammar to nursery rhymes, rarely elaborates educational arguments. In the absence of greater explicitness, it is revealing to place the National Curriculum in two contexts: the pattern of New Right campaigning around curriculum matters and the assumptions to be found in neo-Conservative writings.

In the first context, the curriculum seems a primarily political intervention. It implements years of campaigning around 'sociology' and 'social science', peace studies, sex education, religious instruction, anti-racist and multicultural education and around 'progressive education' and 'second-order subjects' more generally. It is the culmination of the Black Paper campaigns, many themes of which were revived in the formative period 1985–7. Like these campaigns, the curriculum favours conventional subject categories to exclude what it disapproves of. It imposes its 'standards' negatively; it stops the rot. This helps to explain the astonishing silences on multicultural education, social studies, personal and social education, cross-disciplinary combinations like integrated humanities, political education, and careers programmes. In the Consultative Document of July 1987 none of these areas was mentioned even as 'additional subjects' (Consultative Document, p. 7).

Yet they are all areas which provide opportunities to explore different social orientations to knowledges and values. Partly for this reason, they attracted the energies of left-wing or feminist or anti-racist teachers and acquired a radical reputation. Of course they were not the only areas so affected; English and the newer history, geography and religious studies syllabuses were important too. Even so, exclusion under the writ of subject disciplines was an effective way of intervening politically without appearing to, cutting out a whole generation of innovations. How could it be political to assert the centrality of regular school subjects! Where, as in core and foundation subjects, wholesale exclusion of critical perspectives was impossible, control was sought through direct prescription, the minister having the last word.

This interpretation makes further sense in the light of neo-Conservative notions of knowledge and nation. One lesson I learned in my New Right education was that neo-Conservativism works with an utterly non-relative or absolute conception of values (see Chapter 3 below). As the term *National* Curriculum implies, these values are seen as national. At the same time, national culture is itself defined in exclusive, nostalgic and frequently racist terms. This helps to explain why, of all the innovations of the 1980s, multicultural and anti-racist education created most anxiety and aggression on the right, the *Daily Mail*'s tale about 'Red Ken's race spy advisers' matched by Scruton's sonorous dismissals:

> In the light of these considerations, it seems to me that there can be no real argument for a 'multi-cultural' curriculum. To adopt such a curriculum is to fail to transmit either the common culture of Britain or the high culture which has grown from it. And no other culture is put in the place of those: the result is nothing more than a void. (Scruton in Palmer, 1986)

In formulations like these, culture is thought of as a homogeneous way of life or tradition, not as a sphere of difference, relationship, or power. No recognition is given to the real diversity of social orientations and cultures within a given nation-state or people. Yet a selective version of a national culture is installed as an absolute condition for any social identity at all. The borrowing, mixing and fusion of elements from different cultural systems, a commonplace everyday practice in societies like contemporary Britain, is unthinkable within this framework, or is seen only as a kind of cultural misrule that will produce 'nothing more than a void'. So the 'choices' are between hermetically sealed national cultures of an incompatible kind, or between a national culture and no culture at all.

Something of this dogmatic and absolutist spirit did lodge itself in the idea of a national curriculum, specifically in its implied monoculturalism, the non-recognition of ethnic diversity (including dominant Anglo-ethnicities), in the refusal to recognize Asian languages and respond to multilingual situations more generally, and in the ethnocentric preferring of European foreign languages. More generally the National Curriculum used traditional subjects, their common-sense definitions and canons (e.g.

'English', 'a modern language') to override the cultural diversity of contemporary Britain and to privilege a particular version of Britishness. It was significant that one of the few campaigns successfully to modify the curriculum framework was that led by Baroness Cox to re-install Christianity as the dominant religion in the schools, while some of the most despairing comments on the Consultative Document came from the Commission for Racial Equality (CRE) and the national body of LEA advisers, the Association of LEA Advisory Officers for Multicultural Education (ALOAME) (e.g. Haviland, 1988, pp. 46–8).

It was, then, the different fractions of the New Right who had most to celebrate in the Bill, but other groups in and around the Conservative Party received some crumbs of comfort. LEA Conservatives and 'wet' Tories were critical of many aspects of the Act. The ACC, for instance, flatly rejected opting out (Haviland, 1988, p. 123). Yet there must have been some relief that inroads into the LEA system were not greater. By delaying more decisive free-market moves the Act evoked some support from Conservatives still committed to improving the public system. Large-scale rebellion was avoided.

The strength of the 1988 Act, politically, was its versatility. It could be presented in different ways to different audiences. Baker's line – his 'Great Education Reform', improving standards and bringing order, sometimes by central prescription, sometimes by enhanced parental choice – was the most consensual version, capable of appealing to a wide audience. A second, neo-liberal version (that the Act prepared the way for a free market in education) kept the radicals in line after their increasing rebelliousness under Joseph. A third version was associated with the moralism and populism of Mrs Thatcher herself and such campaigning agencies as the *Daily Mail*. Here the Act was presented as a key move in the moral, social and cultural regeneration – 'My New Crusade' – of the third term. It was a crucial item in the alliance with moral and religious orthodoxy, with 'responsible citizens' and with the principle of parental choice-and-responsibility (therefore 'the family') more generally. In this way, some of the most difficult conflicts within the ruling bloc were deferred. In the meantime the many 'voices' of the Act helped to hold together and even expand a complex social alliance of a distinctive right-wing kind. The main antagonists of this alliance and the objects of its control were the educational professionals themselves and, in curriculum matters, the diverse groupings of critical educators – 'radicals' old and new – who had produced many of the curriculum innovations of the 1970s and 1980s.

The 1988 Act as political strategy II: professionals disabled?

The North of England Education Conference of January 1988 was held just two months after the first reading of the 1988 Act. The event took a form which suggested an attempt to put pressure on the secretary of state to modify the Bill by parliamentary concessions or instant consultations. The chosen speakers provided critical angles on the Bill. The 1988 president, Sheila Browne, ex-Senior Chief Inspector and Principal of Newnham College, was also critical, especially of 'the sad decline of working trust between and among the partners'. The target of this rolling conference-as-lobby, Mr Baker, was there in person. Beaming hugely, he was presented with objections to his Bill, consistent threads, the chairman said, running through this 'non-political' conference. So here were the experts, in their careful, rational, non-confrontational way, warning the secretary of state that his measures would damage the service, and willing to negotiate to the last. Baker's response – immovability on essentials, apparent ease and blandness among these enemies – underlined the powerlessness of the gathering. How had this particular disempowerment been achieved? And through what strategies, at least on the government side?

The earliest New Right strategy was to evoke parent power against the professionals. The 1988 Act depended on the political ground won, by this strategy, from the Black Papers onwards. The Bill was presented as a solution to the dissatisfactions so assiduously promoted by its authors! One of the reasons for Baker's greater than usual complacency in January 1988 was that the government could now appeal over the heads of experts to a larger educational public. By now, expert advice was irrelevant, as was mere defence of the service. What the situation demanded, was a counter-strategy: an alternative to the Baker Bill and the willingness to campaign for it.

So the main gain of the first strategy was that the government could now act against the advice and the interests of teachers and educational administrators. It could even make a virtue of bullying them. In its 'Nothing Will Stop Us Now' front-page story of 15 September 1987, the *Daily Mail*, clearly using briefings and leaks from Baker and Thatcher, pilloried 'the upper echelons of the civil service' and of the LEAs: 'Mr Baker himself is known to have been frustrated at the negative approach of the educational establishment.' This intervention came at a critical moment in the Bill's preparation. In January Baker knew his real public lay outside the conference hall, mediated by television and press. He came to the conference with power, in the shape of votes already in his pocket: votes won in the election, votes making up the parliamentary majorities awaiting his Bill. He did not need to consult the experts; he could tell them what to do. No wonder he grinned!

Until the introduction of the Bill, however, the government was vulnerable to the charge of not caring about education at all. The argument about standards sat ill with the emphasis on cuts. The Bill changed this. By installing an alternative to the existing service, it evaded the accusation of negativity. It also provided further ways of neutralizing professional resistance. In the future, the more the professionals complain about their difficulties, the more parents will be tempted to flee the LEA sector. The more teachers resist the deterioration of the service, especially by industrial action, the more they risk encouraging further 'exits'. We might call this second strategy the creation of a dual or triple system.

The first two strategies undermined the position of professionals in the political sphere. But they retain some power because they are indispensable to education and administration itself. There are two ways in which this confers some power.

First, teachers and educationists have power to influence detailed recommendations on such matters as the National Curriculum. This power is hard to circumvent. The minister may show off about his competence in poetry or history, but when it comes to teaching English, mathematics, or science his genius has limits. Given professional hostility to Act and curriculum, and the paucity of educational ideas on the Right, the government depends on the very groups it attacks. The Act minimizes this dependence but cannot abolish it entirely. The minister has given himself great power over the membership of the task groups and the National Curriculum Council (NCC). He can determine the final Orders on specific subjects. He is, however, obliged to consult through the NCC. And he cannot dream up something to consult about all on his own. Where a subject discipline has already been reshaped by radical thinking, where the profession has a relatively unified voice, real fight-backs are possible.

Though it is early to risk such a judgement, there have been successes in the case of the various English committees and reports (Kingman, 1987; Cox, November 1988; National Curriculum Council, March 1989) with substantial ground held on issues of language, literature, multiculture and media studies (see Minns and Dombey, n.d. [1988] for a detailed commentary). Less room was created for mathematics teachers, with science somewhere in between. The modification of the original proposals on testing, despite Mrs Thatcher's personal interventions, is another example of the government's inabilty to exercise the control it seeks (*Guardian*, 13 January 1988; *Guardian*, 23 January 1988).

The second level of professional power is in the schools themselves. Even where the government is successful at the level of National Curriculum documents and Orders, it cannot control detailed classroom practice. This seems to be accepted by the DES. It seems probable that teachers already influenced by debates on multiculturalism, anti-racism, cultural studies, 'the new history' or any of the new tides, will find space to continue and deepen their practices. It will be harder, however, to introduce new critical approaches. The situation in anti-racist and multicultural education may be particularly adverse: a complex of features in the new Bill, from opting out to the silences in curriculum matters, checks or erodes the gains made so far. But even where government wins down the line, it will pay in what is sometimes referred to, euphemistically, as 'low morale'. This includes many conservative resistances, from absenteeism to refusing headteacherships and leaving the profession. Baseline resistance of this kind is already massive and worrying.

In these circumstances the government will apply its third strategy: de-professionalization. Plans to transform teacher education, to introduce untrained teachers, to break up national pay rates already point in this direction. These measures will increase direct control of the curriculum; they amount to the proletarianization of teaching. Educational values will suffer in this. The inadequacies of English education, including the persistent undervaluing of teaching as a practice, will be deepened, not reformed. There is a world of difference between professionals who can take pride in what they teach because they have some control and expertise in it, and 'staff' who 'deliver' a curriculum which actually controls *them*. Increasing time will be spent on self-monitoring for management; decreasing time on productive educational thinking and preparation. There is no better instance of the need to anticipate the government's 'reforms' by reforms and alliances of our own.

The New Right assault has meant that professionals have been faced with learning new relations. Professionalism has had to criticize itself, to redraw relationships, to enter a larger political arena. These themes are explored more fully in Chapter 3; their implications for alternatives are developed in Chapter 10.

Contradictions of the 1988 Act
1. The curriculum

In 1989, despite the achievements, Conservative policy-makers still face major difficulties. In the sections that remain I want to explore these.

One way of understanding changes since the mid-1970s is as the reduction of educational autonomies. This does not mean that state schooling was autonomous of the social order in the 1960s and 1970s; it does mean that there were particular reasons – including the growth of the state-professional bloc – why educational institutions worked free from serving the division of labour and legitimating inequalities. One main project of Thatcherism, especially in the third term, has been to make the institutional superstructures, including the education system, conform more tightly to the requirements of the market society. The New Right educational project is a project for 'capitalist schooling'. Schooling must play its part in a general revival; the spaces which it offers to alternative social values must be closed down.

'Accountability' is the way this project is pursued. Schools should be accountable to parents for the education of 'their' children. Power should be given to parents by enabling them to choose one kind of education over another. This discursive figure of accountability to the parent is, however, ideological in the strongest sense: it hides more than it reveals.

Accountability is not about empowering parents as such, still less about empowering children. The New Right made alliances with parentdom because it took it to be a conservative social category. Actually Conservative discourse incites *a particular version* of parenthood – the parent who owns his children, the parent who consumes education. This model of the parent (and by implication of the child) is valued because, on the neo-liberal side, it coincides with competitiveness and individualism. On the neo–Conservative side, it corresponds to the emphasis on authority. The implied parent is an ambitious and strict father who wishes to reproduce himself (including his unfulfilled desires) through his children (though mothers may take up this point of view as well). This version – the choosing but authoritarian parent, the 'responsible' parent – appears in other policy debates: in propsals to make parents responsible for crimes of under-age children; in campaigns to deny access to professional advice against parental wishes (e.g. in matters concerning sexuality and contraception). This parent is a very particular late-twentieth-century New Conservative Daddy or perhaps conventional 'couple', presented, naturally, as 'natural'.

What about parents who do not want to 'own their children' or make the central choices for them? What about adults who want children to grow up co-operative rather than competitive? Parents may wish their children to be independent, but also to recognize their dependence on others and the dependence of others on them. Conservative ideologists must present such families as actually 'subversive'; they cannot handle the conflict of values. Nor can they cope with the view that children are not passively made by their parents or their schooling, but make their own outlooks on life *in relation to* parental and other views.

There are therefore some tricky questions for the New Conservatism here. First, how far can parents be trusted to act in choosing-and-authoritarian ways? The answer to this question has major implications for the strong state/free market dichotomy which I discuss in the next section. Second, what is the appropriate curriculum for a schooling more attuned to a capitalist world?

Should the government move towards a modern curriculum, reorganizing subject distinctions on lines of capitalist utility, extending 'the new vocationalism'? Or should it preserve the existing 'academic' routes to elite status, where the link between knowledge and social inequality is less manifest? What matters most about education: usefulness for economic development, or certainty about what knowledge is, certainty about 'ability', 'standards', 'excellence' and 'the national culture'? Different answers have been pursued by different sections of the New Right, producing policy oscillations. The swing from *Better Schools* to the National Curriculum is a case in point.

Joseph's strategy was to modernize but with guarantees. The curriculum was to be restructured to correspond to the skills and outlooks required for different positions in the division of labour. Joseph attempted an alliance with modern management and the MSC, even with certain kinds of educational progressivism. *Better Schools* implied some rejigging of curriculum values at all levels, including a critique of traditional academic versions of elite education.

But preparing young people for class-, gender-, and race-related destinations in the social divisions of labour is not the only function of education, even from a Conservative point of view. Education also provides the means to legitimate social inequalities and to recruit to elites. It is part of a larger process of winning consent to discrepancies in power and opportunity. The key requirement here is that curriculum values should be accepted as fair and neutral, so that assessment seems relatively independent of existing social differences. Children must be seen to succeed or fail in education in line with their abilities. Abilities must be seen as relatively independent of social orientation or position. Traditional academic disciplines and school 'subjects' have been the typical forms of this 'neutrality'. The naturalization of disciplines like English, history, or science, each with very specific social histories of its own, disguises the social orientations from which the knowledges have been produced and are usually taught. This installation of specific social orientations to knowledge as neutral or 'objective' is a key cultural operation of modern education systems. It is faith in the value of the Old Curriculum that distinguishes traditionalists from modernizers.

In the history of English education the tension between these two aspects of hegemony – reproducing appropriate forms of labour power and justifying the dominant social relationships – has been particularly acute. It has usually been resolved by splitting off academic subjects and reserving them for elites and those proved competent to join them. More vocational conceptions have been applied to the majority. Ruling groups in England have struck a particular compromise: means have been found – the academic curriculum – to provide an 'objective' character to ascent into the middle class, while popular education has been held at the level of the 'practical'. The cost of this, as Andy Green argues in Chapter 1, has been an underdeveloped system, with little access to advanced secondary education, and a weak technical education tradition.

In effect, the academic/vocational split has come to correspond to class differences. 'Vocational' has been a metaphor for 'working-class'; 'academic' has meant 'genteel', later 'middle-class'. These curriculum categories, produced primarily in the educational system, have interacted with larger social and cultural differences. They have been sustained not only

institutionally, but through cultural resistances too. Working-class orientations towards knowledge – a preference for the practical, the useful, the
handy – have been reproduced in resistance to the dominant academic
criteria of school knowledges. On the other hand, a minority of children
have learned how to manipulate these knowledges instrumentally in order
to join elites, especially the professions. Very similar dynamics around
curriculum categories, cultural formations and social identities can be traced
in relation to gender and race (Johnson, 1988). The marked inegalitarianism
of the English educational tradition had been maintained not only by formal
exclusions, but also by informal cultural processes around the curriculum
categories themselves.

These historical associations help to explain the strength of traditionalism
on the right. If curriculum distinctions have been so important to English
class cultures, Conservatives might well fear to disturb them. It is subversive, from this point of view, to be too conscious or critical of the forms of
knowledge themselves. Approaches that involve thoughtful reappraisals of
existing knowledges are to be eschewed. These are Scruton's 'second-order
disciplines': not real knowledges with real objects, but 'expressions of a
mind working at one remove from its subject' (Scruton, 1980, p. 153). In
other words it is important not to be too critically detached from academic
subjects; it is important to work inside them, accepting their frameworks
and limits. Modernizing strategies, however pro-capitalist they may be, are
also a problem: they resemble left-wing reforms in that they criticize
existing knowledges and suggest alternative criteria of value too.

The resolution of these difficulties in *Better Schools* was to edge carefully
towards a modern curriculum but to stress differentiation by ability at
every verse end:

> Pupils vary widely in their capacity to benefit in education at any given
> point in the process . . . Able pupils are insufficiently stretched and
> waste time practising skills already mastered while the diverse individual
> weaknesses of the less able . . . are not tackled appropriately . . . There
> is insufficient differentiation of teaching approaches . . . There should
> be careful differentiation: what is taught and how it is taught needs to be
> matched to pupils' abilities and aptitudes . . . Suitably differentiated
> papers, or differentiated questions within papers, in all subjects. (DES,
> 1985, *passim*)

Joseph sought to change the curriculum, but to find new markers for
differentiating pupils. Yet even his emphasis on grading failed to reassure
traditionalists. Their suspicion of new approaches underlay the campaigns
against GCSE and tampering with 'A' levels.

The National Curriculum, in its original conception, takes the opposite tack. The curriculum categories are held constant, even revert, but every-thing else is encouraged to vary around them. The curriculum is a fixed point ('set of benchmarks') in a fluid educational workd. Subject disciplines are retained; approaches that might relativize them or make their social orientations clear are excluded. On the other hand, the Act encourages differentiation in two ways: first by stressing testing and grading, second by encouraging variation in schooling.

The overt purpose of testing is to allow parents to judge between schools and to 'choose'. But it also means that individual children will be ranked and ordered as never before. Only aggregate results will be published, but teachers, parents and presumably children must know the individual outcomes so that progress can be judged. The National Curriculum is not only a device for 'accountability'; it is a mechanism for differentiating children more rigidly against fixed norms, *the social meaning and derivation of which are not available for scrutiny*.

A similar combination can be seen if the curriculum is related to the new pattern of school provision. Criteria of success or failure are fixed and given a spurious objectivity. Yet the pattern of provision is to be more varied than before. Opting out and CTCs will produce new types of school. Delegated management, open enrolment and the loosening of LEA control will increase differences between schools. Differences in institutions and resources will be colonized by social groups in ways hard to predict in advance. As so often in the history of English education, institutional separations will become social segregation, especially on lines of class and race. There may be a greater tendency than today for school populations to be relatively homogeneous socially and to differ strongly from school to school. In this way social antagonisms may be intensified along all the lines of 'Us' and 'Others'. Yet no educational means will be provided for negotiating them. Baker's hopes are instructive here. In 'a sometimes visionary speech' at Manchester University he said:

> I see the national curriculum as a way of increasing our social coherence . . . The cohesive role of the national curriculum will provide our society with a greater sense of identity. (*Guardian*, 16 September 1987)

This nostalgia for 'cohesion' is interesting, but the great delusion is that all pupils – black and white, working–class and middle–class, boys and girls – will receive the curriculum in the same way. Actually, it will be read in different ways, according to how pupils are placed in social relationships and culture. A common curriculum, in a heterogeneous society, is not a recipe for 'cohesion', but for resistance and the renewal of divisions. Since it always rests on cultural foundations of its own, it will put pupils in their places, not according to 'ability', but according to how their cultural communities rank along the criteria taken as the 'standard'. A curriculum which does not 'explain itself', is not ironical or self-critical, will always have this effect.

The only kind of 'coherence' achievable in a complex society is one in which differences are recognized and inequalities negotiated. This requires educational guidelines opposite to those proposed. Instead of being presented as 'objective', the curriculum must subjectify itself – it must acknowledge its own roots in culture, history, social interests. Instead of treating all pupils the same, 'regardless of sex, ethnic origin and geographic location' (National Curriculum Consultative Document, July 1987, p. 4) teachers must recognize the different social positionings and cultural repertoires in the classroom, and the power relations between them. A commitment to really equal treatment, to commensurate results or outcomes, involves a recognition of differences, especially where these empower or disempower pupils in relation to each other and the school. Baker's mixture of differentiation in provision and absolutism in the curriculum, *unless modified in the teaching itself*, will produce inequality and social disintegration. It is far from being the orderly, cohesive solution which he imagines it to be.

There are other implications for alternatives in the National Curriculum too. So strong is the association between New Right and Old Education that it produces an opposed alignment: progressive educationists, reforming administrators and industrial modernizers. At the 1988 North of England Education Conference, for instance, it was argued by an educationist (Professor John Elliot) and a businessman (Sir Bryan Nicholson) that such an alternative was already available in the 'progressive education' strand in MSC programmes.

So seductive is this option that warnings are in order! The division between government and modernizers is clear, but may be temporary. I would expect even a Conservative government to move in favour of a new curriculum, with its own forms of interdisciplinarity, justified in terms of (employer) demand. I would be surprised if the Joseph option did not eventually prevail. This will be a painful change for the New Right, perhaps politically perilous; a government of the centre would find it easier. But I think it will be made, under one politics or another.

So the danger of allying with progressive business, without a distinctive position of our own, is that we end up with no alternative movement in education at all. It would be a different matter if we had a worked-out position and made strategic alliances accordingly. An education based on business criteria makes its own closures on knowledge and on the social future. Progressive business people often support a liberal education for graduates and sixth formers; how often do they speak out for a critical education for potential workers, their consumers or their environmental 'neighbours'? This is why the development of a *third position* in curriculum

politics, different from traditionalism and from modernization (or conservative progressivism), is a major preoccupation of this volume (see especially
Chapter 4 below).

Contradictions of the 1988 Act
2. Free market versus the strong state?

How far are these two sides of the 1988 Act in contradiction? How far are
they complementary? The answer depends on the historical perspective we
take: short-term and tactical, mid-term and strategic, or long-term and
structural.

The immediate history of Conservative politics suggests tensions
between strong state and free market as tactical options. For Josepth
centralization was an alternative to the free market which he preferred.
Similarly his erstwhile neo-liberal allies deplored his new dependence on
the DES. His junior ministers, Patten and Dunn, took opposed positions.
Similar parts were played out under Baker, with Joseph now doubting the
wisdom of the National Curriculum (though his opposition may have been
related to his pro-modernizing inclinations too). Pure neo-Liberals in the
IEA saw curriculum and market as alternative strategies, not as complementary ones. These examples suggest tensions between the free market
and strong state strands, with 'Bakerism' as an interim settlement.

Yet it is also possible to argue for the complementarity of free market
and strong state in the mid-term, as a strategy. The combination may
coincide with the historical task which Thatcherism sets itself.

To see this, we need to insist on a point which is more fully developed
in Chapter 3: that the market is a system of social relationships, not a
technical mechanism. It involves the attempt to return to more coercive
relationships between labour and capital, and to conventional gender and
age relations. This market, this social form, has to be created or re-created
in the first instance and then defended, sustained, expanded. To use the old
Marxist language, it needs appropriate 'superstructures'. This includes laws
to act as the coercive shield of the system, appropriate forms of politics to
disorganize opposition and construct and reconstruct hegemonic alliances,
and ways of making culture and values conform to the project in hand.
These insights are important in understanding the rise and historical tasks
of the New Right, and in linking its political, ideological and economic
programmes.

The strong state has initial tasks of destruction: smashing up the old
forms of regulation – in this case 'welfare', trade union organization and
the incursions of the public professionals. The free market requires the
strong state as an initial condition. In education this corresponds to the
assault on the local authorities, on 'partnership', the professions, university

and polytechnic autonomy, and on the state bureaucracies (e.g. disciplining HMI).

New Right theory in its 'dirty-liberal' form – 'Thatcherism' – is more than adequate to this stage. It incoporates a clear sense of the need to free capitalist economic dynamics from the resistance and opposed ideals of workers and state professionals. It provides guides for tackling the power-points of institutionalized resistance and emergent alternatives: whether in welfare provision, or trade union law, or the relative autonomies of public education. It is daring, 'radical' even, on this negative side. It grasps some of the cultural conditions of such a transformation, increasingly so into the third term. It understands that education must be changed to fit better with 'enterprise' and exclude opposed philosophies.

Some 'pure' neo-liberals argue that these interventions are temporary only. They resist the idea that strong state solutions are permanent, at least where they duplicate the market: hence the IEA's opposition to the National Curriculum. Once installed, the market is self-regulating; the wishes of consumers will secure standards instead. I think this is a misreading of likely outcomes, based on the Utopian anarchism that runs through this part of the liberal tradition. It corresponds theoretically to the failure to see that power is socially diffused, a matter of everyday discourses and social relationships not simply of government. Civil society is not a sphere of equality and freedom: it is riven with antagonisms and unfairness; it is the site of different kinds of power and resistance. These may be linked and condensed in state forms, but they do not only originate there. It is at this point that pure neo-liberal theory wavers, and the strengths of 'dirty' neo-liberal or more 'Whiggish' theorists show up. Hayek, like the neo-Conservatives, recognizes that the strong state is a *permanent* feature of the (economically) 'liberal' order (see Chapter 3 below).

The initial reimposition of market relations is not the end of the strong state. Hayek understands the continuing need for the strong state in terms of the rule of law; yet when he specifies this framework (e.g. on trade unions), it is clear he means the protection of market relations, or of capitalist economic organization from forces which might destabilize it. Unfortunately these are not seen as contradictions or problems in the system, but as enemies who must be kept at bay. There is, however, another way of seeing this carapace of law. The market, or more strictly the consumer, is not altogether to be trusted to deliver benefits or to shape the kind of society which Hayek wishes to see. So the typical solution is the market with *guarantees*. In Hayek's case this leads to proposals for elaborate constitutional arrangements, the purpose of which is to guarantee 'freedom' against the people (Hayek, 1979).

The National Curriculum is our best example here. When all is said and done, it is a device for the political control of knowledge. Nor is it temporary or transitional: it has every appearance of permanency, though its forms will be qualified by resistance. It is very clear that the government does not trust parents any more than it trusts teachers. Parents may 'choose' but only what the government says children should have. The government's liberalism, its concern with choice, is qualified by its authoritarianism, its underlying prescription. Even this contradictory form of choice, however, is not distributed fairly. Some parents may 'choose' to be exempt from the government's authoritarianism – as long as they can afford a private education. Thus the children of the wealthy are exempt from the kind of political control exercised over the children of most citizens, a situation very similar to the distinctions between elite and popular education in the nineteenth century. The forms of choice produced by this structuring of education are not so different from those offered by the market generally: there you may choose, but only between the goods which businesses choose to produce and can persuade large numbers to buy. You can venture into more exotic and less constrained choices the more money you have. The social logics of market and strong state are therefore very similar, only differently enforced. The common element is that inequality of access to social benefits is systematically ensured.

In both these ways then – creating conditions for the market in the first place and 'guaranteeing' its social forms – the strong state is an integral part of the strategy; in this sense, in the mid-term, strong state and market are complementary sides of the same historical process.

It is possible to push this argument a good deal further than Hayek or even Scruton would wish to see it go. Hayek appears to assume that in a 'free society' there will be a stage at which the growth of the state will be stabilized, especially if contained by consitutional checks and limits. But it seems to me he is sanguine here, and also misguided in believing that the major threat to liberty comes from popular demands or from the supporters of welfare policies. What if the major threat now comes from the forces which Hayek and his philosophy have helped to create, from the New Right itself?

There is no reason to assume a stabilization of state intervention under the conditions of the free market. Historically, after all, social-democratic and radical-liberal (i.e. social reforming) solutions grew out of the crises of an earlier stage of *laissez-faire* capitalism. Fascism too arose under conditions of capitalist crisis. It may be polemically effective but it is not intellectually compelling to present the whole course of 'social reform' in Britain since the 1840s, as One Big Mistake with no organic connection to the contradictions of capital or market. As I argued earlier, market societies are high-risk social orders. They do not reconcile freedom and security. They are productive of social disorder. They intensify social inequalities and generate deep-seated conflicts. They despoil the environment. From the early nineteenth-century Factory Acts onwards, these conflicts forced into existence the social means to handle them: social legislation, 'inspectors', specific forms of expertise, the 'caring professions'.

Today there is an attempt to sweep away these protections. the negotiative roles of state professionals are weakened. The work of curing and caring, as anything other than an imposed duty or a private philanthropy, is being discredited. In practice it is 'privatized' or handed to 'the community', heaped on the backs of individual women. It is hard to resist the conclusion that the long-term consequence of the New Right project is to increase social divisions but also to reduce the possibility of resolving them in productive ways. This goes for the attempted forms of cultural control as well. We have already argued that the National Curriculum, unmodified by the beaverings of teachers, parents and children, will tend to heighten all the different forms of antagonism between 'us' and 'others'. It certainly provides no way in which these multiple antagonisms can be recognized and productively worked through.

We are not only talking about 'law and order' here, or human wear and tear in an a-political 'social problem' sense. Unviable societies produce political dissent, alternative ways of living, movements of social opposition. Governments of this complexion will be challenged not just by indices of social disintegration and calls for social policy, but by demands for radical change, and, typically in Britain, radical disaffiliation at the moral and cultural level.

New Right frameworks are most deficient at this point. Neither version of New Right theory gives credence to the idea that social arrangements may be contradictory and inherently unstable. Resistances to the liberal or conservative Utopias can look only irrational or malevolent – suitable cases for authoritarian solutions. It is hard for liberals or conservatives to see that attempts to deepen capitalist relations actually erode the supports they seek in 'the family' and/or in traditional (yet waning) gender and child-adult relations. They canot see that the whole scenario of 'growth' and 'man's domination over nature' is as destructive of the human environment as it is reproductive of inequality and conflict, on a worldwide scale.

Even more worrying is the possibility that the New Right works with a fundamentally self-defeating view of human wishes and desires. Again, the failure to understand contradictions or ambiguities is a key feature: here the psychic ambiguity between wishing to be 'free' or autonomous on the one hand and depending on each other emotionally (as well as materially and socially) on the other. The New Right handles this contradiction by splitting off these inner impulses and allocating them, asymmetrically, to particular spheres of life and particular kinds of person, on lines especially of gender. It polices social and especially sexual identities accordingly, punishing some (like homosexualities), rewarding and promoting others. But human impulses are not so neatly allocated on gender or on any other

lines, so that such splitting, installed in social practices and public representations, remains a fertile source of unhappinesses and resistances too.

It is arguments like these that convince increasing numbers of people,
even in the west, that there never can be a satisfactory meeting of human
needs via the western capitalist and patriarchal route, even in its 'post-
modern' forms. New Right theory and politics, sharp and accurate as a
polemic against certain positions, are fatally shallow in their grasp of larger
historical movements. The New Right is pre-modern (not even modern)
in the way it understands human beings.

The great fear is that New Right governments (they may not be
'Thatcherite') will try to solve the problems which are beyond their
comprehension by mainly repressive means, rather as conservatives in
China have done, in another variant of the free market and the strong state.
The cycle of campaigns about law and order and moral conformity and
against new social diseases or immoral 'others', the erosion of civil rights,
the intensification of surveillance and the militarization of the police, form
by now an all too familiar pattern (cf. Hall *et al.*, 1978). Of course, actual
historical outcomes are never the product of one tendency alone. Many
other determinations intervene. It is possible, for example, that New Right
strategies will be continued or modified, by some other party or political
alliance. Still, the political judgement may stand: in the social dynamics
which it promotes, the New Right does not lead us to 'freedom' (in any
meaning), but towards a deepening coercive regulation of civil society, to
forms of serfdom indeed.

Notes

1 This chapter is dedicated with love and solidarity to Jill, Becky and Paul – active
   participants in this story in two ways: first, in the events described (as a teacher
   and school students respectively); second, in the interminable writing of it.
2 The method of research adopted for the more narrative parts of this account is
   worth describing in full. I took as my starting-point the entries in the *Times
   Index* under Education and its various subheadings (the *Times Index* includes
   references to the *Times Educational Supplement* (the *TES*)). I also recorded entries
   under the names of successive secretaries and under-secretaries of state for
   education. On this basis I drew up a very detailed year-by-year (later phase-by-
   phase) chronology of the main public events in education policy. Though
   indications of events in the *Index* are very brief and can be misleading, they
   provide an interesting synoptic view of developments over time. I then
   consulted the *Times Educational Supplement* (especially) and more selectively *The
   Times*, the *Daily Telegraph*, the *Sunday Telegraph*, the *Guardian* and *The
   Independent* at particular policy turning-points (e.g. the 1979, 1983 and 1987
   elections; annual Conservative Party and North of England Education Conferences; the Conservative Party debates of 1981–3 and 1986–7). Among populars,
   I used the *Daily Mail* at key points, since it has had a major function in
   representing Mrs Thatcher's own views and those of the New Right in education

generally, and, less revealingly, the *Daily Mirror*, which has campaigned against cuts. From 1986 I started making my own collection of press cuttings, mainly from the *Guardian*, with occasional photocopies from other newspapers, 'quality' and 'popular'. Where no other source is cited the dating of events is likely to have been through the *Times Index*.

A method that relies on public sources in this way must have many limits, especially lack of access to the inner deliberations of those who make policy. I did not conduct interviews with those in power, nor do I have a 'mole' somewhere in Whitehall, but the internal differences of the powerful do often show up in their squabbles and the way they use the media to try to resolve them. For these reasons I have always tried to be deliberately tentative, even interrogative, when the motives of policy-makers are in question, not claiming to know more than I do. None the less I must confess I do greatly enjoy reading the outer signs of policy for their inner motivations, especially when I think I have a theory and a method of reading which offers me some explanatory power. This pleasure may sometimes carry me away!

3   I am grateful to Gary Clarke and Kerry Bretherton for material and ideas about the 1979 election generally, but especially its historical themes.

4   I have learned much about multicultural and anti-racist education in the current context from Waseem Ahmed, Sharan-Jeet Shan and Avtar Sherri, both in MA discussions and from their written projects on these themes.

3

My New Right education

Richard Johnson

I first began to study New Right ideas to handle some personal feelings. I felt assaulted by government ideas and policies. The media brought fresh horrors daily. In a common fantasy of mine, I sought to control events by understanding them. If I criticized Thatcherism devastatingly, it might even go away!

The strategy did not work this time, even subjectively. My reading told me that I really was the enemy! Paranoia turned to informed panic. My work, my profession, my subject, my politics, my 'whole way of life' was threatened now. I was obviously unteachable as a New Right pupil. I got to thinking how my life had prepared me for middle-aged privatization, wrong-footed by history it seemed. Born with Thatcherite credentials, I made all the wrong choices: the academy not the family firm; social history not business history; E. P. Thompson (whom I emulated), not G. R. Elton (who taught me). And why hadn't I stuck with history (a 'real' subject) instead of deserting to cultural studies? With no National Curriculum to guide me, my mis-education intensified. I struggled manfully (I'm afraid) with feminisms in books and persons. I learned how my Englishness, my Anglo-English ethnicity, was a problem for self and 'Others'.

Yet, as often happens (is this the therapy?), I became intrigued by the subject itself. I started to wrestle with the New Right as a philosophy, as a kind of education, not only with its educational policy. So my New Right education began in earnest, though still with a critical intent.

There are several dimensions to New Right education in this expanded sense. First, the New Right has produced its own knowledges – in a strenuous, collective and accumulative work of analysis, polemic and prescription. It has developed new categories or stolen old ones. It celebrates its own gurus in a self-proclaimed 'Liberal Revival' or 'New Enlightenment' no less. It colonizes the academy. It invents intellectual traditions for itself. It recruits 'big names' (Locke, Hume, Adam Smith, etc), over their dead bodies so to speak.

Second, it educates opinion more widely. It wins consent, makes yesterday's heresies desirable, puts pressure on dissenters like me. It campaigns in the press and other media. Asked what she enjoyed most about being Prime Minister, Mrs Thatcher replied: 'Getting a new idea, getting people in to talk about it, talking it through, thrashing it out.' But she also enjoys 'deciding how we can present it' (*Guardian*, 4 January 1988). In 'getting a new idea' she employs advisers and think-tanks; in presenting it, she teaches public lessons on economics and morality. Her self-education and her educational crusades, her 'conviction politics' and her populism, are closely related (though they must also be kept apart for fear of 'leaks').

Quite late in my New Right education (such is the power of marginalization?) I realized I was in really good company. I was one of an army of enemies, dug in on front-line positions, whether we chose to be there or not. My new 'we' conjured up widening solidarities and made me feel less isolated. I call us 'state' or 'public' professionals: teachers and lecturers; doctors, nurses and ancillary workers in public medicine; social workers and probation officers; physio- and other therapists; many layers of civil servants in central government and employees of local authorities; those responsible for monitoring our health and physical environment; keepers of museums and libraries; workers in the more 'public' media; and many other groups not directly employed by capital, serving public agencies including the voluntary sector. The differences within this social stratum are many: diverse skills and unequal rewards. I am clear that a professional politics is not enough on its own. I know my imaginary politics of this group was initially just that – a saving fantasy or wish. But this piece is written from a self-critical position within this professional world; and I hope to hearten others as their struggles have heartened me.[1]

The government is disorganizing, often destroying, the work of public professionals and, with it, one source of hope for a viable and decent world. The most desperate need is for alternatives to campaign around. Many elements of alternatives already exist: as explicit theories or philosophies, as political movements, and as more implicit ways of thinking, feeling, living. I want to contribute to these alternatives in an area I know well – in 'education'.

So this chapter is an exploration, not of New Right policies primarily but of New Right ideas. I compare them throughout with critical theories, generated by the social movements of the 1970s and 1980s. I try to show where the New Right is weak morally and conceptually, and where the New Politics has an edge. I also suggest that New Right theory itself has already been shaped in the struggle with modern critical thinking. Since a main aim of the chapter is to face up to the systematic targeting of public professionals by the New Right, I end with some discussion of strategies.

Neo-liberalism and neo-conservatism: complementarity or contradiction?

It can be argued that there is no unified New Right theory. Certainly there are important differences between 'neo-liberal' and 'neo-conservative' wings. Neo-liberals stress freedom and the market; they attack socialism as coercion and state monopoly. Political economy is in command. Neo-conservatives deny that freedom is the leading value; social order, authority, tradition and consensus matter too. Morality and a strong state dominate this argument.

Some commentators equate New Right theory with neo-liberalism, so ignore the division altogether (Bosanquet, 1983; Green, 1987; Graham and Clarke, 1986). It is true that the economic arguments have been dominant within Thatcherism; neo-conservativism has been stronger in the United States. Other commentators see the liberal/conservative *combination* as the hallmark of the modern right (Gamble, 1981; Gamble, 1985; Gamble, 1988; Hall *et al.*, 1978; Hall and Jacques, 1983; Hall, 1988). Most later accounts are centrally concerned with this duality (e.g. Levitas, 1986), especially as cultural themes have assumed more significance within Thatcherism itself (Edgar, 1988).

How, then, does this duality work? Does it cause difficulties for the New Right or is it an asset? Some writers stress the difficulties (e.g. Jessop *et al.*, 1984). I follow Hall and Gamble who argue for a more complex pattern. Some differences may be assets, in the short term. They allow for different investments in the Thatcher Revolution, expanding its social basis. In the middle term, the strong state/free market combination may correspond to particular tasks: creating conditions for the free market, defeating 'vested interests', razing resistance. But there are longer-term issues too: will the strong state prove endemic to the new order? If so, what of neo-liberalism's main value: what price 'freedom' then?

These issues are best addressed in the work of Friedrich von Hayek. He is the 'fundamental' theorist of neo-liberalism. He is also, however, a self-confessed 'Whig' (Hayek, 1960, p. 409). His thinking throws a bridge between liberalism and conservatism, much as Thatcherism does.

Knowledge and society in New Right theory

Hayek is a radical sceptic, especially in his early work. Explicit knowledge of complex societies is inherently flawed. This modern stance, 'post-modern' even, stresses relativity, the flux of time, the intense subjectivity of knowing. Hayek anticipates, in the 1940s, radical and feminist assaults on hard-nosed notions of science and 'objectivity' ('scientism'). He caters to contemporary tastes for particular description over grandiose explanation (esp. Hayek, [1942–4] 1952; Bosanquet, 1983, pp. 28–31; Butler, 1983, pp. 132–50).

His grounds for scepticism are distinctive. The increasing complexity of modern societies plays a part, but the limits are natural or logical: the difficulty of grasping, from one centre, the diversity of human intention and motive; the complicity of knowledge with feeling and opinion; the mind's inability to grasp its own workings. Scepticism selects specific targets, Keynesian economics and Marxist 'historicism'. Hayek resembles his friend Karl Popper in using epistemological arguments to attack 'totalitarianism' (cf. Popper, 1961).

Conviction of 'our ignorance' runs deep (e.g. Hayek, 1960, pp. 22–38). Knowledge of self and society is necessarily limited. But Hayek resembles more conservative thinkers. Wisdom is denied to planners and social scientists, but is found in institutions, laws and customs instead. There is a wisdom in unselfconscious social activities, in tacit knowledge. Hayek shares Burke's regard for the good sense accumulating in institutions which stand the test of time – 'spontaneous' not 'constructed' in his vocabulary. Explicit knowledges depend on an infrastructure of habits or dispositions: some biological, all copied rather than consciously fathomed. According to Gray, who claims him as a conservative, Hayek believes 'tacit knowledge is lost by its translation into overt, propositional form', not to be recovered by reason:

> The inarticulate character of the great submerged part of our knowledge means that we always know far more than we can ever say. It also means, crucially, that the rational criticism of social life must come to a stop when it reaches the tacit component of our practices. (Gray, 1988, pp. 256–7)

So a traditional conservative orientation finds a lodging-place with a key neo-liberal theorist. Hayek replays Burke's answer to Tom Paine, the conservative's rebuke to Enlightenment rationalism, but he combines this with the liberal themes of individual and market.

Hayekian scepticism is typical of the New Right as a whole. It permeates the tendency: the suspicion of 'intellectuals', of 'know-it-alls' and 'do-gooders'; the preference for 'common sense' over 'philosophy'; the appeals to the people versus the experts; even Sir Keith Joseph's dislike of 'social science'. The outlook on knowledge chimes well with New Right populism, a distinctive tone in the political style.

There are major implications for education. New Right theory values prejudice over reason, instinct over knowing, in an anti-educational logic. Learning is not the changing of self and society, nor the raising of 'consciousness' in the radical sense. Change through education is a rationalist illusion (Hayek, 1960, pp. 377–8). There is something familiarly

English in this: a conservative suspicion of 'intellect'; a distrust of popular education (Chapter 1 above). From another angle, how strange, how paradoxical this attitude appears! Here is the New Enlightenment, which must have taken some thought, whose activists disbelieve in this activity. Would they reserve philosophy to themselves, discouraging it in others, knowing its power? Or are only certain areas (of spontaneous growth and intuitive wisdom, like 'the family') no-go zones for Reason?

We may usefully compare Hayek's scepticism with other criticisms of 'science'. I have in mind the critiques associated wih the students' movement (incuding various 'neo-Marxisms') and the profound recastings of politics and study associated with feminism, black politics, movements around sexual difference and campaigns around the environment. Naming is difficult here: 'New Left' implies a socialist hegemony; 'new social movements' risks lumping everything in together. Yet these labels represent distinctive waves of politics and intellectual work, with commonalities as well as differences.

In these critical traditions, knowledge is seen as limited by social relations and cultural processes. It is always produced from a particular point of view; always constrained by a framework of attitudes and premises. It is complicit with social interests and power. It takes shape from the contradictory processes it describes. It is formed in desire, in unacknowledged or half-conscious wishes, including a desire for mastery or control.[2] This orientation to knowledge differs profoundly from New Right scepticism in its educational implications. It incites us to greater consciousness of self and social relations, not to censorship or closure. New branches of study arise from the ending of a scientific innocence: the history, philosophy and sociology of science, the analysis of ideology and of discourse, the modern 'cultural' revival of psychoanalysis, cultural studies in general. A similar fertilization occurs around the study of social relations, especially their subjective dimensions. So the intellectual streams that New Right thinkers refuse, block and try to dam up, spread out into a whole new topography of knowledges on another side of the intellectual and political universe. No wonder this causes anxiety among conservatives!

Hayek's scepticism, a kind of conservatism, is not arbitrary, but tightly linked to his politics. Knowledges are so diverse and dispersed, so fleeting and individual, that it is impossible to plan to meet all needs. The market, by contrast, is an exquisitely sensitive mechanism for testing the experimental forays of entrepreneurs through the barometer of prices. Central planning is crude and brutal: crude because it cannot gauge wants; brutal because versions of them are forcibly administered.

Neither scepticism nor anti-statism need lead to these conclusions. There is a strand of anti-centralism in the postwar social movements too, though, again, grounded in social analysis. For Hayek, no amount of social change could make planning rational. His argument about market and state is characteristically absolutist or 'essentialist' (Hindess, 1987, pp. 147–55). There is the 'thesis' of the market and the 'anti-thesis' of the state, but no synthesis (Bosanquet, 1983, pp. 5–24). Once the state is involved beyond its proper task, the slide to socialism begins. For other critics, the consequences of state (or market) are more contingent, dependent on many other conditions (e.g. Hindess, 1987). State intervention is ambiguous rather than irreparably damaging: it may secure gains for popular movements or for dominant alliances. For neo-liberals the state is the grand source of unfairness. The market is likewise idealized as guaranteeing betterment. For other critics, specific forms of market and state are involved in interaction. Neither state nor market is neutral in its effects (as in social-democratic orthodoxy) but nor are they wholly bad (as in old Marxism). As with knowledge, so with state and market, it is important not to foreclose on social possibilities, dogmatically, in advance.[3]

The individual and market: anti-social ideas

It is a commonplace that neo-liberalism has no social theory. It is literally 'anti-social'. Society consists of individuals, perhaps families, no more. The individuals themselves are not formed in social relationships, in and through connections with others. They inhabit and strive to maintain an autonomous sphere. It is hard, from this point of view, to appreciate that markets are social relationships (those between employers and employees, for example); or that the model individual (the entrepreneur) depends on social conditions (e.g. gender relations).

Less familiarly, neo-liberalism has no theory of systematic cultural difference or cultural power. Hayek insists on subjectivity as a property of individuals, hence his scepticism about social science. It is hard to conceive of cultural patterns in this view. Neo-liberalism therefore treats subjective motivations crudely: as self-interest, rational choice, or Machiavellian conspiracy. It neglects the shared and contested frameworks of feeling and thinking, through which human beings make sense of their world.

More critical theories may acknowledge individual diversity, but see individuals as shaped by social conditions too. In everyday interactions, people are not individuals merely, but workers and managers, husbands and wives, salesmen and customers, doctors and patients, mothers and children. These and similar relationships regularly recur in our social experience and persist and change historically. Our sense of ourselves (our 'individuality') arises socially: through language, ideological and moral frameworks, socially sanctioned ways of seeing and feeling, forms of social recognition. Marx argued that 'individualism' – belief in the free, self-producing individual – depended itself on past development, especially the emergence of 'free labour' – wage labour – from serfdom or slavery.

Modern western notions of the individual are relative, not universal. Perhaps 'the individual' is a misleading starting-point; perhaps we should analyse the social bonds that produced him [*sic*] initially (cf. Marx, [1857] 1973). Modern critical theories extend this perspective, breaking down the individual-versus-society opposition, a liberal hallmark.

The neglect of social relations is practically damaging too, hiding difficulties in people's lives, making remedies harder. It promotes blame and superficial solutions. Personal oppressions are often caused or intensified by power that has accrued unequally to social positions over time: husband over wife, boss over worker, national, racial, or ethnic majority over minority, professional over client and so on. Some social relationships seem 'primary' because they produce particularly far-reaching asymmetries. In our society, class, gender, race, sexual orientation, age and ability/disability seem basic, though any such list is an abstraction and must be open to new political claims. More institutional processes – laws, policies, administrative regulation, media representations – arise in the context of these asymmetries, often to handle contradictions. Such routines act back on the problems, and reproduce and modify the relations. Because theorists like Hayek do not acknowledge these imbalances, they dismiss demands for justice too. If injustice is admitted, it is ascribed to bad law, or monopolistic conspiracy, or a failure to compete. Market relations are taken at face value: we are free and equal, monopolies aside. Actually we enter market situations formed by unequal social relationships, already empowered or disempowered. Though fame is sometimes a spur, we prosper most easily if we prosper already.

Anti-social ideas may be viewed in relation to a particular complex of social relations. I choose gender relations here because of their centrality to New Right politics and to the discussion of alternatives (David, 1983; David, 1986).

That neo-liberalism depends on a particular construction of gender is clear from frequent evocations of 'the family'. 'The ties of the family . . . are at the heart of our society and are the very nursery of our civic virtue' (Mrs Thatcher, *Guardian*, 23 May 1988). 'Basic ties' gestures to an array of relationships and practices: the domestic sphere or household; relations between men and women, children and adults; kinship generally. 'The family' is an index for sexual relations, standing for the unnamed norm of monogamous heterosexuality. It may even be a metaphor for 'society'. Rhodes Boyson ascribes to the growth of single-parenthood a great range of evils, stemming from fatherlessness and 'the wildness of the uncontrolled male young': 'violent crime, football hooliganism, mugging and inner city revolts' (e.g. *Guardian*, 10 October 1986).

Such references play a limited role in New Right philosophy. The public worlds of economy, politics and even 'active citizenship' are in sharper focus. The private, domestic worlds of household, emotional life, child care, sexuality and domestic labour are blurred. Mrs Thatcher may sometimes draw on her femininity politically, but has also to handle her own fiercely 'masculine' stance as a public woman (Brunt, 1987; Rose, 1989). 'The family' is evoked as a norm, but rarely understood concretely, as contradictory and variable. It is a sort of national monument, piously preserved and treasured, occasionally cleaned up, but viewed without curiosity or insight for most of the time.

This seems a very masculine point of view, though it can be shared by women. The public world is privileged. The private sphere is acknowledged, but in an ideal form – as Mrs Thatcher's 'basic ties', 'heart of our society', 'very nursery', etc. The economy does indeed depend upon this place where competitors are refreshed, little 'individuals' produced, rewards enjoyed, and social penalties paid. Just as most men assume that women will carry these tasks, so neo-liberalism takes caring roles for granted, with occasional exhortations.

Beneath the gender blindness, the neo-liberal argument is thoroughly gendered. So is the strident insistence on autonomy. In practice, the capacity for independent action ('standing on your own feet') depends on the meeting of emotional needs for intimacy and dependence which only others can supply. Autonomy depends on dependence, just as individuality depends on sociality. Neo-liberalism insists, heroically, naively, on 'individual freedom'; it refuses to admit the vulnerabilities (which are there just the same).

This is the public (and inner?) narrative of conventional masculinity. It is the story of the classic middle-class career, of the buccaneering entrepreneur, of the hero of the Falklands 'task force' (before he is struck down). It is also the story of 'man's mastery over nature'. Here science and technico-social interventions subordinate a complex natural-social reality ('Nature'), with which women and black people are often ideologically aligned. If there is a rich example of the intellectual hubris which Hayek criticizes, surely it is this masculine 'mastery'. Often it is left to women to deal with the social and personal costs of all the adventures, which men, as companions, colleagues, or theorists, seldom seem to recognize until too late.[4]

Neo-liberalism shows a process of splitting, characteristic of gender polarities in our society generally (Hollway, 1984; Hollway, 1989). Masculinity is constituted by splitting off caring roles and tenderness, with attendant vulnerabilities. These emotional-social features are projected on to women, but are also marginalized as social activities. Splitting constructs imaginary or ideal polarizations; in practice men are not invulnerable but dependent. The caring that women are supposed to give (but not to get from men apparently) is actually necessary for all.

The gendered contradictions deepen as neo-liberal policies bite. Market societies are high-risk social orders. They threaten existing social relations and the natural-social environment. Costs are pervasive, not limited to 'failures' or 'deviants'. Human and environmental wear-and-tear is already well advanced in a world of 'mixed' economies. I doubt if true market societies are viable, either in their internal relationships, or in their dependence on Third World deprivation. They imperil all life by plundering and despoiling the earth. The evidence of environmental damage, of diseases caused by a way of life, and of massive social problems is inescapable. More perceptive theorists, like Hayek, understand that capitalism has a destructive side, but condone it for its dynamism. But in celebrating 'dynamism', neo-liberalism shares all the dominant western assumptions about science, technology, progress, unending consumption and 'mastery of nature' which, unless changed, will end the possibility of any progress by wrecking the eco-sphere. A different ideal of human nature is required for mere survival, let alone more desirable living.

The western tradition of social-reforming politics has recognized some of this human wear-and-tear. Perhaps there is a spontaneous wisdom here as well! Welfare institutions mitigate some consequences of competition. They offer some security as a social right. Standards are set around health, safety and the environment. Professionals are employed for these purposes. Women are strongly represented in the public professions, forcing entry most successfully into those involving caring roles. These endeavours are limited by the context of unequal social relations, yet the real connectedness of persons has been recognized. The tradition was re-articulated by Labour, without environmentalist dimensions, during the election campaign of 1987.

Neo-liberalism is committed to dismantling this tradition. It devalues the outlooks of the public professions. It worsens the problems and weakens the solutions, inadequate as they are. Its own plans are contradictory: to pile person-care on to individuals and family members, especially on mothers, daughters, wives, unpaid domestic workers. This is called 'care in the community' with no funds. This comes after a period when women have been claiming a larger public role, have entered massively into paid labour and have participated in significant minorities in feminist politics. Even today there is a strong demand for women as low-paid, temporary and casual workers, so that the burden is doubly doubled and a feminization of poverty ensues (David, 1986, pp. 163–4). Modern capitalism, depending so much on conventional gender polarities, will continue to produce acute contradictions in this area, inciting revolts and alternatives among women and among men. The politics of gender and of sexuality will remain critical front-lines.

Issues around autonomy and dependence, public and private, competition and caring, entrepreneurs and professionals, capitalism and the environment, are points of vulnerability in neo-liberal theory and practice. They are examples of a more general weakness: the failure to grasp social relationships, cultural processes and the social-natural individual within this framework.

Neo-liberalism modified: enter neo-conservativism

Neo-liberalism was a critique, first, of the state-enhancing reforms it calls socialism. But it encountered newer rivals in the New Politics. These stressed the deep embeddedness. of human beings in social relationships and cultural forms, but shared a view of tragic contradiction with the socialist and communist tradition. The tragedy is that the social forms through which human beings co-operate are the main sources of oppression too. Connections are chains, but not external only. They bind inside. The task is not to 'abolish' society, with its material and emotional investments, not to stand magically free, but to create social forms which empower us mutually, not always at the other's expense.

The New Right had to find answers to this new politics, to anti-racism, feminism, sexual politics, and ecological thinking. An anti-anti-racism was elaborated. A strategy evolved against sexual radicalism, including press attacks on 'the loony left' and the banning of the 'promotion' of homosexuality in the Local Government Act of 1988. The language of rights and of oppression was turned against feminism in the Pro-Life campaign. Its focus on the personal was re-appropriated (David, 1986, p. 136). Thatcherism even acquired a slightly green tinge.

Neo-conservativism was useful in meeting the new rivals. It has a heavily social, deeply cultured conception of the individual. It clings desperately to organic social forms which are seen to be natural, or rooted in instinct or intuition. When historical changes and social differences cannot be denied, they are seen as pathological or abnormal. In this case solutions may be frankly imposed. Roger Scruton uses a telling analogy to describe his ideal:

> The analogy with the family is useful if we are to understand the role of authority in politics. It is clear from the start that a child must be acted upon by its parents' power; its very love for them will accord them that power, and parents no more escape from its exercise by being permissive than does an officer cease to command his troops by leaving them constantly at ease . . . The kind of personal love that we envisage as the end of family union requires, as its precondition, the sense of established power . . . And it is a similar recognition of constraint, helplessness and subjection to external will that heralds the citizen's realization of his membership of society; in this recognition love of one's country is born. (Scruton, 1980, p. 32)

Here the social returns with a vengeance as abject dependence. Far from autonomous, Conservative Man is perpetually childlike. Human beings are not free: they are everywhere entangled in moral and religious imperatives, in culture, history and nature. Social connections, expelled in neo-liberalism, are embraced without qualification: as duties not rights, as sanctified traditions, as the strong state. The tensions between liberal and conservative frameworks are obvious, but so are the complementarities.

If Neo-liberalism lacks a cultural theory, neo-conservativism reinstates a non-relative notion of 'values'. In his critique of the 'cultural relativism' of anti-racism, Scruton insists on the value of preserving a national culture (Palmer, 1986). A similar theme, which Paul Gilroy has wickedly dubbed 'ethnic absolutism', runs through New Right discourse from Enoch Powell to Alfred Sherman (first director of the Centre for Policy Studies) (Gilroy, 1986). Though outright racial or cultural superiority is usually avoided in this discourse (but not always), notions of peculiar appropriateness are not. Cultures are ascribed to nations and implicitly to races as absolute conditions for identity. 'British' cultural traditions may not be absolutely good and true, but they are probably as good as they could be and are essential to Britishness anyway! They should not be changed to accommodate others. Cultural absolutism is often a new form of racism (Barker, 1981). It implies the assimilation or repatriation of culturally indigestible peoples and cultures. It never permits cultural fusion or changes in the dominant ethnicity. But racism is not the only closure here. 'British' cultural traditions are selectively invented in other ways. It is hard to conjure up a symbol of Britishness that does not privilege a group or region, and put all the citizens in their places. In the social alchemy of nationalist myth, 'British' often turns out to be middle-class, southern and Anglo-English, with strongly masculine connotations – as specific an ethnicity as any!

Neo-liberalism lacked a social theory; neo-conservativism supplied it – and how! The new social movements had questioned the innocence of 'spontaneous' institutions like the family; conservativism re-naturalized or re-sanctified them – no more impertinent questioning here! Conservatives firmed up values around nation, race and the natural. The fusion is stressed in Scruton's first editorial for the *Salisbury Review*: the need 'to integrate the philosophy of the market into the underlying principle of order which . . . motivates Conservative politics' ([1982], quoted Seidel, 1986, p. 108). 'Order' signals an authoritarian element with specific targets. Conservatives 'esteem democracy only in so far as it contributes to conciliation, and are wary of abuses which democracy makes possible in the hands of demagogues, activists and doctrinal fanatics'. It is not only the ' "armed doctrine" of revolutionaries' which threatens peace, but 'a politics which puts "movements" in the place of "associations" ' (Scruton, 1988, p. 12).

Thatcherism might therefore be described as 'dirty neo-liberalism': predominantly 'free-market' with Conservative infusions. In a spate of speeches and interviews in spring 1988, Mrs Thatcher and a chorus of ministers proclaimed their individualism:

We are all responsible for our own actions. We cannot blame society if we disobey the law. We simply cannot delegate the exercise of mercy and generosity to others. (Thatcher, *Guardian*, 23 May 1988)

The achievement of the Thatcher governments has been to make hitherto unthinkable freedoms and responsibilities a reality for millions. This has been accompanied by a huge spread of wealth. (Baker, *Guardian*, 28 April 1988)

But as the judicious Baker implied, individuals must be 'responsible', especially if British.

I don't think individualism is anything to do with selfishness . . . But individuals have to recognize – and this has been an absolute character-istic of the British – they have to recognize that as they do well, their obligation to their fellow citizens, to the community increases. (Thatcher, *Daily Mail*, 29 April 1988)

Those who already have much should not look down upon the desire to own of those who do not. I do not accept that his [*sic*] drive for self-improvement is selfish. However I do recognize that there is another side to the coin of economic individualism. That other side is social responsibility. Those who succeed have obligations above and beyond that of celebrating their own success. (Baker, *Guardian*, 28 April 1988)

'Responsibility' is insisted on, not as a social product, but as a desirable propensity of individuals, to be evoked by politicians:

The politicians and other secular powers should strive by their measures to bring out the good in people and to fight down the bad: but they can't create the one or abolish the other. They can only see that the laws encourage the best instincts and convictions which I am convinced are far more deeply rooted than is often supposed. (Thatcher, *Guardian*, 23 May 1988)

Perhaps alternatives should be 'fought down' too. The rise of Thatcher-ism can be charted in a list of 'folk devils', from 'muggers', 'Marxist socialists' and 'trade union bosses', to single parents, lesbians and gay men. The new politics and critical theories have increasingly figured in this list. In attacking single parents, Boyson uncovered more sinister presences: 'The family was under attack from extreme feminists, the youth cults, and homosexual lobbies, he said' (*Guardian*, 10 October 1986). Mrs Thatcher has stressed 'theory':

That [the sixties] was a period when it was considered that you had to flout the rules, otherwise you were old-fashioned. This business of breaking the rules began in universities, where most of these theoretical philosophies always start. They never start with ordinary people. (*Daily Mail*, 29 April 1988)

These later versions of New Right philosophy, to which we might have added books by Roger Scruton on *Theorists of the New Left*, and even on *Sexual Desire*, are not the last word (or not in this text!) in the struggle of theories. The New Politics reaches to parts of the social-emotional order which the New Right leaves unexamined, and might hope to protect from further blasphemy.

Policing politics: freedom and coercion in New Right theory

The idea of the New Right as a defensive, frightened (and therefore dangerous) response is worth exploring further. Perhaps neo-liberalism is an attempt to contain the political contest itself.

This certainly fits Hayek's treatment of freedom and coercion. Freedom is 'personal' or 'individual freedom': 'the possibility of a person's acting according to his own decisions or plans' (Hayek, 1960, p. 12). Already politics is restricted here, because 'individual' action is favoured over collective. Intervention or political solutions are justified when freedom is threatened by coercion. To coerce means to exercise 'such control of the environment and circumstances of a person, that in order to avoid greater evil, he is forced . . . to serve the ends of the other' (ibid., p. 21). Coercion is the loss of self-direction, of autonomy. Yet true coercion is, apparently, rare:

> Neither the powers of a Henry Ford nor those of the Atomic Energy Commission, neither those of the General of the Salvation Army nor (at least until recently) those of the President of the United States, are powers to coerce particular people for the purposes they choose. (ibid., p. 135)

Coercion is arbitrary power, not bound by general rules known in advance like a written constitution. This is why old-style presidents do not coerce. So state power, if it abides by rules known in advance, is not coercive, and in this sense is not 'political'. Curiously then, having restricted its initial scope, Hayek even attempts to depoliticize politics itself. His later attempts to construct a constitutional domain beyond politics are elaborate (1979).

As the Ford example hints, economic relations are not coercive either:

they are contractual (1960, p. 135). Competitive market relations guarantee minimum coercion, since parties can go elsewhere if conditions are unacceptable. This applies even where coercion might be thought endemic. If I lose my job, I can seek another employer, just as purchasers seek another supplier. Only absolute monopolies break this rule. Even so, economic coercions are 'rare exceptions in a prosperous competitive society' (ibid., p. 137). Hayek risks extreme examples. What if I am forced into a 'distasteful job at a very low wage' with 'the only man willing to employ me'? I and my family are threatened with starvation. Yet even this is not coercion, since I am not forced 'to serve another person's ends' and the effect on my freedom is similar to 'that of a natural calamity' (ibid., p. 137). Again the scope of legitimate politics is being restricted here: if I am not being coerced, I should not invoke a counter-power. A whole sphere of economic struggle is depoliticized.

What about the General of the Salvation Army? The example is included partly to make another exclusion: 'generally speaking . . . the morality of action within the private sphere is not a proper object for coercive control by the state' (ibid., p. 145). But such actions may be subject to conventional disapproval or 'pressure'. Here Hayek takes issue with John Stuart Mill who feared 'moral coercion' (ibid., p. 146). Mill is thought squeamish and impractical:

> Whether or not we wish to call coercion those milder forms of pressure that society applies to non-conformists, there can be little question that these moral rules and conventions that possess less binding power than the law have an important and even indispensable role to perform and probably do as much to facilitate life in society as do the strict rules of law. (ibid., p. 146)

State, civil society and politics

What are the practical implications of Hayek's stance? First, despite all his limitations on politics, he is not, strictly, a theorist of '*laissez-faire*'. Individual action is best, but state intervention is not ruled out.

> It is important not to confuse opposition to this kind of planning with a dogmatic laissez faire attitude. The liberal argument is in favour of making the best possible use of the forces of competition as a means of co-ordinating human efforts, not an argument of leaving things just as they are. It is based on the conviction that where effective competition can be created, it is a better way of guiding individual efforts than any other. It does not deny, but even emphasises, that, in order that competition should work beneficially, a carefully worked out legal

framework is required, and that neither the existing nor the past legal rules are free from grave defects. Nor does it deny that where it is impossible to create the conditions necessary to make competition effective, we must resort to other methods of guiding economic activity. (Hayek, [1944] 1976, p. 27)

Note the stress on *creating* competition, a reformed legal framework and reserve powers of 'other methods': 'it is the character rather than the volume of government activity that is important' (Hayek, 1960, p. 222). There is no libertarian disavowal of state power here; on the contrary, powerful interventions, tightly defined, for specific uses, are indispensable.

Intervention is clearly justifiable when an individual's private sphere is threatened by a monopoly. According to Hayek, trade unionism is 'a good test of our principles' (1960, p. 283), but the argument may also apply to professional bodies. Meanwhile, the restricted definition of coercion has charmed away employer power. If workers are not coerced, how can trade union action be justified? It becomes legitimate to coerce trade unionists as fiercely as a Thatcher government. All those reasonable distinctions mean that governments may use the power of the state to empower capital against its workers, and attack professionals too.

Similar arguments apply to more social issues. Hayek recognizes that coercion is a diffused social presence, but quickly negates the insight:

In some degree all close relationships between men, whether they are tied to one another by affection, economic necessity, or physical circumstances . . . provide opportunities for coercion. The conditions of personal domestic service, like all more intimate relations, undoubtedly offer opportunities for coercion of a peculiarly oppressive kind . . . And a morose husband, a nagging wife, or a hysterical mother may make life intolerable unless their every mood is obeyed. But here society can do little to protect the individual beyond making such associations with others truly voluntary. Any attempt to regulate these intimate associations further would clearly involve such far-reaching restrictions on choice and conduct as to produce even greater coercion. (ibid., p. 138)

Here everyday oppressions are trivialized or robbed of remedy. The definitions again empower some agents and weaken others. Those coping with domestic violence or child abuse or racist attacks find no help, unlike conservative moral crusaders. By dismissing everyday oppressions, Hayek undercuts welfare policies. They become sources of 'even greater coercion', so must be restricted to certain minimum standards below which none should fall. To go beyond this is to do for citizens coercively what they do better for themselves voluntarily. Most removable oppressions arise from wrong-headed intervention: illegitimate 'politicization' of an 'economic' or of a 'private' matter. The New Right constructs a series of dichotomies, with positive values on the right and negative ones on the left. Note how problems are associated with public agencies, solutions with private:

coercion   freedom
state   market
politics   economics
monopoly   competition
compulsion   voluntary action
public   private

Neo-liberalism, then, can be seen as an attempt to contain politics (which it identifies with more or less justifiable state coercion). Apparently about freedom from coercion, it is much more about limiting the legitimate sphere of struggle or of collective contestation, policing politics itself.

Expanding politics: the critical alternative

Again comparison is useful. The new social movements also centre on issues of autonomy, coercion and control. But their accounts of coercion move in the opposite direction. They *expand* notions of politics and power. 'Innocent' practices are critically viewed. For feminism, for example, power extends to the personal, to intimate relations, to the private domestic sphere, to sexuality, identity, pleasure. Feminist politics cannot be limited to state, formal politics, or the law. This has major implications for the whole dichotomous scheme above, and also for the politics of containment.

Again, the oppositions between the New Right and its shadow are dialectical and political not just formal. Neo-liberalism organized itself around the defence of capital and 'the rule of law'. Its enemy was the left. It handled areas like gender and sexuality by denying they were 'political'. This defence was undermined when the social movements re-politicized these same spaces. So conservatism was refurbished in reply. This dialectic can be seen in its fear of the politicization of everything, its terror of all boundaries down!

For the conservative, state and civil society are *separate* aspects of political order, the former consisting of sovereignty, law and the institutions whereby they are upheld; the latter consisting of free association, and institutions with their *own internal purposes*. *Movements*, doctrines and ideologies, in so far as they threaten the balance between state and civil society, invite also the politicization of the social order, and that *total invasion of society* by political decision-making which is the mark of totalitarian power. (Scruton, 1988, p. 12; emphases added)

This typical reply involves major misrecognitions. The new enemy is misrecognized as the old 'Stalinism'. Actually, the 'movements' do not demand universal regulation. They shift the idea of politics itself. Power is not repressive merely: it is 'productive', 'positive', 'educative'. The range of remedies is widened. Subjective oppressions are recognized: problems of identity, social recognition, the public representation of groups and issues. Self-organization, communal solidarities and alternative ways of life are stressed. Where law is invoked, 'rights' are uppermost. Public agencies can give material support, offer information, negotiate solutions. It is not the movements that identify politics with coercion, but the New Right. Maybe it also signposts a surer road to 'totalitarianism'?[5]

The New Right's politics of class

The New Right refuses Marxist class analysis, but has its own politics of class. It also develops its own class theories with some surprising resemblances to Marxism. The challenge here is to explain the opposition: since the market is beneficient, why do some persist with 'over-government'? If principles are plainly on *our* side, *their* motive must be self-interest. The moral culture of the right (and of sections of the left) is like this.

Part of the problem, according to Hayek, is the hubris of intellectuals. Genuine liberals (true Whigs) distrust ambitious social knowledges; 'constructivist rationalists' think society can be planned. Hayek's scepticism translates into straightforward anti-intellectualism in the Friedmans' blast against 'intellectuals', 'experts' and 'high-minded reformers'. Egalitarianism is an intellectual's obsession:

> There is little support for the goal of equality of outcome despite the extent to which it has become almost an article of religious faith among intellectuals and despite its prominence in the speeches of politicians and the preambles of legislation. The talk is belied alike by the behaviour of governments, of the intellectuals who most ardently espouse egalitarian sentiments, and of the public at large. (Friedman and Friedman, 1980, p. 173)

But government growth is fuelled by 'interests' as well as 'illusions'. Again the right draws on some cruder figures of Marxism. Different New Right theorists from Hayek to the Public Choice School have developed a kind of class theory of the state, an 'economics of politics', which explains why bureaucrats, state professionals and politicians might favour interventions (Green, 1987, pp. 92–108; Bosanquet, 1983, pp. 62–74).

Hayek distinguishes 'the employed class' from 'the independents'. The former are primarily workers; the latter include employers and persons of independent means. Marxist evaluations are reversed: the heroes in this manifesto are 'the independents' and 'the idle rich'. The increase of the employed class constitutes a threat to liberty, since their opinion 'largely governs policy'. If policy favours the employed masses and discriminates against the independents, everyone's liberties will suffer.

> Freedom is thus seriously threatened today by the tendency of the employed majority to impose upon the rest their standards and views of life. It may indeed prove to be the most difficult task of all to persuade the employed masses that in the general interest of their society, and therefore in their own long-term interest, they should preserve such conditions as to enable a few to reach positions which to them appear unattainable or not worth the effort and risk. (Hayek, 1960, p. 120)

This is a rather perceptive analysis of the difficulty of sustaining inegalitarian policies in a democracy. It poses the problem to which New Right populism supplies the answer.

More typically and expediently another elite group, not the people, is blamed for serfdom. Hayek himself quickly shifts targets: 'public servants become the most numerous and influential group among the employed'. They constitute a separate interest group and set standards for employment. Most intellectuals are members of this 'employed class'. They are not 'independents', not men of private means, not 'gentlemen scholars':

> However important the independent owner of property may be for the economic order of a free society, his importance is perhaps even greater in the fields of thought and opinion, of tastes and beliefs. There is something seriously lacking in a free society, in which all the intellectual, moral, and artistic leaders belong to the employed class, especially if most of them are in the employment of the government. Yet we are moving everywhere towards such a position. (ibid., p. 128)

The front-line enemies are not just intellectuals then. They are professional intellectuals employed by the state. Later accounts stress the complicity of all state agencies with private interests: 'There is no escape from private motivations' (Green, 1987, p. 107). Again, Marxism is parodied: the state is an instrument which bureaucrats and state professionals use for security and self-promotion. Protective legislation creates special interests which also defend the status quo. Politicians buy votes by promising state-supported benefits. It is the taxpayers who suffer. Like Marx's peasants, they are scattered and unorganized, more put upon than agents of history. An example of this argument is Friedman's 'iron triangle'. An alliance of bureaucrats, politicians and special interests frustrated the

reduction of state expenditures in the early years of the Reagan administration, thus exploiting taxpayers (Friedman and Friedman, 1984,
pp. 157–9).

It seems to me misleading to present these relations as quite so 'iron': is
there not more than one form of interaction around the triangle, including
the New Right reaction itself?

The social politics of public provision

I find it is useful to clarify Friedman's account by translating it into the
terms of a social politics. This involves redescribing his main agents. In
analysing state institutions, for example, policy-makers and managers must
be distinguished from ordinary professionals. While professionals confront
clients directly, and are 'responsible' in their eyes, they actually lack control
of the organizational and financial conditions of this encounter. Professionals are also different from groups commanding powerful positions
in market relations. These groups – the bourgeoisie of old Marxism –
disappear in New Right theory, reappearing, more acceptably, as enterprising individuals. State employees are the enemies of the people instead.

Friedman's exploited taxpayers are the most mystifying group of all, as
faceless as 'public' or 'people'. These terms hide the radical heterogeneity
of popular groups and classes. If it was less of a mouthful, we should
always have to talk about a cross-class, cross-gender, multiracial, multi-
ethnic, multicultural, thoroughly composite public! Relationships to public
education, or public housing, or the benefit system depend upon social
position. What are your needs? Have you command of cultural resources
to fight a case? Does your way of living fit criteria for aid? Could you
afford alternatives? Public services are encountered, like the market, from
radically different starting-points. It is not just state provision which creates
the differences: they are there already; the forms of provision reproduce
them, modifying them in the process. The ideology of 'choice' takes no
account of this.

The iron triangle is also set in concrete: invariant, unhistorical. Gains and
losses to different groups have been complex, not one-way. Simple
dismissals of welfarism as exploitation won't do.

Welfare modified older tyrannies. Employees are less dependent on
employers when cushioned against working-class insecurities. From this
point of view, workers won welfare from capital, allied with others, to
make their position more habitable. It was part of the battle to have
something to lose but your chains. The fundamental discipline of nineteenth-century capitalism – St Paul's 'if a man will not work, he shall not
eat' – was mitigated by 'the social wage', in which, as Phil Carspecken
shows, education has been included (Chapter 9). It is no surprise to hear

Mrs Thatcher quoting St Paul again (or his nineteenth-century interpreters) in her 'sermon' of May 1988 (*Guardian*, 23 May 1988). Her policy is to reimpose the disciplines by thinning down the cushions.

Welfare institutions have been a focus and a shield for other movements and demands. The 1960s saw attempts to use public services to equalize class chances. In the 1970s campaigns around gender-based inequalities revived. There were moves to recognize the force of institutional racism and the multi-ethnic character of the society. In different ways, state services provided spaces for alternatives. State employment, the dole and the semi-dependency of studentdom were focuses for alternative values and oppositional movements. Alternatives also developed around the youthful appropriation of commercial products, especially, like the popular musics, where infused with black resistance and cultural innovation from urban America or the Caribbean (Hall and Jefferson, 1976; Hebdige, 1979; Gilroy, 1986; Jones, 1988). Environmentalism developed in tension with capitalist business, often among (professional?) groups with 'alternative' life-styles.

Welfare institutions posed problems and opportunities for the New Right. In Britain, where the crisis of capital was deep, its policies were dominated by the economic agenda: the drive to reimpose the sanctions of the market. Thatcherism had to discipline capital's workers, weakening their organizations, discrediting their political party, marginalizing social-ism and labourism. But now it struggles to break through the welfare shields as well, and so must attack state workers and public professionals. It must take on the experts. It must reverse the social and cultural movements and destroy their basis. It constructs a demonology of 'the sixties', implicating the critical social theories too (Thatcher, *Daily Mail*, 29 April 1988; Edgar, 1986; Edgar, 1988). This is as much a work of restructuring as the economic tasks. There must be less space for critical teaching and research. 'Enterprise culture' must enter the academy and professional training. Imposing the free market (trying to make capitalism work) involves war on many fronts, not just the economy.

Friedman's version of the iron triangle has its value in sketching some conditions of New Right successes. The growth of state provision has indeed involved new forms of regulation, new kinds of coercion, a new dependence. One might doubt if the main victims are taxpayers. The clients or claimants of state services are more vulnerable. But Friedman is wrong, at least in Britain, in assuming that taxpayer is the wider category. Most of us, except the very rich, can envisage having to rely on welfare services, through redundancy, major illness, accident, or old age. It has taken hard ideological work to present claimants as a minority of scroung-ers. It will take much more to construe National Health Service patients as improvident, or parents who use state education as negligent or uncaring.

Universal provision is qualified, however, when conditions for aid are imposed. The meaning and character of the social wage changes. It becomes aid to a minority, not to us all potentially. This minority (which may be very large) becomes an object of surveillance and control. Welfare becomes public charity, at worst a form of policing, imposing family forms or sexual practices or conceptions of parenting or attitudes to work. Dependence on the DHSS, or on the Council Housing Department, or on public bodies like the Gas or Electricity Board is as acute a form of oppression as dependence upon an employer. Even so, fear of dependence is not limited to the actually ill, old, poor, or unemployed. If you are already in these situations, you have no choice but to depend. Thatcherite solutions are more likely to appeal to those with some margin to provide against hard times, yet who fear the future and are determined to remain independent. Groups on the margin may also be more likely to project their fears on to 'the scroungers' – whom they dread to be. *Fear* of dependence is a powerful motive for the Thatcherization of society.

The ambiguities of welfare make it vulnerable to political manipulation and ideological representation. From this perspective, New Right criticisms of welfare are paradoxical, hypocritical even. The main trend since 1979 has been to *make* state services more coercive, cutting benefits and imposing conditions. Today's nightmare of insecurity is not just unemployment, bad though that is, nor even the dole, but the insistent promptings and actual coercions of Restart or Employment Training, battles over unpayable rents or mortgages, queues for hospital treatment, and long-term dependence on an inadequate pension and disorganized care for the old. The struggle against harassed and underfunded officialdom has intensified, through no fault of the officials themselves. The aim of manipulation is actually to make private provision seem more desirable than a deteriorating public service and encourage what is called 'exits' (Seldon, 1986, p. 12, note 1). Finance here is decisive, but it matters how services are represented – as strike-torn, or 'not good value for money', or insensitive to choice. 'Exits' increase as services deteriorate or seem to. Exits may be reluctant at first, but may harden into affiliation to Thatcherism. These dynamics are central to the educational scene. Friedman's 'iron triangle' or Hayek's discourse on intellectuals should be read in this context: as ideological representations which make such manipulation easier.

Public professionals: villains, victims, or victors?

Those who work in the public services are centrally placed in these relationships. What kind of power and autonomy do we possess? Are state professionals a new and separate class? What is distinctive about our position?[6]

Compared with ordinary workers, doctors, teachers, or lecturers still have much control over their daily labour. There are divisions between and within professions, especially between ordinary professionals and those with managerial functions. Those who argue for the tendency towards the proletarianization and de-skilling of professions like teaching have a strong long-term case (Apple, 1985, pp. 140–64; Aronowitz and Giroux, 1985, pp. 25–30; Lawn and Ozga, 1981). The intensification of control through conditions of service in teaching or through 'appraisal' in lecturing are recent examples. A distinctive managerial layer is emerging in most professions: 'management' is everywhere the new word for 'control'. New Right drives to 'accountability' coincide with longer-term tendencies here.

The most important feature, politically, is the ambiguous or contradictory position of state professionals. On one side, we are a large social group not directly employed by capitalist business. Unlike business managers, our work has not been judged until recently by profit and loss. Professionals may be self-interested and monopolistic, but may also be committed to their work to the point of self-exploitation. Some of the most trenchant critiques of professional power come from professionals themselves.

Gender is as important as class in placing professions socially. Access to some professions, including the fight for education, is a major achievement of women's movements since the mid-nineteenth century. It has been easier to enter professions defined in 'feminine' terms, by notions like 'the caring professions'. These notions, appropriated by women and by some men, help to distinguish professional values from those of business more generally. Many professions deal directly with social and environmental issues, monitoring changes, picking up personal consequences. Professional work typically deals with the social results of capital's contradictions and of its interactions with other social systems, especially with the family/household. There are strong affinities between the occupational, gender-related cultures of some professions, or of minority oppositions within them, and the 'social' concerns which New Right ideology denies and the New Politics stresses.

The professions, however, are themselves divided. The classic masculine career (which women sometimes opt for – at a cost) moves on from professional work into hierarchies of administration or management. Women's careers (which some men opt for) are more likely to remain focused in the profession itself rather than in management, partly because other obligations and desires delay or interrupt career 'progress'. At the 'top', the male-dominated worlds of public administration, business, finance and high politics converge in the single destination of Management. 'Management' is also the new word for elite, Establishment, or even the ruling class! Coincidences of interest and outlook in this layer explain the adoption of business methods in public institutions. When government wishes to divide professionals into workers and managers, it finds plenty of accomplices.

An alternative thesis, on left and right, is that professionals are really working-class or becoming so. Hayek treats them primarily as 'employed'. I have already acknowledged the force of the proletarianization thesis, but it does not help us to understand current relationships between professionals, workers and clients. We need to understand the other face of professionalism, the power we wield – if only to change it.

Command of knowledge, science, expertise and other cultural assets (e.g. 'creativity') is crucial here. Access to the education system is central. State professionals are, first and foremost, producers and disseminators of knowledge: from natural science or medical expertise to aesthetic judgement and even religious belief. Generally, we control the criteria of legitimate knowledges, and act as gatekeepers to acquisition and accreditation. Control over entry and qualification to professional bodies is only one, rather conservative, aspect of larger dealings in knowledge-as-power, in the capital of culture. Discourses of surveillance and control invariably take the form of professional expertise. Professionals are experts in the production of all sorts of subjective categories (Foucault, 1979; Foucault, 1980): the innocent and the guilty, the mad and the sane, the healthy and the ill, the normal and the deviant, the 'bright' and the 'dim', the able and the disabled.

This knowledge-power can be deployed very oppressively. Detailing the oppressions of professional expertise has been one of the leading insights of the critical social theories of the 1970s, not only among followers of Foucault. The woman who is dogmatically refused an abortion by a doctor, the 'schizophrenic' compulsorily assigned to a mental hospital, the student failed in an examination, the claimant whose benefits are docked, are certainly coerced. These forms of power typically appear as 'objective' knowledge, with their own 'regimes of truth'. Public services are presented as neutral sources of good for their client populations. Failure may be seen as the clients not knowing what is good for them.

These sides of professionalism supply Thatcherism with political resources. There are accumulated popular injuries here. There is enough truth in New Right charges against public professionals to make them stick, even though professionals rarely control the financial and other parameters. Antagonisms between clients and state professionals can be given as much significance as conflicts between working people and their employers, or between men, women and children in domestic relations. *Causes célèbres* like the Cleveland child abuse cases and the more routine denigration of teachers or social workers are cases in point. Popular anger is deflected from those with most power (the owning and managing middle class) to those with some power (state professionals/workers). Discrepancies in terms of income and life-style may also fuel popular resentment (despite the declining incomes of many professionals). The groups stigmatized in right populism are, at best, a subaltern group, or 'the dominated fraction of the dominant class' (Bourdieu and Passeron, 1977). They are not those enjoying most wealth and power.

The New Right versus the professions: opportunities, difficulties

So New Right politics rests on the legacy of welfarism and its historical contradictions. Playing on these contradictions is a new way of defending other inequalities, especially those arising more directly from the economic and gender systems. These historical opportunities, however, also bring *difficulties* of their own, in the short, medium and longer terms.

The short-term difficulty has been the opposition of state professionals. This is quite comprehensible in New Right terms: a vested interest is fighting to defend its monopoly. Yet even in education, this difficulty is not easily overcome and has shaped policy profoundly.

The medium-term difficulty is that state professions are focuses for alternative social values. Minimally, professionals (in the various inspectorates, for example) are charged with monitoring social and environmental ills and continue to come up with findings that are awkward for the government. Again, the government has some solutions, including the manipulation of research, the control of appointments, and outright censorship. Maximally, the professions have been a basis for alternatives to New Right ideas and programmes, one source of rival social philosophies and movements.

The longer-term difficulties are more intractable. I argued earlier that there are limits to 'anti-social ideas'. New Right programmes are based on a one-sided version of human beings, which neglects or splits off our social character, our material and emotional dependence on each other. Practically, they will create deepening social disorganization and environmental deterioration. It is hard for the New Right to incorporate more 'social' insights, except in the alienated form of Conservative authoritarianism. Practically, it will respond to the social disorganization which its policies produce, by higher levels of state coercion and moral policing.

So though New Right governments may marginalize social theories and professionals, and may even de-professionalize them, they have still to find ways of dealing with the social-natural processes which are the subject of their expertise. The New Right programme will meet this and other historical limits. These will force it to change into something else or to yield to some successor movement: a different form of conservatism perhaps, or a refurbished social reform, or some hybrid between these, or a version of the New Politics? The rigidity of New Right frameworks makes adaptation seem unlikely, even without the current leaderships. The most likely outcome in future years is a protracted historical testing of each of these possibilities, a contest unlikely to be settled soon.

Some political choices

I hope this chapter gives reasoned form to the feelings I started with – being personally got at by Thatcherism. I hope I have shown how public professionals are deeply and centrally caught up in the dynamics of the New Right's 'revolution' and that our anxieties, for ourselves and for society, are justified.

There remains some room for choices. Professionals are part of the problem, but can also be part of the solution. We can also choose to be victims or to have a more active role. We can sue for benefits, from managerial status to early retirement. We can battle on through the next struggle over pay, autonomy, or 'the service'. But we can also choose not to defend a past, but to create a future. We can work, 'inside' and 'outside', towards alternative ideas, practices, policies and politics.

One reason for this choice is the vulnerability of existing defences. The public professions and welfare institutions are deeply vulnerable to right-wing populism, and to manipulation by the government. This is one reason why a simple return to 'social reform' which privileges expertise seems inadequate as well as undesirable. In many fields, including education, the government has already developed its own alternatives. An effective counter-strategy requires taking on board an analysis of our own power, our own relationship to clients and users. At a time when professionalism is under dire threat, this is hard to do. It adds vulnerability to weakness. It is hard even to find the time. Yet one way to turn the tide may be for professionals to redefine their power in ways that make alliances with users possible. Such a strategy would modify the relations on which the New Right Tendency, as a type of politics, depends.

Similar arguments apply to philosophies and movements with a professional or polytechnic/university base. As an academic myself, I want to end by addressing the more negative aspects of my own profession and its effects on an alternative politics. The academic character of much left and some feminist theory is an example of the problematic nature of professional power. Most academic production is geared towards forwarding an academic career and addressing a readership of 'peers'. Even when we address others, the habits stay with us, making others feel outsiders. The New Right has a wider range of voices. With appraisal and other controls intensifying, the struggle to develop other points of view on knowledge will probably sharpen.

There are shorter-term and longer-term strategies here too. The longer-term task is to start to modify the underlying conservatism of English cultural formations (much less marked in Scotland and Wales), the present forms of which aid the New Right and will aid similar conservatisms. This involves working on the split between academic and other knowledges, in terms both of access and of form. Everything is not resolved by undertaking to communicate accessibly, or grumbling about academic language. There are structural *relations* of power to be transformed. This means not only more access to higher education, but also more useful courses, and more open forms of teaching and organization, and more educative forms of politics (educative for academics too, that is) outside the 'educational' institutions.

There are plenty of immediate tasks too, many of them within our control as academics, as groups, even as individuals. There is a need to shape pointed truths from over-elaborated theses. There is a need to work on knowledges to make a genuine synthesis, not a fashionable 'name': identifying convergences, picking out essentials. We need to see where our knowledges converge with popular preoccupations and, where they don't, to research and write with specific groups. We must learn to perform in different ways, not always so analytically. We need to answer New Right polemics directly, those, for example, against anti-racism, equal opportunities and 'cultural relativism'. We need to give our own 'truths' a longer, deeper historical range than narrow polemic or the most politically contingent writing will often stretch to. We have to have the courage to recognize that some cycles of return from intellectual work to political effectivity are long and complex and unpredictable, partly because one author (even if it is a group) cannot possibly make all the connections. There is need for fundamental philosophical and political *critique* of New Right ideas, as well as more 'located' criticisms, not just critical appreciations.

We will need to be as effective as educators as the New Right has been, but much more effective in educating ourselves.

Notes

The ideas in this chapter were formed through many discussions on present discontents. Special thanks to Bob and Mariette who have, with good reason, exceptional insights into the current politics of professionals, to members of the MA group (1988–9) in the Department of Cultural Studies (who helped me put together New Right ideas and critical theories), to the Birmingham University Historical Materialism Group for discussions on Hayek, Scruton and the New Right, and to Education Group members for advice, support and faith that this would eventually appear.

1   As I wrote this over the winter and spring of 1988–9, doctors, nurses and midwives and other workers in the National Health Service, polytechnic and college lecturers, barristers and solicitors, my own Association of University Teachers, keepers at the Victoria and Albert Museum, all were involved in critical struggles with the government.

2 For a fuller discussion of the educational implications of these epistemological outlooks see Johnson, 1989. My views have been formed in a series of encounters with Althusserian rationalism (Althusser, 1969; Althusser and Balibar, 1974), Marx's own epistemology (Johnson, 1982), Foucault's analysis of intellectuals (e.g. Foucault, 1980), and feminist critiques of objectivity (e.g. McKinnon, 1983; Jaggar, 1983).

3 This paragraph owes much to the discussion of neo-liberalism in Hindess, 1987, though I do not always agree with his presentation of Marxism.

4 I am grateful for discussions with Maureen McNeil and other members of the Science Group at the Department of Cultural Studies on these and other issues covered in this essay. I also draw on the work of the Popular Memory Group, still unpublished.

5 My general approach here is influenced by Antonio Gramsci's revision of Marxist theories of power (Gramsci, 1971), Michel Foucault's stress on the radical diffusion of power centres and on power as 'incitement' (Foucault, 1979), and my understanding of some of the actual practices of feminist politics. By contrast the New Right appears to work, theoretically at least, with a fundamentally repressive theory of state and law.

6 Much of what follows is based on my own observations and experiences as a professional. I have also been influenced by the notion of cultural capital as developed in the work of Pierre Bourdieu (Bourdieu and Passeron, 1977; Bourdieu, 1984; Bourdieu, 1986). My ideas about professionals have been sharpened through debates with the Ehrenreich's thesis of a 'managerial-professional class' (Walker, 1979), with Poulantzas's 'new petit-bourgeoisie' (Poulantzas, 1975), and the idea of a 'service class' as developed in English sociology. The argument here also develops parts of *Unpopular Education* but attempts to draw out the gendered formation of the professions. For an interesting full critical discussion of professionalism, see Larson, 1977.

4

The strange fate of progressive education

James Avis

This chapter considers the 'strange fate of progressive education' in the postwar period and explores the way in which its ideas and themes have been taken up and distorted by the new vocationalism of the 1970s and 1980s. The concerns of progressive education had to some extent been reflected in liberal and general studies in the 1960s and were echoed by the 'humanism' of the Crowther Report. The aim of liberal and general studies was to move students beyond narrow vocational concerns to examine broader issues related to society. The new vocationalism of the 1970s and 1980s represents a retraction from this position and its replacement by a vocational focus. The first part of the chapter discusses the nature of progressive education in the postwar period, followed by an examination of the curricular models of the new vocationalism. I have considered the Certificate of Pre-Vocational Education (CPVE), *Core Skills in YTS*, and various documents produced by the Further Education Unit (FEU).

From its inception the theory and practice of progressive education have been profoundly contradictory and marked by disjunctures between its rhetorical justifications and the actions of its practitioners (Jones, 1983; Bernstein, 1977). It has often been claimed that focusing on student interest would enable progressive education to move the student on to a higher level of abstraction and so develop potential for critical thought. This aim has frequently been stalled when practitioners become stuck in the present by simply remaining on the terrain of student interest. The contradictions and disjunctures are unsurprising as there is no agreed-upon set of principles on which progressivism is based. This enables its practice to be malleable and capable of being adjusted to meet the institutional requirements of different educational settings (Gordon, 1986; Jones, 1983). The word itself is ambiguous reflecting as it does the divergent directions progressivism can take (Williams, 1981, p. 245). On one level the notion of progressivism can be collapsed into a biological developmentalism – the idea of a step-by-step move from immaturity to maturity. On another level it can be

counterposed to conservatism as its antithesis – thus having a resonance
with radical sentiments (Walkerdine, 1984; Walkerdine, 1986).

Despite the inconsistencies that surround the theoretical underpinnings
of progressivism there are a number of underlying themes. In 1986 Tula
Gordon constructed an ideal type of progressivism present in secondary
schools:

   i. mixed ability, vertical groupings work together and or individually
      in an open plan classroom under a team of teachers;
  ii. the day is 'integrated', the curriculum is problem- or concept-based;
 iii. a wide range of resources is drawn upon;
  iv. the teaching–learning is child centred, based on the pupils' interests,
      needs and skills;
   v. the teacher is a guide and supporter in the child's pursuit of learning;
  vi. academic learning is balanced by social and emotional learning,
      emphasizing creativity and self-expression;
 vii. decisions in the school are made by all those involved in it. (1986,
      p. 29)

Gordon's description has the merit of drawing our attention to a number
of elements within progressivism and its potential ambiguities.

In the postwar period the central underpinnings of progressivism are its
child/student centredness, its focus on relevance, its concern to relate to the
interests of the child thereby enhancing motivation and willingness to
learn, and its concern with integration. The important thing for progressivism is not so much what is learned, but rather the process of learning, and
this is why there is emphasis on activity-based learning. The offshoot is
that learning is individualized, children are perceived to develop at different
rates and the pedagogic milieu should accommodate this.

The mentors of progressivism have been many, but both Dewey and
Bruner figure prominently among these and their ideas have been selectively utilized in theory and practice. For Dewey, by drawing on learners'
practical interests, motivation and commitment to learning would be
sustained. The educational exchange should go further and was intended to
transcend the present and the localized. Learners' immediate interests were
to be developed and engaged in such a way as to enable the acquisition of
conceptual, abstract and analytical modes of understanding. Aronowitz and
Giroux in *Education under Siege* have, by stressing these themes, attempted
to regain the radical potential of Dewey's approach through the development of a critical education. The work of other progressive theorists is
equally capable of being appropriated and used radically, in as much as
these echo a desire to move from the immediate to higher levels of
understanding. For example, Andy Green (1986) has discussed the work of
Bruner whose notion of the 'spiral curriculum' attempts to move children

from simple generalization to the more complex and thus to develop their conceptual understanding. Paradoxically, within practice the potentiality of progressivism has often not been developed. As a curriculum form it is in the curious and unenviable position of being both supported and criticized by the 'left', as well as being subject to attack from the right, and yet being a hegemonic element in the curricular forms of the 'new vocationalism'.

The right in both England and the USA has launched an attack on the work of schools and the practices of teaching and learning that take place in educational institutions. The concern with standards, both academic and attitudinal, is paramount. Schools, it is argued, have been lax, whilst child-centred curricula which work from children's interests are considered antithetical to a disciplined and serious engagement with knowledge. Thus there is a call for a return to basics. The attack from the right has keyed in with popular sentiments and paradoxically is supported and reinforced from the 'left'. Aronowitz and Giroux write:

> Thus, the radical reformers were prey to the charge that they had betrayed the interests of the poor and minorities who desperately needed to learn how to read, write and calculate. (1986, p. 8)

For commentators such as Sharp and Green (1975), progressive education was merely a more sophisticated form of student control and a means of reproducing capitalist social relations. These ideas have a resonance with Bernstein's discussion of the invisible pedagogy and Walkerdine's strictures on the nature of progressivism as a system of social regulation and surveillance, whereby all aspects of the child come under the total gaze of the teacher (Bernstein, 1977; Walkerdine, 1986).

The paradox of progressivism is that it faces both ways and can be appropriated by both left and right in attempts to use it for quite different political purposes. Smith and Knight, for example, suggest the right's attack on progressivism is a result of its potential to evoke social criticism.

> It is in order to ask why the radical right in England, Australia, and the USA fear and attack progressive education. This is not only a reflection of their ideological opposition to liberal democracy but also an index of their apprehension of progressivism's perceived intention and potential for social and cultural change. They fear it because of its perceived failure to train students to docility and obedience and its perceived potential for developing more autonomous and responsible individuals and for fostering a more democratic and aware community. (1982, p. 229)

It is this sense of critique that Aronowitz and Giroux (1986) are trying to reinstate.

There is an inherent difficulty in the practice of progressivism that has enabled it to point both ways. This has been its inability to develop a fully worked-out politics and politically engaged curriculum. Bernstein (1977) commenting on the theoretical underpinnings of progressivism suggests that it is constructed out of diverse elements.[1] Atkinson, commenting on this aspect of Bernstein's work, states:

> it [progressive theory] is a very mixed bag. It is, as I have implied, the outcome of *bricolage:* that is, the cobbling together of whatever bits and pieces are to hand, rather than a custom-built design. (1985, p. 159)

Ironically, it was this theoretical and political lacuna that enabled radical teachers in the 1960s to incorporate progressivism into their practice. As a result of this vacuum, however, neither progressivism nor radical teachers were able to defend themselves from the onslaught of the right in the 1970s. This failure opened the way for a rightist take-over of progressivism and came in the guise of a realistic and vocationally orientated approach that masqueraded as being of the left.

What then have been the radical failings of progressive education in practice? The central flaw has been its individualism. Each child and student is categorized atomistically and expected to pursue their own separate and autonomous development. The difficulty here is that there is no grasp of collective processes or indeed the formation of collective ways of appropriating and using educational forms and knowledge. Education is reduced to the pursuit of individual development. The social processes involved in the production of knowledge are ignored and knowledge is rid of its social uses.

Whether or not knowledge is of use depends on the vantage point from which it is viewed and the social interests to which it can be put. Progressive education either neglects or trivializes social differences, the consequence being its failure to address forms of knowledge that could be used collectively by oppressed groups. This relates to a number of other difficulties. In progressive education the classroom becomes a small-scale model of society without the social relations and as such provides a distorted and astructural view of the social formation (Walkerdine 1984). This results from its empiricism, its focus on relevance and on what the student knows. Despite the strictures of the mentors of progressivism it has often become fixed on the immediate and has therefore failed to develop in its charges a wider understanding of social processes that can transcend the present and provide 'really useful knowledge'. As Andy Green writes:

> The danger of 'instant relevance' is that in its earnest desire to 'meet the kids where they're at' *it ends up leaving them exactly there*. (1986, p. 115; emphases added)

This tension within progressive practice results from its mode of deployment. Progressivism is taken up differentially in various educational sites. Thus it will be subject to subtle transformation between pedagogic locations. In addition, within particular sites its accenting will be dependent upon the type of student or pupil to whom it is addressed. In the case of the Raising of the School Leaving Age (ROSLA), the move towards progressivism was more an attempt to solve the problems schools encountered when faced with pupil hostility to the traditional curriculum, than a well thought-out curriculum intervention aimed at developing 'really useful knowledge'. In these instances it was used as a form of surveillance and student control. Progressivism became reduced to technique. It became part of the armoury of educationists to be used judiciously when the need arose. Its apolitical nature enabled this shift and conspired in its transmogrification into conservative education.

The selective take-up of progressivism

The central themes of progressivism were ready-made for an appropriation into a new conservative educational/training paradigm. Its focus on the student, its orientation towards relevance and its perceived ability, through the combination of these elements, to motivate the learner, rendered it the paradigmatic form for the new vocationalism. A number of related educational currents also fed into the new paradigm in both positive and negative ways. The often reported resistance to traditional pedagogies and their stultifying effect on many pupils provided a negative push away from this type of curriculum towards the more vocational. This shift was located at a moment when traditional education was in crisis, bearing much of the blame for the growth in youth unemployment. The bifurcation between traditional educational relations and those embodied in progressivism was also reflected in the polarity between competency-based education and traditionalism. The deep-seated behaviourism of competency-based education was able to align itself with the truncated progressivism of the new paradigm. Consider, for example, the distinctions made between competency-based education and traditional education in the following passage from *Competency in Teaching*:[2]

Competency Based Education	*Traditional Education*
1. The main indicator of student achievement is ability to do the job effectively.	The main indicators of student achievement are knowledge of the subject and the ability to do the job effectively and efficiently.

2. Once a student has demonstrated ability to do the job, his/her preparation is complete.	Students operate within specified time limits.
3. Criterion of success is demonstration of ability to do the job.	The criteria of success are better grades.
4. Entrance requirements are not of paramount concern.	Entrance requirements are important.
5. Flexible scheduling of learning activities is essential to provide for individual difference.	Students are scheduled for instruction into fairly rigid blocks of time.
6. No fixed rules as to how, when or where learning is to be accomplished.	Classroom teaching.
7. Opportunities are provided to acquire competences in practical field or on the job experience.	Practical field experiences are limited.
8. Learnings are presented in small learning units.	Learnings are organized into courses.
9. Provision is made for differences among students with various alternative paths for acquiring competence.	Lecture–discussion is the most common mode of presentation. Little attention is given to student style of learning.

This passage is of interest as it is indicative of another route to the new vocationalism that draws upon behaviourist psychology and the objectives school of curriculum design (Mager, 1962). It shows the way in which progressivism can become distorted and yet allied to an amazingly restricted educational form. It should be remembered that, whilst progressive educators in the 1960s were often opposed to the psychology of measurement, the two were intimately linked, as Walkerdine (1984) has shown in her discussion of Piaget. In the same vein a similar link is present between the looser forms of progressivism in the new vocationalism and behaviourism. The social and life skills element in the early Youth Opportunities Programme (YOP) reflects this tendency. Davies notes:

It [social and life skills training] has been used for many years in work with the mentally handicapped, with prisoners and even those seeking help with personal and behavioural difficulties. However, in these fields of practice it has usually been possible to regard those undergoing the 'training' as victims of some personal incapacity . . . It has, therefore, also been possible to act as if their 'problems' could be defined 'objectively' and as if their 'treatment' were entirely a 'technical' matter calling for no implicit ethical choices. (1979, p. 4)

Integration was another element of progressivism that was taken up in the new vocationalism. It allowed a distancing from the perceived irrelevance of academic studies, the sterility of much that passed for technical education, and was able to key into anticipated student responses to the newer curricular forms.[3] These changes were responses to the new relations in which further education (FE) was placed in the 1970s. The advent of the youth training schemes and the growth of unemployment meant that youth who had previously been denied access to FE entered in ever-growing numbers. Progressive pedagogic styles were seen as meeting the needs of these students/trainees, as well as avoiding control problems arising from the use of traditional pedagogic models (Stafford, 1981). Teachers involved in this type of work were accorded low status. It was also at this time that the Further Education Curriculum Review and Development Unit was established (FEU).[4] The significance of this unit has been profound and has been crucial in the generation and dissemination of new curricular models that have represented the vocational appropriation of a truncated progressivism. In part its activities have conjoined with those of some practitioners of the new vocationalism who have sought a greater legitimacy for their curricular practices.

It is something of a paradox that the linchpin of integration in the new forms has been contrasted to the restrictive and hidebound theoretical orientations of traditional academic and technical education. Yet the ideologues of the new forms have sought to provide themselves with a theoretical justification for an atheoretical and concretely based practice. This can be contrasted against the heavily theoretical and pedagogically unsupported practice of traditional education. There has been and continues to be a struggle within further education between the new trainers, attached to the newer curricular forms, and those attached to the older. In this struggle careers have been made and a variety of resources have been manipulated. One such resource has been the quite correct denigration of traditional academic education for its elitism and another has been the new trainers' pretence to left-wing commitments (Boffy and Cave, 1982).

The new educational paradigm and curriculum interventions

In this section I consider a number of curricular interventions that reflect the development of the 'new educational paradigm' and its preferred pedagogy. A close-in analysis will be made of a number of documents, *The Certificate of Pre-Vocational Education* (CPVE blue books), *Core Skills in YTS,* and a selection of the publications of the FEU.[5] These documents have been selected as they reflect different institutional responses to the curriculum. The CPVE, for example, developed by City and Guilds London Institute (CGLI) and the Business and Technical Education Council (BTEC), arose out of a response to youth unemployment by the Department of Education and Science (DES) (DoE/DES 1986); *Core Skills in YTS,* was a publication produced by the Manpower Services Commission (MSC) for managing agents and was funded through the EEC social fund; FEU was established, amongst other things, to review and evaluate the FE curriculum. Each of the documents represents a different vantage point from which FE can be viewed. By exploring these documents various contradictions and tensions may be uncovered that open the way for an appropriate political intervention. It should be recognized that there are links and overlaps between these institutions which will be reflected in their documents. In the discussion I do not focus on the entirety of the documents, rather I explore three interrelated themes: models of society, of the student, and of education. These themes are implicitly or explicitly reflected in the documents.

The analysis should not be viewed as restricted to the specific documents and I would contend that a similar reading could be made of current publications emanating from these bodies. In addition, these documents should be viewed as part of an ongoing struggle to define what counts as educational knowledge in our schools and colleges and what are suitable knowledge and curricula for certain types of students/trainees. These documents not only reflect a particular form of appropriation of progressivism but are also attempting to further a specific form of education. As Apple would suggest, they are involved in a process of cultural production. Commenting on the American experience he states:

> It is important that we focus on reports of this type since they act to alter the very discipline of education. The terrain of debate shifts from a concern with inequality and democratisation (no matter how weak) to the language of efficiency, standards and productivity. Alterations in the terrain of debate affect our collective memories in major ways. We lose sight of the years of effort it took to establish the progressive tendencies that do exist within state institutions such as schools, and these changes provide an ideological horizon against which we locate policies and practices of curriculum and teaching. Thus, these documents are not only useful indicators of ideological shifts. *They are themselves part of the cultural production of such altered public discourse* and as such need to be seen as constitutive elements of a particular hegemonic project. (1986, p. 174)

The Certificate of Pre-Vocational Education (CPVE)

The CPVE is a full-time pre-vocational course designed for those who have completed their compulsory schooling. It caters for students with varying vocational commitments and levels of ability. It aims to assist in the transition from school to adulthood; to provide an 'individually relevant educational experience which encourages learning and achievement'; to provide a qualification which embodies national standards and provides scope for progression. There are three elements to the CPVE course framework: the core, vocational studies and additional studies. It is intended that the core and vocational studies be integrated. There are ten core areas and these should cover

> A range of experiences and competences (which include skills, knowledge and attitudes) which are essential to the students' chances of making a success in adult life including work. (CPVE Pt A, p. 4)

The CORE

Personal and career development	Science and technology
Industrial, social and environmental studies	Information technology
Communication	Creative development
Social skills	Practical skills
Numeracy	Problem solving

(based on CPVE Pt A, p. 4)

Vocational studies aim to encourage motivation by building on student interests. They thus enable students to explore and develop their talents and interests as well as providing a focus for the development of core competences. In addition they provide a route for progression as well as generally developing 'broad Vocational Skills applicable to a variety of adult roles found both inside and outside of employment' (CPVE Pt A, p. 5). Vocational studies are grouped into five main categories, each being divided into a number of clusters based on groupings of occupational and non-occupational roles found in the category.

a. Category 1 – Business and administrative services.
b. Category 2 – Technical services.
c. Category 3 – Production.
d. Category 4 – Distribution.
e. Category 5 – Services to people.
(CPVE Pt A, p. 5)

Within each category and cluster there are three stages.

a. Introductory – providing a general introduction to activities within each *category*
b. Exploratory – providing a more detailed exploration of roles in a *cluster*
c. Preparatory – encouraging the development of a range of skills and knowledge within a *cluster* as a preparation for progression within occupational routes in this or related clusters. (CPVE Pt A, p. 5)

The third element of the CPVE framework is additional studies. The core and vocational studies comprise 75 per cent of the course; integration is encouraged, with a minimum of 20 per cent of the core and vocational studies being integrated. The remaining 25 per cent comprises additional studies and this is to provide time for 'community activities, leisure, recreation and for reflection', as well as providing for 'particular educational needs'.

Model of society in CPVE

Within the CPVE, society is conceived of in pluralist terms and comprises different interest groups and cultures. There is, however, an underlying consensual base to society in which fundamental conflicts of interest are absent. In the third aim, 'personal and social development', which is concerned with morals and ethics, the student is to 'recognise the relationship between rights and responsibilities of citizens in a democratic society' (CPVE Pt B, p. 5). And in the fourth aim, 'industrial, social and environmental studies', objectives include:

understanding the legal rights, duties, and responsibilities of the individual.
identifying the role of the police and courts in the enforcement of law and the protection of the rights of individuals and groups. (CPVE Pt B, p. 7)

Implicit within these quotes is a view of society as ultimately democratic and fair, for if it were not, how could one justify an emphasis that stresses the duties and responsibilities of the individual? Where conflicts do arise these are perceived in frictional terms. Individual bias or prejudice may lead to conflict. These are resolvable on the level of the individual and represent a dysfunctioning of an otherwise democratic and therefore just society. Thus students should be able to

formulate personal values by . . . recognising bias and its effect on human relationships – race, sex, age, class, and religious discrimination. (CPVE Pt B, p. 5) and to

> recognise and analyse the signs used to allocate individuals to categories, and to be aware of the prevalence and abuses of such categorisations by . . . assessing the usefulness of such categorisation [gender, class, race, dress, speech, age] in developing effective working and social relationships [and by] recognising misuses of categorisation of individuals and groups – working, social, cultural and religious. (CPVE Pt B, p. 11)

There is a recognition of the social structure, for example, as a cause of unemployment, though curricular stress on the individual limits its centrality (CPVE Pt B, p. 7). The core, to be fair, is potentially contradictory and could be used to raise important questions, but its critical edge is subsumed to a truncated vocationalism that limits this possibility. This is the result of its integration with vocational elements of the curriculum.

> The design of courses and the balance of the various components are the responsibility of the schools and colleges. Courses can vary from a totally integrated programme in which the Core competences are achieved entirely through the Vocational studies, to a structure in which only partial integration is achieved. *Courses in which Core and Vocational studies are wholly separated will not be approved.* (CPVE Pt A, p. 7; emphases added)

> The nature of the CPVE framework recognises that the achievement of core aims and objectives will be met in a variety of ways but *specifically identifies the role of the Vocational studies as a way in which the core will be developed and applied.* (CPVE Pt B, p. 3; emphases added)

If the vocational aims of the CPVE are to be met, the critical potential of the core has to be neutralized and this is done by placing 'vocation' in a hegemonic position. Anything that undermines this aim is thus rendered illegitimate. The vocationalism of the CPVE is constructed as a form of anticipatory socialization through the focus on role exploration. The student is to explore the roles available in a particular occupational category or cluster. The experiences provided by the CPVE seek to develop the personal autonomy of the student:

> To develop ability to make effective personal and working relationships and to promote self-reliance. (CPVE Pt B, p. 10)

> The student should be encouraged and guided to adopt active rather than passive learning methods, with the aim of generating autonomy and a pro-active approach to learning. (CPVE Pt B, p. 32)

However, this concern with autonomy and self-reliance emerges in a restricted form which is stripped of a sense of empowerment. The student is simply to acquire the characteristics of the responsible worker which are reflected in the nature of the CPVE with its stress on occupational socialization (see Friedman, 1977) and its concern that 'The CPVE will allow students to demonstrate readiness to . . . *respond and perform effectively at work*' (CPVE Pt A, p. 3). Whilst the student is to develop a degree of personal autonomy, this stops short of a concern with control and with an understanding of industry and society. The autonomous individual may reject the ideology of vocationalism and may perceive the exploitative relationships that arise in paid labour, but the whole weight of the curriculum is designed to negate such an outcome. The curriculum core does recognize the existence of a range of social inequalities; for example, those based on race and gender. However, these are not considered as patterns of social relations but rather as the effect of individual bias, are treated as dysfunctional and are resolvable within the existing structure of society. Unfortunately the official version of the CPVE provides no space for the recognition of contradictions whose resolution would require structural change.

Education in CPVE

Within the CPVE there lies an implicit critique of academic and 'traditional' vocational education, both being construed as inappropriate. Traditional vocational education is seen as being too specific and failing to develop transferable skills. On the other hand academic education is criticized for its sterility, its lack of relevance and its 'construction' of the student as passive. An adequate education is seen as being activity-based and involving negotiation between student and teacher.

> The learning strategies adopted must support the aims of the course as a whole. The following [activity-based learning, work experience, guidance and student support] are particularly important and will be an integral part of all CPVE courses.
> *Activity-based learning*
> Achievement of a large number of Core and Vocational objectives requires the use of practical activities to develop the students' experience and to provide opportunities for applying and re-applying knowledge and skills.
> Activity-based Learning also provides the basis for encouraging student self-development and increasing autonomy. To achieve this it must be based on the needs, interests and resources of the students themselves. (CPVE Pt A, p. 8)

The teacher becomes a facilitator. The whole educational experience is organized around the perceived needs of the learner and here student guidance is stressed.

> A system of Student Counselling and Guidance is an integral part of all courses and must be closely related to Formative Assessment and the Profiling system. It will include regular meetings between the student and a personal tutor at which problems and progress can be reviewed and future patterns of learning agreed. This involvement of the students in the planning of their own programmes and learning contributes to course integration by helping them to perceive the course as a coherent whole. (CPVE Pt A, p. 8)

Many of the themes raised in the CPVE are an appropriation of progressive education. This is reflected in the concern with a student-centred, activity-based education that relates to the interests and needs of the learner. This progressivism, which presents itself as radical, is in fact deeply conservative. The focus on relevance, needs and interests is the bulwark of progressivism, and in radical versions these are used to transcend the present, to consider possibilities and to develop critical insights into the nature of society. Yet the curriculum framework of the CPVE limits this possibility. The teaching exchange is seen as benign, discrepancies of power are ignored, and education is perceived solely as developing the individual rather than empowering collectivities too. The knowledges that students bring with them are treated differentially. Those that accord with realism and appropriate forms of subjectivity are valued, whilst those that do not are counselled against. Thus the importance placed on profiling and negotiated learning becomes a way of monitoring student subjectivity.

Whilst prominence is given to the notion of vocation there has been a narrowing of the term. Vocationalism could mean not only an exploration of occupational roles, functions and activities, but also an active engagement with the nature of work. This would not solely be at an individual level, focusing on occupational suitability, but involve a more rigorous critique, implicitly raising issues of value. The form of vocational education envisaged by the CPVE subsumes skill to competence and attitudinal dispositions. There is a devaluation of the notion of control that is implicit in the conception of skill. Within the CPVE the split between mental and manual labour is reproduced, as is the separation between academic and vocational education. There is no consideration of their interrelation, or that an adequate and critical education could combine both, drawing on their strengths and in this way transforming them.

Students in CPVE

Whilst the CPVE is purportedly for the vocationally uncommitted with a wide range of abilities, this emphasis should be viewed within the educational relations in which it is placed historically and contemporaneously. Historically it developed from low-level, pre-vocational courses; as a route to high-status occupations it is clearly limited in comparison with traditional academic courses.

In order to motivate the learner, it is argued that an activity-based, experiential, vocationally related course is required. There is a stress on learning by doing and the student is perceived as oriented towards the practical. Vocational studies in their different modes illustrate this. Where there is time for reflection, this is shaped in such a way as to encourage consideration of difficulties experienced by students that inhibit adequate role performance. This approach stresses the practical, is focused on the individual, and to the extent that reflection is encouraged this is in terms of individual inadequacies. Reflection on work experiences, sessions on personal development, counselling and formative assessment all lead to the construction of the student as an atomistic individual. There is a concern with the surveillance and policing of student subjectivity. Even when the term autonomy is used this is in a restricted sense which reduces it to one of compliance and self-discipline within the worker. There is no sense of collective empowerment, and even when the individual is placed in a group context it is to encourage the acceptance of group evaluation of their performance.

> Contributing to the self evaluation of others by sharing perceptions of them through constructive one-to-one and group evaluations.
> Summarising and reviewing opinions and judgement of self in groups and in one-to-one discussions. (CPVE Pt B, p. 10)

Here we see a concern with monitoring the student in order to encourage the formation of a conformist subjectivity. This is all the more insidious in that students are to be party to this process. The vocational nature of the CPVE advances a subjectivity that is fitted to employer requirements, that is, the construction of a flexible, reliable, responsible, self-disciplining worker.

I am aware that many of the core objectives and aims of the CPVE could point to alternative outcomes, and that radical teachers, with their students, will draw on its fissures and tensions to struggle for these. However, the curricular framework of CPVE is such that its core objectives are subsumed under a vocationalism that limits the effectiveness of such struggles.

'Core Skills in YTS'

This document was produced by the MSC for the guidance of management agents in the provision of work experience and off-the-job education and training.[6] The document avoids an engagement with educational theorizing and the acceptance and legitimacy of its educational underpinnings are taken for granted. Core skills aim to encourage managing agents to adopt its definition of good practice. The document secures its legitimacy through its form which is that of the glossy, authoritative report akin to annual reports produced by business firms, and its written style which uses easy platitudes of common sense to authorize its claims. In the discussion I do not consider the implicit model of society found in the document as this is similar to that of the CPVE's. Instead I focus on models of education and the trainee present in the document.

The foreword to *Core Skills* (Pt 1 foreword) summarizes the aims of the Youth Training Scheme (YTS) as providing the trainee with

> initial competence in a job;
> a broad range of occupational and transferable skills; and personal effectiveness.

Core skills themselves are defined as follows:

> Core skills underpin the concept of skill transfer, and the development of personal and occupational competence in the work place. They are of major importance in a school to work transition programme, since they are concerned with the *application of skills and knowledge to tasks at work and in the world outside work. For this reason they cannot be learned or assessed as single subjects in the classroom.* (*Core Skills* Pt 1, foreword; emphases added)

What then are these core skills that are to be developed in YTS trainees? There are 4 core areas which contain 14 core skills groups which together involve 103 core skills.

Core Area	*Core Skills group*
Number	1. Operating with numbers
	2. Interpreting numerical and related information
	3. Estimating
	4. Measuring and marking out
	5. Recognizing cost and value
Communication	6. Finding out information and interpreting instructions
	7. Providing information
	8. Working with people

Problem Solving   9. Planning: Determining and revising courses of action

10. Decision making: Choosing between alternatives

11. Monitoring: Keeping track of progress and checking

Practical   12. Preparing for a practical activity

13. Carrying out a practical activity

14. Finishing off a practical activity.

(*Core Skills* Pt 1, p. 37)

Training for core skills is intended to develop both competence in an occupational area and in transfer skills; and to encourage the acquisition of knowledge and skills that will enable the young person to progress 'to further education and training in the same or different occupations and to cope with the world outside employment' (*Core Skills* Pt 1, p. 4), even if this is unemployment. The acquisition of core skills is far more than the mere learning of technical know-how, as it involves not only transfer skills but also the formation of an appropriate subjectivity. It is, in effect, an attempt to construct the generic worker. What, however, is meant by skills of transfer? There are two ways in which the question is handled. First, itemizing core skills makes visible what was previously taken for granted: for example, the communication skills involved in talking to people at work.[7] By naming these, core skills are uncovered that can be universalized and can transcend any particular occupational site. The acquisition of these skills, it is suggested, will lead to a more adequate performance at work. Secondly, the notion of transfer involves being able to apply knowledge and skills appropriately in new contexts. This element of transfer involves not only the application of knowledge and skills but also the subjective wish to do so.

Education and the trainee

The document implicitly assumes schooling has failed to equip young people with the appropriate core skills because of the dominance of traditional educational techniques. These techniques can be summarized as subjects, abstraction, lack of application to the real world, teacher-centred learning. All of these are counterposed to the good practice that is recommended in *Core Skills*. If trainees are to receive an adequate education/training this must be of a type that is activity-based and student-centred and links what is learned to the real world. Whilst the document is focused on YTS trainees and is primarily concerned with their training and off-the-job education, it does have a wider application to educational debates. This is because its arguments are constructed in such a way as to point to what is considered to be good educational practice. The emphasis throughout is on learning by doing and the *process* of learning.

> Training for core skills often has as much to do with how trainees are learning as it has to do with what specific knowledge they are acquiring; *situations in which trainees learn through active experience promote a greater range and depth of skills.* (*Core Skills* Pt 1, p. 2; emphases added)

This is contrasted to traditional subject teaching which is seen as unnecessarily restrictive and separated from the real world of practice. The document is critical of methods of assessment that 'measure theoretical abilities in isolation from their application' (*Core Skills* Pt 1, p. 8). An adequate assessment of students' core skills must consider their 'performance in real situations'. It is suggested that core skills cannot be 'taught' as subjects but must be related to an integrated programme. This position is grossly anti-educative. For whilst these strictures echo the tenets of progressivism, on another level they are profoundly conservative. This is because the assessment of core skills goes beyond the evaluation of capability and involves an implicit appraisal of moral worth. There is a paradox in the way in which the document deals with attitudes:

> Some skills are more important in a task than others, and some are so insignificant as to be not worth recording . . . for example the collection of mail calls for no real exercise of *skill*. (This is not to say that it is not important in the task. If the trainee did not bother to collect the mail, all the other skills would be irrelevant. But this would be a shortcoming in *attitude* not skill.) (*Core Skills* Pt 1, p. 10, note iii)

Here, there is an attempt to separate attitude from skill and yet in the performance of the task it will be paramount. If assessment is concerned with performance it cannot help but be involved in the appraisal of attitudes. When discussing communication the document states:

> Within both of these groups [customers/clients] trainees should be given contact with a variety of people in order to learn *appropriate* ways of communicating with people in a variety of departments or sections and with people at a variety of levels in a company, for instance. Often communication skills can only be effective if the trainee has first decided when it is best to use them and planned the best ordering for information or enquiries. (*Core Skills* Pt 1, p. 23)

Clearly in these relationships, there is a concern not just with some abstract capacity to communicate, but rather with relations of power and authority and the trainee's response to this. The ability to communicate, in this instance, is not separable from the trainee's attitude as it will be through the perceptions of others that this ability is measured. Thus if a supervisor feels a trainee is insufficiently deferential this will be perceived as the trainee's inadequacy to communicate effectively. It is within this sphere that core skills become problematic. Because they are tied to a particular set of relations, namely employment relations, their accomplishment is limited by them. This means that if occasions arise when the trainees reflect on their position, a contradiction emerges. Reflection is encouraged in core skills; the trainees are to reflect on their training, on their own skills, on the generality of the skills that they possess. However, if reflection transcends the employment nexus, if trainees start to question the authority relations in which they are placed, and if they start to contemplate the exploitativeness and meaninglessness of much that passes for work, they will be seen as having failed to develop the appropriate core skills. The suggestion that core skill training is educational is a misrepresentation, for it is in fact an anti-educative device, though some trainees and teachers may struggle to turn it into something of value.

The FEU: 'conservative radicals'?

In this section, rather than a close-in discussion of a particular document, a more eclectic and pragmatic approach is adopted. The FEU, a semi-autonomous body, was established in 1977. It was set up to realign and co-ordinate curriculum developments in FE and has managed to survive ten years of Conservative government. It is far from being a homogeneous or monolithic institution. The nature of its work, involving the commissioning of research and the dissemination of results, makes for variety in what is produced and recommended. The FEU has persistently seen itself as an agent of change: it was to transform the outmoded practices of FE and to introduce a more modern, streamlined and realistic form. This project connects the FEU to the previous developments discussed, and it has been portrayed as radical and progressive. But is it? What would be the effect if the educational developments suggested by the FEU were taken on board by FE? Would this result in a more 'radical' and therefore useful educational experience for students? What are the limits and possibilities of FEU practices? Is it trapped within the rhetoric of the 'social-democratic' view of education so that its radicalism shields a deep-seated conservatism? In the following discussion there are two sections. The first considers questions of access and waste, and the second the nature of the educational experience.

Access and waste

A recurrent theme in the FEU documents is a concern with access to education and the subsequent waste of human resources that arises when this does not occur (FEU, 1985a). There is an emphasis that educational experiences should provide access for older people, women and members of ethnic minorities. For example, the 'culture' of FE is thought to inhibit the performance of women and girls: 'These female students who find themselves in an FE college are likely to be part of an establishment *organised by men for men often with a monocultural ethos*' (FEU, 1985a, p. 7; emphases added). The intervention of the FEU is designed to overcome these inhibitions. They suggest the way to do this is to transform the curriculum, the institutional framework and indeed the monoculturalism of FE. This stance is applied to all those groups who experience 'disadvantage' in FE: the older students, women, ethnic minorities and the disabled. Thus for the older students traditional further education fails to recognize the significance of their experience. It is proposed that

> Present provision of adult education/training is often the target of widespread criticism. Many schemes of traditional academic and voca-tional training seem to create barriers and disincentives and to inhibit adaptability as a result of their *reluctance to recognize learning derived from work experience*. (FEU, 1984b, p. 2; emphases added)

A set of measures is proposed that will eradicate these blockages and without which we would all lose out; the nation would lose valuable human resources. In *Changing the Focus* the MSC is cited approvingly (FEU, 1985a, p. 8):

> from a national point of view the waste of resources inherent in the failure to make full use of the ability of women needs to be corrected.

There is nothing new about these ideas. They were a recurrent theme throughout the 1960s and became embedded in the social–democratic view of education (Centre for Contemporary Cultural Studies Education Group, 1981). This model of education held out the promise of meritocracy and equal educational opportunity. If these aims were met it was felt that all of society would benefit as its human resources would be stretched and developed to the full. This was the time when the notion of human capital was developed; it underlies much of the FEU's work and can, for example, be seen in the idea of 'skill ownership.'

Like the earlier debates the current discussions treat 'disadvantage' in isolation. The issue of race is treated separately from that of age or gender, and nowhere is the issue of class discussed. A recognition of these relationships would challenge the FEU's project which is to provide an effective, streamlined and adequately motivated labour force for a dynamic capitalism. The 'disadvantages' experienced by older people, women and ethnic minorities are seen to block moves towards economic recovery. To ensure a revived economy, educational processes need to be transformed. Here the FEU introduces something new. Rather than just providing access to traditional FE, its curriculum needs to be changed to facilitate effectiveness.

The educational experience

The FEU is stringently critical of traditional education, both academic and vocational. Both are considered defunct as they fail to extend the student or develop skills needed by a modern, technologically advanced society. The linchpin of these criticisms is that not only does education lack relevance to the wider society and to the world of work, but that the student is cast in the role of a passive recipient of knowledge.[8] In this way the educational experience of the student is rendered incomplete. The losers in this exchange are not only the students but society as a whole. Whilst the FEU's work has been focused on vocational education in FE, its influence has also penetrated the school.[9] For example, the joint publication of the FEU with the School Curriculum Development Committee, *Supporting TVEI*, argues that across the range of abilities there is a need to develop new teaching and learning styles (FEU/SCDC, 1985). There should be a shift away from teacher-led styles to those which are experientially based, curriculum-led, and, importantly, student centred.

There is a move away from the classroom, towards a negotiated curriculum. In other words teachers and students negotiate an appropriate curriculum package that meets the needs of the individual student. There is a consistent critique of the dominance of subject teaching. It is argued that an integrated approach be adopted that overcomes the separateness of subject disciplines. Roy Boffy (1984) also calls for integration. He explains the dominance of subject disciplines as resulting from the power of educational elites in universities who have distorted the curriculum and led to the dominance of inappropriate curriculum forms. The hegemony of subjects renders education an abstract and unreal experience.

Progressing to College: a 14–16 Core states:

> The core should be 'compulsory' for all 14–16 pupils, otherwise it is unlikely to be used and referred to by either educational institutions, examining boards or employers. The way it is provided, applied and made available to individual pupils should be a matter of negotiation and consultation between teachers, parents and pupils themselves. Although

this appears radical, in practice many core subjects such as mathematics, English, etc, are already agreed in this way. The only differences, as will be described below, are that we are suggesting a core broader than a collection of single subjects. (FEU, 1985b, p. 2)

The core is restricted to fifteen aims and all pupils have an entitlement to have access to these. The aims are:

Adaptability	Role Transition
Physical Skills	Interpersonal Skills
Values	Communication/Numeracy
Problem solving	Information Technology
Society	Learning Skills
Health Education	Creativity
Environment	Science/Technology
Coping	

(FEU, 1985b, pp. 3–5)

The significance of the core with its emphasis on negotiation is that areas of study and student capacities that in the past were not assessed are opened up for scrutiny and social regulation.

Personal qualities are, for many young people, their main strength. If these qualities matter, which they certainly do, and if they can be developed, which they certainly can, then we should plan to make them a real part of the curriculum. As well as affecting the approach we adopt to the learning process, this also means that we should work out the implications for assessment. *Not to credit young people with (for example) their ability to work with others, whilst insisting on reporting their lack of ability (such as in essay writing) would seem to be perverse.* (Stanton, 1984, p. 18; emphases added)

These new emphases are indicated in the learning and teaching strategies that teachers are encouraged to adopt: negotiation, experiential learning, counselling and guidance, teaching for transfer, recording and profiling, continual assessment of need and progress, participative learning (FEU, 1984c; Boffy, 1984). Many of the ideas and arguments advanced by the FEU have a fine ring. They do connect with a real criticism of the nature of educational provision and yet their logic is fundamentally flawed. This becomes apparent when the measures used to assess the effectiveness of these interventions are considered. Examine the following aims that are part of the core entitlement:

Adaptability
to develop a flexibility of attitude and ability to learn sufficient to cope
with future changes in technology, career and life style.

Role transition
to bring out an informed perspective as to the roles and status of a young
person in an adult, multicultural society including the world of work in
order to inform responsible and realistic decision-making as to future
opportunities.

Interpersonal Skill
To bring about an ability to be sensitive to and tolerant of the needs of
others, and to develop satisfactory personal relationships.

Values
To foster a reasoned set of social and moral values applicable to issues in
contemporary society. (FEU, 1985b, pp. 3–4)

These aims are predicated on a number of disturbing themes. There is, for
example, an implicit acceptance of the status quo, an attempt to encourage
realism, an acceptance of one's place and a move towards self-blame for
failure. There is a deep concern with the formation and assessment of an
appropriate subjectivity, one that accords with a particular view of the
needs of a capitalist society.

Many of the competences young people need . . . owe little to the
content of traditional subjects. They rely on more generalised process
skills of analysis and problem solving, personal qualities such as resilience and responsibility, and the ability to transfer knowledge and skills
acquired in one context to other problems and situations. (FEU, 1984c,
p. 1)

When one considers the FEU's emphasis on competence, in more directly
vocational education, the conservative nature of the concept and its
attempted subjective effect becomes apparent.

Competence can be defined as: *the possession and development of sufficient
skills, knowledge, appropriate attitudes and experience for successful performance
in life roles.* Such a definition includes employment and other forms of
work; it implies maturity and responsibility in a variety of roles; and it
includes experience as an essential element of competence. (FEU, 1984e,
p. 3)

These issues are underpinned by the assumption that there is no difference
between education and training. The two become merged, the hegemony

of the vocational is secured and with it an acceptance of the social relations of work. Herein lies the essentially conservative nature of the FEU's project and its ideological role. Its version of modernism and progressivism is one that is able to attract a type of 'radical' teacher whose radicalism is reduced to a posturing in the name of socialism and whose practice is conservative in its effect. This is not to deny the valuable work of radical teachers in countering the effects of the 'new curriculum', or of those radicals who work in the FEU and attempt to develop critical educational practices.

Conclusion

This chapter has focused upon the contradictory nature of progressive education, an educational form pointing both to the right and left. It has also been amenable to various inflections at different locations in the educational system. The discussion of educational documents points towards one such appropriation, an appropriation that has been made in the name of progressivism but that disguises a fundamentally conservative education. This is not to deny the malleability of progressivism and the contradictory elements that surround the new vocationalism which may be worked on by students/trainees and teachers in order to generate 'really useful knowledge'. One of the aims of this book is to transcend mere critique and argue for the development of more promising pedagogic forms. Concerns with relevance and students' interests hold the possibility of moving towards more politically relevant understandings.

None the less we have to recognize that the new educational paradigm, forged through the work of such bodies as the FEU and MSC, has had a profound effect on our educational system. The new ideas are fast becoming part of educational orthodoxy. This new paradigm has not only transformed the nature of pre-vocational and vocational education, but is also having an impact on academic education, in particular on the development of GCSE. On one level these moves could be applauded. It is eminently sensible that an individual's educational experiences relate to their interests and to what they consider to be important. On another level, the current developments are deeply disturbing; relevance has become transposed to the immediate, theory to technique, and knowledge to the empirical. The epistemological basis of the new paradigm is fundamentally positivistic and empiricist: the world is directly observable and understandable. This view of knowledge legitimates an atheoretical approach that denies the social processes involved in the production of facts and theories. The knowledge and facts that are so generated are given a hardness and certainty that are unwarranted. This delivers a technicization of knowledge and theory that reduces these to technique that can be used in problem-solving.

The effect of the new paradigm on academic education has been uneven.

Knowledge can be generated through empirical methods and be applied in a technical manner to solve problems. But sometimes theory can become concretized in as much as it is reduced to simplified statements that are empirically testable. Bernstein in his discussion of academic subjects suggests:

> By the ultimate of the subject, I mean its potential for creating new realities. It is also the case, and this is important, that the ultimate mystery of the subject is not coherence, but incoherence, not order, but disorder, not the known but the unknown . . . Only the few *experience* in their bones the notion that knowledge is permeable, that its orderings are provisional, that the dialectic of knowledge is closure and openness. For the many, socialisation into knowledge is socialisation into order, the existing order, into the experience that the world's educational knowledge is impermeable. (1977, pp. 97–8)

Bernstein's argument reflects the provisional and relative nature of educational knowledge. It is also important to take into account students' relationship to knowledge. Students in the course of their studies will have developed particular stakes or investments in certain forms of knowledge. Vocational students and some sectors of the working class may have a stake in those 'objective' forms of knowledge that offer 'practical' mastery, whereas 'A'-level students, oriented towards higher education, may have a stake in more esoteric forms that articulate with the cultural capital of the dominant class. These different relations to knowledge herald different social positions and interests. The working class, for example, has a stake in 'craft' knowledge that provides some control over the production process. The provisional and esoteric nature of academic knowledge, once admitted, can serve to exclude those with a stake in 'objective' and impermeable educational knowledge. It therefore secures the dominance and exclusivity of academic forms which play some small part in the reproduction of the cultural capital of the dominant class.

Many students on vocational and GCSE courses encounter knowledge of a concretized form, by which I mean unproblematic, empirically based knowledge. Should they wish to pursue the elite educational route of 'A' level and beyond, previous educational experiences may be less than beneficial. Students may seek to compensate for these shortcomings by drawing on cultural capital they have inherited or acquired elsewhere. The introduction of elements of progressivism to academic and vocational education, it is claimed, has led to their broadening. By providing a more relevant and interesting educational experience, access is opened up. However, my earlier discussion has shown how these aims have been transformed into their opposite, creating an even more deeply divisive educational system that is able to obscure its divisiveness in the language of openness.

Broadfoot (1986) suggests that the new educational forms hold some 'progressive' possibilities; for example, in extending equal opportunities, particularly in Scotland. She is deeply pessimistic about their implementation in England because the traditional system of examinations remains in place, which means the new developments in assessment and examination, such as CPVE, the Technical and Vocational Educational Initiative (TVEI), etc., will be considered inferior. This will lead to differentiation between students who follow the traditional academic route and those who follow the perceived inferior route of new educational forms. However, this differentiation also arises within the academic route itself and is based on the cultural capital students bring with them and the type of educational experiences they have had. Thus even in terms of the provision of equal educational opportunities the new forms fail and as Broadfoot has put it:

> In all those countries where industrial growth is increasingly being identified as of prime importance, and social justice correspondingly devalued into an associated, rather than a prime goal, the effects of such policy initiatives are likely to be to reinforce social divisions. (1986, p. 122)

It seems likely the new educational forms will exacerbate social divisions and represent, despite the intentions of those who formed them, a conservative education that attempts to reproduce the kinds of subjective disposition and orientation thought to be required by industry.

These tendencies have been exacerbated in recent years by the development of the National Curriculum, which represents a return to an older form of Conservative education (Coles, 1988). Ironically in much the same way as critical educators have ruminated and struggled over the possibilities and limitations of progressivism, so too has the New Right. It seems likely that the incorporation of the new vocationalism into academic education will be halted and will remain focused on the working class.

The 'strange fate' of progressive education has been its transformation into a form of conservative education. Perhaps its fate has not been so strange after all, for those radicals who practised it failed to develop a really radical appropriation. Progressive education has come to be seen as a teaching technique, one part of a teacher's armoury to be used to solve educational problems, rather than as part of a political project. This absence has left the space for the New Right to move in. Here lies the struggle for those committed to the development of a critical education: the need to reappropriate progressivism and move beyond it to provide a 'really useful' education.

Notes

David Maund, originally to co-author this chapter, suggested the title.

1 Bernstein (1977, pp. 122–3) writes: 'Such Pedagogies will adopt any theory of learning which has the following characteristics:

1. The theories in general will be seeking universals and thus are likely to be developmental and concerned with sequence . . . are likely to have a strong biological basis.
2. Learning is a tacit, invisible act.
3. The theories will tend to abstract the child's personal biography and local context from his cultural biography and institutional context.
4. . . . the various theories in different ways point towards *implicit* rather than explicit hierarchical social relationships. Indeed, the imposing exemplar is transformed into a *facilitator*.
5. Thus the theories can be seen as interrupters of cultural reproduction.'

2 FEU, 1984a, p. 7. The passage is an edited version of the quote on p. 7 of the document, the original source being C. E. Johnson (1974), 'Competency based and traditional education practices compared', *Journal of Teacher Education*, Winter, pp. 335–6.

3 See E. Venables, 1967 and D. Gleeson *et al.*, 1980 for responses to the older forms of educational relations.

4 'The Further Education Curriculum Review and Development Unit (FEU) is an advisory, intelligence and development body for further education. It was established in 1977 by the Secretary of State for Education and Science to make possible a more co-ordinated and cohesive approach to curriculum development in FE by

1. reviewing the range of existing curricula and identifying overlap, duplication and deficiencies
2. determining priorities for action to improve the total provision and suggesting ways in which improvement can be effected
3. carrying out specific studies, helping with curricular experiments, and contributing to the evaluation of objectives, and
4. disseminating information about the process of curriculum development in FE' (FEU, 1979; see also Grosch, 1987)

5 BTEC/CGLI, *The Certificate of Pre-Vocational Education*, Part A, B, C, (hereafter cited as CPVE A, B, C) Blue books, 1985; MSC, *Core Skills in YTS* Part 1 and 2 (hereafter cited as *Core Skills* Pt 1, Pt 2).

6 'The MSC YTS Core has been developed within the ESF YTS Core project, which is jointly funded for three years by the European Social Fund [ESF] and the MSC'; acknowledgement, Core Skills Pt 1.

7 '6.1 find out information by speaking to other people' (*Core Skills* Pt 1, p. 37).

8 There are links here with the work of the de-schoolers and with the radical critiques of education that flourished in the early stages of progressivism: Illich, 1973; Freire, 1972, a and b.

9 See FEU (1979), *A Basis for Choice*; FEU/SCDC (1985), *Supporting TVEI*; BTEC/CGLI (1985), *CPVE*, Pt 1, Pt 2; FEU (1984c), *Common Core Teaching and Learning*.

Part Two
'Choices that are not your own': Views of educational agency

Introduction to Part Two
'Choices that are not your own':
views of educational agency

Our main theme in Part One was 'New Right education' in its different aspects. Our investigations identified major contradictions and difficulties on the right. Some of the limits stemmed from gaps in New Right theory; some from the broader historical context; some from the political logics of Thatcherism, especially its anti-professionalism. The neo-liberal denial of social relations, the neo-conservative presentation of them as natural, and the insistence on a singular national identity or 'ethnicity' are blind spots with practical implications. They underpin impossible policies like the National Curriculum. It only goes to show that the spontaneous un-wisdom of powerful groups wreaks havoc among us all! With no under-standing of cultural difference, or of social power, or of systemic and justified conflict, the modern right handles social problems in moralistic, coercive, and non-negotiative ways. It resorts to ideologies of 'Us' and 'Others' and to law-an'-order solutions in a totalitarian cycle. Mrs Thatcher hails the emerging democracies of Eastern Europe, but steers our own society in the opposite direction, talking of liberty all the while.

Similarly, there is little we could properly call history in the writing of New Right theorists like Hayek, though there is a certain amount of historical polemic and a programme for history-writing as nationalist indoctrination or capitalist celebration. Systematic comparison similarly gets no further than the usual invocation of national essences (as in Mrs Thatcher's speeches on Europe). Paradoxically, in view of Hayek's critique of rationalism and *a priori* thinking, New Right intellectual work is frequently generalized, 'philosophical' and abstract.

Taking up contextualizing perspectives ourselves has enabled us to shift right-wing claims from centre stage and see the project in a new light. The historical and comparative perspective of Chapter 1 showed how New Right education, despite its gloss of reform, reproduces many of the long-term difficulties in our educational traditions. New Right policies will not modernize, and are recipes for disaster in our future in Europe and the world. Chapter 2 investigated the contradictory oscillations of policy up to the later 1980s, the limited political successes of the 1988 Act, but also the long-term contradictions: modernization versus traditionalism; 'choice', 'freedom' and 'autonomy' versus a centralizing and totalitarian drift. Our overall conclusion was that New Right policies do not identify the most urgent agenda of English education, and are likely to fail in their own terms in the longer run, producing unstable and socially undesirable outcomes.

The secondary – but important – theme of Part One was the search for alternatives. Opposition to government policy often presupposes – with decreasing plausibility – some future restoration of public education in its pre-1970s forms. Alternatively there has been a tendency to move on to Thatcherite territory, or, as Chapter 4 warned, on to the terrain of a conservative 'progressivism', within the confines of a narrow vocationalism.

In Part One we had to clear a lot of ground, before coming to alternatives. Even so, we hope some arguments already come through. Discussion of the localism and dispersion of the English education system implies a need for a more rational and intelligible structure as one condition for greater fairness. The New Politics and critical social theories provided us with alternative philosophies from which to critique New Right assumptions. One way of developing alternatives is to pursue this critical comparison much further, in situated critiques (around policies for the National Health Service or the environment, for example) and more philosophically too. Our critique of the National Curriculum, from a perspective informed by the politics of gender, class and race/ethnicity, hints at some features of a more acceptable 'Core': more open about its own relativity, more negotiable in its points of view, more genuinely national in its tolerance and inclusiveness. Our analyses of progressivism, of 'objectivity' and of curriculum categories endorse the argument that power relations and cultural differences are central to the classroom. It is essential that teachers recognize the social points of view or social orienta-tions from which all learning is approached, including those which inform existing curricula, formal and 'hidden'. The critique of 'conservative progressivism' suggests the possibilities of a progressivism linked to a more social understanding of culture and identity and not just to economic utility. The careful reassessment of the welfare tradition is central to any alternative: our discussion of the politics of the public professions suggests the need for a radicalized professionalism, in education and elsewhere.

These developments remain fragmentary and often contradictory, especially no doubt in our own text. They are continually disorganized from the right. There has as yet been no really respectful alliance between the continuing claims of an 'older' class politics (and the organizations which represent this legacy) and the autonomous, diffused forces of the New Politics. There has been no thorough re-thinking of the politics of class itself in the light of postwar social changes and the complexities introduced by feminism and anti–racism. What we hope to have shown is that the *resources* for more fully developed alternatives already exist if only these connections could be made. The main blockages are often political and organizational, though there are cultural differences too. Some alternatives have most currency with particular social groups where they are part of daily living. The problem is to relate them, positively, to mainstream or popular ways of life.

The studies in Part Two allow us to take up these themes in a closer relation to everyday local practices. The critique of New Right education is again a major theme, across the case studies, detectable especially in our hot pursuit of 'choice'. The critique of right-wing (and liberal-pluralist) notions of choice is central in all the case studies. How can school leavers be said to 'choose' the Youth Training Scheme (YTS) when they see it as 'the last resort' (Chapter 5)? How can the choice from a bewildering diversity of training schemes as seen from the outside, be anything more than a 'jungle of contradictions' or 'a lottery' (Chapters 5 and 6)? How can parents or pupils or teachers be said to choose an education when the curriculum is imposed from on high through the directives of the National Curriculum, or public examinations boards, or the financial blandishments and 'management delivery systems' of the Technical and Vocational Education Initiative (TVEI) (Chapters 8 and 9)? How can students in further education (FE) be said to choose their jobs or careers (on the basis of not only vocational but 'pre-vocational preparation') when access to courses of all kinds is policed by teacher judgements and exclusive curriculum categories, linked to gender, class and race (Chapter 7)? How does mere choice compare anyway with the opportunity of running a school yourselves, not least as a learning experience (Chapter 9)?

The case studies pile up difficulty after difficulty against any simple opposition of choice and coercion: the freedom of a market versus the coercion of the 'state', for example, or the freedom of the individual versus the coercion of social claims. Actually, choices are never free in this sense, nor truly just 'our own'. Perhaps the most important finding is the importance of organic *cultural* processes in underpinning choice: moral and cultural preferences, often long-standing but not fixed, which grow from the conditions of life of social groups and their repeated strategies. Choice is always relative to the power that can be exercised within a particular social position. It is something different for the middle-class student, the would-be factory 'lass' or 'lad', the socially aspirant 'youth-enterpriser' or the emergent 'politico' (see Chapters 6 and 7 especially). All students, parents and teachers do indeed choose sometimes, in some sense, but the evaluative basis of choice is never individual only, but always conforms to some code or set of values shared with someone else, or part of some 'imagined community', or defined in relation to (not necessarily in agreement with) an insistent social norm. From most social positions most of the time, choices are between evils: between 'last resorts' and something better.

The other major focus of the case studies is a stress on agency as an aspect of everyday action. Agency seems a richer, less one-dimensional notion than choice; it implies more of context and conditions. The ability to act in ways that produce new outcomes is not reducible to picking and choosing, matching and mixing, as in the choice model. The popularity of the idea of choice on the right owes more to a defensive limitation or *policing* of politics than to the desire to deepen democracy or promote popular control (Chapter 3). Ordinary popular agency is routinely more creative than the choice model implies. The strategies of some agents actually extend the range of choice, or show that a particular choice is illusory or meaningless. The practical knowledges of the agents in the case studies are full of ironic insights like these. They rebuke official knowledges at every turn. They are creative in this sense: they transform what is given to them by public ideologies, e.g. Manpower Services Commission advertisements (Chapter 5), or fixed or bureaucratic responses, e.g. exclusive trade union routines (Chapter 6).

This doesn't mean that all this agency is equally transformative of social conditions of course. As we have stressed already, some agency (cultural studies calls it 'resistance' usually) is profoundly conservative, producing again the old dilemmas – choices – relatively unchanged. Some level of agency seems built into social practice and certainly into cultural reception; it is guaranteed by the fact that communication is crossed by social difference and power. But though power is always challenged by resistance, its flows are not necessarily reversed or transformed. It may need a further set of practices – of representation, social recognition, or political organization – to make resistance into more than challenge.

Typically in education, resistance condenses around the teacher-taught relation in its generational aspects. The commonest finding of all these studies is the young-adult flight from school, the experience of schooling as childish or infantilizing in its later years. There are a few exceptions where young adults need to revert to the protection of school, but the picture seems similar whether viewed from within school itself (Chapter 5), or retrospectively from the training scheme (Chapter 6), college (Chapter 7) or, with interesting ambiguities, from working-class adulthood itself (Chapter 9). This base-line resistance to schooling is a difficult lesson for educational professionals to learn, but its recognition is fundamental to reform.

Most commonly resistance on one front – to class and generational oppressions, for example – makes agents vulnerable to traps and pitfalls on others. The resistance of working-class girls may deliver them to conventional feminine identities – the domestic sphere combined with factory work or the feminine sexual allure of a 'glam' career (Chapter 6). The same, it seems, goes for teachers: a politics limited to a radical or progressive professionalism risks making enemies of parents who have a different set of educational and cultural expectations (Chapters 8 and especially 9). Really transformative agency, that steps free from the tangle of social contradictions and opposed strategies, is rarer it seems. The political problem is how to ensure that one man's resistance is not another woman's oppression, that my legitimate struggle really is qualified or informed by everyone else's needs.

One major preoccupation in all the case studies is unravelling the consequences of everyday kinds of agency like these. A major conclusion, for teachers, is inscribed in the writing of the case studies themselves, especially Chapters 5, 7 and 8, which were written by teachers about situations they are still active in. If we want to be effective as teachers, we need to grasp the social and cultural patterns around us, especially the orientations and knowledges of our students. For it is on this basis that they receive, block, or transform our teaching. Such knowledges would have to be a major component in any new professionalism.

This leads us to the third preoccupation of Part Two, the search for alternative practices. We hope the commitment to these comes through in the studies themselves, with many detailed practical suggestions. Perhaps the best place to pull out the more general conclusions is in our Introduction to Part Three, itself entitled 'Alternatives'.

5

The last resort: making the transition from school to YTS

Andrew Vickers

In January 1982 I took up my first teaching job in a 14–18 upper school in Leicestershire. I was teaching in the Humanities Faculty where a core humanities course was taught leading to certification in community studies and English. I taught with a view that stressed the importance of engaging students with real problems, tackling controversial issues and exploring students' own knowledge and beliefs. In the faculty there was a commitment to a student-centred approach, and process was generally considered to be more important than content. What was important was that students acquired skills and confidence in an environment which stressed the value of good relationships. The faculty was also broadly committed to encouraging critical thinking, undermining prejudice and breaking down the barriers between subject disciplines.

It was while I was teaching there that I became interested in the question of how the advent of the Youth Training Scheme (YTS) was changing the experience of working-class young people as they made their transition from school to work, or to what? My most immediate problem was that I did not know how I should talk to a fifth-year student who was thinking of taking a YTS placement. What sort of advice should I give to all fifth-years who were considering YTS as an option? I was pretty clear in my own mind as to what the overall intentions of YTS were, but this was not the same as having a clear view of what it meant for my students and my analysis did not provide me with any idea as to how I could respond to this situation as a teacher in the classroom.

The emergence of YTS was preceded in the school by the introduction of the Technical and Vocational Education Initiative (TVEI), a development which prompted the second theme which I want to pursue in this chapter. The TVEI was seen by many members of the faculty as part of a 'new vocational ethos' which was and would continue to be a threat to the position of humanities and humanities subjects in the curriculum. I was one of these teachers and I wanted to know how as a humanities teacher I could respond both positively and critically to this 'new vocationalism'. What place should the concept of work have in a broad humanities course?

Through a study of the 1986/7 fifth-years in four schools in Leicestershire I began to try to find answers to these questions. The study concentrated on how these young people, faced with the possible prospect of doing a YTS, viewed different sources of knowledge about YTS. It quickly became clear that formal sources of information about YTS were largely inadequate, particularly when young people wanted to know about the chances of getting full-time employment out of a particular scheme. It was from this that I arrived at the third theme for this chapter: what in the context of YTS would radical careers work look like, and what counts as 'really useful knowledge' for the school-leavers facing the new 'choices' offered by YTS?

As part of my discussion will involve questions about classroom practice and philosophy, it may help if I outline some of the teaching experience I had while working in humanities at this school. All fourth- and fifth-year students took the humanities course mentioned above and some took separate humanities options such as history, English literature, or mass communications as well. The content of the core humanities course had originally been prescribed by ten units of study. The ten units expressed a progressive or developmental view of the world in which students were taken from studying themselves and their family at the beginning of the fourth year through to studying global issues such as the arms race at the end of the fifth year. A quote from the Student Guide illustrates the aims of this course and the educational philosophy behind it:

> The Humanities Course aims to give you an opportunity to discover more about yourself and the world of people in which you live. It is intended to increase your awareness of other people's experiences and of your own – of beliefs, thoughts, attitudes and relationships. It is to give you a chance to explore your feelings, to express your ideas and to create your own versions of the world which you find. The Course is arranged as a sequence of ten units. In each unit a topic is taken as a subject of study and as a basis for various forms of expression, factual, critical and creative. (Humanities Faculty, 'Redmond College')

The Course Guide dates from the early 1970s and by 1982 the ten-unit model had been greatly modified by experience and by a growing desire amongst teachers to stress process and skills rather than content. What the students did in lessons was the outcome of debates and planning carried out by teams of teachers. I experienced this period between 1982 and 1986 as an opportunity to be involved in an innovative and creative process in which the humanities course was constantly being rewritten and revised by teams of teachers on a term-by-term, year-by-year basis.

A description of some of the educational practices I was involved in at this school will serve to illustrate the sort of educational values that many humanities teachers saw as under threat from the new vocationalism. The idea of progression still influenced the thinking of teams, and many students beginning the course in the fourth year would do such things as construct memory maps, family trees and diagrams which located themselves in terms of their personal history, their interests and their community. Memory boxes would be collected and teachers would join in by bringing in their own memory boxes, or photos, school reports and other pieces of personal evidence. This work could be developed into an oral history project. Education could be studied through a consideration of the 'Seven Up' series, which also introduced students to the idea of social class. A study of social class could also be developed by looking at soap operas; by, for example, comparing the way in which the different families were constructed and presented in scenes around the kitchen or dining-room table in *Brookside*. Comparisons could be made with the supposed social class of characters from other soap operas. Students might also construct their own soap opera using their local community as stimulus. Students were encouraged to gain understanding through creativity as well as through analysis. In studying bias a teacher might say, 'Here is a range of information on a particular issue. I want you to use it to construct a poster which puts across this point of view. How could you use it to put across a different point of view? What audience are you aiming your message at? Does this make a difference to the way you try to deliver your message?' Throughout the two-year course students were encouraged to acquire the skills of constructing and carrying out surveys and questionnaires, collecting evidence through interviews, visits and participant observation; in short they were taught to explore all possible sources of evidence in relation to different human issues and to see learning as something they were actively engaged in.

It was during a faculty meeting that was discussing the development of the Certificate of Pre-Vocational Education (CPVE) within the school that I began to formulate the questions that I am discussing in this chapter. The meeting was trying to come to a view about whether we should participate in the planning and teaching of this course. The discussion was informed by a wider concern about the push to a more vocationally relevant curriculum and by a belief that this was undermining the position of humanities. There was a general feeling that space was being lost and that although the language of CPVE may be in the progressive student-centred mould, emphasizing relevance and activity, its intentions were by no means in line with the values and aims of teachers in humanities. To me it was part of a Tory-inspired package of measures funded by the Manpower Services Commission (MSC) and designed to structure schooling in line with the 'needs of employers', as defined by the government. It would not prepare students for work, as it was designed primarily like YTS as an answer to the consequences of youth unemployment and not as a solution to the problem of declining employment opportunities. It would, like YTS, encourage young people to see their own lack of employment prospects as a personal problem having a personal solution and not as a social creation which requires political action.

Personally I was not going to see involvement in CPVE as a priority, but I was left with a feeling that I ought to find a positive way of responding to the new training ethos. Schooling, however it was constructed, had to have some relationship to the world of work and in a period of mass unemployment students and parents are rightly concerned that schooling should improve the employability of young people. School-leavers want jobs and even though schools cannot create jobs they need to relate what they do to the aspirations of young people. Working-class youth has traditionally viewed school as largely irrelevant to the 'main reality' of finding work, making money and raising children. The work of Paul Willis (1975, 1977) and Christine Griffin (1985) has clearly made this case, but it is still true in a situation where school-leavers cannot now look forward to the prospect of full-time work giving them status in the adult world that they wish to join.

In the place of full-time jobs thousands of young people are now trying to make an uncertain transition to adulthood through the YTS. The Youth Training Scheme is projected as a unified package of training which can at the same time create 'equal opportunities', while in reality it is becoming more and more differentiated in a way which reflects and maintains the sexual, racial and class divisions in the labour market. Furthermore the quality of YTS in a particular locality will be largely determined by the condition and character of the local labour market. In a severely depressed local economy, what jobs is YTS going to provide a bridge to? In areas of high unemployment there are not enough employers to provide the employer-led schemes the government says it wants. Private training agencies (PTAs) have sprung up in these areas and with so little local employment to plan for they frequently train young people in the employment areas that have the lowest training costs and hence the highest profit margins (YTS Monitoring Unit, 1985). YTS cannot provide young people with a 'permanent bridge into work' and the notion that it offers them 'choice' is also highly questionable. Their 'choice' is defined by class, gender and race and is clearly structured by the condition of their local labour market (Racial Equality in Training Schemes, 1985; TUC, 1987; Cockburn, 1987; Finn, 1987). YTS is a jungle of contradictions which affords to young people a vast range of possible experiences. It is extremely difficult to discover exactly what a particular scheme may have to offer and in this sense the 'choice' provided by YTS is more like a lottery (compare the more detailed account in Chapter 6 below). In this overall context, how did the 1987 school-leavers in Leicestershire view YTS, what knowledge did they have of it and where did they get this knowledge from?

Learning about YTS in Leicestershire

To find out how the 1987 school-leavers in Leicestershire viewed YTS I carried out research in four schools, two in the city of Leicester and two in the county. I was not primarily interested in how they saw their choice within YTS, but rather in how they viewed YTS as compared to other 'opportunities' which might or might not be open to them. Two themes constantly arose in the dialogue I had with these school-leavers: the difference between YTS and a 'proper job' and anxiety about whether you would get a job when a scheme finished. Youth unemployment was a reality and a constant threat which seemed to deny them the prospect of becoming truly adult. A survey carried out by Leicester City Council in 1983 indicated that in the 16–19 age group in Leicester, 26.6 per cent were unemployed, with 23.6 per cent of white youth unemployed, 38.5 per cent of Asians and 45.5 per cent of West Indians (Leicester City Council, Leicestershire County Council, 1983). Since 1983 the participation rates on YTS have risen as the number of young people officially registered as unemployed has declined. In Leicestershire as elsewhere YTS has provided the means of filling the gap created by youth unemployment.

Let us consider the operation of the YTS in Leicester in a little detail. The original implementation of the scheme in 1983 was described by one careers officer as 'chaotic'. In Leicester the then Manpower Services Commission (MSC) had great difficulty in achieving the government objective of delivering 70 per cent of schemes as Mode A schemes run largely by private employers. An employer-led YTS was necessary if the government were to fulfil its wish that YTS should meet the 'needs of industry and commerce for a well-trained, adaptable workforce'. Employer-led schemes would also give credibility to the claim that YTS would provide 'a permanent bridge into work'. Mode B schemes were run by a network of sponsors including colleges, training organizations, information technology centres (ITECs), training workshops and local authorities. The MSC acted as managing agent and the training allowances provided were higher than those given to Mode A schemes. The Mode A schemes were seen as being more likely to provide job opportunities than the Mode B schemes. As with other studies (Racial Equality in Training Schemes, 1985; Cockburn, 1987), data for Leicester showed that the ethnic minorities were concentrated in Mode B schemes (Leicester City Council, 1985). Not only were these schemes less likely to provide jobs but in the move to the two-year YTS the distinction between Mode A and Mode B schemes was dropped and the training allowance was equalized. In effect in

Leicester this caused serious financial difficulties for many Mode B schemes which were catering for the ethnic minorities. The city council and local trade unions were concerned about these cuts and by the growth of private training agencies and the extensive use of small non-unionized workplaces which were difficult to monitor. According to the City Council Report (1985), 27.5 per cent of Mode A schemes were run by PTAs. In Leicester YTS was not fulfilling the government's objective of providing an employer-led training programme which would meet the needs of industry and young people. At least there was very little evidence to suggest that it was succeeding and those concerned with monitoring YTS found a number of recurrent problems. A working paper produced by the local Community and Youth Workers Union (CYWU) in 1987 stated:

(1) That the growth of YTS in Leicester has resulted in a massive decline in apprenticeships available to young people, e.g. a 50 per cent decline in the number of engineering apprenticeships.

(2) Grossly inadequate funding leads to a poor quality of training.

(3) Local authorities and trade unions are being eased out in terms of control over local schemes, leading to a reduction in monitoring, and a subsequent decline in standards.

(4) The growth of the private training sector has led to a decline in standards through cost cutting.

(5) YTS is a key instrument for depressing young people's wages.

(6) Discrimination with reference to gender and race is rife throughout the MSC structure, e.g. in one large company unit in Leicester, out of 150 trainees only *three* were black.

(7) YTS is a key instrument in disguising youth unemployment rates.

(8) The two year YTS will exacerbate the problems mentioned above, i.e. the decline in Mode B schemes, allied with the increase in private placement agencies, will lead to increased discrimination and training standards will decline as money is squeezed. (CYWU, 1987)

YTS in Leicestershire: formal knowledges

The MSC commissioned a study of those trainees who left YTS in Leicestershire during the period April to September 1985. Of the 5,600 trainees who left in this period replies were received from 2,850. This is a response rate to a postal survey of 51 per cent. One can assume that those young people who did get jobs after YTS would be more likely to answer a postal survey. Yet with a 51 per cent return this research is used uncritically in the 1986/7 School-Leavers pack to show that 60 per cent of YTS leavers get jobs. For young people thinking about YTS this is an important piece of knowledge. The actual survey claimed to show that 'the proportion of ex-trainees in employment at the time of the survey was 66 per cent overall, but this increased to 78 per cent if only those who completed the course are considered. On the other hand only 46 per cent of those who had left early were found to be in employment' (MSC, Leicester, 1986). The survey also claims to show that 80 per cent of trainees in the Occupational Training Family (OTF) which includes engineering got jobs through YTS, but the survey does not indicate what sort of jobs they were or what rates of pay ex-trainees received in them. All respondents were also asked 'Was YTS training a useful preparation for what you are doing now?' One wonders how an ex-trainee out of work would take a question such as this when it comes from the MSC. In answer to the question, 52 per cent said yes and 36 per cent said no. The 1986/7 School-Leavers Pack says under the heading 'Some facts you should know': '90 per cent of young people say that YTS is a useful way to train.' In the areas of most concern to young people, the quality of training and the job prospects that may arise from participation on a particular scheme, information is difficult to find and that which is available to young people as an inducement to take a YTS is of dubious origin and is not indicative of the complexity of possible experiences which they may have on different youth training schemes. If one views YTS in Leicestershire from the point of view of school-leavers it is difficult to see what 'really useful knowledge' about YTS is available to them.

Informal knowledges of YTS

If the 'formal knowledge' available was so dubious, what 'informal knowledge' did school-leavers in Leicestershire have, and how did they position themselves in relation to these forms of knowledge? To try to answer these questions, I chose two schools in the county, 'Redmond College' and 'Bedtown College' and two schools in the city of Leicester, 'Dendale College' and 'Walden School'.[1] Both Dendale College and Walden School are 11–16 secondary schools and are situated on the north-east edge of Leicester. Walden School is a largely white working-class school which serves a large council estate. At Dendale College there is a mixed student intake of Asian, Afro-Caribbean and white. The school has a traditional atmosphere and many students perceived teachers as being pro-YTS. Bedtown College and Redmond College are both 14–18 upper schools, but there the similarity ends. Bedtown College is in north-west Leicestershire and serves the town of Coalville and the surrounding villages. It is a white school with a largely working-class catchment area. The economy of north-west Leicestershire has suffered considerably in recent years particularly from pit closures and the decline in employment in the mining sector. It is a school where talk of leaving school and finding work inevitably

Table 5.1   *The intended destinations of the 1987 school-leavers*

	Redmond	Bedtown	Dendale	Walden
response rate	70%	80%	46%	58%
full-time work	25%	31%	26%	27.5%
YTS	10%	28%	5%	33%
YTS 'first choice'	9%	13%	4%	18.5%
YTS 'never'	20%	14%	25%	10%

becomes talk about lost jobs and few opportunities. In contrast Redmond College, also discussed by Dan McEwan in Chapter 7, is a school with a much more middle-class catchment area which stretches from the edge of Leicester to the Warwickshire border. It is mainly white with a small number of Asian students coming largely from the suburbs of West Leicester.

A questionnaire was distributed to all fifth-years in the four schools and the main results of this are shown in Table 5.1.

Let us consider these statistics critically. Table 5.1 does not include those students who said they were going to study 'A' levels or who said they were going to study full-time in a college of further education. In general my study tried to concentrate on those students for whom YTS would be a likely option. The response rate to the questionnaire can be taken to indicate the level of fifth-year attendance over a period of a few weeks in each school. At Dendale a vice-principal had commented that 'many students drift away towards the end of the fifth-year' and were thus difficult to track. The small number of students who said they expected to be going on YTS at Dendale can be explained by a number of factors. Many of the students who would be going on YTS could be in the group of school non-attenders. The students at the school were generally antagonistic to YTS. This antagonism certainly came through in the interviews that I did in this school and was identified by a vice-principal who saw it as a problem which the school had to address. Very few of the Asian students at the school knew anyone who was or had been on a YTS and this is indicative of the low status which YTS has in the eyes of Asian students and their parents. This position was also indicated in the interviews and other sources also reveal a preference for further education (FE) amongst Asian students, though a view is developing which sees this particular antagonism to YTS being eroded.

At Bedtown College there is an obvious discrepancy between the number who expect to be on a YTS and the number for whom this is 'a first choice'. The school estimated that of the 1985/6 leavers, 38 per cent went on a YTS and as nothing would suggest that this figure would fall in 1986/ 7, this could mean that a significant number of students would be going on

YTS who did not expect to. The sense of a need to become reconciled to doing a YTS came through in the interviews that I did in this school.

At Redmond the school tracking records indicate that of the 1985/6 leavers, 24 per cent found work and 15 per cent went on YTS. The results of the questionnaire and the interviews in this school showed that the students intending to go on a YTS had taken this decision positively. Those who did not intend to go on YTS were much more negative towards it, and the students who wanted to do YTS experienced a sense of isolation because they perceived the peer group to be generally hostile to YTS. The academically successful students frequently regarded YTS as having no status and many of the students with a critical perspective on YTS would not be those for whom YTS was a realistic option.

At Walden School the number of students who thought they would be on a YTS was very close to the number that the school expected to go on it. However, as at Bedtown College, there was also a large number of students who did not choose YTS as 'a first choice'.

Making sense of YTS

In a time when all young people could expect to be in full-time employment when they left school the 'really useful knowledge' which informed them about this transition would have been found in the working–class adult community. The slump in the youth labour market has made this knowledge itself redundant and in these circumstances young people are developing a culture of knowledge which is not directly informed by the experiences of adults. To find a route into this informal knowledge I asked on the questionnaire what they had found out about YTS from someone they knew who was on or had been on a YTS. Only students who had informal knowledge of YTS and who were not expecting to be studying 'A' levels or studying full-time in FE were called to interview. Before conducting these interviews I categorized the informal knowledge into negative, positive and responses which were mixed. Table 5.2 gives a breakdown of the 'informal knowledge' revealed in the total questionnaire response.

Students were called to interview so that they represented a cross-section in terms of expected destination and category of knowledge held. Here are some examples of the different categories of knowledge held:

> Slave trade rip off, no training, just given rubbish jobs to do.
> (Boy, Bedtown, Expected Destination (ED) on a YTS)

> The persons say it is cheap labour and no job to look forward to. It is a waste of time.
> (Girl, Dendale, ED full-time job)

Table 5.2 *The informal knowledge in the four schools*

	negative	positive	mixed
all schools	46%	30%	24%
Redmond	43%	30%	27%
Bedtown	52%	28.5%	19.5%
Dendale	44%	22%	34%
Walden	39%	36%	25%

I found out that everyone thought it was slave labour and that you hardly ever get a job after the course is finished.
(Girl, Bedtown, ED full-time job)

They said it was OK and they got a job at the end of it.
(Girl, Walden, ED on a YTS)

They learn you quite a bit and he got a full-time job at Lee Byron at the end of it.
(Boy, Walden, part-time FE)

He said it is OK but he doesn't know if he'll get a full-time job.
(Boy, Bedtown, Ed full-time job)

An analysis of this data shows that the students who had 'negative informal knowledge', also had a more negative overall orientation to YTS and that students with a more 'positive knowledge' also tended to be more likely to be generally more positive towards YTS and the idea of going on a scheme. A significant number of students held 'negative informal knowledge', but were able to maintain a positive or more resigned attitude to YTS and towards the idea of going on one. During the interviews it became apparent that any knowledge which these young people held about YTS was located in terms of their perception of the overall range of opportunities open to them. The dialogue around this area threw up a number of consistent themes in the interviews. A particularly common theme was a view that the whole question of making 'choices' at 16 was largely a matter of avoiding 'the last resort'. What 'the last resort' was depended on how the young people viewed themselves in relation to the range of opportunities that they saw as available to them. For Karen at Bedtown the last resort was definitely a factory job, because it offered no career prospects and it was thus not consistent with her view of herself and her future.

> Karen Well me sister works in a factory and she likes it but she don't want a career or anything but I do. I want something with a

trade so I want to be an hairdresser but I won't get me training unless I go on a YTS . . . I don't really want to but that's the only way to get the training. (Bedtown, 2 April 1987)

This view that YTS offered a career structure was frequently held by girls, many of whom also saw it as a way of avoiding the factory. The girls who were intending to take factory work were much more likely to view YTS as slave labour; at least a factory job was a 'real job' with 'real wages'. Their suspicion of YTS was supported by parents, by knowledge that they had, and by a general understanding of how employers operate the YTS. At least in a factory job you know quite clearly where you stand in relation to the employer. On YTS your relationship to adult society generally seems unclear and ill-defined. Put simply, being in work was seen to be an important marker in defining entry into adult society whereas YTS was seen as a sort of halfway house between school and work, which contained within it vestiges of the practices and values which were regarded as demeaning at school. Going on YTS definitely lowered your status in terms of peer group and this was particularly so among the boys. If YTS was commonly seen as slave labour, where you do 'scabby' jobs, how could any young person feel good about doing one? This view was based on 'informal knowledge', and on the general perception of antagonism to YTS in the peer group: YTS itself had an accepted social meaning which informed the attitude of adults and young people towards it. This is summed up in the phrase 'everyone knows what YTS is', and was used to predict the sort of experiences which you have on a YTS.

Nick   Saying you're on YTS is like . . . it's like when you're at school and someone asks you what maths group you're in you know and you have to tell 'em you're in the lowest maths set or something. (Walden, Boys, 6 March 1987)

Mark   Another difference is the impression that I've got if you're in full-time you're treated like a member of the staff, if you're on a YTS then you're like a dogsbody, 'do this do that', that's what I've heard anyway, you're just treated like as if you're a little kid.

Santosh Most people go on YTS because they ain't got no qualifications so people think YTS, he ain't got no qualifications, that's why he's going on the YTS . . .

Alan   People think of YTS as a last resort so if you go on a YTS it means you can't get anything else. (Boys, Dendale, 20 March 1987)

So YTS is seen by these students as reflecting the distinctions and divisions which have already emerged at school and, as such, young people who go on it are viewed as being trapped by the low status which school has already conferred on them. Only by pursuing the 'real jobs' with 'real wages' can they hope to turn the status which they are assigned at school on its head. The interviews provided more evidence that 'the lads' are still aspiring to and hunting for the lost jobs, the 'men's jobs', where really hard work was rewarded with reasonably good pay and in this exchange 'the lads' would become men with truly adult status. They wanted to escape from school, indeed they couldn't wait to get out; but at best YTS was just 'one small rung up the ladder'. These sorts of attitudes were particularly strong among the boys at Dendale and Walden and among the girls at Dendale, although these girls concentrated their criticisms on the lack of proper training on YTS and on the impossibility of being financially independent on £27.30. All the girls aspired to financial independence and were greatly annoyed at the idea of being dependent on their parents for another two years at least:

> Sue I'd have to pay board and they'd give me whatever I need and that but thinking about it when you only get £27 and you give them so much then you're not really going to be able to get anything for yourself . . . buy your own clothes and that . . . so I don't think the money's worth it . . . I wouldn't like to feel dependent on me Mum and Dad, I'd like to show 'em that I could live like independent.

In the county, where students can return to the school where they did their fourth and fifth years, some students used a return to school as a way of avoiding going on a YTS, seen as a step into the unknown. School afforded them a sense of security as a place which they knew and where they also were known. On a YTS they might get exploited, and the general feeling of their peers would indicate that doing a YTS was a low-status 'choice', whereas stopping on at school was traditionally viewed as something which improved your status, at least in school:

> Louise I'm stopping on at school I think to do me exams again to get better marks . . . because I don't know if the YTS is worth it for how much you get paid . . . better to stop at school. (Bedtown, Girls, 2 April 1987)
>
> Jason No that's why I'm stopping on because I think if I leave school I'm not going to be able to go on the dole, I'm going to have to go on a YTS scheme, that's why I'm stopping on. (Redmond, Boys, 3 April 1987)

So it is students' self-identity, or the identity to which they aspire, which defines their attitude to the range of opportunities that they see before them and the position of YTS within this range. It is this that gives meaning to the 'choices' they face and it is this that defines the differences they perceive between the 'glam' jobs offered by YTS and the 'real' jobs offered by the factories. This dialectic of identity and opportunity also gives meaning to the distinction between 'YTS jobs' and 'proper jobs'. In the working-out of this relationship between self-identity and the perceived opportunities available, it is clear that gender and race play a crucial role in structuring both the individual consciousness of the young person and the material conditions within the labour market which define their opportunities. It is in this context that knowledge about YTS needs to be viewed, as an interrelational social reality: something which happens over time and is conditioned and carried forward by a range of contradictory pressures. The different elements in the process cannot be separated from each other: the self-identity of a young person also contains a view of the labour market, just as the labour market contains the elements of this self-identity expressed in term of class, gender and race. Schools need to try to intervene 'critically' in this process and this intervention must recognize the range of contradictory pressures which students face and must value the knowledge and the perceptions which they are already developing.

Contradictory knowledge and classroom practice

When considering possible sources of information on YTS, virtually all students interviewed regarded all adult sources as likely to be unreliable. They were unreliable because they were not directly informed by the experience of being on a YTS. To fill this gap young people are developing a culture of knowledge which arises out of the specific circumstances which they are experiencing. It is my contention that schools need to take account of this knowledge and, more than this, they need to utilize it positively in the planning and in the delivery of their careers and guidance programme.

The data in this study show that the majority of school-leavers who go on YTS do not do so as a 'first choice'; indeed for many of them it is a 'last resort'. YTS is regarded by school-leavers as an essentially juvenile activity, rather than as an important marker in a transition to adulthood. That transition is still to them dependent upon acquiring a full-time job which provides an income capable of sustaining an independent and adult life-style. Young people are all too keenly aware of what this costs. On average a two-bedroomed terraced house in Leicester will cost about £40,000. YTS is forcing young people to remain dependent on their parents for at least another two years, creating a situation where adult status is denied to them, replaced by a period of extended adolescence.

Through careers work in schools young people are becoming reconciled to the reality of what YTS has to offer. Unless careers work is constructed critically it will fail to question the limited nature of the opportunities provided by YTS; it will also act to marginalize the informal knowledge which students have and will fail to explore the contradictory reality which is actually defining the situation of young people and through which they locate their sense of self and their sense of their future.

Whatever the nature of the informal knowledge that students held they saw it as having strength when juxtaposed with knowledge from more 'formal' or adult sources. Their main criticism of the television advertisements for YTS was that not only did they not give you any 'hard facts' about the quality of training, the different schemes available, or the job prospects arising from participation on a scheme, they did not contain any sense of reality at all. Even students who really wanted to go on a YTS were angered by the suggestion in the early advertisements, that employers were so keen to have you that they would come running on to the streets to pull you into their shops. It is interesting to note that the later YTS advertisements have stressed the theme of 'the best advertisement for YTS is the people who've done it', where a sense of reality is linked to vague promises of a successful high-tech future. One student had a particularly perceptive view of the attempt in one advertisement to appeal to young people's desire for adult status and of the crude and insulting way that it tried to do this.

Jason   Well it's funny, it's a joke . . . people come up to 'em and offer 'em jobs just 'cos they kick a coke can into a bin or something like that . . . all them adverts are amazing, all them job club adverts as well, they're really funny . . . and that car mechanic one where he says, 'I can't do that', and they all seem to sound dead thick, and they go on it and they go, 'Oh I can't do that' in a really divvy voice, and when he's mending the engine he goes down, and then he comes up and he's got a moustache, it's a bit weird that is, as if he's turned into a car mechanic just because he's got a moustache. (Redmond College, Boys, 3 April 1987)

Let us compare this knowledge which Jason has constructed with some other pieces of knowledge. First an example of some knowledge provided by one of the television advertisements structured around the theme of 'the best advertisement for YTS is the people who've done it'.

Ben Squires, who works at Brush Electrical Machines in Loughborough, joined Brush as a YTS trainee and was taken on as a technical apprentice when his scheme finished. He is now training for a career in electronics with one of the biggest names in the business – and he reckons he owes it all to YTS.

(*Youth Training News*, July 1987, p 7)

Ben is obviously a real person who has benefited from participation on a YTS. However, imagine the sort of advertisements which could be constructed using the YTS experiences which the following young people were aware of. All of these pieces of knowledge were revealed through the questionnaire which was carried out in the four schools.

> This person is not very pleased with the money he earns and in his job all he does is sweep up and very small easy jobs.
>
> (Girl, Bedtown College)

> My brother went on one and he hated it because it was slave labour.
>
> (Boy, Walden School)

While these experiences contradict the theme of the television advertisements, others do clearly support the main argument that the best advertisement for YTS is the people who've done it.

> He enjoyed it and got a job afterwards as a painter and decorator.
>
> (Boy, Walden School)

In considering the variety of knowledges available to young people about YTS, it is important to remember that all formal sources of information about YTS tend to support the contention expressed in the then MSC advertising campaign:

> 90 per cent of young people say that YTS is a useful way to train.
>
> (Leicestershire County Council, 1987)

In juxtaposing these particular pieces of knowledge about YTS I am obviously trying to make a point about YTS. I have selected them to illustrate that YTS presents young people with a 'contradictory reality'. By exploring this kind of contradictory knowledge in the classroom, radical teachers can provide fifth-year students facing YTS with the space to make sense of their situation.

A classroom practice and a careers programme which wish to generate 'really useful knowledge' must address the fact that students are already involved in this process of making sense of a 'contradictory reality'. Useful knowledge about YTS can only be constructed by students themselves, through a dialogue which is informed by the whole range of knowledge which is available to them.

The knowledge available can be broadened if the schools become actively involved in monitoring YTS by tracking the experience of their own school-leavers. Any information collected needs to be fed back into the school, through displays and bulletins, so that it too can inform the dialogue which young people are constructing around this issue. Only this dialogue is capable of empowering young people so that they can take greater control of their own lives. A careers education which is constructed solely on formal sources is asking for the response which produces YTS posters covered with graffiti proclaiming that YTS is slave labour.

Careers education also needs to recognize that the 'choices' offered to young people by YTS are defined by particular forces, in terms of class, gender and race. YTS has done little to challenge the inequalities in the labour market which are structured by these divisions. However, YTS arrived in schools at a time when a greater emphasis was being placed on 'equal opportunities' particularly in terms of gender and race. Recognizing this, the then MSC was careful to produce literature which stressed the value of 'equal opportunities'. Many students have been faced with literature that implies that YTS can offer girls opportunities which have previously been restricted to boys and black youth have been given the idea that YTS is attempting to challenge racism in the labour market:

> Sharon Mohammed works at Holyhall school in Dudley, after studying electronics at Dudley ITEC as a YTS trainee. Sharon, 18, hit the headlines almost two years ago when she became the first Midlands girl to specialize in what is thought to be the 'man's world' of electronics.
>
> (*Youth Training News*, July 1987, p. 7)

This theme of 'equal opportunities' continues to be stressed by local education authorities in the literature that they distribute to school-leavers.

> There have been important changes in the law to improve the protection and rights of young people taking part in YTS, in Health and Safety, Race Relations and Sex discrimination.
>
> (Leicestershire County Council, 1987)

However, how is this commitment to 'equal opportunities' actually experienced by young people in schools? Here is one example:

AV   Have you all had careers interviews?

Sue   I've been to one . . . and they wrote down what I liked and me interests and that and I got a letter back the other day about a vacancy for engineering but it says you need your maths and physics and I haven't done me exams yet so I don't know . . . but me brother says I've got no chance with them anyway 'cos you're a girl' . . .

AV   Do you believe you've got no chance of it?

Sue   I wouldn't mind engineering . . . it's always what I've wanted to do really, but I don't think I'll get the chance so I just don't bother now.

AV   Why don't you think you'll get the chance?

Sue Because you're a girl really, there's . . . when there was a thing at school about YTS, one of 'em told me that, they said that they weren't allowed to say that you've got no chance because you're a girl and then I went to another one and he says that really they'd train me but that I've got no chance of getting a job at the end of it because you don't see many women engineers, so . . .

AV   Does that annoy you?

Sue It does a bit 'cos one says one thing and then someone else says another so you don't know where you are . . . but I've always wanted to be an engineer.

(Bedtown College, Girls, 2 April 1987)

Sue was clearly aware that in attempting to pursue a career in engineering she was faced constantly with a range of contradictory pressures. A careers programme which recognized the importance of 'equal opportunities' was only one in a number of influences which Sue was dealing with; and when the representatives of YTS managing agents said things like 'I'm not allowed to say this but', they were operating under the climate of 'equal opportunities' as well. Sue could also have had friends at school who may have told her about the experiences of other girls on YTS, such as the ones quoted below:

She goes to college two days a week and for the other four she sweeps the floor, mashes tea and washes people's hair on occasions.

(Girl, questionnaire response, Bedtown)

Me sister went on one at a riding school and she didn't like it . . . all she did was chop down the nettles in a field all day and she had a diary to write things what she did and she were doing the same things everyday, she didn't do anything about horses.

Here I have deliberately selected pieces of informal knowledge which are negative about YTS. I have done this because all formal knowledge about YTS tends to be positive. I am not attempting to suggest that teachers and schools should themselves deliberately select material which is negative in order to construct a selective reality which is itself negative, but merely to emphasize that a practice that only uses formal sources cannot address the contradictory reality which is YTS.

Although I have made suggestions about the way that careers education in schools ought to be constructed, I am not and never have been directly involved in careers work in schools. I want to end this chapter with the questions which are directly relevant to my position as a radical teacher of humanities who is trying to find a positive response to the new vocational ethos, a response which recognizes the concerns which young people have about earning a living, but which also looks critically at the 'main reality' which they face. I believe that a structured attempt to deal with the contradictory reality which is YTS can provide humanities teachers with a means of raising with students the sort of questions and problems which can act to subvert the blatantly political aims of the new vocational ethos. A classroom approach which values the informal knowledge of our students also places the teacher as learner and the students as the source of that learning; one definite way of subverting the notion that school knowledge is necessarily superior to forms of knowledge that originate in the world outside the classroom. In supporting this form of classroom approach I am not attempting to indoctrinate my students as many on the right would have people believe. In recognizing that the process of knowledge formation involves a dialogue structured by contradictory forces I am also saying that I have no definite plan as to where that dialogue will take my students. This process is also essentially innovative and creative and will not follow any plan. The real source of bias in this area is the Tory government which, like its YTS advertisements, wishes to present a selective view of reality.

The Integrated Humanities GCSE syllabus, which emerged from the desire of humanities teachers for a course which stressed skills rather than content, provides the perfect space for doing the sort of classroom work that I am proposing. It also creates space because it stresses the necessity of perceiving social reality as being integrated and yet potentially contradictory. At the end of this chapter you will find Appendix 5.1 which outlines a patchwork of possible ways of approaching this whole area in the classroom.

At the height of the debate about the 'new vocationalism' a few years ago I, like many other teachers concerned by the dominance of this view, tended to bury my head when confronted with the proposition that schooling should be related to the world of work and preferred instead to fall back on a defence of the 'broad liberal curriculum'. Such a position leaves us vulnerable to criticism on many grounds, not least of which is the justified claim that we are failing to make contact with the matters which are of real concern to the young people whom we teach. If we confront the main proposition of the new vocationalism, we can indeed turn the whole question on its head. When it is clear that the labour market is structured by the inequalities created by racism, sexism and class, does preparation for entry into this market mean that students have got to become reconciled to these inequalities, or does it mean that schools should act, if only marginally, to question these oppressions and give young people the opportunity to discuss their rights in relation to such discrimination? The push to a more vocationally relevant curriculum, the emergence of the National Curriculum, the growth of modular studies and the growing commitment to 'equal opportunities' both in terms of race and gender are all in many ways contradictory forces. We, like the young people we teach, must negotiate these contradictions, but in many ways their continued existence *can* provide radical teachers with the spaces in which to maintain a truly radical practice.

Notes

1   The pseudonym 'Redmond' comes from Hannan, 1978, and is also used by Dan McEwan in Chapter 8. 'Bedtown', 'Dendale' and 'Walden' are also pseudonyms.

Appendix 5.1   *Classroom ideas for looking at jobs, YTS and work*

student knowledge	input	activity	comment
Students list personal skills and the paid and unpaid work that they do. List the jobs which they know are available and wages paid in those jobs.	Copies of local newspapers	Students make a display which shows skills of class, work and jobs done by class and cuttings from local newspapers illustrate paid work available locally.	This allows for informal discussion about local labour market.
Ask students to make informed guesses about how much people earn in different jobs.	Copies of national newspapers	Students compare jobs advertised nationally with those advertised locally and include these in their display	This could facilitate discussion about paid and unpaid work and about illegal paid work – missing school and earning money.
Students list jobs that they would like to do, how much they think they could earn and how they think they could get into those jobs.	Information from careers service and other sources about different jobs	Note down all the different jobs you see being done in your community and record the age, the sex and the race of the person doing the job.	These sort of activities can allow for more critical discussion about the jobs that different people do and the rates of pay received in those jobs. Criticism and questioning related to class, gender and race can be introduced into displays.
Have the students had careers interviews? What did they learn from these interviews? What 'choices' are they offered?	Visits from the careers service and from people in different jobs	Write letters to different organizations to get more information. Write to particular people, e.g. local MP, asking about their job.	Does any of the information contain any particular bias? How do people get to do these jobs? Can anybody get to do these jobs?

student knowledge	input	activity	comment
What do the students know about the jobs their parents and their grandparents have done?	Oral history tapes and other historical sources	Do an interview with parents, grandparents or another adult about what it was like when they left school and about the jobs they have done	This can facilitate a dialogue between students and adults who are important to them and can stimulate discussion about their own historical position.
What do the students know about YTS? Do they know anyone who is on or has been on a YTS?	Visits from YTS managing agents and from young people who are on YTS	Make visits to YTS sites. Tape discussions between students about jobs, parents, leaving school and YTS.	This can introduce the idea of 'informal knowledge' about YTS and students can begin to think about the different sources of information that are available.
Do the students know about the range of schemes available? How many people do they think get jobs through YTS?	Information from 'formal sources' about YTS; videos of YTS advertisements	Carry out surveys, questionnaires and interviews with other fifth-years about YTS, jobs, etc. Students interview someone they know who is on YTS.	This can allow students to compare and contrast the knowledge available from different sources and to begin to consider the question of bias.
What do they know about local YTS schemes?	Use information from 'formal sources' about local YTS schemes. What does the local education authority say about YTS?	Students can swop the information they have collected from their research and make displays that illustrate what they have found out. Design posters to persuade school-leavers to do a certain job, to go on a YTS, not to go on a YTS, to go to college or not to go, to join a trade union, etc.	Students can now begin to juxtapose information from all different sources and present this contradictory picture to other students in the school. Are they trying to persuade young people to think particular things about YTS or are they presenting the whole picture? What are the facts about YTS? The students can now use the information to act on their world to try to change or influence it.

6

Working-class youth transitions: schooling and the training paradigm
Robert G. Hollands

Schools of the vocational type, i.e. those designed to satisfy immediate, practical interests, are beginning to predominate over the formative school, which is not immediately 'interested'. The most paradoxical aspect of it all is that this new type of school appears and is advocated as being democratic, while in fact it is destined not merely to perpetuate social differences but to crystallise them in Chinese complexities. (Gramsci, 1978)

The impact of what has been called the 'new' vocationalism (or more specifically the 'training paradigm')[1] on working-class youth transitions has been formidable. The traditional movement from school into work has been interrupted and altered through the vigorous development of post-16 training policies. According to one source (Unemployment Unit, 1988), by May 1988, 70 per cent of 16-year-old and 25 per cent of 17-year-old school-leavers were going on to the Youth Training Scheme (YTS) and numbers in training had risen from 70,000 in 1979 to 396,000 by January 1988. Working-class school-leavers are now virtually compelled to take part in post-school training schemes in place of unemployment or full-time work.

The implications of this training 'revolution' in altering the link between school and work are really twofold. First, schemes have now taken over some of the primary functions of education in structuring working-class transitions into adulthood and wage labour. Second, as Andrew Vickers argues in Chapter 5, training methods and pedagogy have begun to challenge and influence current educational theory and practice in fundamental ways. One need only think of the introduction of the Technical and Vocational Educational Initiative (TVEI) back into schools or the development of vocationally oriented courses in colleges of further education (FE) (i.e. the Certificate of Pre-Vocational Education – CPVE) as examples of a much wider move towards vocationalism (cf. Chapter 4 above).

The debate about vocationalism in both education and training has been beset by contradiction and disagreement. One perspective has seen the move as a welcome shift away from traditional education structures and practices, towards a more relevant and practical curriculum which reflects working-class youth interests and aptitudes. Strangely, this position has been taken up in various ways across a wide spectrum of political opinion. The common reference point here is a recognition of working-class dissatisfaction with the formal structures of schooling and a realization that education has continued to reproduce social inequalities. Another view, more typical of the left, has castigated training schemes and vocationalism as a Conservative-led conspiratorial attack on the working class and as the introduction of naked capitalist interests in those institutions involved in preparing citizens for the labour market (Goldstein, 1984: Scofield *et al.*, 1983).

The direction of these comments has served to conceal some crucial, underlying issues and contradictions surrounding training, education and the young working class. For instance, if the training paradigm is to be viewed as an alternative to educational reform, then it is surely the case that very few analyses have sought to examine rigorously how training schemes have specifically influenced young people's identities and orientations towards working life and adulthood. Put another way, we must ask what kind of workers/citizens does the training paradigm produce, before proceeding full steam ahead towards articulating a 'radical', vocational curriculum. Similarly, in attacking the most obvious negative features of vocationalism, theorists have often been guilty of completely disregarding the failure of social-democratic educational reforms in attracting, motivating and advancing popular class interests and desires (CCCS, 1981). The result has been a complete lack of imagination in constructing a viable, popular and radical education/training alternative.

In this chapter, it is precisely these issues that I want to bring to the forefront of analysis. First, I want to examine how the debate around education and the working class (including their own experiences) lends genuine grounds for the need for a revised school curriculum and structure. Second, it is crucial to show how the training paradigm shifts from being 'the last resort' (see Chapter 5) to becoming the 'main reality' for many working-class kids. Third, I hope to provide some new evidence which details the various ways in which training has altered traditional transitions and worked to differentiate the young working class in such a way as to eliminate any simplistic analysis of the effects of vocationalism. Finally, I want to evaluate what these new class transitions and identities mean in terms of formulating an alternative policy and politics around youth, education and training.

This chapter stems from a larger and more detailed piece of published ethnographic research I conducted on working–class transitions and training (Hollands, 1990). This research sought to examine the transitional experiences and identities of a group of working–class youths (women and men) as they made their way through one of the most established and comprehensive training schemes – the Youth Training Scheme (YTS). My concerns here were to chart the main elements of young people's responses to the training paradigm, discuss their wider transitional effects and relations (in a range of social sites – i.e. work, the home, the street, non-work sphere, politics, etc.) and assess how a highly differentiated young working class articulates with the longer-term prospects of the labour movement.

The study was based upon two and a half years of fieldwork, examining young people's experiences of YTS in a large city in the West Midlands. Over the course of the research, a series of in-depth interviews and observations was carried out with forty-six young people as they made their way through YTS into work, further training or unemployment. During the fieldwork phase, over 200 trainees were contacted and twenty individual schemes were visited. A representative cross-section of schemes was chosen and trainees were selected for interview on the basis of their type of training and work experience, gender and race breakdown[2] and scheme categorization. Those selected were initially interviewed and subsequently visited at the scheme, out on placement and sometimes in the home and in other venues (pubs, cafés, on the street, etc.).

It is important to give a few brief details and an update on the structure and organization of YTS to provide a background to the analysis and argument which follow. Officially launched in 1983, YTS was designed to provide a year's training and work experience for young school-leavers unable to find employment. It is more than coincidence that the programme developed in the context of mass youth unemployment and its official rationale of providing a 'permanent bridge from school to work' was soon tarnished by various government leaks and admissions that YTS was clearly important in reducing unemployment, easing wage rigidities and reforming young people's attitudes to work (Department of Employment, 1985; *Labour Research*, 1983). Since this time the scheme has been extended to two years, had its funding basis and organization into 'modes' changed and has become compulsory under the Social Security Act.

Yet clearly, youth training was far more than a vehicle for disguising unemployment figures, reducing wages and lowering expectations. The training paradigm was also a crucial lever in aiding the crisis in schooling, reorganizing the youth labour market and ensuring that industry and business began to get a foothold into those state institutions linked to labour market supply. The 'crisis' of progressivism in schools constructed in the early 1970s by the right (CCCS, 1981), culminating in Labour's

'Great Debate' over education, represented by James Callaghan's speech at Ruskin, opened the way for the ascendency of vocational training in the late 1970s (Youth Opportunities Programme (YOP), amongst others) and the mid- and late 1980s (YTS, TVEI and more recently Employment Training (ET)). If schooling was indeed part of the problem, then vocationalism, with its emphasis on relevance, work experience and practicality, was held up as the answer to pupils' desires and industry's needs. Furthermore, the new language of 'skill' (transferable skills, occupational training families and personal effectiveness) implicitly signalled a move to new employment patterns, relations and aspirations for young workers.

The problem, however, was to play down some of the training failures of the past (YOP, for instance) and to match institutionally the mixed desires of school-leavers with the disparate and often confused needs of industry (Finn, 1982). In order to marry effectively these needs and construct a consensus around training, the day-to-day running of schemes was contracted out by the then Manpower Services Commission (MSC, now the Training Agency), through area boards (consisting of employers, government and trade unions), to a wide variety of managing agents. These agents are responsible for organizing off-the-job training and arranging work experience placements; they encompass private employers, local authorities and the voluntary sector and private training agencies (PTAs) in the business of training young people for a profit (YTS Monitoring Unit, 1985). It is interesting to note that the more recent adult scheme, ET, has adopted a similar training/work experience model, provided by training agents and managers similar to the managing agents. More recently, it has been announced that all training schemes (including YTS) will now be run by 'employer-led' training and enterprise councils (thereby further squeezing out local authorities and trade union representation).

Young working-class people find themselves within the midst of these changes and debates about education, training and transitions. How have they experienced some of these changes and what implications might their perceptions, cultural orientations and actions in these spheres have for rethinking politics and policy? I begin by looking at working-class youth's memories of school.

Experiences of schooling

Experiences of formal schooling are an important context for understanding young people's orientations towards vocationalism, training and job choice (Griffin, 1985; Willis, 1977). In the UK a significant proportion of young working-class people still choose to leave school at the earliest possible moment to seek work, despite the fact that job prospects for this age group are less than plentiful.[3] Chapter 5 in this volume outlined some of the key processes involved in young people's perceptions of training options while still in school. In contrast, here I look at how trainee recollections of school form a backdrop to their expectations and experiences of training schemes.

One of the prime reasons why many young people choose to leave school is their desire to move into the adult world of work and out of the child-like relations of schooling. Many working-class school-leavers come out of education deeply wounded by the experience. Here, a trainee painfully recounts her experience of compulsory schooling:

Julie   Educationally, I'm no good . . . on the education side I'm not that good. As thick as two short planks. But um, practically . . .
BH   As what?
Julie   I'm as thick as two short planks. It's a saying. I'm thick. Um, but . . . I'd say educationally I'm no good, but practically I am good. I'm good with children, I'm good with handicapped, I'm good with everything . . . and shop work and everything. But educationally I'm no good. I tried to go to college . . . I had this feeling that if I went to college to try and get this course then I'd be all right. But it just doesn't happen with me.
BH   Do you think at school they don't appreciate those other things? I mean you were saying . . .
Julie   You have to be educationally . . . if you're not educationally good, in this place they just put you in um, elementary classes. And they stick you in there and that's about it. And they help you try and build up your education but . . . you know, more help.
BH   Were you glad to leave school then?
Julie   I wasn't, I didn't really mind leavin'. There were no tears or anything [laughs]. I just left on goodwill with everybody.

This personal confession expresses a number of broader processes at work in a class- and gender-biased education system. For example, it demonstrates how streaming and the curriculum merge to produce self-blame and evaluations that one is 'thick' or a failure. And while many young people realize that they do indeed possess real practical skills (some of them gender-related), they also recognize that these are often undervalued in relation to academic knowledge. Finally, Julie's comments hint at how young people's frustrations at school might get translated into more positive evaluations of vocational training schemes which, in comparison to education, can be seen as 'relevant', 'practical' and related to the 'world of work'. Her follow-up comment makes this latter point explicit:

Julie   From school . . . from school to college you don't know what's, what's goin' on in the world. You don't, it sounds terrible, but you don't. And when you come on this [YTS] you find out that you've got to look after yourself . . . that you've got this backing, you've got like at work, you can, if anything goes wrong you can fall back on this and they push you back up and you get on your way. But you know after this you haven't got anybody to push you back up on a pedestal, you know.

Other young people provided additional critiques of the education system and curriculum, particularly as it related to preparing them for life in the 'real' world:

Mick   All these things you learn at school . . . is not really genuine knowledge at all you need out in the world . . . you don't need nothin' of that . . .

BH   What was the worst thing about school? Ah, what subjects and things?

Billy   English and maths are the worst subjects you can get.

Chris   Science . . . you ain't gonna be a scientist, you ain't gonna end up a scientist in secondary school are you?

BH   What about mathematics?

Billy   It's useful in some ways . . . but the things they teach you, you know, logs and all that sort of stuff . . . simple addings and minusing and timesin' . . . that's all you really need. You don't really need all these er logrhythms [logarithms], Pathagorese, Pathagorus theories and all . . . I was at school right, got this K+A=B or somethin' like that. I thought, where did they get these letters from and what do they mean? It really got me lost that did.

If the 'real world' is defined primarily in terms of work, home and community, then school was definitely not the institution in which one expected to gain 'really useful knowledge'. Similarly, within working-class culture generally, abstract theoretical knowledge pursued in some school subjects is often viewed as completely unintelligible, as Billy's final comment so cogently expresses.

More specific criticisms of the school curriculum revolved around the stress on the examination system and the ranking of traditional academic subjects over technical and practical courses. If the proponents of vocationalism are right about anything, it is their criticism of the continuing elitism and lack of relevance of much of the educational curriculum. This should not imply that the insertion of work-based subjects back into schools is only a recent phenomenon or is automatically a positive thing in its own terms. Indeed, many educational theorists have argued that the rise of vocationalism in the school curriculum has actually been used to justify and exacerbate the distinction between 'hand' and 'head' labour (Bates *et al.*, 1984; Chapter 4 above).

Pupils have had their own criticisms of the irrelevance of schooling for many working-class jobs, prior to vocationalism making its assault on education, and these two views should not be conflated. Working-class kids have long seen through the value of compulsory schooling (even liberal teaching methods and career guidance)[4] in 'helping' them make the transition from school to work and, instead, have relied on their own cultural forms and family/community contacts to make the transition. This rejection of formal schooling has often manifested itself through oppositional cultures and strategies (for a historical view see Humphries, 1981). Clearly, even a vocationally oriented educational curriculum which does not recognize these cultural forms, or is unable to demonstrate a direct relationship between school and real jobs, will face elements of opposition.

In conclusion then, many young working-class people felt alienated by the social relations of schooling. School was an immature setting, while work, and even training schemes, represented versions of the adult world. The irony is that working-class pupils may be labelled 'childish' precisely for developing coping behaviours necessary for enduring compulsory schooling, which they rightly see as blocking their transition into adulthood.

While schooling experiences and relations remain an important social context in preparing the ground for post-16 vocationalism, it is not the sole factor in contouring either young people's 'choices' to go on training schemes or what kind of transitions they help construct when they get there. In the next section, I look briefly at a range of additional factors which help to make the training paradigm the 'main reality' for many young people, as well as limit their 'choice' of scheme and type of occupational training.

Leaving school and 'choosing' a scheme

While the main option for the majority of young working-class people I interviewed was to leave school in search of work, there were exceptions. However, there was often a huge gap between expectations and realities in relation to minority choices. One of the key elements in constructing a new transition into work for school-leavers is the substitution of training schemes in place of the range of existing options.

For example, for those few young people who wanted to stay on in full-time education (either sixth-form or further education), there were often unforeseen circumstances and lost opportunities:

Shabaz   I wanted to go back to Broadhurst because ah, all the people I
         was with then, I had, they all got good marks in the exams and

I was all right in school. I didn't take any exams though (at the new school) . . . I didn't get the chance.

Liz   I was going to go to college full-time, but I couldn't get any help. I couldn't get a grant or anything . . . You don't get any help at all from anywhere.

Furthermore, the apprenticeship route into a trade had literally collapsed and only an exclusive few found themselves lucky enough to gain proper skill training (many apprenticeship schemes had converted over to YTS). Events such as having to change schools, a lack of financial help and a declining apprenticeship system meant that options were indeed limited.

Choices were even further restricted when it came to employment. As I mentioned, the vast majority of working-class kids left school with the expectation of finding work. This proved to be substantially more difficult than was initially anticipated.

Dan   I didn't particularly want to go on a scheme, but I knew I had to do something. So, I hadn't really thought beforehand what . . . I thought I'd get a job as well, but that soon proved to be wrong [laughs].

In the period of this research, less than two out of twenty fifth-formers in the city had found employment six months after leaving school. The impact poor job prospects have on increasing expectations of training schemes as a work substitute cannot be overlooked.

The final structural factor influencing school-leavers' perceptions of training was their experience of unemployment. During this research, young people were still eligible for social security, although there was a waiting period for early leavers. Schoolday perceptions of the dole as a 'bit of a lark' quickly altered for many young people:

Baz   I thought oh great, get outta school . . . on the dole now. Everybody thinks oh God, let's all go on the dole, doss around, just get money for dossin' around . . . you go out and, it's more or less boring.

Since this time, changes in the Social Security Act have meant that school-leavers are no longer entitled to Income Support, and instead must rely on a 'bridging allowance' until they are placed on to a scheme. There would now appear to be little need for the slick, professional advertisements promoting YTS, as attendance is virtually guaranteed by government legislation. It is through these mechanisms that YTS shifts from being 'the last resort', to becoming the 'main reality' for working-class youth.

These structural and indeed coercive factors, however, tell us little about the specific mechanisms and forms by which young people 'choose' a scheme offering a particular type of training. In this regard it is useful to compare and contrast young people's informal knowledges of YTS with the information they receive through official agencies like schools and the Careers Service.

Schools have an important role to play in providing young leavers with information about training. Andrew Vickers's research (Chapter 5), shows that while some institutions heavily promote schemes, others are more reserved about the types of information they provide. Teachers and career guidance counsellors are crucial actors in how training schemes are portrayed:

BH   Who did you hear from that the schemes were no good?
Mandy   Teachers . . . ah, yea, some teachers.

Finchy Well, when I was, when I, yeah, when I was at school that was all they [careers teachers] told me I could have, like. They didn't mention the job side, it was what training scheme do you want to go on when you leave school, right?

The local Careers Office was also central in providing positive evaluations and information about schemes, and it was clear to most young people that the role of this agency was increasingly limited to advice about training rather than job prospects.

In addition to information gained through these formal institutions, all young people had prior knowledges about YTS. These culturally based evaluations circulated through the more 'unofficial' channels of family life (parents, older brothers and sisters), school mates and the neighbourhood:

Margaret It's terrible this trainin' scheme wage . . . my Dad calls it slave labour.
Mick   That's what the YOP was, that's why they scrapped the YOP. 'Cos you didn't go to the training centre, you just went straight to the firm . . . they'd just use you as slave, slave labour.

Despite the fact that much of this information was critical in tone, some trainees actually utilized such contacts to get on to 'a good scheme' or avoid ones described as 'cheap labour'. On the other hand, while many parents were wary about YTS, there were few alternatives to boost the family wage.

With the aid of professional career help, one might initially expect that a young person's choice of scheme and type of training would reflect their interest in a particular occupation area. Instead, there were often multiple and conflicting factors which influenced this decision. One of the key elements affecting young people's choice was their orientation towards different types of jobs and how susceptible they were to career officers' suggestions. Some young people were predisposed towards abstract and more generalized forms of manual labour and were usually directed towards broad-based training schemes offering a wide range of work experience. They often possessed very real cultural knowledges that many working-class jobs do not require a specialist skill or in-depth training. On the other hand, there were a number of young people who were influenced by officers' portrayals of YTS as a career stepping-stone. They genuinely came to believe that schemes could be used to work one's way up in an occupation and develop a career (this usually, although not always, occurred in the service sector). These general intra-class orientations – what one might refer to as 'destinations' and 'careers' – will surface later on in the next section and will receive a more detailed discussion in terms of scheme transitions.

A second element of class culture which often overshadowed any straightforward choice of scheme, was locality. The location of a scheme in relation to the family household was an important consideration for many young people. Garnie, who desperately wanted to pursue training and possibly a career in electronics, gave up the idea because of the scheme location:

BH   Did you just come to one scheme?
Garnie   No, this scheme I came to because I don't wanna go to no
         scheme that's in the Isle of Wight or somethin' like that . . .
         you know? I prefer to just get out of my bed and just walk
         down this road here and come here. I don't want to go, he
         wanted to send me to Ashton . . . I told him no, I don't wanna
         go out there, it's too far.
BH   So it was the location of the scheme that was . . .
Garnie   Yeah, it was electronics he said, but it was too far though.

Despite the fact that most school-leavers were given a number of schemes to visit by Careers, the vast majority picked one near their area, even if it did not suit their first occupational choice. Part of the reason why a training scheme is chosen on the basis of locality, I would argue, is a continuing working-class preference for familiarity, neighbourhood and easy access to the family household (Clarke, 1979).

Finally the choice of a scheme offering training in a particular occupa-tional area, did not automatically guarantee work experience in that field. Once accepted on to a scheme, training choices also depended upon whether an appropriate work placement could be found or one's interest in a certain field matched one's 'aptitude'. Hence there were many training and career changes made in the transition from school to schemes. In summary, the ultimate decision to go on to a scheme must be seen in the broader context of working-class youth attitudes to formal schooling, a lack of jobs and an aversion to the dole. The process of getting on a specific scheme was a product of a combination of official channels, unforeseen circumstances and informal knowledges drawn from the culture and community. 'Choices' in vocational training rarely reflected bourgeois notions of rational decision-making and calculation, but rather more closely resembled a great training lottery.

Working-class youth differentiation and YTS

In this next section I want to consider, in some detail, the impact YTS has on constructing working-class identities and transitions into work and adulthood. One of the most significant features of the training paradigm is that it appears to offer many young working-class people an alternative route into working life outside the unpopular structures of formal education. However haltingly, all young people actively help to construct some kind of transition through YTS, partly because it is seen as different to school and partly because it may be a route into a job. If training indeed becomes an alternative to education for the young working class, then what kind of identities and transitions does it in fact produce? Additionally, if one of the strategies is to argue for a more radical version of vocationalism in schools, it is important to know what kind of impact current vocational paradigms are having on class identities and experiences.

Of course working-class transitions into work and adulthood through such an institutional sphere as the training paradigm cannot be looked at in isolation from broader class processes and the impact gender and race have on class formation. Similarly, such an analysis needs to recognize how the 'new' vocationalism has altered historical working-class transitions as well as be aware of the impact a range of contemporary social sites is having on youth identities.[5]

A number of key starting-points for coming to terms with working-class youth differentiation under the new vocationalism stem out of the work of Phil Cohen (1982; 1983; 1984; 1986). He has argued that historically, working-class youth transitions were organized around two structures or 'codes' – those of 'apprenticeship' and 'inheritance'. In other words, the transition into adulthood (and reproduction of classes) took the form of a cultural apprenticeship, rooted in the inheritance of particular skills transmitted through the family, the shop-floor and the wider working-class community. For working-class males, this apprenticeship was specifically related to their celebration of the techniques of manual labour and through a highly masculine shop-floor culture. Young working-class women's apprenticeship took on a very different form and was largely focused through the domestic, rather than (though not exclusively) the wage labour sphere.[6]

Cohen argues that in the postwar period, this particularly strong combination of codes began to dissociate and the way in which young people experienced and lived out their class position changed dramatically. While the factors behind this transformation are extremely complex, what is most significant for understanding the specific impact of vocationalism on youth transitions, is the rise of the 'career' code and the decline of traditional working-class notions of craft skills. Clearly the training paradigm, with its radical redefinition of skills and the youth labour market, has been a central fulcrum in differentiating youth transitions.

In his own work, Cohen (1984; 1986) hints at some of the broad changes in working-class youth responses to vocationalism. Changing definitions of skill have led to a weakening and pulling apart of both apprenticeship and inheritance codes. For some working-class males, the lack of jobs and status gained through the acquisition of craft skills, has meant a disavowal of the masculine culture of the shop-floor and the search for alternative identities in the non-work sphere, youth politics and 'white collar' jobs. For others, the breakdown of this inheritance has led to the adoption of exaggerated masculine and racist identities in the context of a declining manual culture. For young working-class women, the weakening of the power of the domestic apprenticeship and the rise of 'careerism' through the 'new' vocationalism, has led to a more diverse set of female identities and transitions. Other spaces in the non-work and political realm have also led to the beginnings of some interesting gender patterns.

My own work has been more specifically concerned with unearthing the range of class transitions and identities carved out on YTS (Hollands, 1990). Clearly within the working-class youth population, gender identities form a key fault-line in structuring young people's experiences and choices on YTS (Cockburn, 1987; Stafford, 1981). Race, also, has a specific impact on YTS take-up rates and the type of schemes black youth are placed on (Racial Equality in Training Schemes, 1985; Youth Employment and Training Research Unit, 1987), and racism in the wider labour market also makes itself felt on work-experience placements (see Pollert, 1985, p. 19).[7] While remaining aware of these divisions, I have sought to provide a more differentiated pattern of working-class identities and transitions which are not reducible to any simple combination of social relations or the result of any single social site. The following typology of youth transitions is a highly condensed version of my research on YTS.

In the case of young working-class women on schemes, it is clear that the traditional domestic apprenticeship pattern continues under the surface of job 'choice' and training opportunities (Cockburn, 1987: Fawcett Society, 1985). Local career service figures reveal that 83 per cent of female trainees were receiving training in only four occupational areas (clerical, retailing, catering, personal services). However, it is equally obvious that trainers have sought to redefine some of the more traditional forms of female labour and create the illusion of increased career opportunities for young women. Crucial to this process is the way in which a particular type of labour was imagined or perceived by young women, as well as how it was constructed under the new types of skilling regimes on YTS.

The main routes into work and adulthood for the majority of young working-class women on YTS are best expressed by viewing their 'choices' along a continuum – ranging from 'glam' (glamorous occupations) to para-professional, domestic and factory transitions. This should not imply the use of a simple labour market metaphor for explaining young women's movement through YTS; rather one must understand such female transitions within the broader context of a range of social processes and interactions (i.e. sexuality, domesticity, type of scheme, work culture/placement, non-work activity, politics, etc.). For example, it should be noted that all the training/job choices above are infused with varied notions of femininity and are clearly shaped in some degree by the traditional domestic apprenticeship.

Young women's definitions of 'glam' jobs included secretarial services, some types of shop work (i.e. selling high-fashion clothes, jewellery, cosmetics), hairdressing, fashion design and beauty therapy, and training places in these areas were highly sought after. These schemes (many of them PTAs) often promoted the glamorous and exclusive nature of this type of work, and notions of careerism and possibly self-employment were fostered on both placements and off-the-job training. Office work has been viewed by some young women as a possible glam job, particularly through the illusion of moving up the office hierarchy and becoming the boss's personal secretary (Downing, 1981). Even for those YTS trainees starting at the bottom, it was seen as a good job in terms of 'standards':

> Kamni   Yeah, I think I'd like to have a really good job as secretary or an office junior. You know, I think that would be up to my standards . . . Yeah, I think that's it, I think that would, ah, be the main thing I'm aimin' for in life.

The non-work sphere was often used as a site for working on the self-image necessary for these types of occupations (i.e. the correct clothes, hair-style, exercise, manners). Engagement in particular life-style activities then helped to supplement visions of upward mobility and status at work and on the scheme.

While the transition into 'glam' occupations may provide somewhat of a buffer on the traditional domestic apprenticeship (generally, these young women were least likely to retain traditional domestic roles), the hierarchical nature of this transition and the substitution of selling feminine sexuality in the market-place in place of domesticity, often blunted any real collective understanding of one's class position or gender issues. The stress on individualism and working one's way up through training was crucial to the formation of this type of transition as the following quote aptly testifies:

Julie   I've built up my own little thing. I'm in charge of the shop sometimes for a half-hour at a time. I'm in charge of me own jewellery, when I started I didn't have that. So I've worked up to the position I'm in now. I'm needed there.

As Julie went on to say, she'd rather work in a good high-street shop selling better-quality clothes and receive less money, than continue on her present placement (a small owner-occupied store) at a higher salary. Politically, this group was highly reliant on an individualist philosophy (self-blame if they failed to achieve), with little interest in formal politics or collective work issues.

Para-professional and domestic orientations, while representing quite distinct poles of opinion, developed in relation to 'people-minding' jobs such as child care, care of the elderly and disabled and various other service/care occupations. While Ursula Huws (1982) has described many of these jobs as 'doing other people's housework', it is clear that within the training paradigm, particularly in the off-the-job training element, there has been a concerted effort to para-professionalize various strands of this type of work. By this I mean brushing up existing feminine skills and preparing young women primarily for the social aspects of these jobs, at the expense of technical training and qualifications necessary for real advancement and promotion within these fields of work.[8] For example, the following quote from Margaret, a black trainee working in the child-care field, clearly demonstrates the link between existing female knowledges and the low-level training on offer at the work placement:

BH   So do you think you're getting good training at your work placement?
Margaret They don't train you exactly, you just pick it up. You know, they say, 'Can you change nappies?' and what they do, you just ah, watch 'em and do it . . . what they're doin'.

Off-the-job forms of training, however, clearly attempted to project the image of a professional career within these fields through their location within established educational institutions (i.e. further education colleges). Personal and social education, rather than technical and academic training, characterized these types of schemes.

The implied movement into a para-professional career for female trainees in many ways represents a compromise between having a 'people-minding' and/or a domestic career. Jackie, another trainee in child care, reveals the close link between a domestic career at work and at home, in this short quote:

> Jackie   At least this will come in handy when I get married and have children.

This domestic duality throws up a stronger veil of femininity over this transition, despite its careerist tendencies. Although critical political issues such as low pay, part-time work and a lack of promotion opportunities within these fields are sometimes raised within this group, often they are mediated by ideas about professional responsibility, work hierarchies and/or young women's future roles in and expectations about family life.

Finally the gendered transition into factory culture on YTS for young women is perhaps best representative of the strength of the domestic apprenticeship and the traditional route of the working-class lass. Manual jos such as assembly-line production (electronics, textiles, etc.), warehouse distribution and stock-taking, are all examples of these types of work. The crux of this transition is the move into a gendered version of an informal shop-floor culture of work stressing humour, friendship networks and the rejection of careerism. This orientation is represented here by Michelle:

> Michelle   I work in a big warehouse, filling orders and things. It's quite hard work but I really like my mates and the other people working there . . . we're always havin' a laugh about somethin'.

The movement into factory work for young women has often been understood by them as a temporary stop-off *en route* to marriage, and those taking up this transition generally performed the highest amounts of domestic labour at home while on YTS. Non-work activities were highly organized around boy-friends and work was viewed as a temporary fling before moving full-time into a domestic career.

Politically, while this transition/orientation is perhaps the most 'class-conscious' of all the female routes on YTS, its potential is clearly undermined by patriarchal notions of skill and the exclusivity of craft-based worker organizations (Cockburn, 1983). Many of these lasses had to struggle against male bias at work (i.e. for doing a 'man's job') and rarely were they taken seriously by manual trade unions. Also limiting was their own reliance on strong definitions of femininity and domesticity which ultimately, as some researchers argue, actively work to deliver them into the 'double burden' of wage and domestic labour (Pollert, 1981).

While the possibilities and options for young working-class men have always been more open than those of their female counterparts, they too have been quite firmly anchored around transitions into manual labour, through a highly masculine cultural apprenticeship. Generationally, this transition has been accomplished through young men's insertion into a counter-school culture (Willis, 1976) and their transition and integration into the highly masculine aura of the shop-floor (Willis, 1979). With the ascendancy of the training paradigm and the destruction of craft skills, this traditional route from school to work has been dramatically altered in many respects.

This pattern today is most symbolically represented and taken up through the semi-skilled manual labour route characterized by the 'lad culture', described in some detail by Willis (1977) in his study of counter-school culture. Despite the changing nature of industry, particularly with the decline of manufacturing, the manual-labour lads still constitute one of the main transitions on YTS. Nearly two-thirds of male trainees in the locality were training in the manufacturing or construction sectors, despite a massive downturn in employment prospects in these areas. Additionally, many of these jobs have become less strenuous due to technological changes. However, such masculine cultural attitudes remain out of all proportion to the number of jobs requiring heavy physical exertion. Here one lad describes his perception of a 'manly' job and the work culture it is a part of:

Chris   I wanna be a butcher.
BH   Is that a long day?
Chris   It's a, it is a long day . . . yeah. You start about six o'clock and about six o'clock you finish and then you go to the pub until about nine o'clock . . .'cos if you worked that hard he, the gaffer, takes you out.

The link between manual labour and working-class counter-school culture continues through YTS and is represented here by the views of one of the lads on work and his scheme mates:

Billy   There ain't nothin' like a hard day's work . . .
BH   What do you think about the rest of the lads in here?
Billy   They're a great laff. I don't know whether they'll get a job. They should do . . . if not for anything else for their laff. You know 'cos they're quite good company . . . even if they're a docile load a' bleeders. They'll get one I reckon just for their laff.
BH   So that's important then?
Billy   This job would really get boring without kids like that . . . really boring.

> BH   So you wanna have people around you can have a laugh with?
> Billy   Um, that is most important, that is I reckon. Next to wages it is,
>   yeah . . . A good laff and wages, that's all I want.

Humour, group solidarity and a predisposition for physical, manual work continue to be part of this still significant transition.

'The lads' remain exuberant and lively opponents of the 'life-skilling' emphasis of off-the-job training on YTS (particularly anything 'school-like'), but the strength of this semi-skilled transition has been clearly undermined by the training paradigm. The decline of manual skills has already eroded the lads' already weak position in relationship to apprentices and the construction of a new transition into work through YTS has broken many potential linkages between the informal culture and the labour movement. Additionally, the loosening of white, male working-class control over traditional craft skills has deepened some of the lads' long-standing attachments to racist and sexist practices over a range of social sites, thereby further isolating them as an oppositional force.[9]

A growing male working-class pattern is the development of a white-collar, middle-management transition on YTS. This identity develops almost exclusively in the service sector area (retail, office administration, etc.), and involves notions of managing other people's labour (i.e. managerial ambitions) or possibly self-employment. The essence of this transition included a belief in a career hierarchy, a concern with company and/or self image and a view that work should be interesting and challenging. This persepective is more than adequately expressed by this young black male training in office administration:

> BH   Do you know what you'd like to go on to do next after YTS?
> Nigel   Definitely management, definitely. Actually, I would like a job,
>   to have the experience after working in an office and seeing the
>   pressures you go through, the ups and downs . . . build you up
>   in yourself so you get a bit stronger inside. But definitely
>   management of some sort. My future plans really would actually
>   be to go self-employed. In what, I don't know.

Within the service sector, new opportunities for upwardly mobile young men to supervise and police the labours of their contemporaries are clearly being promoted. This adherence to forms of individualism, loyalty to the company and the adoption of so-called 'progressive' people-managing techniques, reflects a growing conservative and corporate view of industry. Leisure, life-style and political interests for this group are also decidedly middle-class and individualist. While there are obvious limits to how far such working-class trainees can progress up the company ladder or move into self-employment, this transition and the accompanying identity have important implications for a future differentiated class structure.

A final transition or identity promoted by YTS which relates to future work destinations, might be broadly described as 'enterprising youth'. In reality, this is not really a route in and of itself, but rather should be seen as an extension of numerous other transitions mentioned previously. In some cases this route was promoted by entrepreneurial forms of off-the-job training and schemes influenced by the enterprise culture ethos (e.g. private teaching agencies). Clearly, glam jobs, some types of para-professional training and white-collar male transitions are sometimes linked into visions of self-employment. Aspects of lad culture (e.g. the semi-skilled handyman) may also sometimes feed into this category. In the majority of cases, this is a destination projected into the future by young people, who are motivated by a wide variety of reasons to consider small business as an option.

Notions about being 'one's own boss', taking on the family business, viewing self-employment as a form of social mobility or simply selling youth culture and style for profit, are all different variations of a general 'penny capitalist' spirit influencing a small proportion of working-class trainees. Liz, a trainee in the clothing industry, for example, saw her working future very much as a part-time 'youth culture enterpriser' – selling her own unorthodox clothing designs and styles to stores on a commissioned basis. Leisure and style, rather than the traditional values of thrift and hard work, influenced her vision of self-employment. This version of self-employment/sub-employment, although politically ambivalent, at least signals a different female orientation towards wage and domestic labour, as well as the non-work sphere (in Liz's case, partly motivated by her particular sub-cultural style). On the other hand, Margaret, a black trainee in the child care field, mentioned opening up her own nursery day-care, because she simply wanted to 'be the boss', while a small group of lads mentioned self-employment primarily in the context of not being able to get a job working for someone else. Overall, while enterprising youth was a small category, its significance and variation merits additional consideration and research.

So far, all the youth transitions and identities thrown up by YTS have been characterized by varying degrees of attachment to work. The majority of the young working class (both male and female) continue to have a desire to move into work, however much this orientation is deflected by the domestic apprenticeship or new upwardly mobile identities constructed under the training paradigm. This is not to argue, however, that all young people make the transition with equally strong attachments to work. Education and training have never been able to produce ideal sets of young workers eager to be slotted into the occupational hierarchy. Some young people develop identities outside of, or in opposition to, work and wage labour. In some respect, the domestic pull on young women's transition into factory culture initially produces only a temporary commitment to work *en route* to a future of family and children, despite the fact that such a situation often results in a double burden of labour. Furthermore, the female youth culture enterpriser is at least as equally committed to style, non-work and pleasure as she is to full-time employment.

However, there are more distinctive 'workless'[10] cultures produced on YTS, which draw their strength from a number of other sources. One of the more interesting patterns I observed on training schemes, is characteristic of a group I called the 'survivors'. Experienced in the philosophy and politics of street life and highly suspicious of any formal organization, the survivor used the training paradigm to develop skills independent from the often unquestioning attachment to wage-labour expressed by the lad culture. Garnie, a black trainee on a community-based scheme,[11] provides an explicit example of this perspective in this discussion:

BH   So you're quite happy with the training but you're pretty suspicious about going out on placement?

Garnie   Yeah, I'm not suspicious . . . I know. It's just that I know, right, they're just using us as slave-drivers. Now I'm not gonna work for no man, no employer right and get £35 in my hand or £45. I don't want that, he can take that and buy his chicken or whatever he wants to buy with it. 'Cos I'm not, you ain't gonna find me out there workin' for him at that low price. I know what I'm worth, everybody knows what they're worth. See everybody knows what they're worth and I know what I'm worth and I'm worth more 'n that. You see? And you get out there and you be workin' your bollocks and you come home right, you wouldn't be able to eat your food, you have to jump in your bed, jump in the car again, work your bollocks off. By the end of week comes, right, you've done so much workin' right, you come home with £45 right . . . they tax you, insurance after that and listen man, you don't, you just look back to £29, you might as well, you know what I mean? It's a waste 'a time. What I got here, you know what I mean, I'm satisfied.

Garnie had, in fact, chosen to go on to a community-based scheme because he could work at his own pace, have some control over what he did and what skills he learned and develop a good working relationship with his supervisors. While many of the strategies adopted by survivors tended towards a certain kind of individualism, this transition is clearly in opposition to the dominant work ethos of the enterprise culture. While work skills are valued in their own right, identity formation relies more on leisure, style and one's links with the informal economy rather than with an adherence to wage-labour as such.

The other major category of young people in opposition to youth training and the available transitions into work, has been labelled the 'politicos'. Within this general categorization, there are important subtypes, which need to be distinguished. For example, in my research, the female version specifically developed out of an acute disappointment with training and work experience on YTS (particularly in relation to the realization that many para-professional jobs were really glorified forms of domestic labour). The conscious recognition of exploitation on YTS is expressed here by a young female trainee who was involved in a placement caring for the elderly:

Tracy   When I first went on the scheme I thought great, I'll be able to get some training in the field I want to work in. But then I couldn't get a placement in that area and I got put in a rest home instead. All I was doin' was moving people around and doin' all the shit jobs. I know now that these schemes are just slave labour.

The demeaning and repetitive nature of the combination of feminine wage and domestic labour, as expressed through YTS and the home, led some young women to pursue the training issue in a political way, hence developing the necessary skills to extend and connect their experience through to its gender and class basis. Tracy, for example, initially became tentatively involved in various labour-movement organizations and later moved into exploring gender and class issues in the media/drama field.

The male politicos are of two types. The first group were involved in largely class-based forms of politics prior to YTS and they utilized this framework to develop further critiques of youth training schemes and the erosion of young workers' rights. As Dan said, 'I basically knew they were glorified slave labour schemes, before I started.' Some of these people attempted to struggle against the worst excesses of their scheme and organized other trainees into councils or unions. They were often seen as 'troublemakers' by scheme personnel, and many had difficulty moving into and staying in manual labour jobs following their training. Their personal identities were largely defined by their engagement in a range of political struggles and they were often frustrated with the labour movement's patriarchal and patronizing stance on the youth question. Overall, their identities were rooted largely within a broad political field, rather than in a strict workerist/wage labour tradition.

The second type of male politico became involved in youth issues solely through experience of YTS. These trainees were even further removed

from a 'labourist' political position. Instead, their truly vocational orientation (occupational 'calling') was initially directed towards socially useful
work rather than struggles over wage labour:

> Ben   Since I first began thinkin' about having a job, I wanted to be a
> scientist all the time, when I was young. And then as I got towards
> middle school, I began to get interested in the outdoors. I wanted
> to make a career in the outdoors, you know a lumberjack sort 'a
> thing. And now . . . funnily YTS has provided me with an
> opportunity, which I shouldn't have really, doing union work and
> trainee rights . . . that sort of thing. That's where I'll probably be
> going . . . but I wish I wasn't [laughs].

The experience of YTS served to confirm Ben's dislike of meaningless,
boring manual labour and the exclusivity of its masculine and labourist
culture. Instead, future transitions were very much understood in terms of
doing something useful (as testified by Ben's engagement in the youth issue
and his later involvement in voluntary and social care work) and through
the development of personalized and issue-oriented forms of political
activity like youth rights, ecology and questions of gender.

   These then are some of the main transitions made by working–class
youths as they moved from school, through YTS, to the labour market/
adulthood. I do not claim to have unearthed all of the transitions in
existence, there may in fact be finer variations or different routes altogether.
The main point has been to show the sheer variety and diversity of
working–class youth identities and to demonstrate how these different
orientations are actively constructed out of the interaction between vocationalism and the training paradigm and young people's own active cultural
level of experience. In the conclusion I want to utilize the case study
material to explore some of the potential political and policy implications
for education and training.

Conclusion: youth, politics and policy

The central thrust of this chapter has been to detail the impact the training
paradigm is having on young working–class identities and transitions.
Throughout, the emphasis has been on the active and partly 'self-making'
character of young people's daily lives and experiences in education and
training. Institutional structures are not simply foisted upon the young,
instead they actively impart something of their own culture and focal
concerns in their transition from school through YTS.

   My main point has been to show how working–class youth transitions in education and training have been affected in the shift towards vocationalism. The complex differentiation of youth responses and identities on YTS is evidence that traditional class routes have fractured in response to numerous social changes. The implications this differentiation has for debates about education and training and for some of the key actors involved in these arguments (progressive teachers, trainees, theorists and politicians) are profound.

The wide variety of transitions developed on YTS tells us much about the strengths and limitations of the vocational training model. For example, it is clear that unlike some of the completely pessimistic analyses of the training paradigm (Allum and Quigley, 1983), young people are not being moulded into 'just another brick in the wall'. The fact is that many young people remain wary of the 'training revolution' and attempt to make what they can out of an often difficult situation. Trainees' use of vocational training to gain space for their own focal concerns provides evidence of a critical engagement with the YTS curriculum (see Hollands, 1990, ch. 3) and the transparency of notions of training for a 'career' is recognized by many young people who continue to rely on family and community knowledges about schemes and the local labour market.

For instance, the fragility of the training paradigm is exposed by the formation of politicos on YTS. How, in effect, if schemes are so indoctrinating, can this transition be explained? Similarly, other groups of young people utilize schemes to gain skills (sometimes for the informal economy) thereby sheltering themselves from unscrupulous employers, and realistic appraisals of job opportunities and the poor quality of work-experience placements can also produce strong 'workless cultures' amongst sections of the youth population. Despite being the dominant paradigm, vocationalism is unable to contain the plethora of responses and maintain a monopoly on all the youth identities and transitions produced on YTS.[12]

These are some of the soft spots in the new vocationalism's armour which are revealed through young people's own responses and cultural dispositions to the training paradigm. At the same time, however, vocationalists have always understood something about working-class youth experiences of formal education and their desire for training for the real world of work. The success in mobilizing a kind of consensus around the youth-training issue has been, in part, the way the training paradigm builds upon aspects of the cultural level, while responding to changing class conditions. Trainers, vocational bureaucrats and training agencies have in fact learned a great deal from the failures of education.

In responding to these lessons, I believe there has been a slow shift in the dominant manpower training paradigm. The first element has been a move away from a strictly 'deficiency' model, to one which stresses 'opportunity' and 'choice'. This developing position is clearly consistent with the careerist ideology evident in some of the transitions examined in the last section.

The shift from personal blame (a negative image) to fulfilling one's potential (a positive one) is I would argue, a more general feature of the third term of Thatcherism. For example, the training television slogan 'I can't do that . . . can I?', paints a rosy picture of progressive skill development and unlimited career prospects on YTS. The main idea here is to provide the image of new opportunities for already existing working-class skills and desires, through a directed and disciplined vocational training programme.

The other key element of this new paradigm is the way in which vocationalists have successfully dealt with the relationship between the developing careerist transitions and traditional working-class routes into work. For instance, training agencies and the government have heavily promoted the idea that new career opportunities for early school-leavers exist in the service sector of the economy. When challenged, these opportunities are contrasted to the highly limited nature of traditional working-class transitions into wage and domestic labour. In this service scenario, new jobs and working practices signal a move away from 'outdated' notions of class to a modernized, corporate and socially stratified work-force. The existence of a variety of new work identities and transitions on YTS – such as glam and para-professional orientations, male white-collar and youth enterprisers – are evidence of the success of this growing ideology. At the same time, the training paradigm's emphasis on 'transferable' and 'broad-based' skills and equal opportunities has begun to strip away the internal collective power of traditionally male craft occupations.

It is through this mechanism, that one can see how vocationalism effectively critiques formal schooling and attempts to reform traditional class identities, while underhandedly seeking to construct a new type of generalized, compliant work-force. Such an ideology clouds real working-class issues such as decent employment rights, the right to a skill and the unspeakable terrain of worker control, socially useful production and equal opportunities in a truly egalitarian society. Nevertheless, it is on this issue that the liberal educators' and the labour movement's own social-democratic repertoire of abolishing class and creating equal access is cruelly twisted back on itself. For example, vocationalists have simply to point towards a history of working-class resistance to schooling (even the comprehensive experiment) to prove their point about relevance. Furthermore, Labour's failure to construct a popular educational alternative and the trade union's historical complicity in maintaining the generational, sexual and racial division of labour through the exclusiveness of the apprenticeship system, are boldly exposed by the proponents of vocationalism. At one fell swoop, the training paradigm has effectively silenced any radical alternative from the labour movement.

The point is, it is impossible to go back to some 'golden age' of working-class transitions. Such a traditional scenario never existed in a pure form, and besides often it benefited only a minority section of the class (white, male, skilled). The fact that elements of traditional transitions remain, and still possess some sort of oppositional potential, does not in itself justify a move backwards. To base an alternative on minority and declining transitions, is a sure recipe for political disaster.

Today, the young working class is highly diverse in its orientation to work, politics, the home and community life. Many of the transitions described in the last section appear to be largely anti-labour movement in the traditional sense of the term. The construction of new transitions into work, based around notions of social mobility, individualism and the enterprise culture, clearly does not square well with the current image and functions of the labour movement. If we are to begin to construct an alternative, what contribution can this study of youth transitions in training make to both a politics of everyday life and policy-making?

For those actors working directly with young working-class people in some capacity, there are some immediate implications raised by this article. For example, 'radical' teachers can no longer ignore the thrust of vocationalism back into schools or attempt to counter such developments within a detached liberal/humanities framework. They must face up to the real needs and desires of working-class pupils and help them to address the 'main realities' thrown up by education and training. It may be possible to vocationalize radically humanities courses in such a way as to create spaces for exploring the available options and desires young people hold. Andrew Vickers in Chapter 5 provides some practical examples of how school students can explore their own knowledges and feelings about training schemes in relation to 'official' accounts (i.e. television advertisements, glossy publications, careers advice, etc.). Similarly, many of the images of work held by young people and promoted by the training paradigm could be explored through the use of guest speakers (from the 'real' world) and other visual/written material. The whole gamut of institutional 'options' needs to be explored, detailed and made clear to young people (i.e. apprenticeships, further education, cultural field, etc.) and racist and sexist elements influencing transitions need to be challenged and analysed. In short, while 'radical' teachers certainly can't change everything, there clearly is a lot to get on with.

'Progressives' within the training paradigm itself (and there are socialists working within YTS) can extend some of these activities without suffering under the undue weight of school-leavers' disaffection. Off-the-job training provides an ideal context for exploring 'the world of work' (i.e. work placements), training options and youth identities. Individuals such as this can often act as a buffer against crude work 'socialization' and false 'career-building' on YTS, by performing 'radical educational work' (in the best sense). Again, the widest possible set of 'choices' and futures needs to be realistically set out and equal opportunities ensured wherever possible.

Some off-the-job tutors already include exercises on youth identities, challenge racism and sexism on the scheme and elsewhere, and include discussions on the role of trade unions on YTS.

Of course, these everyday actions, in order to be sustained, require an organizational form and focus which might be expressed at the departmental, institutional, or even regional or national level through a variety of channels (unions, pressure groups, completely new organizations, etc.). Over the long term, however, even these collective structures can probably only be maintained through broader political commitments and initiatives. Politicians, political parties and organizations of the left too must come to terms with the kind of transitions and identities that are being constructed amongst young people. Cohen (1983) has argued that is is precisely the left's inability to comprehend the youth question, that has led to a crisis of confidence in the Labour Movement. The trade union movement's historical role in maintaining the generational division of labour and the Labour Party's patronizing utilization of statist rather than populist solutions to the education and training debate, have both played their part in making the movement largely irrelevant to the majority of working-class youth.

More recently, there has been a series of hopeful signs and discussions around the youth question in certain quarters. Various trade unions have at least begun the task of responding to young people's needs and fruitful discussions have taken place in Labour's Youth Forum. However, much more needs to be done. In terms of policy and organization, the party needs to consider merging education and training as a way of opening up young people's options and choices. Such a merger could open up 'choices' (by providing equal financial incentives and easy movement between technical and general forms of education) and the unhelpful distinction between the 'academic' and the 'vocational' could be reduced and/or eradicated. Education and training policy could also link itself up with a much broader approach to youth affairs across a range of spheres of interest to young people (i.e. cultural and arts policy, entertainment, independently run youth venues, etc.). Local political initiatives like the Wolverhampton Youth Review (Willis, 1985) and various loosely organized campaigns (e.g. Red Wedge) have stressed the need for a comprehensive youth policy rather than a simplistic training 'solution'. Any effective and long-term development of a genuine youth/class politics must begin to build upon some of these initiatives and develop policies which above all reflect the cultural experiences and desires of young people themselves.

Notes

1   The 'new vocationalism' as a term of analysis has been most well developed in the work of Cohen (1982; 1984). As Cohen, 1982, p. 46 explains:

Under the old system, 'vocational courses' were a misnomer for quite specialised training in the practical skills for a particular trade or occupation, in other words a form of apprenticeship . . . In 'lifeskilling', however, the relationship is reversed – the image of apprenticeship is used to obscure the fact that the one thing most of these courses aré not about is the mastery of specific techniques or skills of manual labour.

In this chapter I use the term to refer generally to vocationalism in both education and training, thereby reserving the concept 'training paradigm' to refer to the specific organization and utilization of vocationalism on the Youth Training Scheme (YTS).

2   Just under 50 per cent of the trainees interviewed were women and 29 per cent were classified as black (Afro-Caribbean and Asian). Both these figures are 'roughly' representative of the overall composition of YTS in the area.

3   In my own study there was a small group of trainees who indicated that they wanted to stay on in school, but were forced to leave for various reasons. This group was predominantly female. A more representative sample of young people in a nearby town showed that a higher percentage of males than females wanted to leave school 'very much', the most disaffected group being working-class males. The same report also presented figures which suggest that young Asians were more likely to attend school sixth form than either whites or Afro-Caribbeans. See Willis, 1985, p. 203 and p. 27.

4   This comment is not intended to make teachers the scapegoats for working-class resistance and opposition to formal schooling. While some young people I spoke with mentioned teachers in a negative light, it was the whole social relations of schooling that they objected to. I return to the role progressive teachers can play in relation to early leavers in the conclusion.

5   What follows is a highly condensed discussion of a much larger body of work concerned with the impact vocationalism and the training paradigm have had on working-class youth identities in the contemporary period. See Hollands, 1990.

6   By this comment, I mean that female working-class involvement in wage-labour (except in wartime) tended to reflect and was largely restricted to domestic and/or traditionally feminine jobs.

7   While I have remained acutely aware of some of the structural consequences of race and racism on youth training, my own ethnographic material suggested that black youth are spread across a variety of the transitions, from 'careerist' and 'enterprising youth' through to manual labour orientations and 'survivors'. Just as there is no one 'pure' class response to vocationalism, neither is there a monolithic black response. This point, however, does not negate the fact that racism on schemes and in the wider labour market often limits, influences and constructs obstacles which make some transitions and identities more difficult to adopt than others (e.g. 'glam' jobs, lad culture, politicos, etc.).

8   In making this point I should make it clear that I am in no way attempting to downgrade these feminine 'social' skills. I am simply trying to point out how the training paradigm builds upon them while creating the illusion that they can be utilized in some sort of 'career' progression.

9   The role that white racism plays in working-class youth culture and youth transitions is explored in greater detail in Hollands, 1985 and Hollands, 1990, ch 8.

10 By 'workless' I am not implying that these young people are either lazy or feckless. Rather, these attitudes often represent a very perceptive and realistic view of the drudgery of much work in capitalist societies.

11   I should re-emphasize here that the 'survivalist' approach is only one approach black youths take in response to a racist training and labour market (see note 7). White youth may also adopt a version of this kind of transition.
12   Creative and varied working-class responses to vocationalism in schools (such as TVEI) would presumably also apply.

7

Curriculum categories and student identities in FE

James Avis

Colleges of further education are an important educational site for young people and play a significant role in defining what it is to be young in the 1980s. Youth may encounter further education (FE) through a number of discrete routes. Schools may run, with their local FE college, link courses whereby school students go to college to pursue vocational studies. Youth Training Scheme (YTS) trainees may encounter FE through the provision of off-the-job education and training, echoing the experience of those sent to college by their employers. Another route into FE is by becoming a part-time or full-time student.[1] It is with the latter group that this chapter is concerned.

The 1990s herald demographic changes in the size of the school population. One response to these changes has been the development whereby an authority's educational provision for the 16–19 age group is located in tertiary colleges. If this strategy is widely adopted it means that increasing numbers of young people will experience further education.

The material in this chapter whilst restricted to a particular time and tied to specific students has a more general applicability. It is concerned with the ways students made sense of and experienced the educational relations in which they were placed. It therefore more generally discusses the way in which students experience FE and raises a number of issues that a critical educational practice has to address.

This chapter considers the experiences of two disparate groups. The first consists of students following Certificate of Further Education (CFE) courses in four colleges in the West Midlands. Research on this group was conducted in 1982. The CFE was a predecessor of the Certificate of Pre-Vocational Education (CPVE) and many of the experiences of CFE students can be transposed to those following the CPVE. The second group is smaller and consists of ten 'A'-level sociology students in a particular college. Research on this group was carried out in 1983 (Avis, 1983; Avis, 1984; Avis, 1985). The research was ethnographic in orientation and aimed to gain an understanding of the way in which students made sense of the college relations in which they were located; to this end unstructured group interviews were used. There are elements of discontinuity between the two studies in part as a result of the time gap between the work on each, and in part a result of the openness of the methodology adopted: where interesting themes were developed these were followed up in the course of the interviews. The two studies were not designed to parallel one another though the second did bear a relation to the first.

The two groups of students are of interest because they reflect different educational trajectories. The Certificate of Further Education was designed as a pre-vocational course for students with few if any qualifications. There were three variants: a CFE in engineering, a CFE in pre-nursing and caring, and a general CFE. The CFE courses were themselves differentiated, with the vocational courses being more selective. These courses have since been incorporated into the CPVE.[2] The development of the CFE in colleges reflected at least three factors. First, it was a response by educational institutions to the development of Manpower Services Commission (MSC) youth training schemes. Secondly, teachers reflecting on the high failure rate of 'O'-level students felt a more vocationally oriented qualification would suit such students and that those likely to fail 'O' level should be 'deterred' or rather 'counselled' to take the CFE. Thirdly, it was a response by educational experts to the perceived failure of the academic curriculum to motivate non-academic students and a desire to develop a more relevant curriculum which would neutralize such students' resistance to schooling.

The CFE students in this study had few if any qualifications and either had been redirected from 'O'-level courses or had a vocational orientation. By and large these students did not perceive themselves nor indeed were perceived by teachers as having high status. One teacher commented:

> For the first time there was a course [CFE General] which could be easily identified. They were all black, that was the thing about them, they were a group that was low level and they were all black as well. I think there was a certain amount of prejudice that was picked up there and they were blamed for everything [by teachers]. (Quoted Avis, 1983)

This feeling of being made culpable was echoed by students:

Jo   We also get blamed for things, this course is blamed for everything in the college . . . because most of them come to learn and not mess about.

All   Yeah . . .

Bev   If you're in the college with another group an' they can make as much noise as us but they'll [teachers] blame the FE course.

Students in the second group were following the traditional academic curriculum, being full-time 'A'-level students in their second year. The two student groups represent different strands in the tripartite division of FE. Gleeson has described this division as follows:

Tertiary Modern	The new FE; incorporating the unqualified, unemployed and unemployable. Curricular emphasis is on 'generic' skills via remedial vocational education, 'voc prep', work experience and social and life skills.
Craft	Mainly day release craft tradition (male dominated); but now incorporating female craft skills . . .
Academic-Technical	Full and part-time academic/technical tradition.[3]

It is important to consider the continuities and disjunctures between the two groups' experience of FE. How do these students 'live' within the relations of FE? What sense do they make of, and how do they experience, the pedagogic relations in which they are placed? What is their response to vocationalism? What is the relation between their experiences and the formation of particular vocational orientations? How do they experience being young people in a college and how does this relate to their previous experience of schooling? The answer to these questions may point towards a more adequate and politically relevant educational practice: a practice that starts with students' interests and recognizes their different positionalities in terms of class, race and gender. These positionings will relate in part to their orientations towards the college and the courses they pursue. In part they are reflected in the way teachers respond to them and place them on various courses. It is also important to recognize that students are actively engaged in self-production and therefore may appropriate cultural forms that cannot be read from their origins. Students are both positioned and actively position themselves in their relation to educational knowledge. It should be recognized that student experiences within particular courses are not all of a piece, being mediated by a number of factors – age, sex, race, class, subjects taken, relationships with peers and with teachers.

School and college

Nearly all the 'A'-level and CFE students found college to be better than school. They experienced college as a more mature and adult milieu. In the comparison between school and college, college invariably won out and at least initially school provides the yardstick against which it is judged (King, 1976). Mary, an 'A'-level student, commented:

I went back to collect my certificates from school, an' um, there were all these little people running around, all pulling faces and spitting in the corridors, and I thought I'm glad I've got away from all this.

Similarly a group of CFE students suggested:

JA   How do you find this place compares to what school was like?
Ashvin   Better.
Delbag   It's a lot better.
Iqbal   Yeah.
JA   In what sorts of ways?
Davinder More freer, it's not got the sort of strict, silly rules and regulations that you get at school.

Whilst the majority had been pleased to have escaped from the restrictions of schooling there was some ambivalence. Angela, an 'A'-level student, had liked the warm and supportive atmosphere of her single-sex school and had experienced some uncertainty and confusion when first she had entered mixed-sex classrooms at college:

There's just no comparison [between school and college] when I walked into a classroom, there were of course no boys in the classroom an' of course I hated it here . . . I'd only been used to an education with girls, so you didn't know whether to say anything or not for fear of them laughing [boys].

In the transition from school to college Angela had to negotiate a new form of being in the classroom, a new form of femininity that was accomodative to the presence of boys. This she accomplished, for she added: 'You know, when you think of it now it seems funny' (Stanworth, 1981; Spender, 1982). However, she was exceptional as most of the students had hailed from co-educational state schools.

Given the research results of the sociology of education, from the classic studies of Hargreaves (1967) and Lacey (1974) to more recent studies (Keddie, 1971; Ball, 1981), the finding that CFE students were disillusioned with school is unsurprising. Generally those enrolled on the CFE courses were those who had 'moderate success' at school and whilst there they would have been awarded relatively low status in the academic hierarchy. On the other hand, one would have expected those who were accorded high status in the school to have had a more benign view. Yet this was not the case. The academic 'A'-level students were equally disillusioned with school despite the attempts by their teacher to dissuade them from attending college.

Mary   The headmaster had special talks with me, asking me why I
       wanted to do this [go to college], I was coming off the rails,
       why didn't I want to stay on at school?

Anne   Yeah, I was treated in the same way when they found out I
       wanted to go to college. They were a bit funny with me over it.

However, once teachers had become aware of their pupils' decision to leave
school, this was met with some hostility.

Mary   They [teachers] got really desperate with us and said [imperi-
       ously], 'But if you want things changed you need to stay and
       change them there's none of this running out.'

Ranjit   When we was going to come 'ere we had an assembly, an' you
         know all the teachers are up there an' they say, 'Well at college
         you've got lots of freedom an' you won't do your work, an' it's
         a doss house, an' the standard of education is very low, the
         teaching method an' all that is a load of rubbish.' An' all that,
         really putting across it's a load of crap, an' says that your
         examination results an' all that are very low an' I found out that
         Raleigh Road, compared to this [college], is very low.

These processes do reflect the nature of institutional conflict between
schools and colleges at a time of declining school rolls and reductions in
sixth form size. It is often the case that teachers' favoured pupils are
traditional sixth-formers. In the interviews none of the CFE students
volunteered that teachers had actively attempted to persuade them to
remain at school. This relation to schooling and by implication with
schoolteachers will have been one that in part shaped such students'
relationship to academic knowledge and would have predisposed them to
have a preference towards the practical and the 'practical' style of some FE
teachers. These processes would have had an influence upon student
subjectivity and through this on the type of courses they would have
chosen at college and thus upon potential occupational destinies (Connell *et
al.*, 1982). Thus a subjective orientation to the practical is in part shaped by
the nature of school experiences and is in part validated through the class
cultures which working–class students interactively form, construct and are
located within (Willis, 1977).

It is within this context that the key differences between school and
college should be understood: the one institution pointing towards the
world of childhood and the other to the adult world. The crux of this
difference rests upon the perception by students that they have voluntarily
chosen to attend college and follow a particular course; unlike school they
are not compelled to attend.

Rick   Because most of them [CFE students] come to learn and not mess
       about.
All   Yeah.

As an 'A'-level student commented: 'It's a different situation, it's our choice
to be here, not supposed to be forced and I suppose that's why it's
different.' It is important to recognize that the 'choice' to come to college
is constrained and mediated in all sorts of ways, for example, through the
negative compulsions of youth unemployment, parental pressure and the
lack of any clear alternative to college. Once inside college the choice of
course itself is constrained in more or less visible ways. Some CFE students
had not been allowed to enrol for 'O'-level courses and had been redirected
on to the general CFE.

Well I applied for the 'O'-level course and I hadn't heard anything by
enrolment date so I thought I'd come into college and I went and saw
the teacher and he said I hadn't been accepted . . . so he said go and see
Mr Lipton [CFE course tutor].

In the case of CFE students on the engineering course in one college the
processes of course exclusion were more hidden. Students were given a
diagnostic test and then allocated to a course that staff deemed to be
appropriate. These students tended not to enter the college with a particular
course in mind, just a desire to do engineering; thus a sense of failure and
rejection that was felt by many general students was avoided. To a lesser
extent this also occurred in the nursing CFE in cases where students had
indicated a desire to do a 'nursing/caring' course.

The ideology of voluntarism, the notion that students have freely chosen
to attend college and freely chosen a particular course, ignores the circumstances which limit their freedom: the absence of an acceptable alternative
to college; the course as the only available means to a chosen end. There
are regional variations in courses and employment opportunities and those
offered by YTS. Students bring with them different educational experiences
and levels of qualifications that reflect the structuring of opportunities in
the school system. Students have differing interpersonal skills and abilities
to appropriate the cultural forms of different social groups. Thus the
choices that students are able to make are often limited and of a pragmatic
kind. They select the best choice on offer.

Teachers act as gatekeepers: through their enrolment practices, they open
up and close off educational routes. As we move into the 1990s it is likely
that course gatekeepers will find it necessary to become increasingly
stringent in their enrolment practices. The moves towards teacher appraisal
with the use of a variety of performance indicators, one of which will be
examination success or the successful completion of the course, will mean

that classroom teachers will resist teaching students who they believe are unsuitable for the course. College managements will also place pressure on teachers, for the same performance indicators that are used to judge teacher performance will be applied to assess the efficiency of the institution as a whole. These tendencies will join with the increasing emphasis placed on student counselling and profiling. Whilst both are welcome in a number of respects, they pose difficulties. In an educational sector where course completion and high pass rates are valued, those students who are border-line and who lack the cultural capital to argue their position, may find themselves being counselled away from the course of their choice. This process on an institutional level will be heralded as a success, as students will have acquired a more 'realistic' appraisal of their worth. The development of these practices will serve to diminish choice and when students have debunked the counselling process may lead to greater student resist-ance in colleges.

Pedagogic relations

For all students the transition to FE from school is marked by a clear break between the two institutions. FE is found to have a more adult ambience and Haddon (1983) found students to be oriented towards the social relations of higher education. Yet this institutional difference was not necessarily translated into teaching relations. It was here that there was variability in the teaching styles adopted by particular teachers as well as between courses. A CFE engineering student stated:

> Teachers [FE] are all right, they're not like the teachers at school, you can have a joke with them. I mean, they don't mind, they do it themselves. I mean, it's different from teachers at school . . . If you said something to them [schoolteachers] like a joke they would chuck you out, give you detention, tell the headmaster, but here you can joke with the teachers and they don't mind really.

Another group of engineering students:

> Robert   It's different, they treat you more like grown-ups than at school, and here I reckon they're interested in what you're doing, 'cos at school it was just . . . they'd throw you a book and tell you what to do, what pages or exercise to do, and just get on with it. At this college they explain it better and go over it with you . . .
>
> Winston   He's a teacher not afraid of using words . . .
>
> Delroy   They have a laugh with you.

'He's not afraid of using words' represents a more open and informal relationship between these male students and their teacher: the rough and ready masculinity of the workshop. Thus the teaching relation itself keys in with and supports the ongoing construction of a particular type of masculinity that is articulated towards a particular occupational setting (Connell *et al.*, 1982). These practices are also inextricably connected to class relations. This argument can be further illustrated by considering the pre-nursing CFE. First a course tutor reflecting on her practice:

> Perhaps in the first year I'm a greater disciplinarian. I don't know whether it's right or wrong but it's a matter of – in hospital there's got to be a great deal of discipline, and self-discipline, and things like being on time for classes, behaving in class, general attitudes – I'm strict about that in the first year.[4]

This teacher aimed to impose a fairly strict and disciplined regime on her students. This not only involved timekeeping, general attitudes and class-room behaviour but also included dress and appearance. Students were encouraged to dress neatly, as would be fitting for future nurses.[5] This teacher legitimated her practice through her nursing experience. In this example, there are again strong links between the attempted construction of a particular form of femininity and a trajectory towards a particular occupational destiny and class position (Gibb, 1983). However, the students had a rather different understanding of this tutor's practice: 'If you're away you've got to bring a note from home, a bit childish really.' A different group of pre-nursing students suggested:

> Sheila   It's just like it [school], you're hounded around.
> Brenda You get bullied around by some of the teachers.
> Sheila   You get hounded and hounded just like school, they don't treat you any different.

For these students the teaching relations and classroom practices, rather than anticipating work, pointed back to school. They had 'mis-recognized' these practices as being the age-based relations of the school rather than those of the hospital. However, it would be ingenuous to dismiss their perceptions and accept too readily the common-sense understandings and rationalizations of their teachers.

The 'A'-level students experienced a diverse range of teaching styles. This partly reflected the idiosyncrasies of particular teachers but also, according to students, reflected the ethos of different departments. Those who had experience of the Science Department felt that staff in that department were somewhat authoritarian. However, few of them had such experiences and the majority stressed the differences between particular teachers. Maxine, commenting on a teacher, stated:

It's different when talking to you for instance . . . like in listening . . . with other teachers they're a bit sort of standoffish. You can tell they're, I'm the teacher an' you're the pupil.

and as Dave commented:

it depends on the lecturer, I mean, say with you. We know we can get away with a little bit but we never go too far . . . Whereas you've got someone like Miss Knight an' she'd slash your giblets out if you tried anything.

What is played down in these accounts are those institutional processes and constraints that have a bearing on teaching style: for example, the stress placed in a department on examination results; the form of teaching exchange a teacher has negotiated with students; and the associated forms of femininity and masculinity. In the same way as teachers negotiate a way of being in the institution so too do students. At times the two constructions mesh and at others disjunctures arise.

Mary   Yeah, but some of them treat you as if you're still at school.
Harjeet Some do you know but others don't, all . . . most of mine don't.
Maxine   You've got Hitler down the corridor.

Both Dave and Peter had a similar view of this teacher:

Dave Just when you're expecting it to be informal it gets all formal . . . I keep on expecting Jones to cane me.

And Peter argued, 'I think he's nice to you if you go in an' say I'm inferior to you.' Whereas June suggested, 'I think he's pushing you for your own good really.' The different responses reflect the construction of different types of teacher–student exchanges. June in this case granted a degree of legitimacy to the activities of Jones, activities considered illegitimate and authoritarian by other students. As a consequence June was prepared to surrender a degree of personal autonomy. This was not the case with other students who perceived Jones to be introducing illegitimate school-based forms of discipline into the college. In this instance these students had taken seriously the designation of the college as an adult institution.

In the allegedly voluntaristic environment of the FE college, the teacher–student exchange is based on the teacher as imparter of knowledge, the student as recipient. In this exchange the teacher works on preparing materials for the classroom, marking work and so on. The student is expected to attend, contribute and carry out the set work. After all in the teacher's perception the student has chosen to attend. This teacher perception glosses over the underlying structural processes that constrain student choice: the effects of parental influence, and the social uses students make of college. The teaching exchange is echoed in the parent–child exchange: support for college work, a reduction in domestic labour as a consequence of college studies, an acceptance and support for the person who is 'doing something rather than nothing'. The parent exchange will have an effect on the teaching exchange and can strengthen student instrumentalism. Haddon (1983) found the type of exchange that students negotiate with their teachers is subject to an ongoing re-evaluation; as a result students' commitment to certification is variable over time. In this next statement, a group of CFE pre-nursing students are evaluating the CFE as a qualification:

> Satbir   When you got CSEs, if they weren't good enough [for 'O' course], they say go into this course it's better for you, you've got more chance to pass.
>
> Sheila   Yeah, but I don't see the point of this course . . . this is the year we only get one 'O' level out of this . . . And it's a hell of a lot of work to put into one year.

It would be mistaken simply to focus on students' commitments to their studies; there are a whole range of uses that students can make of college. As one teacher commented on two CFE students:

> Then the lack of motivation in two Asian students. One of them was thrown off the course some time ago but is still involved in the social life of the college. So they geared themselves towards that and had totally neglected the study side of the course.

The CFE and the 'A'-level students superficially held different orientations towards the curriculum and the nature of academic knowledge. For the most part what the CFE students liked about their course was the element of practical work and the opportunity for work experience.

> JA   In what sort of ways would you improve the course?
> Pupinder   I'd have more practical [engineering student].
> Suhky   On first aid we learn about putting bandages on. All about the patient, that's a good subject [pre-nursing student].
> JA   What would make physics more interesting?
> Sheila   More practicals.
> All   Yeah.
> Sheila   More things we could do on our own . . .
> Satbir   And he just goes on with loads and loads of stuff [pre-nursing students].

Another student simply described her work experience as 'It's great.'

These students' experience of the classroom was for the most part disillusioning. They found the more academic lessons somewhat tedious and unrelated to the real world of work. Indeed the ennui that surrounded much classroom work served to highlight the attractions of both practical sessions and the real world of waged labour. Paradoxically the experience of college pushed students to stress their occupational orientations. The tedium of the academic curriculum had become a marker against which the perceived pleasures of the practical and of waged labour could be measured. These practices relate to the formation of the mental – manual divide and draw upon the cultural resources of the working class that serve to produce a hositility to theory and academic knowledge. Student practices also reflected a rejection of the generational relations in which they were placed. After all, the academic curriculum, rather than anticipating work, pointed back to the childish practices of the school.

Commonsensically one would have expected the 'A'-level students to have been strongly committed to their studies. They had been academically successful, were following a high status course and had not only 'chosen' to study 'A' levels, but also had selected their subjects on the basis of interest. Yet this potential for an involvement in the process of learning was rarely present. As Peter stated, 'There's nothing interesting, sorry about this, in coming to lectures.' The interviews took place at a time when the 'A'-level examinations were painfully near and so may have exacerbated these tendencies. However, there are a number of factors surrounding 'A'-level studies that contribute towards a process of disillusionment, some of which were mentioned by students: the organization of the curriculum, the timetable structure, the nature of teaching and classroom relations, the type of student labour involved, the commodification of knowledge and the nature of the examination system.

June   I'm all right in the hour lessons, but when it's two hours I start to fall asleep, my mind starts to wander off after an hour an' I'm just picking odd things up.

Dave   It does get boring all the time, but you have to go through patches . . . So it's the time after twelve, thirteen years of education people's interest is bound to wane . . . But if you've got a two-hour lesson, say from nine to eleven right, an' you only got out at ten to eleven and you've got another lesson from eleven to twelve, by twelve you're bored out of your mind.

Ranjit   An' for two and a half hours or whatever, he just sits there an' dictates – solid dictation . . . I don't think I've been to all his lessons in a week, I mean, I've always missed off two or three lessons in a week. I just can't take it, it kills me.

Paradoxically the response of these students to the academic curriculum echoed that of the pre-vocational students. Both groups experienced it as being stifling rather than enlarging. Yet the two groups had rather different orientations to the future. It is important to remember, as Dave stated, 'You have to go through patches.' At times the academic curriculum will hold the interests of students, some teachers will be better able to negotiate the constraints of the curriculum and some students will likewise be better able to overcome the more tedious aspects of the curriculum.

Both groups of students handled the more tiresome aspects of classroom relations similarly, drawing upon the well-established repertoire of survival techniques that had been developed in school. It was through these strategies that they resisted the more oppressive aspects of the relations in which they were placed.

> JA   How do you play up teachers?
> Sheila [laugh] We either sing or talk, we sing in the physics lesson . . .
> Satbir We've got to have a bit of fun, we can't be all –
> All   Yeah, yeah.
> Sheila Teacher's pets all the time. Like at school, you've been at school you know what's it like.
> All   [laugh].
> Sheila You didn't like just sitting there lesson after lesson, just writing, dictated to, being told what to do. I mean, everybody's been through it.

These strategies of survival were in part dependent on context. Some 'A'-level students commented:

> June   I think the fact that you're getting bored is because you're sitting there not talking to anybody. I mean, if you talk to each other while you're writing, like, it's not so bad.
> Mary   But you find ways, just small ways to overcome it, you know like, you decide to take a lesson off here and there, an' go somewhere, or you go to the pub every dinner time [laugh].

Another group of CFE students commented:

> JA   When you find it boring what do you do?
> Sadie   Make jokes.
> Cynthia 'Cos you'm listening for the first ten minutes and the rest of the lesson you're somewhere else . . .
> Sadie   Well, *we carry on with the work but we laugh and chat* [emphases added].

In responses from both student groups there exists an alienated relation to academic knowledge (Woods, 1983). Resistance to the more tedious aspects of the classroom make it possible for students to remain in class. Their resistance does not challenge existing teaching relations, rather an accommodation has arisen, an accommodation that distances students from the academic curriculum and separates them from its critical elements. This separation is also encouraged by an instrumentalism in which studies simply becomes a means to an end: to work, a vocational course, or further academic study. This instrumentalism undermines the critical appropriations that they could have made of the subjects they were studying. Perhaps what is most surprising is that though many of the 'A'-level students had a somewhat jaundiced view of education they were nevertheless committed to further study.

Infantilization

The most irksome aspects of teaching relations for students were those that recalled school. They resented disciplinary forms and teaching relations that echoed the 'childish' practices of the school. It was on this level of generational struggle that their opposition was strongest. Many CFE students were vocationally oriented, having a much clearer perception of their occupational destinies (though these were not necessarily attained) than did 'A'-level students. Work, through the acquisition of the wage, was seen as providing adult status and the occupational identity of a waged worker. For these students the world outside of education provided a solution to the set of youthful dependencies in which they were placed. Their solution drew upon working–class cultural resources and their own educational and vocational experiences. The effect was to 'push' students towards paid labour and a particular and potential class position. Students' responses to pedagogic relations not only served to validate particular forms of subjectivity but also contributed towards class formation.

Whilst the 'A'-level students felt acutely their dependent situation, they were committed to a different solution from that of the CFE students. A number wanted to take some time off from education – 'a year off'. This was to provide a time to break with dependencies that had revolved around their educational experiences. Many hoped to acquire employment and to use the wage to assert their independence and autonomy. It was as if once this autonomy and independence had been won it could then be surrendered. In many ways this stance represented an imaginary solution and would only have provided a partial solution to their dependence on their parents, given the nature of the temporary youth labour market.

Mary   I'm sick to death of education at the moment.
Val   You feel cut off from the rest of the world, don't you.

Ranjit   Yeah.

Anne   You ain't done anything or seen anything, or gone anywhere.

Mary   Especially when you've got friends who are older than you and are just beginning to do it . . .

Ranjit   I mean all my life, since I was that high, I've been in school and college . . . outside college there's a whole wide world, you know you could do a million things an' I mean that's what I want to do for a year. I want a complete break, 'cos at the moment it's just killing me. You know, at the moment I feel as if my mind's decaying.

What was significant about these 'A'-level students was that their experiences of education had not dissuaded them from further educational endeavours. They had no real desire to acquire the permanent identity of an adult waged worker. In a sense they wished to use the wage to assert a level of personal autonomy which could then be used to claim independence when they re-entered education. They were selecting the middle-class route of studentdom and were prepared to inhabit the breach between school/college and permanent waged labour. It was in part their awareness of their position in the local labour market that led them to reject waged labour.

Mary   You so often get fed up with poverty an' think, I'll pack it all in [college]. To just have some ridiculous job an' lots of money [laugh].

Dave   But 'cos I've had –

Val   Oh yes, you've had haven't you, you've had experience and know what it's like.

Dave   A ridiculous job, an' you know what it's like packing boxes.

Shortage of money was a common refrain amongst the students; most survived by 'scrounging off their parents' which again asserted their dependent position. A number of the CFE engineering students felt they should be paid to attend the course. Another group of CFE students felt their impecuniary state acutely and had a strong sense of injustice having been denied a 'grant' (this was a continuation allowance which then amounted to £5.00 a week).

May   I was expecting a grant and I didn't get one.

Cynthia   So was I.

May   That made me mad.

Cynthia   They said my Dad was working too much.

All   [laugh]

Cynthia   I mean for gas and electricity all his money's gone already, plus his rent that's gone, right, and they claim he's working too much.

May	Yeah, they come to see me Mum, right, and they claim me Mum's income's too high.
JA	That's for a grant?
May	Yeah, for a grant.
Cynthia	That's hopeless that is.
May	'Cos you can hardly manage.

Amongst this group of girls there was a strong sense of the poverty of their families and the way in which their impecuniary state exacerbated their dependence on the family. It also made it difficult for them to dress as they desired.

Cynthia	I mean when you go to college looking like a tramp and everybody dresses up.
May	I mean, you look really . . .
Joann	Yeah, but nobody really dressed up at college.
May	They do.
Cynthia	At [college] they do.
Sadie	At [college] it's like a fashion show I'll tell you.

For these girls lack of money made it difficult to project a desired form of femininity. On the subjective level not only were their practices reproducing a particular form of femininity they were also producing a consumerist orientation to the market. Particular clothes would be used to project a certain style; the college itself would be a backdrop to the projection with its articulation to the adult world and studentdom (Haddon, 1983). Their concern with style and self-presentation can help to explain the importance of place for these girls. The majority of their studies took place in a college annexe which had been a primary school. This annexe at the time of the research retained many of the architectural features of a primary school. It thus contradicted these girls' perceptions of themselves as quasi-adult as its features carried the ascription of childhood.

Sadie	I've never said I'd come to [the annexe] . . .
Joann	I said [college].
Sadie	Not this place.
Cynthia	Everybody says where's the annexe?
Joann	You feel embarrassed coming here . . .
Cynthia	I don't tell nobody.
May	Well I tell everybody I'm at [college].
Sadie	An' if they say 'Can I come up', I say come up on Wednesday, 'cos I'm up at college then.

Vocationalism

The vocational orientations of CFE students were reflected in the courses as was the gendered nature of such occupations. A course tutor on the general CFE in one college stated:

> Again the girls want to be typists – they go for the typing course and because the girls don't want to do engineering they often choose institutional management as a girls' subject. In other words a lot of them choose subjects in terms of boys' and girls' subjects.

The pre-nursing students were oriented to the nursing/caring occupations. Those following the engineering CFE were oriented towards engineering. With the general CFE the picture was more opaque. A number of students had been redirected from other courses. 'I was supposed to do a secretarial course but when I couldn't do that I came on to the CFE course.' For some the CFE was a route to those courses from which they had been excluded. 'It's not a waste of time if you get your distinctions or credits but really it is if you don't.' For this student if she gained a pass that enabled her to enter another course, her time spent on the CFE would have been worth while; if not it would have been a waste. Thus the course was seen instrumentally. However, one of the course tutors on the general scheme felt that the CFE should wean students from their academic ambitions. 'There is a sense in which many of the students have to be socialized away from 'O' level because it just isn't for them anyway.' This aim was only partially achieved in his college as some students did move from the CFE General to 'O'-level courses. However, the course tutor's intention did feed into and reflect both the racial structuring of the local youth labour market and its 'reproduction' given that his practice was an unconscious attempt to place students in potential class positions. For those CFE General students who wished to enter general education courses their occupation orientations were more variable and more akin to those of the 'A'-level students.

Amongst the 'A'-level students there were different orientations to vocation. This reflected the general nature of the 'A'-level route and pointed towards processes that were concerned with the general reproduction of the middle class rather than the more specific reproduction of subjectivities that are related to particular occupations (Gleeson *et al.*, 1980). The variability of the orientations amongst these students served to constitute them as individuals. Whilst all the courses as a result of their forms of assessment and teaching relations individualized students, this was exacerbated in the case of these 'A'-level students. The whole ethos of these students' orientation was based upon individual choice and the freedom from constraint.

There were three types of orientation held by students: the ambivalent, the committed and the sceptical. Those who were ambivalent were uncertain as to where their occupational commitments lay, the committed knew exactly the occupation they wished to pursue. The third category comprised those who were not only unsure of their occupational commitments but were also unsure as to the value of work.

JA   Do you know what you want to do?
Peter   I suppose that's the good thing, it'll be a surprise.
All   [laugh]
Peter   I don't want to get a job, work for thirty years, buy a car, get a house an' then snuff it.

In this next rather lengthy quotation a number of themes are raised that reflect these students' thoughts on work.

JA   What about work? I mean long-term work, I mean jobs and things.
Dave   I don't want one.
Ranjit I do, I want to do something interesting, community work or something like that, that's what I want really to do, but you really need a lot of experience.
Mary   I think, it all becomes a job in the end, somebody making money out of you.
Val   'Cos I've never had one an' I'd like to have some money in my hand.
Dave   You're not missing much believe me.
Ranjit Yeah.
Val   Just to call my own, an' do what I like with, an' not rely on my parents for everything.
JA   Yeah.
Dave   That's not so much a job though as money, you just want a lot of money.
Val   Um –
Dave   So stay on the dole, the older you get the more you get.
Ranjit It doesn't work like that.
Dave   You live on your own, an' you can get your rates paid for you, your rent paid for you.
Mary   No goal in life.
Val   No purpose in life if you're on the dole, if you're working.
Others [confused]
Dave   You're free to do whatever you like. If you're working you're probably stuck in a place you don't like.

The very individualism of these perceptions is crucial to the ongoing formation of a generalized middle–class culture. However, the perceptions and understandings of these students should not be considered all of a piece. Their perceptions are mediated by the lived cultures of class, gender and race of which they are a part but also actively produce. Their vocational orientations similarly 'push' them towards different fractions of the middle class. A key process here is their orientation to higher education. Clearly the practices in which these students are engaged are related to the formation of subjectivities that echo and articulate middle-class cultural forms. However, these practices are not without their contradictions. All the students desired work that would not only provide an income but would also provide interest and a sense of fulfilment. In the current restructuring of the labour market and in a context of de-skilling even if these students can obtain work, this work is unlikely to fulfil their expectations. Paradoxically this failure has the potential of opening up oppositional tendencies within their orientations.

The vocational orientations of these 'A'-level students and the meanings they attached to college and their wider experiences serve to reproduce middle-class cultural forms. Most important amongst these is a deep-seated individualism. For a number of white students their individualism is compounded, reflected and reinforced in their perception of race.

> Mary   I remember there was one afternoon in particular, I was in college late an' if you walked through the common room you'd be the only two white girls walking through, an' there was such a feeling of they're all strong and joined together, an' that everyone was sneering at you because you were white.
> Val   Yeah.
> Mary   That was just Jamaicans.

A notion of individualism and choice which plays down the significance of the social structure leaves the student without the conceptual framework to make sense of the situation in anything other than a racist manner. By ignoring social structure and the racist nature of British society, the black response is broken from its social roots and can be interpreted as minimally a black exclusiveness, if not racism. Thus the atomistic orientations of these white 'A'-level students not only contributes to the reproduction of middle-class cultural forms but at the same time delivers a form of white racism (Avis, 1988b).

Conclusion

I have considered the actively produced orientations of students towards further education. Their educational experiences and active responses generate an anti-educative encounter that separates them from the critical potential harboured in education. Pedagogic relations were endured rather than enjoyed, were stifling rather than enlarging.

Curriculum divisions between CFE and 'A'-levels correspond to social divisions and differing class destinies. Students define themselves in relation to these curricular and social divisions. They culturally and subjectively inhabit their courses and are engaged in making sense of them. Curricular divisions do not in themselves crudely determine students' responses. Rather these are produced by students working on the cultural resources and knowledge available to them.

CFE students experienced a curriculum that was practically focused and that itemized academic knowledge, reducing this to a collection of facts. A similar itemization was experienced by 'A'-level students. In addition their curriculum was, by its abstraction, separated from the everyday world. Both curricular practices failed to generate critical thought. The task for critical educators is to interrupt those cultural and pedagogic practices that inhibit the development of a critical appropriation.

The CFE students liked and valued the practical elements in their course, but found academic aspects tiresome. What is surprising is not the responses of these pre-vocational students to the academic curriculum, but rather those of the 'A'-level students. They too were similarly disillusioned. An educational response that drew upon the same framework as the pre-vocational course would not have lessened their antipathies. What would be an appropriate educational response that could overcome the differentiations between the two groups of students?

The notion of vocationalism incorporated into pre-vocational courses is of a highly dubious kind. It focuses on the 'socialization' of students into appropriate occupational identities, an attempt to form subjectivities that willingly accept the oppressions of work. An important part of this process arises through students' subjective investments in the mental/manual division. The CFE students tended towards the 'celebration' of practical labour which corresponded with a dismissal of academic forms of knowledge. Thus the potentially critical elements of this knowledge became foreclosed.

As far as the 'A'-level students are concerned, a related process was evident. They too had a tendency to dismiss the intrinsic value of academic knowledge. Their instrumentalism treated academic knowledge as a means to an end: knowledge becomes technicized, a solution to particular problems. It becomes a disposable commodity to be used, consumed and discarded rather than a means to interpret and engage the social world (Freire, 1985).

An adequate educational response has to be one that is able to recover the critical elements of the curriculum. Academic practice has undermined its critical potential through its separation from the social world. It becomes reduced to a set of knowledges that the student needs to acquire and manipulate in order to gain credentials. Those elements of academic education that are potentially critical have been turned inward and create

214   *Education Limited*

an alienated educational practice. These critical elements lie in the abstraction, systematization, generalizations and reflexivity that are located in academic knowledge forms. How is it possible to recover this potential? One possibility is the appropriation of one of the key insights of progressivism, its concern with relevance and students' interests. For many progressive educators these concerns were a vehicle through which students could be encouraged to make a critical appropriation of the world in which they lived.

There is a need to combine and transform vocational and academic education so that both become ways of thinking about and changing the society in which we live. There is a need to challenge the individualism that underlies educational relations and is an ideological prop of middle-class cultural forms. It is this individualism that saps an awareness of the social structure and turns students away from collective appropriations. An adequate educational response needs to transform the practices of both academic and progressive education. Students' interests and experiences should be the starting-point. Both curricular models need to be rid of an atomistic individualism which should be replaced by an emphasis on the collective and a recognition of student positionalities. For it is this positioning in terms of class, race and gender that will influence their appropriation of the curriculum. Such changes will require teachers to re-evaluate their relation to the curriculum. A critical educational practice would need to transcend the limitations of academic, progressive, and pre-vocational education. Teachers would have to develop a new conception of professionalism, one that could handle students' differing positionalities and relations to educational knowledge.

Notes

1   **Table 7.1**   *Educational and economic activities of 16-year-olds*

| | 1976 | | | 1986 | | |
	boys	girls	total	boys	girls	total
Percentage of 16-year-olds who were in full-time education						
School	28	28	28	30	32	31
College	10	14	12	11	18	14
Total	38	42	40	41	50	45
in employment (outside YTS)	54	51	53	15	16	15
on YTS				31	24	27
unemployed				7	7	7
total of 16-year-olds (=100%)						
(thousands)	420	401	821	441	419	860
of which in part-time education (%)	20	6	13	7	3	5

Source: *Social Trends* 18, 1988

2 For a detailed discussion of the development of the various CFE courses see Avis, 1983. The incorporation of pre-vocational courses into the CPVE framework has not been without conflict; some courses still remain outside of the CPVE framework.

3 See Gleeson, 1983, p. 38. A similar argument has been put by Green, 1986. This tripartite division should be viewed as a continuum that is comprised of all sorts of internal differentiations. For example, in the case of the CFE there was a hierarchy, with engineering and the pre-nursing CFE in a superordinate position with respect to the general CFE.

4 In order for CFE pre-nursing students to enter nursing they need to take 'O' levels; in this college these students in effect follow a two-year course. In the first year they take the CFE followed in the second by 'O' levels.

5 'They do dress [making] . . . It gives them a consciousness of clothing that helps them to keep their uniform correct which is another thing, and dress themselves neatly, another important thing in nursing' (Avis, 1983 p. 22).

8

Hustled by history: choices before teachers in a progressive school

Dan McEwan

'I teach English literature at a redbrick university and write novels in my spare time, slowly, and hustled by history . . . What will happen now? All bets are void, the future is uncertain but it will be interesting to watch' (Lodge, 1980, pp. 243–4). 'And more interesting to take part in,' he should have added.

In this case study I shall consider how the teachers of 'Redmond College', of whom I am one, are trying to take part in the future of education, though they are being hustled by a history that is being made for them by others. That history is immediately the Thatcherite policy which is being imposed on the educational system of England and Wales; that policy in its turn has to settle accounts with the older history of the system and with forces operating in countries beyond direct British influence. In choosing how to respond, the teachers of Redmond have also to settle accounts with the history of their own institution.[1]

Since the voice of the students is strangely (and sadly) absent from my account, I must give the first word to a student:

> In only a few weeks' time I will be set on my own little trip to the outside world (well, that is, what's left of it anyway) . . . My view is that the promised light at the end of the tunnel is not for me. Our house is already going through a rather depressing time at the moment. My father has just been made unemployed. At one time he would be the big proud Worker, would go to work and see the same old people having a laugh over a mug of tea. But that's all finished now.
>
> I mean that at one time there would be 3,000 men working in one factory. It is just that little bit different now. For instance, there are no more factory outings, because there are only 600. So now nobody would like to go on the trips, because the men you have worked with for many years are just not there any more.

Also I get very depressed when you see a 50-year-old come home and
just sit there crying.

This extract from an essay that 'Patrick' gave me, somewhat coyly, towards
the end of his fifth year reminds us that students, no less than teachers, are
hustled by a history made elsewhere which profoundly affects their choices,
their behaviour, their collective and individual identities, even their gender
identity. The same Patrick who had seen his father cry was known to many
teachers only as a rather threatening, macho presence in the corridors. He
was also secure enough to cause a teacher concern by languorously running
his fingers through the hair of another lad while they watched a film in
class: 'I would not have minded so much had it been a girl's hair.'
Contradictory experiences in their political and social lives lie behind the
behaviour and opinions of students no less than behind those of teachers.

The case study and its context

Redmond College, a reorganized grammar school, opened in 1969 in a
Midlands village, seven miles from the centre of a major city. It is a county-
controlled, comprehensive, coeducational upper school within the Leicestershire Plan. It receives students from three feeder high schools for the
final two years of their statutory education, and many of them stay on for
one or two years in the sixth form. As a community college, it accepts
part-time students of all ages and provides a varied programme of community education. Redmond's large catchment area includes suburban
estates, a small market town, villages large and small, hamlets and farms.
The population of the area is about 30,000. According to the Registrar
General, it has a higher proportion of Class I and II than the average for
England and Wales and a lower than average proportion of Class IV and V
(Cuming, 1983). The area remains relatively prosperous, although even the
'massaged' official figures recognize that the county has an unemployment
rate of 5.3 per cent.[2]
   Since its opening, the college has had a 'progressive' ethos: decision-
making has been democratic, with all management committees answerable
to the General Staff Meeting; students are cared for as individuals, with
individualized timetables; much of the teaching is in mixed-ability groups;
there is considerable integration of subjects. Certain teachers, though
committed to the inheritance from the 1960s and 1970s, were becoming
critical by 1980 of flaws and limitations: a participatory democracy that
devolved power to teachers but ignored the opinions of parents with
something like professional arrogance; a failure to recognize the subordinate
position of women; a failure to recognize and engage with racism; viewing
students as individuals abstracted from their positions in social structures;

an obscuring of the extent to which real power still lay with the principal. The new vocationalism and other elements of educational policy exploit these defects in confusing ways which do not keep faith with the hopes of 1970s progressivism; the very notion of 'progressive' is changing.

In this case study, I have attempted to analyse how the teachers of Redmond College are responding to the structural changes that are taking place. Broadly speaking, they might see that their choices lie in one of three directions, and each of the directions corresponds to a theoretical framework that I considered for this research.

First, there is the guilt trip. Is there something in my attitude and behaviour which makes for discontent in the college? Perhaps if I chose to smile more often . . . This response has much to recommend it. Certainly each teacher is responsible for all that's wrong with the college, all that's wrong with the world. It is in the power of all teachers to smile more often. But this must not blind them to the fact that the college they have been appointed into (like the world we have all been born into) makes them the sort of person that they are. So I cannot be satisfied with the first response, the belief that individuals are simply free to become good teachers, good persons, in the light of abstract moral principles about how to relate to one another and to students.

Secondly, there is the gloomy acceptance of 'reality'. It's only a saint that could be happy in this place. This response also has much to commend it. Certainly teachers have to be realistic in accepting the constraints placed upon them. The intractable inequalities of our society are going to persist and the most teachers can do is to help a few students climb a little way up some ladder from the place where they begin. I am not satisfied with this response either, whether it comes as the superstitious (and profoundly unchristian) belief that God or Nature made things as they are or as the left–wing conviction (of Althusser and others) that an immutable Society reproduces itself mechanically and leaves no space for resistance.[3] Good learning is not just about making realistic choices in regard to an already constituted curriculum, culture, society.

Thirdly, there is the attempt to change the objective situation. Teachers form alliances and seek to effect specific changes through the college's decision-making process. This recognizes that the college, like society beyond, is the way it is because of the actions of people in the past. It is a view that is committed to engaging with, and making visible, the structures which otherwise would determine the sort of people that we are and the sort of positions that we occupy. It is an explicitly political approach, with some vision of how it would like things to change. It is an awareness that only by striving together to bring about the projected change will we discover what the structures really are. This is the approach which I find most satisfactory. Involvement in decision-making is not some choice we have the right to make or not. It is a duty. It is a necessary condition of education.

In organizing the material, I twice found a similar pattern of three emerging. After assessing teacher reaction to Tory educational policy, I examined first their views on intersubjective teacher-student relationships, then on the curriculum as an objective reality and finally on decision-making as the dialogue between agency and structure. Similarly, when I asked teachers what factions they recognized in the staffroom, a pattern of three occurred: some gave priority to student choice; some gave priority to passing on an objective body of knowledge; some saw collective nego-tiation of the curriculum as the central educational task.

As a teacher in the college, I am part of the system that I am trying to examine, and, of course, I experience it from the position that I have within it (a white, male teacher of humanities, born in Scotland in 1941, etc.). I shall try to make myself visible in the report by pointing out which groups include me.

For the research I have drawn on my fifteen years as a teacher in the college. While on secondment in 1984–5, I set up a more specific research project into the ways that teachers make sense of their experience in the college. I interviewed the former principal, two weeks before he retired at Christmas 1984, and the present principal in July 1985. I interviewed a structured sample of fifteen teachers. In the summer term of 1985, I received fifty-six replies (60.9 per cent) to a questionnaire. In the summer of 1986, I received thirty-two replies (37.2 per cent) to a follow-up questionnaire; and in the autumn term of 1987, I received thirty-two replies (40 per cent) to a further one. An earlier version of this chapter was given to the staff; it thereby became, I hope, an intervention in staffroom politics; it also, through reactions expressed, became a further element in the research.

Thatcherite educational policy, or who are the social engineers now?

As a first measure of the choices that Redmond College teachers see before themselves, I asked in the questionnaire of 1985, again in 1986, and again in 1987, whether they agreed with elements of Thatcherite policy.

The sketch of that policy with which I operated included a more technical and vocational view of education, relevant to the needs of the economy; paradoxically, a reaffirmation of the grammar-school curriculum; clearer differentiation amongst students on the basis of their ability, which is deemed to reside 'naturally' in individuals rather than to be constructed within patterns of interaction; a more centralized system within which relationships are those of individual consumers choosing in the market-place; opposition to integration of subjects and to mixed-ability teaching; a 'back to basics' move; a changing definition of 'youth' (excluded from the labour market, young people will be part of the solution to national economic ills provided that they realistically choose low wages and financial dependence).[4]

From a fairly crude calculation of whether respondents 'agreed' or 'agreed strongly', 'disagreed' or 'disagreed strongly' with the elements of Thatcherite policy enumerated, I obtained the following results.[5] In 1985, 23 teachers, including myself (41.1 per cent of respondents) clearly opposed current policy, while 15 (26.8 per cent) were sympathetic. In 1986, 13, including myself (40.6 per cent) opposed, while 9 (28.1 per cent) were sympathetic. In 1987, 21, including myself (65.6 per cent) opposed, while 8 (25 per cent) were sympathetic. At the same time, neutral responses decreased dramatically from 18 (32.1 per cent) and 10 (31.2 per cent) in 1985 and 1986 to 3 (9.4 per cent) in 1987. In other words, attitudes became polarized. From 1985 to 1987, sympathy for Thatcherite policy has remained constant both as a percentage and as individuals: only one person from that grouping has moved to a neutral position. Opposition to it, on the other hand, has increased from about 40 per cent to 66 per cent. Those hostile to the policy are present at all levels of the college hierarchy, are a mixture of male and female, and are mostly in the National Union of Teachers (NUT). By contrast, those sympathetic to the policy are found partly in the NUT but also amongst the non-unionized and in the Professional Association of Teachers (PAT); they are predominantly male; only one of them is a member of the college management committees, unless others are hidden amongst the two vice-principals, one faculty head and one pastoral head who have not replied.

Besides being hustled in their choice by Thatcherite policy, Redmond teachers are also coping with the history of their own institution and the pressures that puts on the way that they think and act. Research into the college carried out in 1973–4 has allowed me to recognize key developments in the history of the institution (Hannan, 1978).

Hannan identified amongst the teachers three groups that were in conflict. First, those who put their trust in the structures and principles of the original plan for the new comprehensive school he called 'conservatives'. A second group he called 'closed ideologues'. These advocate distinct subject disciplines, distinctions between staff and students, distinctions between senior and junior teachers; they celebrate the school or group and favour collective ritual and tradition. A third group he called 'open ideologues'. They obscure boundaries and mix categories; they celebrate the individual and belittle collective ritual and tradition.

As a tool of analysis the distinction between 'open' and 'closed' as used by Hannan is as imprecise as that between 'progressives' and 'traditionalists'. It is impossible to know where to situate political terms between the open, which celebrates the individual, and the closed, which celebrates the school or group (for example, liberal, socialist, conservative, anarchist). In other words, Hannan conflates educational philosophy and political tendency and obscures the relations the two might have with each other.

Despite these limitations, I repeated his research in 1984–5 and reached two main conclusions. First, those that Hannan would call 'open' were more numerous, more representative and more entrenched in the college hierarchy in 1985 than in 1974. Secondly, there is strong correlation between being 'open' or 'closed' and being opposed or sympathetic respectively to the Thatcherite policy. All of those that were 'open' in 1985 opposed Thatcherism, with three exceptions, who were neutral in its regard. All the 'closed' were in favour of it. Even more interesting, nine teachers who were neutral between 'open' and 'closed' were in favour of current policy. Since these nine form a new constituency to which Thatcherism appeals, they need further consideration. Four of them are commerce teachers; four are science teachers; the ninth is a (temporary) humanities teacher. Since recent policy creates jobs for science and commerce teachers, it makes sense that those teachers should support it.

In conclusion to this section, opposition to Thatcherism is numerically strong at all levels of the teaching staff. Support for it comes from those that Hannan would have called 'closed' joined by a new constituency, which is made up mostly of commerce and science teachers. It would be silly and unhistorical to attach too much importance to the place occupied on this map of the staff by each individual. What is marked here could be a stage on a journey rather than a final resting-place.

I shall now consider how, at that stage on their journey, the teachers saw their freedom of choice being affected by historical circumstances in regard to their relationships with students, curriculum and decision-making.

Teacher–student relations.

Visitors to the college often comment, favourably or unfavourably, about the quality of relationships that exist between students and teachers: relaxed, friendly, at times (however) insolent. It is a well-established custom that students call teachers by their first names.

The teachers appear to be happier with the type of relationships that exist with students and with their pastoral work than with the curriculum offered or with decision-making procedures.

Teachers who are critical of the whole style of relationships object in various ways to their being 'too familiar': 'I would have felt happier if there had been more continuity in the standards of behaviour accepted by members of staff'; 'I am not in favour of Christian name terms for staff by students.' Those most committed to the informal manner of relating to students also express reservations: 'We can avoid pushing kids along in class'; 'I am sometimes concerned that some staff have a need to be liked and quite collude in behaviour which is not generally socially acceptable. I think that does our kids a disservice.'

Others are anxious that this 'vastly most positive area in the school' is under serious threat. 'Many people in the hierarchy,' says one, 'are more interested in systems, neat curricula than people.' Certainly one of the vice-principals thinks that they[6] differ from older ways of doing things at Redmond in so far as they are unwilling to enter into a counselling relationship with a student such that they will treat with confidentiality anything that the student tells them.

The hope of building good relationships between teachers and students is erected over a contradiction. The basis of the relationship, whatever else may subsequently enter, is that, until they are 16, students are compelled by law to be there and teachers are responsible for ensuring that they are there. The relationship is further complicated by the fact that students are being assessed, undergoing the preliminary selection for the types of employment to which they may be given access. Teachers, as agents of that selection, enjoy a power which is threatening to all students (except perhaps those who are totally confident of their own ability and those who no longer expect to receive anything useful from school). This contradiction in the material basis of teachers' relationships with students, it seems to me, explains many of the ambiguous feelings that have been expressed.

Curriculum

During the early 1980s and well before the National Curriculum debate, a major plan for reorganizing the curriculum of Redmond College had been developed and then rejected by the General Staff Meeting. It had been an attempt to move away from a grammar-school model of separate subjects. After a further two years of debate, a General Staff Meeting in September 1984 approved a new curriculum to begin in 1985, later postponed, for practical reasons, to 1986.

The new curriculum envisaged that students in the fourth and fifth years would spend 75 per cent of their time in compulsory core courses. The aim here was to provide a broad and balanced education with the possibility of qualifications in five subjects. the remaining 25 per cent of students' time would be given to additional studies, which would be organized as a wide variety of self-contained, eight-week modules. Each student would choose a new module and a new teacher every eight weeks. The work done could be added to the five assessed core subjects to improve qualification grades.

Those students, expected to be relatively few, who wanted to gain one or two further qualifications would not have the benefit of additional studies.

The reaction of many teachers was euphoric. At last a curriculum was evolving which caters for the majority of students within a comprehensive: the needs of the minority who aim for more numerous qualifications are provided for without determining the overall curriculum. Yet within two terms a General Staff Meeting in June 1985 voted that the plan cannot be implemented 'in the present circumstances of cuts in resources and industrial action'; commitment to the already approved curricular change was reaffirmed 'given a resolution of the industrial conflict'. Was this an expression of fickle, cowardly reaction to progressive change? Was it further proof that relatively democratic structures are ineffective for planning and managing? The second question will be explored in the next section. The first question, about staff educational philosophy, will be discussed now.

The reasons that I uncovered for the move away from the plan were diverse. First, the weekly hours of teaching time and class size would increase, a sensitive question during the teachers' dispute. Secondly, some felt that the plan had become the property of top management in the college and that key persons in developing and advocating it would not themselves live with it as ordinary classroom teachers. Thirdly, a curriculum which is designed for the majority of students but provides slots for the minority with academic ambitions runs the risk of streaming by perceived ability. Competition for admission to the academic slots will be keen. It may end by reintroducing the 1944 tripartite system surreptitiously. It may end up by providing a broad, balanced curriculum for the majority who have to be diverted from aspirations that cannot be fulfilled and by providing at the same time a narrower, more straitened route for the minority who will finally be admitted to the professions. It may, as one interviewee put it, 'do Thatcher's work for her'. In a word, good ideas from one quarter can be appropriated and transformed by the other side in the political conflict that is educational policy.

A fourth reason was expressed by only one person, but it deserves full discussion. The organization of the explicit curriculum is less important than attending to the hidden curriculum and underlying structures. What is being referred to, I think, is best illustrated by two stories and a non-story from the same humanities team. 'Wayne' wanted to go to the toilet and proclaimed the fact in a loud voice. The teacher, determined that he would not go, told him to shut up. Wayne then embarked on such persistent, noisy protest that the teacher sent him out of the room to be dealt with later. About the same time, 'Jonathan' asked the teacher to explain more fully what he had said in a lead-lesson about social class. The short-term result was that Jonathan borrowed an E. P. Thompson article from the teacher. The longer-term result was that he returned the article in the marking room and became part of a half-hour discussion of the notion of class with three teachers. In both cases real learning was taking place. Wayne was learning to interrupt the work process in a way that equips him for survival in assembly-line production (trips to the toilet outside the specified times, timekeeping by duress, having a 'laff' at the expense of those who keep him working, ritualistic manifestations of aggression, flaunting of a ribald sexuality). Jonathan was developing his skills of negotiation, accepting tasks to perform in voluntary, unpaid overtime, effecting a dialogue between his personal interests and the advice offered by those more expert than he in certain areas. He was on the route towards the university tutorials and seminars that would have been his immediate destiny had a tragically early death not cut him off. Wayne was on his way towards the manual job which he finally lost when he told his boss to 'fuck off'. And the non-story? I cannot recall what any of the girls were doing around that time; and this despite the fact that that team contained the most impressive and varied group of female students I have ever met in one class. Important learning processes connected with class and gender are at work and we are part of them, whether we realize it or not. Any constructing of students as individuals divorced from the social processes that carry them is an inadequate representation of reality. I shall come back to some of these issues.

From these four reasons it seems to me that the partial reversal of curriculum policy in the college is not to be explained by the fickle attitudes of teachers on lower salary scales. What is at issue are profound questions about the type of society we are becoming, the role of education in producing it, the political nature of all schooling. This points to decision-making, the subject of the next section, as the central question in curriculum development. Before that I shall consider how the Technical Vocational and Educational Initiative (TVEI) has affected the college.

The involvement of the college in the second phase of TVEI has become the central terrain on which struggles have taken place around both the curriculum and decision-making. As the college had been part of the TVEI pilot scheme since its launch in September 1983, it seems to have been taken for granted that in 1986–7 it would make a submission to the second phase. There was little consultation, but it was felt that at that stage the college was committing itself to very little that was specific.

The response of the Manpower Services Commission (MSC) was that the local education authority (LEA) submission (which included that of the college) needed to be clarified in certain ways: it had not ensured that the curriculum of each individual student would be sufficiently broad and balanced; in particular, it did not ensure approaching 20 per cent science nor 10 per cent technology for all students; it had not submitted plans for counselling and guidance systems which would ensure that each student made suitable choices.

The college's re-submission had to be prepared in great haste. It involved for fourth- and fifth-year students the loss of an option subject in favour of complementary studies which could provide, through modules, extra science for those who did not opt for two separate sciences; these would also provide technology and other elements as required for breadth and balance.

Staff apprehension led to the calling of an Extraordinary General Staff Meeting in March 1987 to discuss the proposal that entry into TVEI Phase Two be delayed until certain concerns had been resolved in regard to the effect on the balance of the curriculum, the educational merits of the scheme, the feasibility of modules, and the effect on guidance, pastoral and reporting systems. A counter-proposal that the submission proceed won narrowly.

The reduction in the number of option subjects available to fourth-year students led to a dramatic decrease in the numbers taking design and humanities options as well as biology and typing. This led to the paradox-ical situation that 1987–8, which had opened with a well-argued rejection of much of the proposed National Curriculum, ended with the same teachers looking to the same National Curriculum as their hope for maintaining subjects like history, geography and literature.

'Hegel remarks somewhere that all the great events and characters of world history occur, so to speak, twice' (Marx, [1852] 1973, p. 146). So in 1988–9 the draft TVEI submission for 1989–90 was drawn up by the college's TVEI co-ordinator and one vice-principal, again in great haste and with little consultation. Again staff apprehension, expressed this time in an open letter from twelve staff, produced public debate.

Confusion existed as to whether TVEI was concerned with the whole curriculum or with part of it. This came to some extent from the fact that constraints are imposed both by the LEA and by the Training Agency (TA), which has inherited the MSC mantle. The LEA, in the interests of school-based debate, had not written down its requirements, despite pressure from the TA. In effect, this enhances the power of the TVEI co-ordinator as he can commune with the emerging criteria. The college's proposals focus on the technological, mathematical and scientific areas of experience and make little reference to the aesthetic and creative, human and social, linguistic and literary, moral, physical and spiritual (HMI, 1985). Defining TVEI in these narrow terms has meant that financing has favoured certain areas of the curriculum. Under questioning, the TVEI co-ordinator admitted that he preferred to put budget proposals directly to the principal rather than to the normal Finance Committee. Another sign that TVEI is favouring line management against more participatory forms is that a teacher with some TVEI responsibility was told by a vice-principal that he was not meant to represent the views of the faculty of which he is a member; rather he was part of 'the TVEI/LEA management delivery system'. Finally a proposal that faculties and departments discuss how areas for which they are responsible are being affected by TVEI and that this be part of the TVEI submission was debated beyond the deadline for it to be included. Promoting and evaluating TVEI on its own terms and not in its connections with other parts of the total curricular system were reasserted as the 'common-sense' way to deal with matters.

TVEI is proving to be a powerful means of redefining the curriculum in narrower terms, of undermining relatively democratic structures, of de-skilling teachers (who have to operate under criteria which are kept hidden from debate) and of presenting developments in isolation rather than in the context of the total system. At least that is the case in this one school.

In the previous section, I discussed teachers' perceptions of teacher-student relationships which stand on the contradictory reality that some are compelled by law to be in school while others are paid, partly, to ensure that the law is observed. In the present section, I conclude that curriculum discussion is best seen in a parallel manner. The contradictory ground on which teachers engage with one another is the fact that schools in general and the public examination of 16-year-olds in particular are used for placing people in types of jobs (or modes of unemployment), and thence for allotting their positions in a class society. Most frequently, the assessment gives an illusion of fairness to social destinations that were fixed outside the school. The contradictory reality of the curriculum and the political nature of the debate point towards decision-making.

Decision-Making

When the former principal retired at Christmas 1984, an important aspect of celebrating the college's achievement with him was the confidence that a radically new curriculum had been developed and approved democratically. One shadow, however, lay over the last week of 1984. The weekly *Staff Bulletin* carried 'A Parting Statement' from a Scale One mathematics teacher: the extraordinary energy and commitment of teachers are frustrated in a lengthy participatory process 'where no conclusions are even expected to be reached, thus giving the participants the illusion of democratic involvement, while the real decisions are made elsewhere'; power has shifted from the General Staff Meeting to committees of senior staff and to working parties. The timing was insensitive, and the principal recorded his distress 'at much which is (frankly) inaccurately reported and deduced'. Yet the intervention proved prophetic. Decision-making has emerged as the issue which is causing teachers most anxiety, although from 1987 onwards anxiety about the curriculum has become as significant. Concern about decision-making ranges from the worry that power has been usurped by a handful of oligarchs to the worry that the incapable and inexperienced are hampering efficient management.

Criticisms made by those sympathetic to Thatcherite policy had an anti-democratic tone: 'Democracy leads to delay in decision-making and too much compromise. Very few successful businesses are run by a committee.' 'General Staff Meeting decisions are often based, in the end, on emotional arguments and not always on sound educational judgement or even pragmatism.' Criticisms made by those opposed to Thatcherism feared some sort of conspiracy by senior staff: 'I'm not sure the present executive agree with democracy and therefore not sure of the trust they have in the staff.'

A comparative study of seven schools, completed just before the period I am examining, found that all groupings of staff at Redmond College were more convinced than staff in the other six schools that theirs is an 'emergent participatory school'. The exercise of a veto by the (former) principal was hardly ever noticeable; non-negotiable areas were felt to result from staff consensus rather than from the principal's statutory rights (Bishop, 1984).

The statutory power of heads of school is clear. Other members of staff may make recommendations, but the responsibility for every decision rests with the head and the governors. It is essential then to consult the attitudes of both the former principal and the present one on decision-making. Certainly both are explicit that they want the involvement of all teaching staff. Both strive to encourage student involvement through the School Council and through student representatives on the General Staff Meeting. The former expressed regrets that issues were discussed within unions, which then took unilateral action, rather than discussed by the staff as a whole in order to decide a course of action acceptable to the majority. In November 1985, he wrote in response to an earlier version of the present material that I had not adequately acknowledged 'the major part which union action had played in checking the move towards staff participation'. The college cannot hope 'to maintain democratic structures if sectional interests dictate the terms; and, if there can be no meetings [during the teachers' industrial action], how can the "management" – as you know, I hate the divisiveness implied by the terminology! – consult, let alone delegate responsibility for decision-making? That more than anything else accounts (in my thinking) for the difference between the hopes of 1973–74 and the disappointments of 1984–85.' The present principal expressed sympathy with these comments. He was persuaded that 'the process of making decisions . . . basically does not need changing, although it does need improving desperately, because it is proving more complex trying to deal with contraction and with a loss of resources. We haven't any of us as yet arrived at reasonable management techniques to cope with that.'

The expressed commitment of the former and present principals to democratic processes is clear. The question raised by one head of department must yet be asked. Are 'people with power . . . unaware of how their influence differs from that of [junior teachers]?' In conversation, the same person confessed, 'I got a buzz being in a small *ad hoc* group discussing where the cuts would fall in the faculty and in interviewing candidates for the first time. This buzz will become less conscious but no less real as one becomes used to exercising that sort of power.' I am persuaded of the justice of this way of seeing.

The whole curriculum debate, presented in the previous section, has raised questions about the pressures which exclude people from working parties, about possible manipulation of consent, about the distortion of good ideas as they are inserted into larger contexts which are being changed by political decisions outside the school, about the reliability of the information presented to the general staff, about decisions being made without public debate.

A vice-principal, departing for a year's secondment in 1985, rehearsed his anxieties about decision-making. He pointed out that several progressive schools had just had more autocratic heads appointed. He is, of course, right that democratic structures need to be robust to withstand the widespread anti-democratic pressures in society. But he is wrong, I think, when he goes on to suggest that, for all its importance, the 'process of decision-making is surely not the most important purpose of education . . . Schools exist, not to give fulfilment to teachers to control their collective destinies, but to enable the learning of the students in them to happen in the most effective way.' What is at issue, I suggest, is much more than the working conditions of teachers, important though these be. In the struggle to maintain and develop democratic structures, teachers and students alike are learning to become responsible for the whole of society. If they simply resign themselves to the destiny which is prepared for them by others (be it the triumph of technocracy, the nuclear nightmare, or the educational system as conceived in another place), they limit arbitrarily the sphere of critical intelligence; they impoverish education; they accept a stunted humanity.

What I am arguing for is a version of the ideal that was sketched in his parting speech by the former principal, but a version that is, I hope, more conscious of how our individual and collective identities are worked out in political struggle such that advocacy of apparently sectional interest bears the hope of a more complete liberation than the present community can envisage:

> I often think that the people who have been happiest at [Redmond] are those (both teachers and students) who have been sufficiently confident, adult, mature to respond to the challenge – as I would see it, the human right – of being responsible for themselves. Conversely, those who have

been least happy, it may be – who can judge? – least successful, are those who have looked for the sort of lead from others which has not been so readily available . . . There have always been those who in spite of recent history – in spite of present experience – look to leaders with a capital L to solve the world's problems.

The decision-making structures suffer from real defects. A working party that is reviewing the whole system pointed to the strength and the weakness of the General Staff Meeting: there is 'stark disagreement between those who feel it is a conservative gamesmanship club with fewer members than alienated spectators and those who feel that its function as a court of appeal in which all colleagues participate is irreplaceable'. The majority view on the working party is that both these versions are true. The danger is that attempts to reform as a response to genuine grievances could encourage the tendency to separate teachers into those who are managed and those who manage, especially at a time when the advent of the Local Management of Schools will encourage that separation.

In decision-making, as in teacher–student relations and curriculum, world views are formulated on a contradictory reality: power is very unevenly shared, and attempts are being made to build a participatory democracy on that.

Factions amongst the staff

The meaning of words is changing. I have already hinted at it with 'counselling' as enabling people to find their own solutions or as encouraging them to enter realistically the slots prepared for them. Similarly, 'drama' can mean the practising of deference or of defiance. Again, the college is 'progressive' in the eyes of those opposed to Thatcherism in so far as it retains older ways of doing things. The new constituency, which supports Thatcherism, understands 'progressive' as centred on technological developments and a more vocational notion of schooling. The latter interpretation is reinforced by the realization that departmental claims on TVEI funding will depend on their being progressive in this sense. Likewise career advancement might require it: a teacher interviewed for a senior post in the college had the impression that their educational philosophy was undervalued by the senior management team as out-of-date 1960s optimism. Such changes of meaning, however, are not pre-inscribed in some dictionary. They are the result of some sort of political struggle. What then are the factions in this struggle over the meaning of words?

Clearly the staff are not waiting for my research to tell them what factions exist in the college any more than the native peoples of what became America were waiting for Columbus to discover them. It became clear to me that the most significant divisions in the staff are articulated around attitudes to Thatcherite educational policy. By asking the teachers, however, whether the college staff is reasonably agreed on educational philosophy and what the characteristics of the main factions are, I hoped to form a more adequate picture of what groupings exist amongst teachers, what choices are politically possible.

Teachers' replies suggest that many perceive an alliance forming between 'management' and those teachers committed to a more technological and vocational view of schooling; this alliance presents its approach as politically neutral and 'progressive' in the new sense. A certain perception of the political neutrality of teaching and a belief in the possibility of resolving contradictions for students without reference to their position within objective economic and social structures are the hallmarks of a way of thinking common within the staffroom. It is a world-view that was deeply influential in the early planning of the college (see Rogers, 1971, p. 149). Opposition to this is seen to be formed around an analysis of the social and economic consequences of increased differentiation amongst students.

A classification of staffroom factions proposed by a representative of the new constituency gave me pause, and not just because it was confirmed by much of my evidence:

(1) those who think 'students lead', form groups by 'free choice' and 'learn by research and discovery';
(2) those who believe that 'a body of sequential knowledge must be taught and staff lead students';
(3) those who favour the second approach, 'but fit in the first where possible'.

This resembles uncannily a set of distinctions made by Paul Willis. He suggests that, broadly speaking, there are three ways in which a cultural item may be analysed or appropriated by a social group. (1) The social group gives value to an artefact or art form and gives it meaning. The freedom of the actors is total. This would make it unnecessary to analyse the internal structure of pop music, for example, (or of 'a body of sequential knowledge'). (2) The meaning and value of a cultural item are entirely intrinsic and independent and can be discovered by an analysis of the item on its own terms. No room here for student initiative, freedom, or creativity. Divergence of critical opinion, however, about music, art (or, for that matter, the significance of nuclear physics) shows that values are not autonomous, waiting to be read off by the discerning. (3) Willis's own position is that meaning and value are given in some interaction between a social group and a cultural item (or school curriculum), but always within the 'objective possibilities' that the item opens up. A group can creatively give meaning, but this has to be a response to the item in its materiality (Willis, 1978, pp. 198–201).

It could be said more simply. For present purposes, I think it comes to this. Ways of thinking about teaching may usefully be divided into three. (1) Groups of students have within themselves the resources to make sense of the world and, left to themselves or assisted by teachers who tune into the process, will give themselves the education they require. The virtue here which gobbles up all the others is respect for the free subjective choices of individual students. (2) The world already makes sense. ·Teachers will initiate students into that sense. If students choose to co-operate, they will benefit; otherwise they will condemn themselves to failure. The one virtue here is respect for the world as already constituted, something hard and objective. (3) Teachers and students alike learn by engaging collectively with the world as it is and by striving to make it a place where disadvantaged groups are set free. It is the struggle of collective subjects with objective reality. Wherever else the third view comes from, it is deeply rooted in the Jewish tradition, which feeds into western culture.

Paradoxically, I have derived this way of characterizing those opposed to Thatcherism from a teacher who is in favour of Thatcherism. I suspect, though obviously I cannot prove it, that beneath the teacher's expressed approval for current policies lies a deeper structure of thought which points in another direction.

Opposition to Thatcherism is here characterized as engaging with 'a body of sequential knowledge', with the socioeconomic order as presently constituted, but precisely as advocates for those groups who suffer disadvantage in the present order. It reveals how a 1960s progressivism (pupil-centred, based on the choices of individual students, naive about political consequences and primarily concerned with teacher–student relationships) might discriminate heavily against students who already are at a disadvantage because of their gender, class, or race. It suggests too how the hard-nosed traditionalism of a pre-established, academic culture (primarily concerned with the objective standards of a well-ordered curriculum) might produce identical results: the disadvantaged make 'realistic' choices about their place in society.

The commitment to collective struggles around decision-making, the advocacy on behalf of disadvantaged groups for which I am arguing, compel me to ask whether support for such an approach is to be found amongst the staffroom factions.

Class, gender, race, sexual orientation

Any research into a human institution is also an intervention in the politics of that institution. Any questionnaire is also an intervention in the thinking of each respondent. Being convinced of this, I included some questions that I hoped would encourage each respondent to reflect on their practice.

Only seven of the fifty-six respondents to the 1985 questionnaire said that they did not see as a problem a cultural gap between teachers and most parents: 'Some students may feel we do create barriers but I don't think this is necessarily the case.' On the other hand, thirty respondents added comments which indicate that they see a problem in the class nature of our national culture. Some of these were political ('There is a power relationship. *We* define the worthwhile.') and even stirringly oppositional ('I think we partly perpetuate the "officially recognized knowledge" instead of acting as agents of social change.'). In a word, there is widespread recognition of difficulties for teaching and for relationships that spring from our stratified society.

I had intended to include some question about the significance for Redmond students of the existence of the public schools. After all, the 2.5 per cent of the population that attends those schools provides 90 per cent of the country's top army officers, 83 per cent of directors of major insurance companies, 80 per cent of the directors of clearing banks and 62 per cent of the top civil servants.[7] There does appear to be a privileged route, and students in state education are not on it. An attempt to touch on this in my pilot questionnaire showed that the teachers I asked considered the public schools irrelevant to their students. So I dropped the question. Something in the teachers' mode of perceiving prevents them from seeing aspects related to one another in a total system. It is surely the same cast of mind which made many hesitate to assess TVEI from the point of view of its effects on the different areas of knowledge and experience represented in the college.

I do not see that any reasonable doubt can be entertained about the contention that society is structured in such a way that women as a group are at a disadvantage compared with men. To discuss the complex ways that this interacts with the structure of inequality based on class is beyond the scope of this chapter. My more limited aim was to get some indication of how teachers see gender-based inequalities.

To judge by teachers' responses, boys contribute more to discussion and obtain more attention by being disruptive in the classes of teachers opposed to Thatcherism than elsewhere. Another (more likely) interpretation is that those teachers are more aware of what is going on in this matter. I was made embarrassingly aware of the fact that the teacher may not notice when, a few years ago, a colleague asked me whether females were allowed their fair share in discussions in my classes. I began to notice for the first time.

Messages about what is normal for females are built into Redmond College. The principal and two of the three vice-principals are male, four of the five faculty heads, three of the five division heads and seventeen of the twenty-four heads of department. All this has its material basis in the facts that domestic work and child-rearing are almost exclusively the responsibility of women and are unpaid; women's acceptance for paid employment and their promotion are conditional upon fulfilling their primary 'family duties', whether actual or potential (see Delphy, 1977).

Once we begin to explore gender relations and the patterns of collusion built into our stock notions of 'real men' and 'true femininity', the question of gender identity becomes real, perhaps troubling. Statistically we can expect 10 per cent of students to be gay. Should this have any effect on teaching? The high proportion of those who think that considering gays should not be an aspect of their teaching (62.5 per cent) contrasts with my pilot study. In it only two out of seventeen (11.8 per cent) said the consideration should have no effect on their teaching.

One teacher asked, 'Why introduce this?' I do so with some hesitation, but I think that we should confront the question for, unconfronted, it operates powerfully as an unconscious element in our hidden curriculum. Consider the case of 'Tracey', who taunted at least two male teachers about their masculinity ('Are you a poof or summat?'). She appeared to be challenging them to prove their manliness by hitting her; at any rate, the teachers experienced it like that. Meanwhile Tracey found a boy-friend, son of a very dominant father whom he feared. The boy-friend asserted his manliness by teacher-baiting, some vandalism, some bullying and even some rough handling of Tracey. Structures of gender relations were being reproduced, although the outcome might cease to be inevitable if we do not respond with unexamined spontaneity.

The racial structure of domination is laid on top of those based on gender and class and relates variously to them. I asked whether in their teaching the teachers sought to promote anti-racism and whether they think they should. Of the ten who say that it should not be part of their teaching, three give reasons which are very similar: 'Any promotion by us might be met cynically. I try to treat everyone the same.' Their argument is seductive. Nevertheless, we must beware that treating everyone equally does not leave certain groups being treated very unequally. I am not personally accusing the three colleagues, for a few words on a questionnaire cannot do them justice. I am trying to engage with an argument which presents students as 'individuals' or as 'people' in abstraction from their position in power structures which formally and informally place black people, women, working-class people, youth and gays at a disadvantage.

The staff is attempting to become more aware of these issues. It agreed that the great bulk of resources for in-service training in 1987–8 would be spent on multicultural and anti-racist work. Many of them have been disturbed by a video in which five students of Asian origin talk simply about their experience around the college and about the forms of resistance to racism which they deploy.

Community education

It is apt that a section on community education be 'bolted on' to this chapter for such is how the head of community education feels that her area of responsibility is related to the school. Many working-class people, she feels, are hesitant to use such a middle-class institution. Back in 1973–4, one of the major issues for Redmond College was the unification of the upper school and the community college. (The other was dealing with disruptive students after the raising of the school-leaving age.) The enthusiasm occasioned by unification has borne little lasting fruit. Cuts in community education have, of course, played their part. So too, according to the former principal, did the reluctance of teachers' unions to put these hopes above concerns about working conditions.

Be that as it may, to engage with the parents of the school students and with the local community in general is surely a matter of political urgency. Grand hopes of developing a college that will be truly organic to the local community are probably Utopian, given the geographic and social divisions within that community. Even to encourage sympathy for comprehensive education in the abstract is wildly ambitious in the face of the messages purveyed through the popular media. To work, however, towards making more people believe that at least their college is worth preserving and defending is feasible. As teachers engage with the contradictions of Thatcherite educational policy in their locality, they may effect some change also in their notion of community education.

Conclusion

I set out in the hope that an analysis of the teachers' understanding of their work in Redmond College would reveal the structures which both underpin (or determine) that understanding and which at the same time are themselves reproduced by that understanding.

What emerges from that analysis is that the involvement of teachers in decision-making is seen by the grouping most hostile to current educational policy as the characteristic of Redmond most urgently to be defended. It shows too that a large group of experienced teachers is committed to the task. Two comments need to be made about this. First, vigorous defence of teacher control of the decisions which affect their work risks being blind to the way it excludes parents and students from power; users of a school must not be divided into professional experts and dependent clients.[8] Dialogue with governors, parents, students and other interested parties is essential if an adequate form of participatory democracy is to become possible, if a complete and relevant education for citizenship is to take place. Current legislation addresses the problem. It offers, however, an illusory power to all parents where only some will have genuine purchasing power in the educational market. If teachers, governors, parents and students seek ways of repsonding, they may breathe new life into community education. Secondly, decision-making may be seen by many teachers at Redmond as the most important terrain on which to commit themselves. This results, however, from the particular history and ethos of that institution. Teachers of similar persuasion in other institutions may experience the frustration of staff meetings which are powerless to set their own agenda or to do anything other than rubber-stamp and implement autocratically made decisions. These teachers will find it more sensible to engage with issues in their teaching and pastoral care.

The case I have presented has determined the methods I have used. If I had been the neutral observer reporting how things are (an approach which I consider to be an illusion), many things would have presented themselves to me as 'natural'. It is only by looking for allies and by engaging collectively to change certain things that a researcher can ever learn if those things are immutable aspects of reality or ideological constructs masquerading as 'normal' and 'natural'. The structures of social reality and of teachers' thinking which have been partly uncovered by these methods show the limitations of any knowledge which does not advert to the relationships between items (be it TVEI without the rest of the curriculum, state schools without public schools, heterosexuality without homosexuality). In particular, it is unacceptable to perceive students as individuals abstracted from the positions they occupy in those structures and from all the inequalities thereby implied.

Falling rolls mean contraction of the educational system rather than the opportunity of making more and better available to the decreasing number of young people; but this follows, not from some God-given law of economics, but from the political decisions of those who, by their struggle, are currently making the decisions (see Taylor, 1981). We must not let the power they have won through struggle and organization become invisible, part of the world-taken-for-granted. Our duty as teachers is to help young people to understand critically why the world is offering fewer opportunities to them than it did formerly or could do again.

That is why I cannot rest in the position of some colleagues. They hope, and I feel some sympathy, to establish an island of caring for students and of teaching them to care; this island is to be distinct from the surrounding economic and political turmoil which unions (even teachers' unions) treat as their element. The surrounding turmoil is the element in which education must take place. Only such an education is truly relevant to the world outside the school. Only such an education affirms the full rights of critical intelligence. To offer an education that is politically neutral, unconcerned with the role of schools in reproducing a stratified society is to collude, albeit caringly, with a hidden curriculum which constrains the potential of most students: they would be offered free choice but prevented from seeing the limited range of choice offered; they would have no say in the significant decisions that determine their future, which is all our future.

Notes

Thank you to the Redmond College students and staff (including the teachers), to the Education Group, to the Leicestershire Insights into Learning Group, to Ann, Margaret, Bernard and Clare. It is theirs at least as much as it is mine.

1   See Andy Green in Chapter 1 and Hough, 1984. The pseudonym 'Redmond' comes from Hannan, 1978, and is also used by Andrew Vickers in Chapter 5. Larrain, 1979 and 1983, taught me what reality it is I am examining.

2   Figures given by Leicester Jobcentre in March 1989.

3   This reading of Althusser, 1972, seems fully justified to me. It is the interpretation favoured by Hall, 1981.

4   See Bates *et al.*, 1984, pp. 59–61 and Simon, 1985 and 1988, *passim*.

5   I present this research more fully in an MA thesis at the Centre for Contemporary Cultural Studies, University of Birmingham, 1985.

6   Following a use that began in the fifteenth century, I use 'they' to say 'he or she' (see OED).

7   See Sampson, 1962 and 1982. Even before opting out confuses the picture further, an official publication is trying to blur the distinction between 'public schools' and 'independent schools', which latter accept 'roughly 7 per cent' of the age range. It extends the former term to certain schools which do not belong to the Headmasters' Conference, thereby increasing their number from just over 200 to 'about 500'. It adds the gloss: 'To-day the term [public school] is becoming less frequently used' (COI, 1988, pp. 165–8).

8   Chapter 3 discusses how the professional power of teachers and administrators grew in the postwar period and was resented by masses of ordinary users of the educational system. This was a historical condition which contributed to the popular appeal of New Right interventions in education.

9

Parental choice, participation and working-class culture: an analysis of power and secondary schooling

Phil Carspecken

Kenneth Baker's educational reforms include the interesting combination of a nationally controlled curriculum and a nationally imposed assessment policy, alongside measures which purport to give parents greater freedom to choose schools and involve themselves with decision-making processes within them. 'Parental choice' and 'standards' are among the slogans used to sell this package. But the category of 'parents' is by no means a homogeneous one, and different groups of parents will be affected by Baker's reforms in different ways. This chapter considers in detail the complexities of working-class parental choice and involvement in education. It argues that assessment and curriculum, which Baker intends to place under national control, are in a determining position with respect to other features of schooling. Baker's proposals are very likely to tie achievement ever more blatantly to class lines for a number of fairly obvious reasons (Simon, 1987; Glennerster, 1987), but in this chapter I shall consider some of the less visible ones. I will do so by providing an in-depth analysis of an incident of working-class parental involvement in a Liverpool secondary school during the 1982/3 school year. By focusing upon what was in fact a highly unusual and particular event, it is possible to illuminate general and common conditions affecting the relationship of education to the British working class.

The event analysed is a sort of spontaneous 'action experiment' in parental choice and community education which occurred in Croxteth, Liverpool, in 1982 and 1983. It has been analysed elsewhere (Carspecken, 1985; Carspecken and Miller, 1983; Carspecken and Miller, 1984a; Carspecken and Miller, 1984b) but is discussed in a very new way here, in order to highlight some of the themes of this book. Croxteth Comprehensive School was closed in 1981 by the combined votes of Liverpool's Liberal and Conservative Parties, who pointed to the falling rolls of the school as evidence of parental choices, or 'votes', against it. Thus a parental choice argument was used to justify a closure that soon proved to be highly unpopular for the majority of parents affected (for the entire story of Croxteth Comprehensive, see Carspecken, 1989).

After a year and a half of unsuccessful campaigning to reverse the decision for school closure, a number of the working-class residents of Croxteth illegally occupied the comprehensive in July of 1982. The parents, with wide community backing, then proceeded to invite volunteer teachers into the school to help run a full educational programme for the 1982/3 school year. The school was successfully run for the entire year and was eventually reinstated as a state-funded school. I was myself highly involved in the occupation as a mathematics teacher, a staff co-ordinator and a campaigner.

The occupation of Croxteth Comprehensive is illuminating educationally through its alteration of several traditional relations of power in which schools are normally located. Local authority bureaucrats and professional teachers were replaced by a working-class action committee as the formal decision-making body determining school policy and practice. The teacher volunteers who came in to aid them, moreover, were largely politically aware individuals, many holding to certain 'progressive' (but see below) educational ideals. They were motivated to teach out of sympathy for the political goals of the campaign. Most had no investments in teaching as a *career*, and thus were not subject to many of the limitations pertaining to occupational interests. Furthermore, the teacher volunteers were formally subordinate to the working-class action committee of Croxteth with respect to all decision-making procedures.

However, unusual though this situation was, a largely traditional educational regime developed in the school just the same, in many cases despite the intentions of the people involved. Croxteth Comprehensive, during its year of occupation, taught a highly traditional curriculum, divided pupils into streams based on 'ability' and made examinations a central educational goal. And all this despite the lack of a national curriculum and DES-controlled assessment procedure at that time. There were a number of reasons why such a traditional regime was established, such an *inappropriate* regime in the case of Croxteth where the majority of pupils had extremely limited chances either to pass the standard national examinations or get jobs. Some of these reasons have been detailed elsewhere (Carspecken, 1985; Carspecken and Miller, 1984b) – especially reasons of *constraint*, of lack of alternative educational materials, lack of familiarity on the part of teachers with alternative forms of education, and lack of time to think through and try out an alternative practice. Important alternative practices did arise, but spontaneously rather than intentionally, and their effects were very limited though undoubtedly promising (see Carspecken, 1985; Carspecken, 1989).

In this chapter I will show how deep-seated and largely unquestioned attitudes to politics and schooling, all of which are related to social routines common to the daily lives and social positions of the people drawing upon them, led to the establishment of traditional educational practice in Croxteth Comprehensive. The relationship of attitude to activity, however, was by no means a simple one. Indeed, the pages following will concentrate on *disagreements* between activists on political and educational issues and on how these disagreements were resolved, with traditional (reproductive) effects. While disputes broke out over questions of discipline and campaign strategy in the school a deep structure of views on the nature of knowledge and the necessity of examinations worked in barely perceived ways to determine the actual nature of schooling practice.

Uneasy allies: the working class meets the radical middle class

Croxteth Comprehensive was occupied by between 30 and 40 local residents in July of 1982. In September this group was joined by 260 pupils from the Croxteth estate and a number of volunteer teachers who were invited in to teach courses. The initial situation was frequently described as chaotic by those involved. There was no general consensus with respect to three central questions:

(1)   the form of schooling to be instituted,
(2)   the future direction which the political campaign for the school would take,
(3)   the particular groups of participants who would have authority to decide each of these questions.

Interpersonal conflicts broke out over issues within each of these three areas. To understand the basis of these conflicts it is necessary to understand something of the backgrounds which the activists brought with them into the school.

Immediately after the buildings take-over in July, Croxteth Comprehensive was placed under the control of a local organization called the Croxteth Community Action Committee. But many of the local participants in the daily life of the school were for various reasons not members of this organization and were called 'helpers' to distinguish them from members of the committee. Helpers were allowed to attend action committee meetings but had no voting rights. The committee itself had at any one time between twenty and thirty active members, not all of whom worked in the school on a regular basis. It had a charismatic chairman and secretary named Philip Knibb and Cyril D'Arcy respectively, and followed formal trade union procedures in its official decision-making. Although most members, as well as helpers, were women, men dominated the informal decision-making structure, with Philip Knibb personally enjoying the greatest amount of autonomy and decision-making power.

Most of the activists from Croxteth were unemployed at the time of the occupation and the majority of these had been so for over five years. Of those unemployed who were women, all were either single parents or had husbands who had been out of work for over five years. A few had part-time and/or temporary work during the occupation. The employment backgrounds of these participants, and their parents, were all the unskilled, semi-skilled, or skilled manual labour categories. With respect to education, virtually all of the local Croxteth activists had taken no examinations in secondary school. Six had attended Croxteth Comprehensive itself, one had gone to a grammar school, and the rest had attended other secondary modern schools and comprehensives.

During the year of occupation over 100 teacher volunteers came to help at Croxteth for some period of time, but most of these left after a short stay. Just under thirty teachers worked in the school for significantly long periods of time, and it was this group of long-term teachers which participated most in the decision-making procedures of the school and whose members found themselves taking sides in some of the conflicts to be described below. Twenty-seven of these teachers were intensively interviewed for this study and it is about them that the following regularities are noted.

While nearly all of the local activists were long-term residents of Croxteth with periods of residence varying from ten to thirty years, most of the teacher volunteers had grown up in areas outside of Liverpool altogether. Their socioeconomic backgrounds were primarily middle class, fifteen with parents in professional or semi-professional occupations. Others had been born into working-class families but had been upwardly mobile and had training and work experience in education. Four, however, *had* grown up in Croxteth itself and worked in the school as teachers of science, games and physical education (PE). They came to identify themselves primarily as teachers and usually took the teachers' side in those disputes which polarized roughly along teacher/parent lines.

Of the twenty-seven teachers interviewed, twenty-two had completed a BA degree or equivalent. Seven either had, or were working on, post-graduate degrees, and seven had taken teacher-training courses. Of eighteen asked about their experience of secondary education, twelve had attended grammar or public schools. Three of the four teachers from Croxteth had taken no examinations in secondary school, but their involvement during the occupation led all three to enrol for 'O' levels, and in one case eventually 'A' levels and then university, in the following years. Roughly one-third of the core teaching staff had previous training and/or work experience in education.

Frameworks for action and choice: the social wage versus community power

Now I will examine the subjective orientations held by these activists towards politics and schooling and note reasons for these orientations in their normal conditions of life. I will first give a very brief description of how these activists viewed the occupation of Croxteth Comprehensive *politically* and then, in the next section, *educationally*. Much more time will be given to the educational orientations held by the participants, in order to keep this chapter at an acceptable length, and many interesting aspects of their political orientations will have to be left out for lack of space. However, I hope to make it clear in the analysis that these political and educational orientations were linked.

The bulk of the teacher volunteers explained their involvement in the occupation through an ideological theme I shall term 'community power'. This subjective orientation is termed an 'ideological theme' because it was a cluster of values and assumptions which were discursively drawn upon by most of the teachers when offering explanations and justifications for their active support of the occupation (hence 'ideological'), and yet were used to support differing theories by different teachers (hence 'theme'). Thus while nearly all the teachers interviewed accounted for their involvement in the school as resulting from their belief that the assertion of grass-roots or 'community' power was to be valued in itself, some theorized this through the imagery of 'class struggle' and others simply as the stance of 'common people' (rather than working-class people) against government.

Regardless of how the community power theme was used to support personal theories, its values and many of its most immediate implications were shared by those who held to it. These activists agreed that the occupation of the school was at least potentially a positive step in itself, not just a defensive step, or a mere means for party-political goals – that it was a 'proactive', rather than a 'reactive' movement (Tilly, 1975). They agree that the injustice which had been committed in Croxteth was not just the fact that a school had been shut down, but was rooted in the lack of control the community had had over its school in the first place, even while it was officially there. Later in the first term, those who adhered to the community power theme were to argue politically for more community involvement in the school, and some even for an alteration of educational practices to make them consistent with the political nature of the occupation. They were opposed in these arguments by members of the community who wished only to get their state-run school back and who wished to emphasize a tight liaison with the Labour Party in order to do so.

The action committee also made use of the term 'community', especially in their statements to the media aimed to justify their illegal action, and their use of this term certainly drew upon many of the same associated values as those tied to the teachers' use of the term. But local activists rarely emphasized community *power* as the teachers did. Community 'rights' rather than power was their central concern. To most of them, the occupation was not an end in itself but rather a 'holding operation', as it was often to be called, to be continued until the state was forced into taking back its obligations to the community and providing it with a school. The ideology was markedly different, one which I shall term 'the social wage'.

The social wage theme was a way of justifying and interpreting the occupation which emphasized the duties and obligations of the state. It is a justification which could be described with one of Castell's categories of urban social movements, a form of 'trade union consumerism' (Castells, 1977; Castells, 1978). Implicit to this view is the client-administrator relationship inherent in most welfare services, which parallels in many respects the employer-employee relationship on the shop-floor. The purposes for which the activities of the shop-floor are organized are primarily the purposes of the employers, not the employees. The latter organize in unions in order to struggle over the conditions in which they work and the amount of pay they receive – they do not control the basic logic by which production quotas, type of product produced, etc., are determined. With respect to social movements over welfare services, those movements which fall into the category of trade union consumerism similarly don't challenge the actual nature and form of services, but rather the amounts and 'quality' (where state definitions of quality remain unchallenged) of services being supplied. The key relationships involved are not contested by these movements.

Both the community power and the social wage themes were frequently theoretical objects of the participants themselves. This meant that, unlike features of 'common sense' which are so taken-for-granted that serious alternatives are invisible to those drawing upon them, the proponents of the community power and social wage themes were able to articulate and argue for their points of view in full realization that competing perspectives existed. Hence these two themes were subjective conditions of action existing at high levels of discursivity (Giddens, 1979), and thus amenable to debate and alterations over time. Their high level of discursivity was in stark contrast to many of the conditions which will be discussed below, conditions which fell more within the deeper realms of 'common sense' and which thus exerted their influences in less visible or controllable ways.

Knowledge, control and jobs: attitudes towards schooling of the community volunteers

On the whole, the community volunteers began their occupation of the school with a basically unquestioning attitude towards schooling. They desired their school to be restored to them, and their children to attend it, and they did not really question what went on inside of it. They had their own 'black box' theory of educational equality (Karabel and Halsey, 1977) – a theory which emphasizes the equal *provision* of schools and does not examine the inequalities which may be perpetrated *within* them. This was, of course, consistent with their social wage orientation to politics. Moreover, the residents felt themselves *unqualified* to criticize or comment on schooling. Virtually all of them, as shown above, had been school-leavers, had gained no formal qualifications, and this caused most of them to regard themselves as incompetent to criticize schooling or to have any say in the curricular and pedagogic policy of Croxteth Comprehensive. When the teacher volunteers first arrived, the community volunteers insisted on deferring to them on all questions of actual educational practice.

While noting this perhaps unsurprising attitude of the community volunteers it is important to bear in mind their memories of what schooling had been like when they were pupils themselves. Most of them were prepared to tell a number of personal stories which illustrated a generally unpleasant experience during their school years. Since memories and stories are related not only to actual events in the past but also to presently held frameworks which place patterns of selection and emphasis upon past events, it is important to consider these stories of the past for what they can tell us of the present. In this case the interest is in how an unquestioning attitude towards schooling could coexist with negative personal memories of being in school. By examining the situation it is possible to assemble various elements of the subjective attitudes held by the Croxteth activists towards education into a sort of model of the interpretative framework these activists possessed.

Croxteth volunteers conjoined negative memories of school with present attitudes towards education in several ways. One was to identify inadequacies in their youthful understanding of the purpose of schooling, their personal failure to see how schooling could help them. This almost always revolved around the theme of employability. The reason schooling should be taken seriously is that it is something which can help one get jobs. The following comment from Margaret Gaskell, a local activist with two children in the school, illustrates her negative memories of school given alongside regrets that she had not understood the importance of a qualification for getting a job.

> I didn't really take it seriously. I'm sorry now I didn't, really. I didn't do any examinations. I did hate the school. I thought when you left school you'd just go and get a job and if you didn't like that job you could just change it, go from one job to another.

Margaret had regrets that she had not taken school very seriously because this had limited her chances in life. Her comments were not untypical.

Many community volunteers noted that schooling was important for getting jobs, especially in the 1980s when qualifications are being demanded for more types of jobs than was the case when they were themselves pupils. In so far as this explanation of the usefulness of an education almost never included things like personal growth, critical awareness, 'broadening' and the like, it is another ideological theme – one labelled with the shorthand of 'employability' here. A major purpose of schooling was seen to be to make youth employable. Not to realize the importance of this feature of schooling was seen as a personal failing.

Another way in which local activists recalled their previous dislike of school and yet affirmed its importance uncritically was provided by many of the males. Many of them affirmed their previous dislike of schooling and their corresponding involvement in resistance activities with some pride. They retained positive memories of their own resistance activities in school, but did not interpret these previous activities in a way which found any fault with the schooling process. For example, kitchen helper Marty McArdle had been expelled from three schools for hitting teachers. PE teacher and former Croxteth resident Mick Checkland had played truant and got drunk 'as much as I possibly could'. George Knibb, a brother of action committee chair Philip Knibb who worked in the school corridors, noted:

> We used to do the same as this lot, Phil. I mean we would take our books and work and tear it up and hide it in a hole in the floor. The teacher would go the whole year without knowing. So I can understand them [the 'lads' of the occupation].

But George, Marty, and others who reported either unpleasant experiences in school or their involvement in resistance activities (or both), did not initially question the validity of traditional teaching, neither in terms of content, nor assessment, nor teacher-pupil authority relationships. Their own negative experiences in school were not the basis, at first, of any critique of school practice. On the contrary, the very experience of 'failing' at school, of not taking the examinations, helped to solidify the unquestioning attitude of these volunteers to the competence of those who had not failed. There were several reasons for this, one being the lack of an articulated critique of schooling within their own culture or, indeed, within the Labour Movement itself.

The most fundamental reason, however, that local residents had not developed critical attitudes to traditional schooling from their personal experiences of it, is that these experiences had been absorbed and interpreted in conjunction with two features of their local culture: (1) a particular view of school knowledge and, (2) the customary pattern of adult-youth authority relationships on the estate. I will look more closely at each of these.

School knowledge is traditionally presented in a way which makes it appear as something external to daily life. It is seen as something to be possessed, rather than continuously produced. Its value lies in its marketability for jobs, as 'commodity knowledge' (Whitty and Young, 1976; Apple, 1982). School knowledge was seen by most of the volunteers during the occupation as a desirable acquisition, desirable because it can help one to get jobs. It was not seen as something which was related to the considerable knowledge required and used in daily life, even in this situation of social disruption, where a group of people were carrying out a campaign which required significant amounts of new knowledge and processes of learning. School knowledge did not have value as something which could enrich an individual, alter identities, or serve to promote social change, it was rather something which could at best be acquired as a possession to increase employability.

Corresponding to this view of school knowledge was an acceptance of certain authority relations which went with it. Some people had school knowledge and some people did not have it. Those who had it were believed to be entitled to a certain amount of authority, in some realms of life, over those who didn't have it. For example, the local activists having no qualifications did not feel they had the competence or the authority to question schooling practice:

> Actual standards of teaching are not up to me to criticize, 'cause I don't think I can. I can't say that the kids are doing the right work or the wrong work 'cause I've got no, I don't know, CSEs or 'O' levels meself, I'm just ordinary . . . So actually as criticizing educational standards, I couldn't do it. And I don't think there's anyone else in the school that can, on the action committee. The only thing we can criticize is the handling of the kids. I don't think we can criticize anyone on work standards, I don't think we have the authority to. (George Knibb)

This passage is pregnant with meanings, meanings which were expressed by nearly all the community volunteers talking about schools. George uses the term 'standards', not suggested to him by the interviewer. 'Standards' is a term which we often come across in policy statements, media presentations and professional articles about education. It is itself a product of the education system: a view of schooling which suggests that very clear objective criteria exist by which schooling practice can be judged and assessed (just as the transmission of school knowledge can be assessed with examinations). It implies that only those qualified can make judgements about standards or even know what they are (like teachers, examination boards, and now the Department of Education and Science). George calls himself 'ordinary' in this passage. Those who have school knowledge are not ordinary, those who do not have it are. A distinction is created based on possession of qualifications which has authority implications. George himself uses the term 'authority'. The experience of being a school-leaver is an experience which disqualifies one, subjectively, from criticizing educational practice. School-leavers are 'ordinary', 'thick', or 'slow' – terms which many volunteers used to describe themselves, and terms which point back to a particular view of school knowledge, tightly related to the way in which school knowledge is organized and presented.

This view of school knowledge is one more of our ideological themes, called 'reified knowledge' here. It is a view of knowledge as something external which can be possessed and which is not in an obvious relationship to the sorts of knowledge all people master in conducting their daily lives. This latter type of knowledge is rarely called 'knowledge'. Several things work together to produce the reified view of knowledge. One pertains to the cultural form of school knowledge, which many sociologists of education have noted to be fairly class specific (eg. Bernstein, 1977; Bourdieu, 1973). Thus, when a disjunction exists between home cultures and school cultures, the latter will appear more foreign and 'thing-like' – more separate from the forms of knowledge used outside of school in conducting everyday affairs of life.

However, other and possibly more determining factors help to generate a reified view of knowledge which has nothing to do with the cultural form of the knowledge *per se*. It must be stressed that what is meant by 'reified knowledge' here is an *orientation*, not anything intrinsic to the knowledge itself even though cultural disjunctions between home and school help to produce this orientation (as argued below, middle-class volunteers in Croxteth also had a reified view of knowledge even though they were fairly fluent with it). The first of these determining factors is the process of certification mentioned above – getting qualifications which immediately translate into opportunities on the occupational structure of society. Because an examination pass is a 'thing' which serves as currency on the job market, the knowledge which it represents is easily viewed instrumentally – a possession which can be cashed in for jobs. The second of these determining factors concerns the *advantages* gained by those who take an instrumental orientation to knowledge. For the working class, the view that knowledge is a possession useful mainly for getting jobs may be a form of resistance to a schooling situation which is difficult because of the cultural disjunctions of community and school mentioned above. It may be a way of retaining cultural identity by distancing oneself from the values and general culture of the school, since identifying too closely with these may undermine local cultural modes of attaining dignity (Hargreaves, 1982). For complex reasons, clarified partially in passages below, entering too intimately into the middle-class culture of the school was viewed by many as an effort to be 'posh', which incurred various informal sanctions in the community.

In the quotation above, George Knibb also mentions the one area in which he does feel competent to make judgements about what is occurring in the school: 'the handling of the kids', the state of discipline in the school. He is correct in speaking for all the community volunteers on this; they did, as a group, feel competent to make judgements on how teachers were handling pupils and were in fact very critical of how it was being done. The feeling of competence with respect to judging teacher-pupil relationships is related to the second cultural factor which mediated the negative experience of secondary schooling reported by most of the activists: adult-youth authority relationships.

Adult-youth authority relationships in Croxteth involve a style of interaction in which rough language, and sometimes rough physical actions, are often skilfully combined with humour and affection as well as disapproval. Adults in Croxteth have to negotiate and maintain their authority over youth, who frequently challenge it. Thus it was not seen as unusual but was rather to a certain extent *expected* that pupils would be disruptive, would challenge authority whether in school or outside of it. When George Knibb, Mick Checkland, Marty McArdle and others from Croxteth were themselves pupils, they were very much 'lads'. They challenged school authority frequently. But they did not interpret this in a way which could have led to a critique of school authority. They did not like school, just as they did not like other situations in which authority was exercised over them. But this dislike, displayed in disruptive and defiant activity, was expected cultural behaviour, especially expected of youth. The existence of authority was accepted as given and the way in which they had resisted it as pupils was a way in which youth were expected to act. Hence when these individuals crossed the cultural line between youth and adult, they looked upon their past behaviour as behaviour typical of youth. As adults they could understand pupils carrying out the same sorts of disruptive activities, but they opposed it just the same in their role as adults.

Teacher-pupil relationships in Croxteth Comprehensive before the occupation were reported to have been 'strict', 'firm' and yet caring by community volunteers, former pupils and ex-staff. As George Smith, the former headteacher, put it, 'If they [pupils] step out of line, God help them.' And the cane was used regularly in Croxteth before the occupation. Although some former pupils like Mick Checkland and Marty McArdle explicitly stated their dislike of this type of authority, it was a style of teacher-pupil relationship which worked in Croxteth because it was in harmony with the adult-youth relationships on the estate. The two reinforced each other. This was more than a matter of homology or correspondence: the school actually bolstered efforts of parents to extend authority over youth (a reinforcement of practice). The challenge of youth in Croxteth to adult authority is not always successfully contained within the cultural style of interaction. There was a high rate of vandalism and, now, of drug usage. Parental fears for the welfare of children translate quickly into demands for discipline.

Another ideological theme emerges here: the imposition of authority in school is a goal in itself, not just a means to teaching. There is much evidence to suggest that this view was held by many adults, both among community volunteers and the parents who sent their children to the school. In a number of incidents, parents actually took pupils out of Croxteth Comprehensive and sent them to other schools, explicitly *not* due to any worry about how much they were *learning*, but because they feared that their sons or daughters were not being disciplined enough. Discipline was not a mere means to learning, but a goal in itself.

In the beginning, examinations, like other features of schooling, were not questioned by the community volunteers. They were part of schooling, for teachers, not parents, to make decisions about. Examination results were a way of getting jobs, valuable for those who could get them. This uncritical attitude towards examinations changed for some of the volunteers as the year went on and the plight of the non-examination pupils became more visible to them (Carspecken, 1985; Carspecken, 1989), but initially the educational value of examinations was not in question.

Added to this was the strategic value, for the campaign, of introducing examinations into the school. They legitimized the occupation to parents sending their children to the school, and it served as a weapon in the media battles. Occupied Croxteth Comprehensive was virtually forced into competition with other schools over examination results. In these circumstances it seemed impractical not to offer examinations. But the community volunteers did not reluctantly concede to necessity in this case; they did not question examinations initially at all. This was in contrast, as discussed later, to some of the teachers.

In summary, I have analysed a number of attitudes of the community volunteers to education. They took examinations for granted, had a view of school knowledge which I have called reified, and which formed the basis for their view of teacher authority. They believed that education served two principal purposes: to increase employability and to discipline and control pupils. I have suggested some explanations of these views. The community activists' own experience of schooling made them feel unqualified to criticize school practice and to challenge the authority of those who had succeeded in school. There were good reasons to worry about the discipline of youth on the Croxteth estate and the approved form of school discipline corresponded in style to adult-youth relationships in the local culture. In addition, there were no clearly expressed or widely available alternatives in the residents' culture, nor in the culture of the Labour

Movement generally, to form the basis of a different form of examination or schooling. Finally, it is obvious that this unquestioning attitude towards schooling practice was consistent with the political orientation of the social wage.

The subjective structure of this cluster of orientations can be represented by a chain of reinforcing themes, one supporting the other:

ADULT-YOUTH AUTHORITY RELATIONSHIPS IN CROX-TETH / SCHOOLING FOR DISCIPLINE AND CONTROL / SCHOOL AUTHORITY / REIFIED SCHOOL KNOWLEDGE / EXAMINATIONS / CLASS RELATIONSHIPS (via cultural disjunctions between home and school cultures of knowledge) / SOCIAL WAGE.

Examinations and progressivism

The teaching staff displayed more diversity of opinion on educational issues than the community volunteers. However, teachers did not have the time or the materials during the early months of the occupation to work out an alternative curriculum, although many wanted to. Most relied upon their own memories of what had happened when they were in secondary school and on available textbooks and standard syllabuses to plan their lessons and organize their classroom practice.

Even if enough time *had* existed to develop an alternative curriculum it is by no means clear what forms would have been proposed. Examinations, for example, played a major role in the attitudes of teachers towards the curriculum. Teachers agreed that they were important and must be offered, for much the same reasons as the community volunteers. They legitimated the occupation in the eyes of the public and helped to retain the trust of parents.

A minority of teachers wished the situation could be otherwise. An interesting contrast exists between the data collected in the field notebooks on ongoing events in the school and the responses given by teachers in interviews on the question of examinations. In the field notebooks, there is virtually no significant record of any discussion of examinations, though stormy debates took place frequently on many other issues. It was a matter of course that examinations were a major educational goal of the school. In the taped interviews, however, a number of teachers claimed that they were very much opposed to examinations in principle. Their failure to emphasize this at staff meetings no doubt came from their perceptions of the enormous constraints which existed for developing a non-examination-based curriculum. Drama teacher Graz Monvid expressed their view as follows:

> Then the decision was made that in order to prove the school's worth we had to totally orientate it towards examination results – our first step towards lunacy. Trying to carry that led to the point where kids were being expelled. Smaller and smaller numbers of kids were there because you have to exclude the ones who won't conform to what you've decided is the aim of the occupation: examination results. More and more of the teachers, as far as I could see, spent their time mainly with kids who wanted them [examinations]. The others, as in traditional parts of the education system, were being forced out.

Graz's observations were to a large extent correct. Once examinations were accepted as a goal of the school, the use of a traditional, academic curriculum was strongly reinforced. Although traditional curricular practice became adopted in the school primarily for reasons of time constraints, examinations firmly entrenched its usage. As long as the major currency for the job market remains examination results, no single school can ignore them, even if it is known that only a small minority of the school's population has any chance of passing them. And examinations meant a curriculum based on standard syllabuses.

The need to teach a standard syllabus adequately to those Croxteth pupils who seemed motivated and able to pass the examinations led directly to the use of streaming, which became especially marked in the fourth and fifth years (Carspecken, 1985). The most experienced and dependable teachers became allocated to the higher-streamed classes so that the chances of these pupils in their examinations would not be jeopardized.

Several 'sink' classes, lower-stream classes with a high incidence of disruption, formed in consequence. The sink classes were non-examination or CSE groups who could not be consistently taught because of a shortage of teachers during the first few months. They were exposed to a high turnover of the least experienced volunteers, who taught them watered-down versions of the examination syllabuses for lack of alternative materials and ideas. During the first term especially, many of these teachers left after short periods of time, finding the 'B' classes, as they were called, too difficult to teach.

Graz Monvid and several other teachers believed that an alternative curriculum could have solved these problems, one which captured the interest of the pupils and which had more relevance to their lives. In the second term, alternative projects were tried out on two of the 'B' groups. These projects included photographic studies of the local community and some contrasting, more affluent areas of Liverpool, and they did capture the interest of many of these pupils for some time. They also had the merit of attracting a few adults from the community – producing a mixed-age learning group. Yet because these students were clearly labelled 'B' and because these projects did not lead to any examinations, the pupils involved felt themselves viewed as second-rate and openly resented it. This resentment minimized the positive effects of these projects (see Carspecken, 1989). Graz's point was that the examination system prevented the occupation from developing a truly flexible curriculum, because its immediate impact was rigidly to categorize and rank forms of knowledge.

Most teachers, meanwhile, expressed either moderate or enthusiastic support of examinations. Some tended literally to equate successful education with passing examination. Others argued, and the argument is not an invalid one, that examinations allow pupils from deprived areas to rise above the stigmas of their local schools by proving themselves on nationally competitive tests. But the counter-point made by teachers like Graz was that very few pupils in a school like Croxteth can actually pass examinations, largely due to differences between home and school culture – most do not even try them, or do poorly on them. Meanwhile making examinations a goal of the school reinforced the problems mentioned by Graz, creating sink classes and increasing disruption.

More moderate teachers were less quick to associate 'good schooling' with work towards examinations, but most of these felt they were an important part of what schools do. They recognized the problems which streaming introduced and were aware that Croxteth pupils tended not to pass examinations. The most frequent explanation they offered was a discrepancy between the pupils' 'actual ability' and their self-confidence and/or work habits. Many saw the examination question in terms of 'potential' versus 'self-image', rather than in terms of cultural disjunctions between deprived communities and school culture (Hargreaves, 1982). 'There is a certain false mystique about these exams, most of these kids could pass them' was a comment made at one staff meeting, expressing a not uncommon view.

Here we find a familiar ideological theme but in a new context – 'reified knowledge'. Teachers tended on the whole to miss the connections which exist between knowledge and lived culture and the relationships between the form and content of school knowledge and its transmittability to children from various cultural groups. Teachers tended to think that the same knowledge in the same form and taught pretty much in the same way could be transmitted to children of any cultural group as long as the barriers of self-image and attitude were breached.

Lest this be viewed as an argument for a separate curriculum for the working class, let me stress the point that 'reified' refers to an orientation to knowledge, not to the content of knowledge itself. Within Croxteth a number of students excelled in traditional, academic work (see Carspecken,

1989), and it was important that the school provided them with this opportunity. But the examination system made it hard to respond to the needs, interests, cultural styles and capabilities of other students. Reification takes a limited form of knowledge, identifies it with examination skills, and fixes it – as 'knowledge' as such. A non-reified orientation to knowledge is more open and flexible: knowledge is seen as a social product which changes continuously and reflects the socially influenced orientations of those who produce it. This implies a flexible assessment procedure, so that the ranking of different orientations to knowledge may be lessened.

Of course one might point out that Mode III examinations allow for a great variety in what is tested and how the testing is done. This is true and Mode IIIs could well be a good assessment model which would allow for educational orientations more 'organic' to the working class and other cultural groups (Connell *et al.*, 1982). But Mode IIIs were never discussed during the Croxteth occupation. The volunteers were unfamiliar with them; the need for them, as the above paragraphs have argued, was not recognized.

Teachers too tended to stress employability, but would often mention other purposes of education as well, such as the development of 'personality' and 'character'. Employability was used as an argument against the persistent objections of *pupils* against school work as such. It was not uncommon to hear teachers arguing with resistant students with statements like the following, uttered here by a frustrated chemistry teacher: 'When you get out of here into that jungle out there you're going to wish you had qualifications!' Amongst themselves, however, many teachers also stated their belief that pupils in occupied Croxteth Comprehensive were learning 'special' things just from the atmosphere and the unique political situation of the school. These 'lessons' were never specified very clearly, nor directly taught, but were held to be learned in the school all the same. Indeed, teachers often said that these lessons were possibly more important than academic knowledge. Such statements appeared to be made primarily in order to justify continuing the school under its difficult conditions – conditions which possibly lowered the quality of classroom practice in the occupied school according to traditional criteria – and also to justify their own teaching practices when many did, in fact, doubt the usefulness of what they taught.

The realm in which teachers *did* attempt to introduce innovations in the school was that of authority relationships. When the teachers first arrived they introduced themselves to pupils by their first names, attempting to establish warm and friendly relationships with them. They also dressed informally and insisted, over the objections of many local residents, on banning the cane as a form of punishment. Teachers attempted to give pupils power in school decision-making processes by having a school council with representation on the staff and action committee (to which the action committee agreed).

The relevant ideological theme drawn upon here was 'progressivism', but a progressivism largely limited to the form of authority relationships and not encompassing other features of schooling. Teachers soon found, however, that Croxteth pupils were extremely difficult to contain with such informal authority relationships. Pupils liked their new teachers and supported the political campaign to save Croxteth Comprehensive, but resisted classroom activities strongly and all the more successfully for the lack of coercive sanctions which they were used to both in school and at home. Teachers soon found it impossible not to employ various coercive methods but even then discovered that they were not very skilful in their use. Meanwhile, the student council, and student representation on the action committee, failed to win lasting enthusiasm from pupils and were both dropped within a matter of months.

To summarize this section, teachers differed from the community activists in their advocacy of informal pupil-teacher relationships and some of them were more critical of traditional methods of assessment. But on the whole they subscribed to traditional educational practice and had their own versions of a reified view of school knowledge. They saw an important purpose of education to be making pupils employable but mentioned other, less tangible purposes of education as well.

In looking at relationships between the practices, and between the conditions of practice, of the teachers, we find more relations of tension than of reinforcement. A traditional curriculum has been shown to be in tension with informal teacher-pupil relationships by other sociologists of education. Bernstein (1977), for example, predicts that strong classification (knowledge presented in a sharply defined and categorized form) accompanied by weak framing (classroom activities not subject to a highly visible teacher authority) will produce a tendency to move towards strong framing. This did occur to a certain extent in the school with teachers increasingly making use of coercive sanctions to curb disruption, sanctions such as writing lines, detention after school, suspensions and expulsions, and the creation of a discipline room where disruptive pupils were sent during the day. But this tension was resolved in more complex ways involving the intervention of local adults. Though the implementation of examinations and a traditional curriculum was largely due to constraints of time, materials and the lack of an alternative, it was reinforced by the view of school knowledge held by teachers. This chain of reinforcing relationships between practices and ideological themes was in tension with the themes of community power and progressivism held by the teachers:

REIFIED KNOWLEDGE		PROGRESSIVISM
TRADITIONAL CURRICULUM	*versus*	COMMUNITY
EXAMINATIONS		POWER

So teachers drew upon subjective orientations which polarized into two mutually antagonistic clusters: while a reified view of knowledge reinforced and was reinforced by the adaptation of a traditional curriculum along examination syllabus lines, it existed in implicit conflict with the values of progressivism and community power held by the teachers. The progressivist theme was used by teachers initially to establish informal relationships with their pupils, but as shown above, this produced problems as soon as a traditional curriculum was introduced. The community power theme, moreover, was used by teachers to emphasize, among other things, the value of the school occupation in itself – the fact that parents now 'controlled' their own school was deemed a positive end in its own right. However, the use of examinations and the stress on academic forms of knowledge helped to keep parents away from the schooling practices of most impact on their children.

Unlike the community activists' orientations, those of the teachers were implicated primarily in face-to-face encounters occurring in the school, in processes of social integration. They were not tightly connected to systems of practice that linked the school and other social sites, at least not in the same way or to the same degree that attitudes of the local residents were. Local residents' orientations linked home and school, and the cultural past (being a pupil) and cultural present (being an adult); teachers' orientations were connected only to their own previous success in schooling and examinations, and to the investments they had made earlier in traditional forms of education which had yielded certain pay-offs. The teachers' orientations, in other words, were related to their middle-class backgrounds and tied to very broad systems of practice which did not involve the Croxteth community in an immediate way.

Before starting the next section it should be noted that the subjective orientations held by both teachers and Croxteth activists towards education never became clear theoretical objects but rather existed on tacit or what I will call 'under-articulated' levels. Tacit conditions included reified knowledge for nearly all participants, age relations in Croxteth, and schooling for employability. These orientations informed discourse and practice without themselves becoming objects of discourse. They were largely uncontested conditions as well, shared by most of those involved. Progressivism and schooling for discipline and control, on the other hand, were in tension with each other, generated conflicts as a consequence, and so led to some articulation of each orientation since conflict requires verbal justifications. Yet neither of these orientations was ever given a very clear articulation and thus no theoretical *positions* were formulated about which sides could form in the disputes. These orientations were therefore 'under-articulated'.

A dual system of authority: reconstituting conditions of action in Croxteth School

There was a complete clash really with mainly middle-class teachers coming in with certain views of how, if it were an independent school, different methods of education could be carried out. For instance, right at the beginning it was decided there wouldn't be caning. But we had no tradition to draw upon. We were trying to devise completely different social norms which the kids weren't used to. (Graz Monvid, drama teacher)

Tables 9.1 and 9.2 summarize the orientations discussed in the last sections.

Interpersonal conflicts took place in the occupied school, especially during the first few months of the occupation, as a result of tensions between orientations held by the activists. The conflicts were manifested in two main areas: campaign strategy and the form of schooling. Underlying these conflicts were the differences of orientation we have already examined: the social wage versus community power, in the case of disputes over campaign policy; progressivism versus schooling for discipline and control, in the case of the educational disputes.

These disputes and the way in which they were resolved were conditioned by two factors: by the degree to which the orientations in question were articulated in discourse, and the degree to which the subjective structures involved were self-reinforcing or, alternatively, in tension. The social wage and community power themes were highly articulated orientations, increasingly articulated as the school year progressed, so the resolution of conflicts based on them *had to make considerations of legitimate decision-making power a central concern*. Unfortunately, this first set of conflicts can not be described in this chapter for want of space (they are discussed in Carspecken, 1989).

The conflicts arising from the tension between progressivism and schooling for discipline and control, on the other hand, were not articulated into explicit and competing positions which could be resolved through a decision-making process. Their tacit and under-articulated nature meant that they could be resolved in practice, through a set of 'compromise routines' if you like, while verbal disputes based on them continued throughout the year. Moreover, they were conflicts over what form participants thought routines *ought* to take when these routines were already in the actual process of forming. The principal conflict which will be considered in this section was over the nature of teacher-pupil authority relationships. Since teacher-pupil relationships began to be established as soon as teachers and pupils met together, discursive conflicts over the form they took were very much a retrospective affair – taking either the form of

Table 9.1 *Subjective orientations of community activists and teacher volunteers concerning politics and education*

	community volunteers	teachers
justification of involvement	Community deprivation implies demand for state provision (social wage).	Community deprivation implies demand for community control (community power).
attitudes on education	Knowledge reified and basis for authority of educationists. Examinations important.	Knowledge reified but transmittable to any group (cultural deprivation). Examinations important and/or inevitable.
	Schooling for discipline and control of pupils.	Informal teacher–pupil relationships desirable, (progressivism).
	Schooling for employability.	Schooling for employability and intangible goals.

Table 9.2 *Conditions of action and their degree of articulation*

conditions of action	degree of articulation
age relations in Croxteth	Not articulated for community volunteers and teachers; uncontested and not in discursive formulation.
traditional curriculum/reified knowledge/examinations	Not articulated for most community activists and teachers; uncontested and not in discursive formulation. Where articulated and contested by minority, no articulated alternative.
schooling for employability	Not articulated for both groups. Uncontested. No clear alternatives.
schooling for discipline control	Under-articulated for community volunteers. Contested by teachers. Alternative partially formulated.
'progressivism' (informal teacher-pupil relationships)	Discursive and contested. Held by many teachers, opposed by many community activists.
community power	Discursive and contested. Held by teachers, opposed by community activists.
'social wage'	Discursive and contested. Held by many community activists.

justifying what routines had already been established or the form of urging a change in what had already been established.

Right from the first day of school in September, community volunteers began to criticize volunteer teachers over the way in which children were being handled. Many at first believed that it was a mistake not to use physical punishments like the cane and blamed the prevalent discipline problems in the school on this. For example, Cyril D'Arcy, the secretary of the action committee, once commented: 'I don't see why the cane isn't used. I found a kid vandalizing a door and I cuffed him around the ears. It worked, and the kids don't think anything of it. *Something* has to be done!' In other incidents criticism of teachers for not using physical punishments was more direct. Yola Jacobson, a history graduate who had come from Edinburgh to volunteer her time in the school, was having trouble with the daughter of one of the Croxteth helpers, Tommy, who worked in the school every day:

> She [the pupil] was just giving me hell in a class, just not doing any work, so I asked her to leave the room. Later I said to Tommy, 'Look I'm worried about Annette, she's not doing work, she's being a nuisance.' He said, 'Well, you've got two hands, clip her.' I said, 'No, I don't hit kids.' He said, 'I give you permission, you keep control! If you've got two hands why can't you just whack them? You call yourself a teacher?!'

There were a number of similar incidents involving other teachers, pupils and local residents. Local residents saw most of the teacher volunteers as 'soft' and thus as not 'proper teachers'.

Many local activists also stressed the need for teachers to maintain traditional indicators of superior status with proper dress and with the insistence that pupils address teachers with 'Sir' or 'Miss'. The teachers, on their side, invited the pupils to call them by their first names, a fatal error in the eyes of a majority of the local people.

These criticisms from the helpers and the action committee caused resentment in many teachers. Chris Hawes, the first teacher co-ordinator, called the expectations of the local activists 'cruel'. Other teachers expressed disgust at what they took to be old-fashioned and barbaric methods of discipline, advocated by the local activists. Many teachers noted something like a dilemma in the situation:

> We had parents in the classrooms or helpers who'd be screaming at the kids and dragging them out by the hair, thinking they were helping! But in fact they *were* helping. In fact I can remember fleeing from a class when my helper didn't turn up. They thought I could control the class and didn't need a helper. I thought it was deliberate sabotage at the time. There were real problems. (Graz Monvid)

Yet the community volunteers, much as the pupils, also frequently praised the warmth of the relationships between teachers and pupils. Pupils often stated they liked these teachers better. As fourth-year Steven put it: 'Some of them care about you, a lot of them do!' None of those interviewed seemed to see any contradiction between their appreciation of the warm relations and their criticism of the poor discipline.

So during the first term an informal, dual, authority system took shape in the school. Parents constantly disciplined pupils by giving them a good scolding, often mixed with threats of physical punishment. But usually this sort of discipline was carried out with the assumed authority of the teachers in the background. The most common way the community volunteers disciplined pupils was to scold them severely (a 'good rollicking' as Mick Checkland expressed it) and then take them over to a teacher for the 'real' punishment).

The irony in this situation was that it was the methods used by the local activists, not the teachers, which were most effective in keeping control. The pupils clearly recognized this fact: 'Without the parents this school would be torn apart,' one of them said. But the community volunteers, despite their awareness of their superior abilities, would consistently refer back to the authority of the teachers when carrying out their own castigations of pupils. Local activists used adult-youth forms of authority from their culture, not just to discipline pupils, but to try to force pupils to defer to *school* authority. 'That's no way to talk to your teacher!' could often be heard during a scolding session. 'I'm going to take you to see your teacher!' and so on.

This usage of adult-youth authority relations to bolster traditional relations of school authority (and this usage of school authority to justify local methods of control in the occupied school) did not always work so directly. There are several incidents recorded in the field notebooks in which community volunteers administered their own punishments on pupils, which were effective because they agreed not to tell any of the teachers about it. During the first half-term, for example, some pupils broke into the chemistry room and stole a number of laboratory materials. Two community volunteers discovered who the thieves were and steps were taken by these two to get the items back and admonish the offenders. Yet, at a joint teacher-parent meeting held after the incident, these two helpers refused to reveal the names of those who had been involved. 'We can't break confidence,' one explained. This was crucial to the form of discipline these community volunteers could hold over the pupils within the school. They would have been seen as 'grassing' if they'd given the names. 'Grassing' is something which has meaning only in a 'them-us' situation. The pupils saw the teachers as 'them' and the community volunteers, or at least some of them, as part of 'us', even though they were still seen as adults in opposition to their own status as youth. Many other incidents of this nature occurred during the course of the year.

What is noteworthy about these incidents is that, first of all, pupils were more successfully disciplined by community volunteers when it came to face-to-face confrontations. Yet, secondly, the *form* in which many of these successful confrontations took place referred back to what was really a symbolic, and greater, authority which was not the teachers, but what the teachers represented: school authority. Pupils responded well to promises not to break confidence, because their misbehaviour was often a resistance to the symbolic authority of the school. Not breaking confidence meant that the resistance had still in some ways succeeded, and the pupils could feel, even when punished by a community volunteer, that they and the community volunteer were in some ways on the same side. Order was maintained in this way, disruptions were controlled and thus school authority prevailed under the prop of adult-youth authority relations drawn from the culture of Croxteth.

As time went on during the occupation, certain figures from the Croxteth community took on more visible roles as disciplinarians in the school. George Knibb in particular began to handle many of the discipline problems which came up. He stood in the corridors every day to make sure pupils went to their classes between periods, and he was approached by many of the pupils themselves over disciplinary matters. George began to think of himself, only partially in jest, as 'headmaster'. He was very confident that he could handle the kids better than any other adult in the school, including the various figures on the staff who temporarily occupied highly visible positions, such as myself, and including his brother Phil, the action committee chair. Yet he still held himself below the status of a teacher, a 'proper teacher', even if he believed that no teacher in the school was really competent to fill that status either. The following lengthy quotation illustrates both his self-confidence in matters of discipline and his simultaneous insistence that he was not a teacher but was rather 'just ordinary'. The passage also illustrates the style of adult-youth authority relations in Croxteth, its physically aggressive referents which served more to win the consensus of pupils than to frighten them:

I try to talk to kids as they talk to themselves. I mean, in words that they use like, if they want someone to go away, they'll say 'Do one!' you know, or 'Turn it in!' I mean if they think somebody's snitched on them, they'll say 'He's a grass', you know. So if you talk to kids in their language, you get more response out of them. I'm not saying that's the right language to talk to them in, but I mean just for the time being if a certain situation explodes and it needs quieting down there and then. If you walk into a class and say, 'Now look kids!', like a lot of teachers do in this school, and it's not the teachers' fault, the teachers don't come from this area so they don't know the kids' language . . . And you've got to bring them down in the class and let the class see that you can stop any of them, no matter if it's a 16-year-old who is 6 foot 6 which we've got in this school, who's twice as big as me. But I'll walk up to him and I'll tell him, you know, that if he wants to walk outside I'll go outside and I'll knock his head off. But I would never hit a kid, but they think I would. And then when you get hold of them and you sort the situation out and start talking to them, then, you find out you've got

their respect. 'Cause I think I know why I've got the respect of the kids
. . . I mean, I won't allow them to call me 'sir', I mean I won't allow
them to because I'm just an ordinary, well, local person myself. So, if I
go walking around the streets of Croxteth . . . and I hear kids call,
'Hello sir', you know though the people I'm with know I'm doing a
decent job in the school, but you know I make sure they call me George.

This quotation refers to a complexity of things, three of which particularly
stand out. It begins with George's emphasis on the importance of knowing
the kids' language – winning authority over them through their own
cultural terms. But as George himself says a little later, these terms are not
simply of the youth culture: they are of the culture of Croxteth generally,
and the confrontative style in which George uses them is not a style limited
to the youth culture. It is a style which I have already described as
characteristic of Croxteth adult-youth relations (and partially of Croxteth
adult-adult relations) generally. George next describes this confrontative
style: his skill at communicating a readiness to come to physical blows if
necessary. George, it must be kept in mind, was better than most
community volunteers at disciplining pupils and part of the reason was his
ability to combine features of the youth culture with features of Croxteth
adult-youth authority relations in a skilful way. Finally George says he
refuses to allow pupils to call him 'sir' and stresses that this is one of the
main ways in which he has won their respect. George was drawing upon
the *identity* which was most acceptable for him, according to his interpretative scheme. He avoided putting himself into a position of directly
representing school authority, and thus he was perceived as united with the
pupils in some ways against that authority. He could be perceived by the
pupils as in some ways being 'one of us', where 'us' was defined against
school authority relations. This perception of unity worked even though
George's adult status differentiated him from the pupils, and even though
he used the authority ascribed to the Croxteth adult to try to get pupils to
defer to the school authority they actively opposed! In Croxteth, the
difference between being a pupil and being an adult is less fundamental
than the difference between being a pupil and being a teacher. In this
passage George defines himself as being 'just ordinary', i.e. as *not* being a
teacher, and he feels he earns respect in this way. He insists that pupils call
him 'George' rather than Mr Knibb, again allowing pupils to see him as
one of 'us' against the authority of the school. The roles and standards of
behaviour prescribed by the culture of Croxteth to differentiate between
adult and youth were less of a division than those indicated by the expected
behaviour of teachers and pupils.

George's practice of not allowing children to call him 'sir' or to consider
him a real representative of school authority was widespread in the school.
Many other volunteers from Croxteth took on activities within the school

which overlapped with activities expected of teachers, and they also insisted that pupils refrain from using the linguistic forms which would have ascribed school authority to them. Although the community volunteers were for the most part critical of the teachers in the school when it came to questions of discipline, then, they held the *position* of teacher in esteem, did not feel it was a position they themselves could even in limited senses occupy, and used their authority over the pupils to try to get pupils to hold it in esteem too.

Thus teachers were expected to be authoritative with pupils, or at the very least to have control over them one way or another. But successfully controlling pupils was not seen as the essence of being a teacher; it was the teacher's possession of school knowledge, indicated by their success on the examinations, which was seen as the ultimate basis of teacher authority, the ultimate criterion by which the teachers and the 'ordinary' were distinguished. And, to point it out once more, those who had this knowledge were outsiders, territorial and class others. A coincidence of terms existed, aligning broad class relations with more micro-social relations of authority.

A 'dual' system thus emerged, unplanned and not clearly recognized by anyone. It was a dual system in a double sense. First, it bolstered traditional school authority by drawing on local cultural forms of authority. Second, this double borrowing resulted in a harmonious pattern in which the way community volunteers took on relations with pupils and the way teacher volunteers did so supported each other in the creation of routines. A feature of this stability was continuous argument and conflicts between adults and pupils in the school throughout the year, and worries about discipline, which never ceased. But the routines were stable ones even though few people were satisfied with them. Pupil-teacher relations were often warm and liked by both teachers and pupils, but failed to get as much 'work' out of the pupils as the teachers desired. Community volunteers found themselves intervening in the activities of the school more often than they thought proper, and everyone seemed to think that daily classroom disruption was at an unacceptable level, pupils as well as adults. Yet the social relationships had taken on routine forms just the same, 'compromise routines' if you like, resolving in practice conflicts which were inherent in the situation.

Conclusions

The Croxteth take-over was a disruption; a minute tearing of the social fabric which allows a peek at some of the underlying threads. It could be viewed as an exaggeration in educational choice and participation – similar to a test which magnifies certain conditions in order to discover the limits within which more moderate applications of these conditions would exert their effects. The altered conditions were those of the formal authority relations within which our schools operate. Formally, Croxteth parents were in total control of their school. Moreover, these were working-class parents, and working-class parents with a critical awareness of conditions on their estate combined with an exceptionally high determination to change them. They barricaded their school from the government and invited in a staff of volunteer teachers who were for the most part critical of traditional modes of teaching and sympathetic to the political cause of the Croxteth community. If the resulting educational practice didn't produce significant alterations, one may presume that the major factors which determine the educational experiences of our children exist in realms other than formal parental rights – that having formal rights to enter the decision-making process of single schools is not the same as having control over the most significant effects those schools exert.

It is misleading simply to proclaim the virtues of free choice and formal rights without providing any attention to the social and cultural contexts in which such freedoms must operate. The analysis presented above, which deals only with the first term of the Croxteth occupation, indicates clearly that formal relations of power over schooling processes are subordinate to cultural conditions which influence the perceptions, choices and informal relations of teachers and parents. The schooling regime established in Croxteth Comprehensive was the product of deep-seated assumptions about the nature of knowledge, the purposes of schooling, and the competency of parents and teachers to make educational decisions. Croxteth parents felt incompetent to intervene in the educational processes they were formally in control of. Yet when middle-class teachers with certain progressive ideals failed to generate the forms of schooling these parents were used to and felt to be 'proper', the parents did indeed intervene and did so in ways which bolstered a presumed 'school authority' – an authority partially of their own creation which yet excluded themselves from the educational processes which have most impact on their children.

Baker's measures seek to increase parental rights for both choosing schools and holding their teachers accountable for what happens inside them. When implemented, they will never result in as much formal control as the Croxteth Community Action Committee had over Croxteth Comprehensive. In light of what occurred in the occupied school, one can expect a basically conservative stance of most parents. In working-class areas, this stance will be conditioned by the same factors outlined in the previous pages – beliefs about the nature of knowledge and the need for a disciplining and controlling institution translated into demands (where such parents feel competent enough to make demands) for strict regimes producing good examination results. For teachers, the problem will be that mere parental demand for examination results is not likely to produce them

– schools will be differentiated by the social class from which the majority of the pupils come, and teachers, with the national control of assessment and curriculum, will be unable to adjust teaching practice and goals to the needs of their students.

However, the full story of Croxteth Comprehensive is also about parental *participation* in schools, which is of course fundamentally different from parental rights of choice and formal involvement on boards of governors. As the months rolled by in occupied Croxteth Comprehensive, the value of participation itself began to show. Parents who worked with children in the school became critical of the plight of the non-examination pupils and started to question the worth of some of the subjects taught. Working alongside teachers in the school made many of their formerly invisible assumptions about knowledge, testing and discipline become objects of their critical awareness. Moreover, the critical perceptions of these parents didn't exactly match those of the teaching staff – teachers were finding they had much to learn from parents in Croxteth (unfortunately, this chapter could not explore these developments which occurred towards the end of the occupation; see Carspecken, 1985; Carspecken, 1989). A dialogue between teachers and parents resulted which may well have led to important and positive alterations of schooling practice, beneficial to the Croxteth community.

It took months of participation for this change in awareness to occur, and when it did the potential alterations which opened up were never tried. There were two main reasons for this. One reason was ironically the victory of the campaign – the parents won back their school legally and yet lost it as a consequence, for they were forced out by the incoming professional teaching staff on state incomes and by the short-sighted educational policy of the local Labour Party, which failed to recognize, and thus maintain, study and nourish, the possible advantages of having so much community involvement (see *Schooling and Culture*, Summer 1984 for a decent description of what occurred). The second reason, however, is more relevant to the current climate in British education. Even as this critical awareness developed amongst the parents and as a constructive dialogue developed between them and the volunteer teaching staff, the examination system still existed to limit the realm of possible change. Parents were beginning to think of possible alternative curriculums for their children, yet national exams and the consequent ranking of knowledge were beyond their powers to change.

Kenneth Baker's proposals seek to create a uniform curriculum and assessment procedure for all British schools, allowing for even less variability than presently exists with the GCSE examinations and than existed at the time of the Croxteth occupation with 'O' levels and CSEs. Disjunctions between local cultures and the middle-class culture of schools will be even more tightly fixed. Baker's proposals are justified with slogans for greater parental freedom and parental powers to influence schools, but working-class parents will have little impact on the educational experiences which their children will be subjected to when these experiences are to be determined primarily by assessment and curricular policies which do not take diversity of class and ethnic cultures into account. Hence the Baker proposals offer more choice and formal rights with one hand, while they consolidate more centralized control over the key factors which actually determine educational experience with the other.

Events in Croxteth help to clarify the question of what an educational policy set in opposition to Baker's programme could look like. Above all, it must make matters of curriculum, assessment and the purposes of schooling clearly problematized – not left to operate as covert supports for relations of domination between schools and underprivileged groups. Part of the policy should seek to make actual participation possible, and part to allow for the resulting ideas to have room for being tried and tested. This would require an assessment policy which is flexible – which would not tie a *single* set of examination skills so tightly to the job market. The full story of Croxteth Comprehensive indicates that working-class participation in schools, combined with ongoing dialogues with teachers, could do much to make education more beneficial for the children of that class.

Notes and acknowledgements

I would like to thank Henry Miller for his enormous support during the course of this study and for helpful comments on early drafts of this paper. I would also like to thank the people of Croxteth who were extremely helpful during the period of research. Finally, I would like to thank the other members of the Education Group at the Department of Cultural Studies, University of Birmingham for their invaluable comments on earlier drafts of this chapter and Richard Johnson in particular for his useful remarks on my entire study of the campaign for Croxteth Comprehensive.

Part Three
Alternatives: Public education and a new professionalism

Introduction to Part Three
Alternatives: public education and a new professionalism

In the last fifteen years public education has been through a trial by torture. Almost every aspect has been fiercely questioned, from left and right, including its public character. The professional practices of teachers and others have been sorely tried and tested, often to breaking point. At the same time, there has been a strenuous canvassing of alternatives to the public or state systems, especially from the right. The later 1980s have seen attempts to insinuate a system based on market principles. In the process, the nature and limits of this right-wing alternative have become clearer.

Our own conclusion is that a system of public education remains indispensable in a modern society. If, in east and west, we are to depend on markets, we must not fall into the free-marketeers' delusion that the market provides all. There are at least three vital arguments against this view and in support of public education.

First, it will not do to rely on the market and on parental choice in education since it is inheritance in the largest sense that is the main vehicle of educational inequality and injustice. This is not to blame parents in any way: it is hard not to see the point of view of parents who have recourse to private or selective education, especially in families disadvantaged in other ways. It is important to insist, however, that the very being of the child – *its* choices and agency – cannot be subsumed into that of its mother or father or other carer, just as a mother's rights must not be subsumed into those of her dependants. It is precisely because children (and mothers) have independent rights that other social influences may intervene in the parent's power to dispose of the child. As we noted in Chapter 2, conservative assumptions about inheritance, parental possession, the family and childish dependence lurk in the shadows of good old 'democratic' parental choice. Enshrined as the sacred principle of education, it will ensure that accidents of birth and parentage are even more determining of a child's opportunities than they are today.

Second, as we argued in Chapter 3, market systems, in association with administrative centralization, are far from neutral. They accentuate differences in resources by permitting parents to buy an enhanced educational provision, and opt out of local forms. They withdraw powerful sources of support from communal provision and tempt teachers to greener pastures. They build up layers of purchasable privilege, easier routes to higher education and well-heeled jobs. Aided by the mechanisms of 1988, they will produce a more differentiated education provision than exists today, for all kinds of social power to colonize. There is nothing wrong with difference as such in our philosophy; difference is a positive especially in terms of culture and social identity. It encourages cultural creativity, borrowing, fusion. The problems arise when difference takes socially segrated forms and is associated with cultural privilege and social power. A system of market provision, policed in the spirit of cultural absolutism, gets us the worst of all worlds: separated provision and pretended cultural unity. This way the advantages of a few are always won to the disadvantage of the many and the creativity of cultural difference is misrecognized as deviance or an 'alien wedge'. Because of the asymmetries of the market – a system of social relations not a neutral mechanism – there is always this awkward question for eager, wealthy Mums or Dads: what does my power to choose mean for my neighbour's child? It is because of this contradiction that some social interventions on behalf of *all* the children are completely justified.

A third consequence of the move to market systems, especially in association with administrative centralization, is to remove educational policies from public debate. It is up to individual parents to choose and the hidden hand of unintended consequences does the rest. The idea of a public political sphere in which educational aims are debated is correspondingly weakened. Again, trust in 'spontaneous' outcomes might not matter in a relatively unified and homogeneous society. In a strongly divided, massively heterogeneous and chronically insecure social order like modern Britain, the combination of market and strong state controls is a recipe for further division. The alternative is a public system which in forms of government and internal relations is sufficiently flexible, open, and well-resourced and staffed to allow an ongoing discussion of social objectives and cultural differences, right up to the modification of forms of social power within the institution itself. If this is to restate the case for a 'liberal' or 'pluralist' social order, it is with this difference: educational systems and their specialist workers have to have the resilience not merely to accommodate difference, but to evoke and negotiate real antagonism too. A pluralism perhaps. A 'new' or 'post-pluralism' perhaps? A Marxist or socialist or New-Times pluralism? A pluralism, anyway, wedded to a complex understanding of power, that recognizes multiple oppressions and works to organize things differently.

The difficulty with this argument – perhaps the stumbling-block of our inherited notion of public institutions – is that the public debate tends to be dominated by professionals of different kinds. There are the professionals of the different public regions – education, health, etc. More weighty, often, are the professional power-dealers – politicians, managers and media men – especially those who speak for the power-centres in economy and institutions. This is why a commitment to public education (or a public anything) must lead rapidly today to considering changes in professional outlooks and organization, and to people-professional alliances against the ruling groups. The role of the professional (including the manager) has to be redefined: not to dominate debate but extend and enable it, drawing in unfamiliar and silenced points of view (of working-class mothers, or of children from 'mixed' and ethnic-minority backgrounds, for example). Compellingly expressed, these interventions often shift the dominant viewpoints. This is not only in the public domain itself, but also in practice on the ground. Professional routines have to be responsive to the very different cultural values and points of view, wishes and social orientations we encounter *in the practice itself.*

It could be argued that this is a retreat from the full-blown egalitarianism of some socialist views – and so it is. These were mistaken in believing that state schooling was an invariable social good and that the problem boiled down to access. This optimism about schooling, which overlooked or preached down the rationality of the school-hating and school-resisting popular responses, was always rooted in particular middle-class and working-class fractions. Education systems may actively reinforce and often unwittingly reproduce the gamut of social inequalities that make up a complex social order. It requires a painstaking politics, careful to identify the tendencies of formal and hidden curricula, to construct an education system which acts against negative inheritances or irrelevant criteria (race prejudice or rigid gender norms, for example), without erecting inequalities on some more 'defensible' ground (e.g. the 'merit' or 'ability' of the individual child).

On their own, schools can never remove inequalities; what they can do is to provide a sphere in which they are revealed and contested, and therefore some of the conditions, especially some subjective ones, for their removal. Students and teachers on both sides of some powerful divide can be made more conscious of the power they wield or resist. They can be enabled to weigh up and negotiate contradictory social situations and messages. We return over and over again to a version of the educational institution as a sphere of *negotiation*, a privileged space since it is supposed to be a place for learning, but not innocent because it incorporates many inequalities and forms of power. In case some connotations offend here, we do not see negotiation as a form of pacification, but rather a means to change, including personal transformation.

This places us, in Hayek's system of thinking, as Utopian or 'constructivist rationalists' of the worst kind (Chapter 3). This is inaccurate, as it happens. Unlike true Utopians and rationalists (according to Hayek) we do not pretend to predict the outcome of negotiated interactions and are not planners or engineers in his sense. We share his scepticism of science. We are in among the rough-and-tumble of imperfect and relative knowledges, along with everyone else. But Hayek's own scale of values – even his view of knowledge – is anchored by the fact that he is content that society remains unequal and unfair, and that men like him, and their children's children, and their immediate neighbours no doubt, continue to enjoy great privileges, in systems of inequality that span the globe. The New Right's espousal of spontaneous common sense, tradition and intuition – all relatively 'unarticulated' forms of knowledge (Chapter 9) – expresses the non-negotiability of this social ideal, and the hope that popular aspirations will not be stirred too profoundly. Making things explicit is a step to being sufficiently conscious about social discrepancies to change them. This is most definitely not the only mode of change, but in educational contexts, under the sign of learning, it must surely be an important one.

This is why the biggest failing of public education is the installing of socially relative points of view as neutral, natural, or absolutely valid. This is the biggest difficulty with the National Curriculum and its associated policies, non-negotiable, both at the 'consultative' and at the school levels, without the help, anyway, of a bit of teacher-parent-pupil-DES subversion. The curriculum allows too little flexibility to the teacher and too little opportunity for new knowledges to be produced in the learning. The same holds for all the deeply naturalized curriculum divisions which we have analysed above: those between the manual and the mental, between the practical and the theoretical, between schooling and training, between the technical and the academic, between the academic and vocational, between the arts and the sciences, between the 'arty' and the 'bookish'. We all, teachers and resisters alike, bounce back and forth across these dichotomies, as helpless as ping-pong balls. Actually these divisions express widespread social orientations to knowledge and are closely articulated to class, gender and race/ethnicity, via longstanding cultural associations, often of a peculiarly English kind. Relativizing, revaluing and eventually dissolving them (not encapsulating them in school subjects and academic and other identities) is the essential condition for reform in the public education system. If we could achieve this, we would disturb some of the deepest cultural foundations of unfairness and allow all children to acquire the range of accomplishments, which we ridiculously split off one from the other.

A second serious set of failings is the infantilizing features of schooling in its later phases. Our ethnographies represent what a chorus of young-adult voices have been shouting for decades: why is school so childish!? Making schools less school-like would have much more beneficial effects than making them private. This reform is a particularly good example of the impossibility of well-rooted changes without negotiation, especially here, between parents, teachers and students. As Chapter 9 so convincingly shows, traditional or authoritarian versions of schooling are sustained as much by parent culture as by teacher strategies. There are conflicts between parents and their children too. Patient, intelligent, cross-class work on this knot of contradictions might, as the unintended experiment of Croxteth showed, unravel a whole tangle.

So public education is an indispensable resource in the broader educational apparatus of a modern society, the more so as it becomes more culturally complex. We cannot allow it to be replaced by a New Right alternative or stolen away by creeping privatizations. The argument has to be had out, over and over again, with those who use their agency to harm most children by seeking special advantages for 'their own'. On the other side we have to assert, over and over again, how honourable the task is of teaching in a *really* public school, and reward it accordingly.

On the other hand, public education needs reform. There are two sides of a reform movement: an 'outside' and an 'inside'. 'Outside', the problem is to overhaul and expand the structures and organization of the school system, especially in terms of its accessibility for all. The implications of this programme are spelt out in Chapter 11, together with an assessment of Labour Party conceptions of reform. What must be the main elements of an organizational reform and expansion? How far do Labour Party plans match what is needed here? Do they go far enough? Chapter 11 was first drafted by Andy Green and revised in the light of group discussion; the section on Labour Party plans was added after comments on our neglect of Labour by our reader.

The greatest weakness of the educational tradition represented by Labour has been the neglect of the 'inside' of educational systems: curriculum content and method, the forms of institutionalization of knowledge and its social consequences, the social dynamics of professionalism and expertise, the forms of pupil-teacher relation, the modes of local democratic control, and participation, etc.

Our two other chapters in Part Three concern these issues. Chapter 10 pulls out some of the more general conclusions from our recurrent discussions of teacher professionalism and the curriculum. This chapter was discussed extensively by all of the members of the group and revised, but as with all our chapters bears the marks of individual concerns, especially James Avis's interest in FE.

We felt that the book should end with an account of one person's practice as a teacher and of attempts to radicalize it (though see also Chapters 5 and 8 especially). Reforming public education is not just a matter of expanding access nor even of shifting professional practices and curriculum categories; it involves personal changes too. Negotiative modes of teaching and managing (as indeed of 'leading' generally) put the knowledges of all participants on the line. Since knowledge always involves personal and social identity too, stakes may be high. In Chapter 12, Richard Johnson draws on his experience of teaching in the Centre for Contemporary Cultural Studies/Department of Cultural Studies, in an account which other teachers may care to 'negotiate.'

10

Educational practice, professionalism and social relations

James Avis

I want to raise three issues on the theme of educational practice and social relations: changing the existing forms of professionalism; the implications of fully recognizing social difference for curriculum and teaching methods; the possibilities of a politics of professionalism. The aim is to contribute to a politically relevant response to the new conditions, a project involving recognition of current difficulties.

What is the good side of professionalism? How can this be developed without strengthening its bad side? What are the limitations which are inscribed in curriculum categories, and in how teachers view them? How can we develop strategies which recognize the constraints on our agency as teachers, which use the spaces Thatcherite policies offer, and yet can move beyond the pragmatism such tactics often suggest?

This involves a dialogue with Richard Johnson's argument in Chapter 3. Is it possible to build a politics of professionalism? How can we work for an alliance between radical professionals and progressive social movements? Although my own profession of teaching is central here, alterations are possible only with comparable transformations elsewhere. Alliances with school governors, parents, educational administrators and managers and others are especially important in any emancipatory project.

Professionalism

Dan McEwan (Chapter 8) illustrates the contradictions and difficulties that face teachers working in a progressive school in the 1980s. His school, by its very atypicality, charts the course of the 'new realism' in education, the success of the New Right in influencing schooling and the real difficulty that critical teachers have in sustaining and developing the emancipatory possibilities that inhere in the educational system. One of the paradoxes in Dan's and in much sociological work has been the finding that teachers have a well-developed sense of justice, fairness and a commitment to the development of their students (Avis, 1988a) but that at the same time these lie within an education system that is involved in the perpetuation of inequality and that stifles the development of many of its students. How is this inconsistency handled? I consider two aspects, both of which have a bearing on the way we think about being a teacher and the nature of professionalism. The first concerns the nature of the teaching nexus and the subsequent construction of student and society. The second focuses on teacher professionalism.

The teacher–student relationship is essentially one-to-one and serves to atomize social relations. Teacher culture, socialization and training stress the individual and their performance (Beyer, 1988). This is compounded by 'subject' cultures; for example, in maths, science and languages there is a presumed developmental and sequential process that students must pass through if they are to learn effectively (Ball, 1981). Such subject cultures tend to individualize educational performance. When students fail to develop, this is understood as a consequence of their failure to move beyond a particular developmental stage. Jan Lee (1987) found that teachers' individualism led them to ignore issues connected to class, race and gender that affect educational performance. Even those teachers aware of the cultural and social impediments to educational success are, because of the teaching nexus, led to neglect or play down 'structural' issues. They, like their 'astructural' colleagues, individualize student relations and perform-ance. The teaching nexus pushes teachers towards a practical individualism that denies the presence of structural inequalities or the recognition of the collective social differences that characterize their students. By practical individualism I refer to the orientations of teachers in their relations with students and the tenor of the accounts provided to explain student perform-ance. For teachers who subscribe to left-wing politics there will often be a contradiction between their practical individualism and their more general political understanding of society (Keddie, 1971).

If these impediments are to be overcome we need to work towards a situation where teachers recognize that the constitution of social differences outside the classroom has a bearing on educational performance. This is not just a recognition of individual difference but an awareness of the patterning of inequality in the wider society and the hierarchical validation of social differences. Such understandings would unhinge the atomistic logic of teaching relations which effectively deny the social and collective differences that are present in the individual.

A more collectively oriented teaching practice requires us to rethink not only the nature of practice but also our conceptualization of teaching and professionalism. This would require us to confront the inherently political nature of teaching. Teaching is based on power relations at the root of which is a struggle over meanings and knowledge. We should recognize the relationship between knowledge and positionality. Students are positioned in terms of class, race and gender, but they also actively position themselves in relation to curriculum categories that reflect wider social divisions. Students' relations to and investments in preferred curriculum categories contribute to the formation of social difference. In the same way as teacher individualism denies the collective, it also denies the political nature of teaching. Ironically the assumed neutrality of teaching, present in contemporary constructions of professionalism, delivers a conservative practice.

Teachers' practical individualism is not simply an ideological or attitudinal construct, but relates to the material conditions in which teachers labour and the way in which performance is evaluated by those with power. The construction of the student–teacher relation has a material basis. The state is crucial as it defines and sets the parameters of teacher professionalism. These parameters are to some extent reflected in the curriculum, as well as in the methods used to assess student performance and appraise teachers. The National Curriculum is a case in point. There is an ongoing struggle by critical teachers to mitigate the educational consequences and to strive for the incorporation of good practice into its proposals. However, the National Curriculum may exacerbate the individualizing tendencies of the teaching nexus, as a result of the emphasis on regular assessment.

Teacher professionalism is a social construct the meaning of which changes historically and varies between educational sectors. Grace (1987) illustrates the way in which conceptualizations of professionalism have developed in England in the twentieth century. He is particularly interested in state responses to teachers and discusses four phases in this relationship. Only the last two are of interest here. These correspond first to the moment of the social–democratic educational settlement, and secondly to its breakdown with the state attempting to regain control over teachers. The basis of the social–democratic settlement was the exercise of professional autonomy in the classroom on the proviso that an active politics was excluded. Grace refers to this as the ethic of legitimated teacher professionalism. Such a construction was profoundly limited, both as a pedagogic strategy and as a conception of professionalism. However, it offered teachers the illusion of autonomy, and a space, the classroom, in which to exercise their professional skills as well as allowing an expression of their commitment to their subject cultures/disciplines. Teaching and subject cultures were constructed as if they were politically neutral. Since the 1960s teachers have been castigated for introducing politically biased materials. Those teachers who attempted to introduce radicalized versions of progressive education have likewise been subject to media abuse and accused of offering students a biased education, one that offers a misleading and corrupting view of society. Grace argues the state is currently attempting to regain control over teachers.

Various means have been used to counter the assumed radicalism of teachers. The generous funding of the Technical Vocational and Educational Initiative (TVEI) can be understood as an attempt not only to provide a more meaningful and market-oriented education for students but also as a means of encouraging teachers to develop approaches and forms of subjectivity befitting the enterprise culture. Changes in the relation between schools and the communities they serve operate within a similar logic. Quasi-market relations now exist between schools, with parents able to select schools. Increased parental representation on school governing bodies is supposed to alert schools to the needs of the consumers they serve. Similarly in further education (FE) there is increased industrial representation on governing bodies. This move towards a market focus should not be understood as an attempt to force education to meet the needs of the consumer but rather as part of a strategy to generate an enterprise culture and requisite forms of subjectivity. The aim is as much to bring industrial perceptions into line with the enterprise culture as it is to meet the needs of industry.

However, alongside these tendencies exist others which have a bearing on teachers and the construction of professionalism. The implementation of the National Curriculum is crucial. Teachers may lose control of the curriculum with task groups laying down the material to be covered and the levels of attainment to be achieved. The political context of the National Curriculum is hardly amenable to the development of critical educational practices. Yet those who aim to implement and develop the National Curriculum face a dilemma: they need teacher and professional support. As a result spaces may be opened up which allow critical practices to develop. For example, in the National Curriculum document *Science for ages 5 to 16* (Department of Education and Science and the Welsh Office, 1988) students are to consider the technological and social aspects of science as well as inquiring into its nature. There is also provision in the National Curriculum for group work. There are spaces that can be taken up and developed to provide students with critical experiences.

Andy Green argues a National Curriculum is not necessarily anathema to a socialist educational project provided it recognizes and validates social differences. But the Conservative version is likely to be prescriptive and limiting. In the proposal of the National Curriculum for *English for ages 5 to 11* (Department of Education and Science and the Welsh Office, 1988) there is provision for media education and verbal skill to be assessed in the vernacular. Both are clearly progressive but sit uneasily with Baker's pronouncements on standard English. It is likely that with the National Curriculum teachers will find their role changes, their subject expertise will be downgraded and they will be turned into vehicles for the delivery of a curriculum made elsewhere. These processes can be seen in primary schools where there is a heavy reliance on pre-published workbooks and learning schemes. This tendency towards de-skilling and proletarianization has been and will be exacerbated by the intensification of labour (Apple, 1987). Current reorganizations in schools and colleges which carry heavier teaching loads and more administrative demands mean teachers have less preparation time and are more likely to turn to pre-published material. Even when they are engaged in curriculum development they may find themselves working within predetermined guidelines set by examination boards and subject to collegiate control, policed by interdisciplinary teams who censor curriculum offerings (Lawn, 1988).

I have stressed the limitations and constraints under which teachers labour, a key ideological element being the construction of teacher professionalism. The ethic of legitimated teacher professionalism remains an important prop of current constructions. It fashions the teacher as an expert in pedagogy and their subject discipline, and views teaching as apolitical. Such a model of teacher professionalism leads inexorably towards the depoliticization of teachers, their domestication and incorporation (Lawn, 1988). If we are to develop educational alternatives that challenge the current directions a new radical conception of teacher professionalism is necessary.

Towards an alternative professionalism

Ironically the Conservative government has highlighted the political nature of education. This has conjoined with teachers' real concerns with providing a valuable and relevant education. Teachers have become increasingly concerned with the educational consequences of Thatcherite policies. However, a resurrection of the social-democratic settlement with its construction of legitimated professionalism is no solution. This is because its model is flawed, with teachers perceived as educational experts who possess the skill and ability to determine the curriculum. It was partly the failure and impositional tendencies of this model that explains the early growth and popularity of the New Right educational critique. A top-down impositional model is hardly likely to win general support or contribute towards the development of a popular critical education.

How then should we attempt to reconstruct our conception of professionalism? We need to develop an approach that does not denigrate the skills and knowledge teachers possess but is able to view these as communal resources. A real debate over the nature of education should be fostered in which teachers are but one set of participants. Other participants would include parents, governors, educational managers and administrators, students and their communities, progressive social movements as well as the more traditional political groupings of the Labour Party and trade unions. Such a debate would go beyond the consumerist orientations embodied in the thinking behind annual parents' meetings. Or the notion of parental choice which views education as a market-place where consumers select the appropriate product. Such constructions atomize and homogenize parents, at best as the universal middle-class parent who exercises choice to benefit his or her child. This construction needs to be replaced by one that recognizes the different collectivities from which parents are drawn.

The ways in which a critical educational debate could be stimulated are uncertain but one thing is clear: the recognition of social difference has to be accompanied by an appreciation of social antagonisms. Critical teachers, professionals, managers, parents, black communities, each of these groups is marked by internal antagonism of class and gender, and between each there are also antagonisms of interest. Not only must antagonisms be recognized, they must also be worked through and in their resolution lead to the reconstitution of each of the main parties in the struggle.

Existing models of teacher professionalism embody a conservative morality embedded in the notion of neutrality. A new construction that attempts to develop an organic relationship to the communities and collectivities that education serves requires a morality that is passionately opposed to the hidden injuries of class, race, gender and sexuality. And that sees part of its task as relating to community needs through providing a locale in which 'really useful knowledge' can be generated and disseminated. Such a model of teacher professionalism has real risks for those involved, for it opens up education to a far wider debate, one which at times will be acrimonious and against which teachers will no longer possess the security of legitimated professionalism. This should be offset against the benefits of such an approach. An education which strives to develop useful knowledge may serve to sustain the commitments and interests of those who otherwise would become disillusioned. Such an education could key into local political struggles and usefully advance the spread of democracy. It is important to recognize that in our understanding of radical professionalism teachers are not simply being placed in the role of educational facilitators who are at the behest of local communities. They are part of that community and have a right to participate democratically in educational discussions. It is not merely a question of teachers organically relating to the communities and collectivities they serve. An organic relationship implies that those communities and collectivities support and sustain their teachers. However, what is possible is constrained by the conditions in which teachers labour.

A radical professionalism means that teachers relate to the communities they serve and recognize students' differential positioning and relations to knowledge. The notion of an apolitical or moral education free of politics is rejected. A radical professionalism undermines the construction of immutable expert knowledge and opens up a debate over the nature and purpose of education which facilitates the development of 'really useful knowledge'. In such a dialogue education becomes a centre of debate and democratic participation and so contributes towards the development of an active citizenship (Giroux, 1987). A commitment towards an open, responsive and interactive schooling facilitates the educational development of many of those students who have been traditionally exluded and thus contributes towards the improvement of educational standards. To create an educational framework in which those who have been denied a voice are actively encouraged to participate requires teachers to review their expectations of those who traditionally fail.

A reconstituted professionalism is tied to a transformed pedagogy in which teachers' skill and knowledge become a resource for students. It recognizes social positioning, the power dimensions of knowledge, and aims to offer students access to knowledge and skills that enable them to explore issues and situations that have a bearing on their life worlds. It thereby enables them to engage with the wider society and be in a position to exercise choice and have some control over their lives.

If teachers are to transform their notion of professionalism this not only necessitates an alteration of the material context in which they work, but also requires parallel changes amongst those other groupings that participate in the educational field. Educational managers and administrators need to reflect on the ways in which their activities and roles need to be changed, as do governors, parents and the community in which educational institutions are placed.

Curriculum divisions

In *The Strange Fate of Progressive Education* I discussed the take-up and reorientation of the ideology and practice of progressive education by the proponents of the training paradigm. The themes of relevance and student interest are re-cast and provided with a vocational focus. The practical application of knowledge becomes paramount, and those immediate forms of knowledge that facilitate this are validated. Here the notion of competence becomes important. The successful student or trainee can competently perform the task at hand, be it stacking a shelf in a supermarket or using a telephone to pass on information to a client. Practical knowledge is stressed as this enables the effective performance of tasks. Attitudes are also significant for without an appropriate disposition trainees may fail to perform adequately. In much of the 'new FE' and the Youth Training Scheme (YTS) a practically focused curriculum has been provided. This represents one of the curriculum divisions present in schools and FE. Other divisions correspond to those between technical and academic curricula. These divisions are not necessarily intrinsically inscribed within the discourses of different subject disciplines but arise from the way in which the curriculum is oriented towards particular students. There is, however, a relationship between the way disciplines have developed and teachers' own orientations and commitments towards the subjects they teach. These often sustain curricular divisions formed around the practical, technical and academic.

Andy Green has described the three-tier structure of FE:

> Tier one comprises students on full-time higher, technical and business courses (B/TEC) and those doing GCE O and A levels . . . Tier two includes craft courses and junior clerical courses (with qualifications from the RSA and the City and Guilds) . . . Tier three includes a disparate array of courses, including those for MSC . . . The Certificate of Pre-vocational Education (CPVE) will be the main form of certificate on many of these courses in future. (1986, p. 105)

The 'new FE' is placed within this third tier. Its stress on the practical ties in with the anti-intellectualism and concern with relevance of progressivism. These themes have been taken up and incorporated into the training paradigm. The resulting curriculum form tends to replicate the division between mental and manual labour, as its stress on the practical, the ability to do, and competency leads to the marginalization of the theoretical and corresponding forms of reflection.

Ironically, in the first and second tiers there is also an emphasis on the practical, particularly courses which have a vocational orientation and which validate the practical application of knowledge. For example, National Diploma courses such as engineering would be a case in point. The difference between these courses and those in the third tier is that the practical is more broadly understood and extends to theoretical knowledge that has, or at least is assumed to have, such applications.[1] Students pursuing craft and National Diploma courses in engineering share a common antipathy towards the inclusion of general studies or communications in their curriculum (see Gleeson *et al.*, 1980; Avis, 1989). This rejection is based on the presumed lack of practical relevance of this input. However, in the case of National Diploma students the marker against which knowledge is judged is not the accomplishment of some immediate task. Rather the emphasis is on understanding technical processes which enable intervention at a higher level to solve engineering problems. In this technical curriculum, theoretical knowledge is not valued for its ability to encourage reflection but for its practical application. Knowledge and theory are instrumentalized, becoming a means to an end, the solution of engineering problems. Such a curricular orientation bears a homologous relation to the mental/manual divide, for it explicitly validates knowledge and theory which have practical application and implicitly dismisses those which do not as meaningless speculation. If knowledge and theory are to provide a solution to practical problems they must be expressed in the form of cause and effect. They thus become removed from their social roots and are expressed in terms of value freedom, objectivity and fact – the language of positivism. Thus the social roots of technical knowledge are ignored. The history of knowledge and theory is bypassed, both being given a hardness and certainty that are unwarranted. Technical knowledge becomes locked into the present. The social processes surrounding its growth are obscured and with this the social interests that underlie its development are occluded. The technical curriculum tends to ignore these processes and validates the existing social relations of production. Denial of these social processes makes it hard to consider alternative technologies or modes of working. This instrumentalism lacks a critical or transformative edge. Its insights remain necessarily partial. It must be recognized that both students and teachers have made personal investments in this form of knowledge. Whilst its insights are partial, it does offer a means to understand and control technological processes and implicitly heralds the possibility of extending this and of understanding the social relations surrounding the application of technology.

Curricular divisions exist between the technical and academic. The latter relates to the traditions of liberal education found in the humanities and social sciences. In this tradition the pursuit of knowledge is good in itself and education aims to broaden and develop the individual. This tradition has often been counterposed against the narrowness of technical and practical education and has been seen as offering real possibilities for the full development of the individual (Beyer, 1988). Holt (1987), in strictures against the new vocationalism, considers liberal education to provide an effective alternative, provided it is cleansed of its academism. Much of academic education's potential has been undermined by abstruseness and distance from the lives and interests of students (see Chapter 4). Herein lies a paradox. The value of academic disciplines lies in their encouragement of reflection, systematization, generalization and their promotion of theoretical understanding. Yet these are often embodied in a curricular form that contradicts them.[2] For example, reflection and the development of theoretical understanding are hardly encouraged in curricular forms that operate with a banking concept and which present knowledge as simply facts to be absorbed. There is a tendency in academic disciplines to operate with a corpus of knowledge. The danger here is that such a stance constitutes the curriculum as a body of knowledge deemed to be factually based and therefore beyond controversy. Many teachers have developed a personal stake and commitment in their disciplines. Such stakes may exacerbate the tendency towards treating knowledge as a collection of facts. Holt (1987) argues that a return to the ethos of liberal education would go some way towards rectifying the distortions of a narrowly based academic education. However, within the liberal tradition there is a tendency towards the objectification of knowledge and a neglect of the differing positionalities that students take up in their relations to it.

Current legislation requires local education authorities to produce curriculum statements. Wolverhampton's is a typically liberal document in which there is a desire to develop the individual and an opposition to the injuries of class, race and gender. The issue of bias is addressed.

> There are further issues which are often regarded as controversial. For example, all young people are entitled to be provided with opportunities to develop an awareness of political and economic issues. It is the responsibility of the school to provide the educational opportunities which will allow and enable pupils to consider these and other important issues at an age and stage of development which is appropriate. *Consideration of controversial issues such as politics or personal relationships must be handled in such a way that avoids bias whilst empowering pupils to make informed personal decisions for their adulthood. Unbalanced influences should have no place in these aspects of the curriculum.*
> (Wolverhampton Borough Council, 1988, p. 18; emphases added)

These sentiments can be applauded and there is a clear antagonism to an uncritical and impositional educational practice in which students are told what to believe. However, the document fails to come to grips with the positionality of students: the varying vantage points from which they address knowledge. The document operates within a particular construction of knowledge that veers towards that found in positivism, a construction that sees knowledge as separate from human interest and inherently neutral. Such an understanding implicitly leads towards the validation of those types of knowledge that secure the present in the interests of those with power. The very neutrality the document seeks to foster, delivers a form of bias. It fails to recognize the social struggles that generate a particular understanding of society. Thus the construction of unbiased and unbalanced accounts is a consequence of the differential power of social groups to validate their conception of society. Bias is not amenable to verification according to some universal and transcultural device.

A similar tendency is found in examiners' reports. I will use the example of 'A'-level sociology where in an examiner's report students are castigated for failing to discuss the relevant material in answer to a question on voting.

> The vast majority of candiates failed to move beyond the deviant voting material of the 50's and 60's (Butler, Stokes, McKenzie and Silver, Parkin *et al.*) and appeared to be completely oblivious to the fundamental changes which have occurred since the mid 70's . . . Key concepts in contemporary psephology such as class dealignment and partisan dealignment were notable mainly for their absence as were references to

the work of Crewe even in the form of uncritical descriptions. (AEB, 1985, p. 272)

Paradoxically this academism is what Holt (1987) criticized and it serves to establish a corpus of knowledge that is separated from the student's life. The irony is that within this and other examiners' reports there has been a consistent plea for an engaged sociology. Yet this is accompanied by a dismissal of students' 'conventional' knowledges:

> For some candidates sociology is a body of knowledge to be ingested and regurgitated in the examination room. This body of knowledge is apparently abstracted from the 'real world' and has no bearing upon it. Sociology's potential as a tool for making sense of the world in which we actually live remains completely unachieved and even unimagined for these candidates. (AEB, 1984, p. 258)

There is a tension between meeting the requirements of academic tradition and of providing a valuable educational experience. These two examples serve to illustrate the need to transform the curriculum divisions within which we work. This requires not only teachers to reflect on the nature of the curriculum but also educational administrators and managers.

The curricular categories discussed, which correspond to existing social divisions, are harmful and limiting. Each category is partial and therefore anti-educative. One response is to suggest that these curricular categories be broken down. A solution is to propose a synthesis that enables the strengths of each to be retained and developed. For example, the connection between progressivism and student interests and definitions of relevance could be an important starting-point. Technical education's concern with the practical is valuable for it raises questions about how knowledge is used. Academism through its encouragement of reflection, theorization, systematization and generalization is also important. It could be argued that if these forms were conjoined a more useful and inspiring curriculum would be created. However, such a synthesis would take us only so far.

What are the reasons for this? These derive from the form of curricular categories, their relation to knowledge and their individualism. Knowledge is construed as either immediately observable and knowable or belonging to an already existing corpus. Students are constituted atomistically and as a result their collective positioning and relation to knowledge are ignored. No recognition is made of the different vantage points from which students address and orient themselves to knowledge, such as those related to the social differences of class, race and gender. If we wish to move beyond the limitation of the existing curricular divisions an approach has to be developed that recognizes the differing positionalities of students and their collectivities. This necessitates a different approach to knowledge which understands education as being involved in the creation of 'useful knowl-edge'. Ben-Tovim *et al.* (1986) provide us with a sense of what this would entail. Whilst referring to the rather different context of local politics they write:

> There is a kind of knowledge which can be constructed out of political practice, for which there is no substitute. It demands a continuous interplay of calculation and testing through struggle within a political context. (Ben-Tovim *et al.*, 1986, p. 9)

Thus knowledge is the product of practice, and through active engagement useful knowledge may be produced. Such an engagement involves taking a particular point of view. It is here that student positioning in relation to knowledge and collectivities becomes important. We are offered another way to view education and the curriculum. The aim is not so much to recover 'dead knowledge' but to engage in developing 'really useful knowledge' so that students can act upon the society and are able to make choices.

Students

In schools and colleges students are divided in all sorts of ways. In our discussions we considered students in school, in college and on training schemes and also their cultural responses to the resulting curricular div-isions. Any alternative practice must be alert to the different orientations and positionalities from which students approach schooling and educational knowledge. What stands out from the ethnographic work is the demand that education offers something useful to students. That is to say, education provides students with credentials that have exchange value or introduces them to knowledge that has practical application. Thus the measure against which education is judged is an instrumental one, whereby education becomes a means to an end.

   Clearly, there is a whole range of social practices with which students are actively engaged that serve to construct their needs and constitute identities, which deliver a particular orientation to knowledge and edu-cation. It is important to recognize not just the cultural processes involved in the construction of these needs and identities but also the stakes and investments that students have made in being particular types of people. It is incumbent upon us to take seriously these investments and orientations. What are these orientations? These reflect curriculum divisions as well as the ways in which students transform them and make sense of educational relations. To simplify, some students are oriented towards the acquisition of practical knowledge that has an immediate application in the world of paid employment (for a more complex discussion of student identities see Chapter 6). Many of those following government training schemes will fall into this category as will some of those placed on Certificate of Pre-Vocational Education (CPVE) courses. Those pursuing more 'academic' courses such as 'A' levels are oriented not so much to the acquisition of practical knowledge as to the attainment of credentials that offer vocational routes or entry to higher education. There are also those in FE and school who are following vocational courses which offer theoretical as well as practical knowledge. National Diploma courses would be a case in point. Here there is a direct vocational linkage and knowledge is assessed in terms of its relevance to the accomplishment of a long-term occupational aim.

What unites these differing orientations is an instrumentalism and tendency to commodify knowledge. Knowledge is perceived as already constituted and the student is merely to absorb it. In both progressivism and the training paradigm students are simply to recover the practical knowledge that is existing or to discover that which they already knew. Similarly the pursuit of credentialism and an instrumental relation to educational knowledge can preclude an active engagement. Thus instrumentalism serves to undermine the critical potential that flows from a serious engagement with academic knowledge. Another consequence of student instrumentalism is that academic, vocational and practical knowledge becomes frozen. This is because the social interests, conflicts and practices that have led to the generation of knowledge are obscured. Curriculum divisions also serve to differentiate students and contribute towards class formation. Students' orientations tie in with particular occupational destinies and thereby contribute towards class formation.

Students' investments and interpretations of curriculum categories serve to fracture their relation to knowledge and this posits false distinctions, such as those between the theoretical and practical, the vocational and non-vocational. If students are to be offered an educational experience that goes beyond the present and offers 'really useful education' these distinctions need to be surmounted. Such a move needs to be attentive to student orientations for if these are ignored or trivialized students will simply reject the educational encounter.

Practice

An effective educational practice needs to operate with two different agendas. The first flows from students' immediate goals and interests. Here the aim is to satisfy students' concerns with, for example, the acquisition of practical knowledge or the attainment of credentials. These interests and demands need to be taken seriously and a real and committed attempt made to meet them. Such an educational practice will only become fixed in the present if it fails to go beyond these short-term interests. At this juncture the second agenda comes into play. Here there is a concern to move beyond the immediate and to show the tentativeness and socially constructed nature of the present. If this is understood the future as well as the present becomes seen as the outcomes of social practice and the possibility of different futures is raised.

Andrew Vickers's discussion of attitudes towards YTS and work illustrates one such approach. He builds upon students' interests in work and uses this to lead to a more general discussion, one able to encompass employer and worker strategies. Students are encouraged to recognize the social conflicts, relations and practices that have led to the current organization of work. Andrew's starting-point is with students' interests. He avoids the major pitfall of progressivism, which is to become trapped in the present and its failure to move beyond the everyday knowledge of students. He is not just concerned with the process of learning but is also interested in its content. This interest is not determined solely through pedagogic considerations but rather through political ones. He is concerned with content that would offer students the opportunity of developing a fuller understanding of the social formation. More important is his commitment towards an educational practice that enables students to make 'choices'. The aim is to draw into the classroom as a resource both student knowledges and those of their communities as well as the 'professional' knowledges available to teachers. Students are offered a range of alternative knowledges which can be drawn upon, combined, or rejected in attempts to understand the social world. Thus students exercise choice and are encouraged to seize control of their own learning. The teacher is not the authorial I, for if he/she were, an anti-educational experience would be offered. Ironically an educational practice predicated on a crude positivism delivers just such an outcome.

If we are to deliver a critical practice we need to move beyond positivism. By positivism I have in mind the notion that knowledge has universal applicability, is objective and value-free. However, not only should our practices encourage students to undermine such a conception, we should also actively encourage the generation of new knowledge. If such an aim were incorporated, pedagogic relations would become more open and educative.

Towards a new politics of professionalism

Chapter 3 explores the way in which Thatcherite politics serve to undermine and attack professionals employed by the welfare state. This is particularly the case in education where blame for many of the inadequacies of schooling has been attributed to teachers. Those teachers who adhere to left politics are particularly open to attack. It is they after all who are supposed to have generated the anti-business culture that permeates much of the educational system and serves to disqualify pupils in their search for employment. Thatcherism has been very effective in capitalizing on popular discontents. The connection between state professionals and the protection of vested interests is a case in point. Vested interests and the forms of association that coalesce around these are seen to jeopardize the smooth running of the market and to place a block on the development of the enterprise culture. This critique applies not only to welfare state professionals but also to liberal professions. The argument implies there is a potential alliance between these diverse groups which could form part of an opposition to Thatcherism. This social bloc has yet to be constituted. To do so state professionals and their organizations need to develop a politics that goes beyond short-term survival and pragmatism. A more assertive and openly political stance needs to be developed. Such a bloc should recognize the social antagonism and differences present within itself. These would need to be made manifest and worked through. Similarly there should be an awareness of mutual problems and the relation between positionality and knowledge and a recognition that knowledge is the result of social practice.

A decade of Thatcherism has led to the politicization of the welfare state. The myth that education, health care, social services are outside politics has been exploded. The danger in being reactive and attempting to secure short-term advantage is that this operates within a terrain that has been set by Thatcherism. If we are to oppose effectively we need to develop a counter-hegemonic strategy and develop political alternatives to Thatcherism.

An alliance of professionals opposed to Thatcherism is insufficient. Any oppositional bloc must necessarily be extended to include all progressive social movements: those that have organized around the oppressions of gender, race and sexuality, and around environment issues, as well as the more traditional groupings of trade unions and socialist parties. Such a social bloc would be able to contest Thatcherite hegemony and offer an alternative vision of society. In the same way as the New Right appropriated the language of the left a new social bloc could reappropriate Thatcherite terms. Notions of choice, consumption, human development, education, the good life, society, social responsibility and citizenship could all be reworked with an emancipatory inflexion.

Whilst the preceding argument can be criticized for its naive Utopianism, without these attributes there is hardly any point in political engagement. But there is another more serious encumbrance that needs to be addressed. The argument has been predicated on the 'good side' of professionalism. There is, however, another side. The New Right has addressed this in its notion of vested interests. If we are to develop a new politics our understanding of professionalism has to be reworked to develop its good side. We can take further education as an example to illustrate the negative side of professionalism. I have in mind the cultures of racism, sexism and technicism. I have used the term culture advisedly to refer to their deep-seated and culturally based form in further education. The social antagonisms these divisions represent have to be taken seriously and transcended in the formation of a critical educational politics.

Practitioners can come up with any number of anecdotes that illustrate the racism and sexism present in FE, and no doubt in other sectors too. I would like to share two recent examples. A black member of staff who held a senior position in a college had his communicative skills continually challenged by management. One manager in particular queried his use of the word 'lacunae'. Did such a word exist? Was it English? (We are left to wonder who the philistine was?) The whole exchange was underpinned by reference to a racist discourse on black speech patterns. The second example refers to a woman teacher's complaint about a page-three-style calendar. When it was discovered that she had complained, pictures of naked women were placed in her room with flaps of paper covering the appropriate parts. Incidents like these are commonplace.

If as professionals we fail to take on board our own complicity in sexist, racist and anti-working-class practices and discourses, our wider alliances will fail – and we will deserve our isolation. If we are male and white, we will be doing what Thatcherism accuses us of – protecting our own interests. More positively, such incidents are opportunities for alliances to be formed, as are all the more formal moves towards 'equal opportunities'. These are valuable in indicating that it is not merely individual prejudice which is involved, but institutional arrangements and power. On the other hand, institutional codes are inadequate if they remain formal only. Real commitment, by the relatively powerful in these relationships, involves a determination to recognize experiences different to our own, and to try to change ourselves and our power accordingly.

There are other impediments to the development of a critical professionalism. For those who work in the welfare state, career paths lead away from professional commitment towards management positions. This has been exacerbated in recent years because of the emphasis placed on market forces and the political demand that welfare state institutions adopt the outlook of business. This is reflected in the proposed reorganization of the National Health Service (NHS), in the incorporation of institutions of higher education (HE), as well as the granting of financial control to school/college governing bodies. Increasingly welfare state managers will find themselves severed from their professional roots and adopting a managerial stance that aims to maximize efficiency and productivity. The more effective managers will use the rhetoric of professionalism to extract surplus labour from their erstwhile colleagues. The logic embodied in managerialism is inherently anti-progressive and anti-democratic. A tendency mirroring managerialism is the proletarianization of professionals and the intensification of their labour. This can encourage a defensiveness and sectional politics as well as the danger of incorporation into a managerialist project.

The new politics necessitates a reworking of institutional and hierarchical divisions that will be messy and contradictory. The relationship between progressive social movements and professionals has been fraught with contradictions. In the same way the relationship between professionals and managers has been equivocal. We have argued for an alliance between progressive social forces and professionals which should be extended to include 'radical' managers. They possess knowledge and skills that would be valuable to a social bloc opposed to Thatcherism and the 'new realism'. If such an alliance were to be developed managers would have to redefine their relationships with these groups. What would be the form of this redefinition? It would be unwise and prescriptive to specify in detail the requirements, but a few broad parameters can be suggested. Managers would need to struggle to create a forum in which 'managerial' decision could be opened up for wider participation. In the past, participatory management has been used to develop a compliant and productive workforce (Edwards, 1979; Storey, 1983). Such strategies are particularly effective in education where notions of professionalism can be manipulated to justify the further exploitation of teachers. Managers need to recognize their past and current histories in which they have used the available ideological tools to extract surplus labour from former colleagues. These tensions can be mitigated if managers conceive of themselves as enablers who strive to support and create conditions favourable to a radical educational project. This conception is rather different from one couched in the language of managerialism, efficiency and output. In the conditions of the 1990s, managers and educational administrators are going to find it increasing difficult to hold on to and develop a progressive practice. As in all spheres the new conditions will not only close off a number of options but will open up new spheres for intervention.

In teacher cultures there are constructions of the parent ranging from the over-aspirant middle-class parent of the unacademic child to that of the indifferent working class. A key element in these is the suggestion that parents are concerned only with their own children. Thatcherism constructs parents in the image of the atomistic consumer as does teacher culture. Despite an underlying insight this construction precludes parents' more general educational interests. In teacher discourse parents are only provided with a legitimate voice in terms of their own child. This limits intervention and ironically only allows the more forceful and articulate parents to intervene, thereby encouraging the perception of the over-aspirant middle-class parent and the passivity of the mass. If we are to develop a more radical educational politics and create a progressive anti-Thatcherite alliance parents in all their diversity must be seen as potential allies. However, in the same way as professionals and managers need to be reconstituted to form a progessive social bloc, so too with parents.

Towards a new politics

An adequate educational politics need to be related to a general politics that is oriented towards the development of a progressive hegemony. Such a politics needs to be a whole politics, one able to encompass a range of different social movements. The struggle is not for a return to a monolithic politics that prioritizes a particular aspect of social relations but rather to a form of politics that validates difference and works through social antagonisms. Such a politics is able to accommodate a range of social identities. It seeks to provide and enable a real politics of 'choice' to develop where people are placed in a position to take control of their own lives. This counter-hegemonic struggle is crucial for it sets the terrain in which progressive practices of all kinds can develop. This then is the long-term goal; the development of a new conception of social relations and society that can be counterposed to Thatcherism and its reflection in the 'new realism' of the Labour Party. An important part of this strategy is the ideological contest to re-appropriate Thatcherite terms for the new politics.

Central to our arguments has been the suggestion that state professionals could be forged into a 'progressive' opposition. Such a political practice is constrained not only by the material conditions in which professionals sell their labour but also by the current construction of professionalism. If a radical project is to develop, professionalism must be redefined. Indeed for those who wish to form a progressive alliance a similar re-evaluation is called for. This applies to all who wish to engage in this new politics whether they be teachers, parents, governors, educational administrators, Labour Party activists or trade unionists.

I have stressed the need for a new politics that battles on the ideological terrain, for without a whole politics more immediate and localized responses will be short-lived and amenable to incorporation. However, in our institutional politics sensitivity to the particular and local is crucial. An adequate educational politics needs to be able to handle these differences which require a recognition of the limitations that face practice in particular sites as well as the more general constraints that flow from the new conditions.

Throughout this book we have stressed the new conditions that confront education: the move towards centralized control of the curriculum, teacher appraisal, proletarianization and the intensification of labour to name but a few. It is important that in the development of new educational and political strategies we recognize the danger of overloading those who oppose the new conditions. This could be accomplished by the formation of an alliance between those who work, study and have an interest in education. In such an alliance mutual support and encouragement could be offered to those who struggle for a better educational future.

This chapter has been written by a teacher and collaboratively discussed with others in the Education Group. It includes the strengths and weaknesses that derive from that vantage point. We do not have all the answers nor the resources to deliver all that is needed. There are real difficulties in arguing for alliances, not just those of antagonism and social difference but strategic difficulties of how, what and where. These remain to be worked upon.

Notes

1 These categories can be further differentiated, between the business and the technical, the academic and the creative, etc.
2 See the various works of the de-schoolers; Paulo Freire coined the term 'the banking concept of education'.

11

Expanding public education

Andy Green

We started this book with a brief essay in our educational history; examining the origins of some of the structural peculiarities of our education system. We must now, in conclusion, look to the future, learning some lessons from our distant and more recent past, and attempting, albeit provisionally, to envision the kind of policies and changes that might be appropriate in education as we approach the third millennium. One of our underlying themes has been the persistent relative underdevelopment of English education, most graphically illustrated in widespread early school-leaving and the very low rates of participation and performance in post-compulsory education and training. We have noted, more generally, the failure of schools to become popular institutions, and the divisions and barriers to access which have resulted from the fragmentary and sometimes opaque appearance of the system as a whole. Low expectations of mass schooling seem to have become a national characteristic, lying at the heart of our individualist and pragmatic culture, and underpinning that weak state commitment to a collective or genuinely public education system.

These singular shortcomings in our schooling are not essentially the failure of postwar social democracy: they go much further back into the liberal politics of the last century; however, they are something with which no postwar government has really come to grips. We have repeatedly failed to modernize and democratize our system, and the results are becoming ever more manifest. With the approach of 1992 and the single European market, these problems will be thrown into sharper relief. The UK will increasingly come to look like the dummy of Europe.

Now is certainly a time for change. Social justice demands an improved education for all. Sheer economic realities make it essential. The low average standards of general education, particularly in languages and science, and the inadequacies of our vocational training are already causing problems. The economic upswing of the mid-1980s demonstrated the problems in our training with considerable skills shortages in many areas. Education authorities are trawling the world's labour markets for qualified teachers, there are shortages of engineers and computer specialists, and we are told that if the National Health Service (NHS) still exists in 1995 and wants to retain present staffing levels it will have to recruit 60 per cent of all suitable qualified female school-leavers. In the competitive economic climate of the single European market, we will experience the handicap of an undereducated and undertrained work force. Germany already has double our proportion of workers with vocational qualifications and France turns out three times more craft level engineers than we do each year (Prais and Wagner, 1982).

Demographic change also calls for major rethinking. By 1995 there will be 23 per cent fewer 16–19-year-olds, making it imperative that we retrain older workers and attract new groups of workers into the labour force. With poor employment rights and maternity provision for women workers, and amongst the worst public nursery facilities in Europe, there could be serious problems in recruiting mature women, to give but one example.

A major new national commitment to improving education and training is clearly in order. However, our analysis of current trends and the contradictory directions of Thatcherite educational policy lead us to doubt whether this is feasible with present policies. Some aspects of recent legislation appear to break with past traditions and offer something new. The National Curriculum and the setting of attainment targets are offered as a way of improving standards. Some kind of legislation, along these lines, has certainly been long overdue and would bring us more closely into line with some of those continental systems which have been more successful in raising the general educational standard of their populations. However, the enormous conservatism of the National Curriculum and the crudity of the testing procedures, now set to rely largely on standardized benchmark testing, rather than teacher assessment, do not bode well for this version of a solution. Also the way in which the National Curriculum has been introduced and the other quite contrary 'free market' measures alongside which it sits make its success most unlikely. The measures in the 1988 Education Act have been imposed without consultation, with scant regard for the accumulation of past good practice in the teaching profession, and in a climate of such financial parsimony and manifest malevolence towards teachers, on whom the success of the operation entirely depends, that one can hardly be optimistic about the results. Furthermore, the drift of these measures, which is certainly in some sense towards a welcome modernization and rationalization of public education, is directly countermanded by other measures designed to take us towards a free market education system.

For years the New Right and the ideologues of neo-liberalism have been arguing for a new, semi-privatized market structure of independent schools. The voucher system was their prize card and we may yet see this played, depending on outcomes within the Conservative Party. For the moment, however, it seems the government is going down the same road but more cautiously, or by other means. As opted-out grant-maintained schools and city technology colleges (CTCs) grow in the next few years, freed from local education authority (LEA) control, they will be self-governing institutions well poised at some future date to become both selective and fee-charging: the prototypes of a new system of quasi-private schools which may yet be generalized through the voucher system, if the realities of the educational world do not first prove them to be products of a land of doctrinal make-believe. Open enrolment and per capita funding are designed to bring the ginseng market forces into education and financial self-government for schools and colleges promises to groom institutions into new paragons of educational enterprise. Training is to be handed over to local employer-led training and enterprise councils (TECs) and higher education will be steeled to new peaks of efficiency and industrial relevance through fee-charging, voucher funding and the tough-minded control of new employer-dominated funding councils. Education plc has been launched.

The results of these measures, if they ever come to fruition, have already been suggested by our analysis (especially Chapters 1, 2 and 3). A market education system would not only be characterized by the gravest inequalities, but it would be most unlikely to deliver the general improvements in standards in education and training that are so clearly necessary. Employers have failed to invest adequately in training for a good century or more, and it seems unlikely if things are left to them that much will change now, despite the optimistic rhetoric of government. Free market liberalism did little for education in the nineteenth century. Why should it do much now? Whatever the individual success of new, elite independent institutions, the cost of marketizing education in the public sector will be immense. Not only will funds and prestige be drained from the state system, but planning and rationalization will become almost impossible. The current planning blight experienced by local authorities, unable to rationalize their post-16 provision because of the danger of schools opting out, is one example. The difficulty local authorities will have in implementing strategic plans for education and training or in redeploying staff in their areas when they have reduced control over individual institutions is another. Education is an essential national resource which requires planning, co-ordination and generous state support, and, as nineteenth-century liberals found to their cost, it is not very amenable to improvement through the undirected efforts of market forces.

The alternative to market anarchy is to make a high-quality public education system a chief priority of the state. This, of course, means devoting more public funds to expand and improve the service. The proportion of our Gross National Product devoted to education has now dwindled to around 5 per cent, a pitiful figure compared with the 9 per cent spent by Sweden and the 7 per cent spent by Canada and the USA

(OECD, 1984, p. 85). It means spending more money to improve the appalling conditions of many school buildings and paying teachers enough to recruit the high-quality applicants that a good education service requires. However, it also means some major restructuring of the system, requiring a political will on the part of governments and some deft handling of some of the sectional interest groups that have frequently resisted change and that Labour governments and local authorities have in the past been reluctant to take on. Such reforms can only be achieved by winning a national consensus for educational reform which would require an effort of political education and leadership that the current opposition parties have shown themselves none too good at in recent years.

Several different levels are involved in any restructuring. In Chapters 10 and 12 we look at such matters as changes in the curriculum and in the forms of teacher professionalism. Here I focus on the overall rationalization of institutions which would render them more accessible to different sections of the public and capable of producing more uniformly high results. Though many changes are involved in the reform of public education this one seems essential.

Post-16 provision is clearly the first candidate for fundamental reform. Its currently chaotic and unintelligible institutional structure is inefficient, wasteful and a major reason for low rates of participation; it badly needs reforming. An integrated system of post-compulsory education and training, organized through local networks of tertiary colleges, would be the most efficient and democratic way of dong this. It would mean extending the notion of comprehensive education up to a further critical period and the success and popularity of existing institutions of this kind suggest that it could well be achieved. This would mean abolishing sixth forms and sixth form consortia which are now an archaic and unpopular structure, and the incorporation of the training networks, currently supervised by the Training Agency, within a single unitary system.

To combine education and training effectively, providing maximum choice for students and the greatest possible access, would mean adopting some kind of modular course structure, long familiar in Sweden and the USA, and replacing the divisive and incomprehensible private examination system with some new kind of credit accumulation framework based on a uniform national model and designed to encourage students to combine general education with vocational training, where each would have parity of prestige.

Higher education likewise needs to be democratized and made more accessible, moving towards the kind of expanded higher education system which already exists in the USA and continental Europe. The major barrier at the moment is the examination system, where entrance based on 'A' levels precludes most students from applying. Reforms in post-16 certification would remove this, but it would remain to encourage the institutions to move faster towards adapting course structures for larger numbers and for different kinds of students, as is already beginning to happen in the polytechnic sector. More attention would need to be paid, for example, to supporting students in their acquisition of the essential skills for studying at this level. The most important enabling feature here would be to start to finance a public higher education system unified across the binary divide, in proportion to its economic and social importance. The polytechnics have already increased their enrolments by over 50 per cent without increased funding. One cannot expect institutions to further expand their intake with static resources, as they are now doing, without a decline in the quality of provision.

Reforms in compulsory secondary education must be designed to improve overall standards and encourage all children to attain high levels in a broad range of subjects. This should include, for all children, subjects and interdisciplinary areas which were excluded, for political reasons, from the 1988 National Curriculum, like social studies and an understanding of cultural differences and relationships. But it should also stress subject areas, like mathematics, science, technology and languages, where levels of achievement, especially in relation to other countries, have often been too low. An essential (and currently neglected) condition for achieving these ends is a much more generous attitude towards financing high-quality teachers, adequate school buildings and books and other equipment.

Reform in secondary education also means changing certain attitudes. We have discussed in earlier chapters (especially Chapter 4) some of the limitations of the 'progressive' pedagogues of the 1960s and 1970s. Although the solutions are crude and inadequate, some New Right criticisms of these approaches have picked on real difficulties and confusions, especially in those versions of progressivism that have tended to concentrate more on the problems of the different cultural starting-points of children and less on the objectives they should reach. This is not to deny the importance of starting-points. We have already argued (see especially Chapter 2) that effective educational practice, and any effective version of a national curriculum, has to take account of the different social orientations to knowledge in the classroom and in society at large. But this insight has to be taken alongside a commitment to aiming for high standards for all children. Understanding differing social orientations – including those embedded in the curriculum subjects and approaches themselves – is an essential condition for challenging conservative resistances and defences and moving towards genuine learning and change. The aim is not to confine what the child can learn within the terms of a particular orientation – working-class pragmatism, for example – but precisely to recognize and then challenge this cultural limitation, in order to make new knowledge and identities available.

It may be because 'relevance' was sometimes understood in a conservative way that low expectations of children were allowed to become a perennial problem, particularly in some subjects for girls, for black children, but in truth for the majority of working-class children. From this point of view some of the features of the argument about relevance and starting-point have functioned as a modern form of the very archaic belief that there was a special kind of education appropriate to working-class minds. There were both right-wing and left-wing variants of this conservative cultural theory.

Against this legacy, by no means 'progressive' or even recent, the need is for a revolution in aspirations. This is not just a matter of teachers aiming higher, but implies deeper and wider cultural transformations. The relation between cultural features formed over long historical periods and more immediate organizational change is complex and hard to predict. Given the obstinately conservative character of English education, however, it seems likely that some relatively drastic set of institutional changes of a rationalizing, standardizing kind will be one essential in the necessary educational revolution. A more uniform structure of public education will do much to encourage normative expectations of higher achievement, but we need to go further than this.

One of the great oversights of the comprehensive movement was the belief that you could achieve greater equality in education simply by creating the structures for access. Unlike other countries we failed to realize that co-ordinated intervention was necessary in the way knowledge is divided up, categorized and taught. It is perhaps more evident than ever that the liberal, do-your-own-thing attitude in education cannot be the basis of a progressive educational policy. In the long term it hindered a real alliance between popular classes and groups, educational 'experts' and critical intellectuals of different kinds. It allowed some very conservative cultural conditions, characteristic of English history, to be reproduced.

There is a sound case, then, for reclaiming the project of a core or national curriculum, despite its immediate Conservative antecedents (it has of course a longer history). Any progressive version would have to differ considerably from what is currently being imposed by the government, both in its mode of introduction (where there must be lengthy consultation and research), and in terms of its forms, contents, and whole political philosophy. Under different political auspices, it would be possible to devise a curriculum that would meet the conditions discussed in Chapter 2 and in a different way Chapters 10 and 12, even by reforming the structures, organization and contents of Mr Baker's version. Such a policy would link with the grass-roots resistance to this burdensome monolith which is now beginning.

As Britain moves into a post-Thatcherite political era, and with the possibility of an alternative government emerging for the first time in over a decade, what then are the prospects for education under a new political regime? At the outset of the 1990s, with the uncertain domestic political climate and momentous international historical changes occurring almost daily, it would be foolish to offer hard-and-fast predictions. We cannot even be certain of a new party in power after the next election, only that the next government will almost certainly have abandoned many of the Thatcherite policies of the 1980s. However, there are certain broad trends which we can identify which do augur well for positive changes in education.

First, it seems that at last a historical reckoning is occurring with regard to the deep-seated and long-standing deficiencies in English education. This may seem paradoxical to many in education who feel that things have never been worse than in the past ten years, and who have long since ceased to take comfort from adages about the darkest hour. Nevertheless, it does seem to be the case that long-neglected problems are now being recognized, and not only by the political parties and the media but also by leading sectors of industry. No one can read the press these days and not be aware of our appallingly low staying-on rates or the low levels of our qualifications compared with France and Germany. The recent campaign launched by BP to increase participation in higher education is a clear sign that the more enlightened industrial concerns are beginning to realize the economic dangers of having an undertrained work-force in the highly competitive economic climate that will exist in Europe after 1992. The present government may not have found the solutions but the problem is clearly on the agenda and economic realities and increasing public awareness will probably keep it there.

The second positive trend relates to the likely effects of our involvement in an increasingly integrated Europe. One of our arguments in this book has been that in many respects English education and training is, and has been, poor in comparison with what is achieved in many continental countries. The development of a single European market is likely to throw this into sharper relief as economic competition highlights the importance of training and as our familiarity with continental education grows. Pressure for improvements in our education and training will almost certainly increase. Furthermore, moves towards implementing the Social Charter will force changes in our system. There is already a powerful movement for improving language teaching and for harmonizing qualifications across Europe. Such pressures are likely to force improvements in some of our weakest areas, like languages, and to encourage some welcome rationalization of our system so as to bring it more in line with other countries.

Lastly, and on the broader political level, our involvement in Europe seems likely to undermine the extreme free market ideologies which have dominated the UK for the past decade and which have, despite Conserva-tive and some left-wing protestations to the contrary, made us as much the political exception in Europe as the ideological vanguard. As the UK rediscovers some of the benefits of a modernized social-democratic politics, such as dominates in much of continental Europe, there could be benefits in many areas of public life, and not least in education. The leading role of the state in encouraging high-quality education through effective planning and adequate resourcing could well re-emerge.

None of these pressures will be to much avail, however, .unless new policies are devised which can bring the changes and improvements which are so badly needed in education. After the recent torrent of Tory legislation on education we cannot expect that another Conservative government, of whatever political hue, would adopt any radical new direction in education for some time. The most that could be hoped would be that it would allow the more unworkable parts of the existing programme to be quietly shelved. What then could we expect from a new Labour government? The recent Policy Review document (Labour Party, 1989b), gives some indica-tion of Labour's alternative educational programme and it is to this which we must finally turn.

Labour has had a hard time reviewing and updating its educational programme. Not only has it had to question the wisdom of some of its earlier progressive policies but it has also had to respond to an agenda decisively set by the Tories – a situation it has not faced before in its history. It is not easy to formulate an alternative vision from such a defensive position. There are also other factors which have prompted caution. Some of the recent reforms, like local management of schools, may have results that cannot be easily predicted in advance; others, like the abolition of the Inner London Education Authority (ILEA),. canot easily be reversed, even by a government which wished they had not occurred. The dominant view in the party is that scrupulous care must be taken to advance no policies which could be attacked as expensive or unworkable or which might lose votes. Furthermore, after a decade of traumatic educational change and with the likely economic problems a new government will inherit, there is a certain resistance to grand plans or the 'big idea'. It is perhaps not surprising then that the new policy programme is cautious and incremental in its approach, even to the point of remaining studiously vague at certain points. Nevertheless there is much in it which suggests that a start has been made in developing a workable alternative to Thatcherite educational policies.

The most refreshing thing about Labour's Policy Review proposals is their unequivocal commitment to raising standards. The sheer depth of the problem of under-achievement is now recognized – arguably for the first time for many years – and the document shows a real readiness to tackle the problem even if this means adopting measures which are unpopular with some teachers. The aim is to create a 'talent-based economy' and a 'new culture of education' (Labour Party, 1989b, p. 1) which would raise the aspirations of all those involved in education. Standards in schools would be improved, particularly in languages and science, and participation rates in post-compulsory education and training would be doubled over a period of years. Access to higher education would also be improved.

How would this be achieved? The measures suggested for secondary schools form the most coherent part of Labour's programme. The policy seems to be to repeal, modify, or supplement the 1988 Education Act as necessary to raise standards but in the context of a planned and comprehensive public education service which remains committed to the ideal of equality of opportunity. The Tory policy of improving standards selectively through the uncontrolled mechanisms of the market is rejected, although certain aspects of market choice would remain. Equally the centralist, anti-consensual approach of the present government towards the control of education is condemned in favour of a return to the traditional model of partnership between teachers and central and local government. However, something has perhaps been learned about the limitations of an excessively *laissez-faire* approach by central government and there are signs that a Labour government would now take a more positive and directive approach to matters like the curriculum and educational standards.

In practice this means that Labour is committed to repealing the grosser and most divisive features of Tory market education policy, like the grant-maintained schools and city technology colleges. Assisted Places would be phased out and there are the familiar proposals to reform the Charities Act to limit the autonomy of independent schools. On some of the other market mechanisms introduced by the Tories, like per capita funding, local management of schools and open enrolment, Labour is clearly reserving its position, no doubt to see how they work out in practice, whilst the provisions relating to the curriculum and assessment will be modified.

In order to raise standards in secondary schools Labour now seems prepared to take more decisive steps than it has done hitherto. It is now unequivocally committed to the importance of a national curriculum in ensuring a well-balanced education and in raising aspirations for all children, although it rightly criticizes the version adopted by the Conservative government as authoritarian and dogmatic. It therefore promises more consultation and further reform to allow more room for cross-curricular teaching and to end the undue prescriptiveness of the current Act as regards the choice of foundation subjects which do not form part of the core of English, mathematics and science. The new national curriculum would also become genuinely national in that it would apply to all schools, including those in the private sector. Likewise on assessment, the Policy Review recognizes the importance of regular assessment for attainment but rejects the over-simplistic and restrictive methods embodied in the government's Standard Attainment Task battery of testing procedures. Instead it recommends a mixed economy of continual assessment, exams and diagnostic tests with records of achievement used to record systematically progress and attainments.

Other measures recommended to improve standards include the creation of an Education Standards Council which would incorporate the present National Curriculum Council (NCC) and School Examinations and Assessment Council (SEAC) and would be responsible for evaluating the performance of schools. Labour promises that school performance would not be evaluated through meaningless league tables of results but rather by measuring how much a given school actually adds to its pupils' learning given where they have started from – the so-called value added principle of evaluation. Exactly how it would do this is not yet clear, but the principle is a welcome improvement on the mechanistic approach of numerical comparisons. The quality of results in a public service like education cannot be measured like production outputs in a manufacturing system nor can they be safeguarded by market competition alone. Rigorous and publicly accountable professional evaluation through internal institutional review and external monitoring must remain the basis of quality control. In a country where all public service is denigrated as bureaucracy many may have doubts about this, but it can be an effective way of ensuring standards in a monopoly public service as in Germany where the quality of teaching is maintained without recourse to competitive market mechanisms. In this respect it is encouraging that the Labour Party also seems inclined to strengthen the role of the inspectorate, which has long been hamstrung by inadequate powers in this country.

The Policy Review also has a good deal to say about the teaching profession and the training of teachers. Much of this can be welcomed as sensible and innovative. A new system of teacher tutors would be instigated to surpervise newly qualified teachers and successful schools would be designated as training schools much like teaching hospitals. Teachers would be given more opportunity to concentrate on their professional duties through the creation of a new tier of teacher assistants. These would have a proper career structure and pay scale and would be able to use their experience to count towards part of their teacher training if they so wished. On teacher pay, however, the Policy Review is sadly equivocal. Teachers would have their negotiating rights returned to them but there is no commitment to improving teacher salaries.

The main weakness in Labour's plans for secondary education arises from the refusal to make commitments on additional funding. The question of teacher pay is shelved and little is said about the need to improve the desperate state of school buildings and the widespread lack of books and equipment. One can only hope that this reticence is mainly prompted by electoral pragmatism since without these additional funds it is hard to see how the morale of teachers and pupils and the quality of institutional provision can be improved. Nevertheless there is a consistency and good sense about many of the proposals which carry credibility and would no doubt win support from large sections of parents and the teaching profession. The programme for post-compulsory education and training, on the other hand, is in many ways less credible and consistent, and represents something of a missed opportunity. Symptomatically post-compulsory education and training are dealt with in separate sections of the Policy Review.

The overall strategic aim in post-16 provision is to increase participation rates in education and training to something like average continental levels. This will mean doubling the present proportion who stay on. Labour proposes to require local education authorities to produce comprehensive plans for increasing participation which would include targets to be agreed with the new Education Standards Council. As far as educational provision is concerned, the Policy Review gives little indication of how any new provision would be delivered. Support is expressed for the Higginson Report's proposal for a five-subject 'A' level to increase the breadth and balance of learning at this age. This would certainly be an improvement on the existing 'A' levels which are far too specialized and provide a major barrier to participation at this level. However, it does not go far enough. The present division between academic and technical qualifications needs to be abolished. If a full-blown credit accumulation system, along Swedish lines, is too radical a step at the present time, then at the least we need to introduce a system of grouped exams like the French *baccalauréat*. This would assess a wide range of subjects taken at upper secondary level but would also require a core of essential subjects to be taken so that students could not choose a totally unbalanced curriculum. The French system also goes some way towards breaking down the academic/technical divide by having a technical *baccalauréat* of equivalent standing to the traditional examination.

The Policy Review also ducks the vexed question of the institutional structure of post-16 educational provision and this is one of its major failings. Allowing local authorities to devise their own arrangements for this age group will be a recipe for continuing the present inefficient muddle. As we have argued at many points in this book, there is really no sensible alternative to rationalizing post-16 education. Sixth forms were never a popular option and declining numbers mean that they are no longer viable. Sixth form consortia are an unsatisfactory compromise and sixth form colleges, whilst popular and effective for the more academic students, are not a solution for the majority of the age group. The only rational alternative would be to introduce networks of upper secondary institutions, big enough to combine academic and technical provision but not so centralized as to lose their community bearings. Whether the break is at 15 or 16, this is the common practice in much of Europe and North America and we already have a successful model of it here with the tertiary colleges. Introduced with sensitivity, in a way that combined the traditions and expertise of schools and colleges, such a system could work. The benefits this would bring to students in terms of access, choice and intelligibility must not be forfeited because of the sectional interests of one particular part of the teaching profession. That the term tertiary college does not even appear in the Policy Review is extraordinary and can only be seen as a serious failure of nerve on the part of the Labour Policy Review team.

Post-16 training, unlike education, receives much more detailed treatment in the Policy Review. Labour acknowledges the inadequacy of the existing Youth Training Scheme and recommends its replacement by a new traineeship scheme for those of 16 and above which would last from six months up to four years. The national training strategy would be devised and overseen by a new national organization called Skills UK, supplemented by local and regional skills organizations. Thus far it seems much like a return to the old Manpower Services Commission (MSC) structure but there are innovations here as well. The traineeships would last up to twice as long as youth training schemes, the first two years being predominantly college-based and a possible further two years, leading to Higher National Certificate standards, being predominantly work-based. Traineeship schemes would be developed by LEAs in collaboration with unions, employers and skills organizations. Trainees would receive an allowance from a National Training fund with the possibility of top-up wages from employers, as occurs now on the better schemes. The whole would be financed from existing resources and from the revenue from a Training Investment contribution, a payroll tax on employers, set at 0.5 per cent of payroll. Companies providing training would have to use qualified instructors. A further scheme, known as Opportunities Training, would be developed for adult workers and the adult unemployed.

The explicit aim here has been to design a training scheme similar to the so-called Dual System operating in West Germany, which the Policy Review calls the best training system in Europe. The latter certainly has considerable merits. It manages to train over 60 per cent of the nation's youth up to craft levels and above (Cantor, 1989). Our own YTS trains less than half the age group and less than a third of these gain craft level qualifications. However, there are a number of reasons why this system might not be so easily borrowed in this country.

Employer-led systems such as the West German one rely for their effectiveness on a high level of employer commitment to training. There has been a long history of this in Germany but the same is not true of the UK where the employers have generally taken a very short-term and minimalist view of training. The relative success of the German system also owes much to the existence of a large cadre of work-place supervisors not only well qualified in their own trades and professions but also trained as instructors. The UK does not have an equivalent resource to the German *Meister* and requiring firms to appoint qualified instructors will not suddenly create one. Lastly there are limitations to employer-based training systems *per se*, which apply even to the best examples. They are particularly sensitive to the ups and downs of the economic cycle, and recruitment inevitably suffers in times of recession; the quality of their training is uneven, with the smaller firms typically providing a rather narrow and plant-specific approach which is the antithesis of what is required in modern (post-Fordist?) economies dependent on skills transferability and good general education; and they tend to reproduce the characteristic class, race and gender inequalities of the labour market since the normal employer recruitment mechanisms apply.

A more promising exemplar for the UK might well be the French or Swedish models of college-based training. The *lycée professionelle* and the *Gymnasieskola* can combine a broad general and technical education in an integrated provision; their recruitment patterns are determined by student demand or fixed quotas and therefore training need not suffer in times of recession or because of employer complacency; and we already have a surplus of the trained personnel to staff them. The main objection to the college-based system is that training can become too theoretical and out of touch with work practices. This need not be the case. The use of work experience and work placements can supplement college courses and, in any case, the role of initial training should be to provide broad, generic vocational preparation, not to implant job- and plant-specific skills. This is properly done by the employer subsequently. As regards colleges being out of touch with work practices, there is an argument that training institutions should be innovators rather than followers of the often archaic practices of British industry. In any case institutionalized links between colleges, professional and certificating bodies, and industrial and service employers can ensure college provision remains relevant to work practice.

Whatever system is adopted, training must be closely linked with post-compulsory education. Despite its promise to 'unify education and training' (Labour Party, 1989b p. 46), Labour's Policy Review patently falls short of this in its proposals. The organization and administration of the two remain separate, and there is no consideration of the proposal for a combined ministry of education and training favoured by many. Courses of general education and training schemes are still seen as separate tracks and there are no clear plans to integrate technical and vocational qualifications. Labour promises to set up a National Vocational Council (1989b, p. 21) to develop a 'comprehensive system of nationally and internationally recognized qualifications', but there is no indication that this would be linked with the Higginson-style reform of 'A' levels which does not include vocational qualifications. The latter is a particularly serious omission.

At the present time the National Council for Vocational Qualifications is engaged in a long-overdue rationalization of vocational qualifications. It is encouraging certificating bodies (like City and Guilds) to modularize their courses and base their qualifications on competencies before they can be validated at one of the five levels of the National Vocational Qualifications. The process has been much criticized, not least by the National Institute for Economic and Social Research, because it is failing to integrate academic and technical qualifications and because its insistence on employer-defined competence criteria is making training even more narrowly job-specific than it already is. This despite the fact that one of the shortcomings of British training has always been its over-empirical and narrowly practical focus. By ignoring this vital area Labour is missing the opportunity to effect a complete overhaul of our outmoded and labyrinthine system of qualifications which does so much to limit young people's opportunities to develop a broad general and technical education.

Lastly, Labour's Policy Review says little about financial support for students staying on after 16. The internal policy document, *Passport to Success* (Labour Party, 1989a), called for a system of grants for 16–19-year-olds in education but the Policy Review does not reiterate the pledge. The issue needs serious further consideration since it will be very hard to increase staying-on rates significantly without offering some fiancial support to those families who cannot currently afford to allow their children to continue in education after the age of 16.

The issue is clearly a difficult one since unconditional grants are very expensive. For instance, if half of all 16- and 17-year-olds were to receive a grant of £35 per week it would cost over one billion pounds;[1] that is more than the total current operating costs of YTS. In order to make some such grant available it would almost certainly have to be means-related or targeted in some way. It might also be necessary to consider transferring some of the resources currently spent on grants for those in higher education to the younger age group.

The present system, where fewer than one in ten 16–19-year-olds in further education receive grants compared with most full-time students in higher education, is demonstrably inequitable, especially so since the latter more often come from affluent families. It is also denying the sector most in need. There is no doubt that the weakest area in our system lies with education at the intermediate 16–19 levels and not in higher education where we actually turn out as many graduates as most other European countries. We can never hope to increase enrolment in higher education far without first improving participation amongst the younger age group. However, we are much more generous towards funding students in our higher education, which is currently the most expensive in Europe in per capita terms, due mainly to the cost of student grants.

Labour is undoubtedly correct to reject the government's student loan system which is expensive to administer and will almost certainly deter students from less affluent families from entering higher education. However, it may need to consider implementing some form of graduate tax, whereby graduates who have found employment repay part of the cost of their grants according to their income. This would release some funds to support the most needy in post-compulsory study. In the long term this would do more to increase working-class participation in higher education than the current grant system, which is already inadequate to support students. It would allow more realistic grants for undergraduates and, by releasing more resources for 16–19-year-olds, would help to remove what is currently the biggest barrier to access, which is the lack of traditional qualifications due to early school-leaving.

Other aspects of Labour policy – for instance, on higher education and primary and nursery schooling – lie outside the purview of this book but it should be stressed that these are also vitally important and receive their due attention in Labour's thinking. This is particularly true of their ambitious plans for pre-school education. Our review of Labour's proposals is therefore incomplete and somewhat lopsided. We give most attention to one area – post-compulsory education and training – where their plans seem least developed. It is worth reiterating then, in conclusion, that we do see an alternative agenda emerging and that there are now new policies coming through which begin to meet the case for the changes we see as necessary.

The challenge facing us in the 1990s is to create a public education system adequate to the needs of all workers and citizens as they emerge at the onset of this new millennium with its rapidly changing economic and social patterns. We have not achieved that in the past and now the demands facing the education system are greater than ever before. It seems that education so often lags behind social realities, struggling to catch up. Now, here in the UK, it seems to require a quantum leap. However, two things now seem crystal clear. One is that if more people are to receive a better and broader education than ever before, our system, developed to reserve high levels of education for the elite, now needs to be modernized and democratized. The other is that if we are to improve education for the majority, and not simply the few, we cannot rely solely on the now not-so-hidden and not-so-beneficent hand of the market. Education must become a chief priority of the state. It is a public and collective concern. It cannot remain merely the individual 'privilege' of those who toil away, so often under-rewarded and undervalued, within it.

Notes

1   US usage here; a thousand million pounds.

12

Ten theses on a Monday morning

Richard Johnson

1 Monday morning: alternative appraisals

I have always wanted to start a working week perfectly prepared: teaching planned, assignments marked, tasks listed, strategies sussed out. The other side of this fantasy is panic on Sunday night and Monday morning. Panic, I used to think, was due to unpreparedness. Now I think 'preparing' is the way I handle fears which go back to a history of movements from 'home' to 'work', including leaving for boarding-school aged 8. Significantly, my panic is over 'work', in the dominant masculine sense, not personal relationships, say, or being a father (though I panic over these sometimes too).

It's plainly irrational. I prepare three hours' worth for a fifty-minute talk. The day over, I wonder what the fuss was about. Tuesdays are easier.

These theses are examples of a self-consciousness about my practice which I would like to have in advance, but rarely do – and never on a Monday morning.

Alternatively, I offer them as an alternative appraisal, a process we must increasingly endure? They may suggest the irrelevance of the official version.

2 Impossible tasks (not persons) 'appraised'

Most professional practices are strictly not possible, especially today. Doctors cannot 'cure' all their patients, teachers don't actually 'deliver' curricula, and social workers cannot solve all their clients' problems. Honest professionals, among friends, admit this. This does not mean that the work is worthless and should be cut – though this fear prevents us being more honest. So why are indispensable tasks so impossible?

The conditions so many public professionals now work under are partly to blame: punishing hours, inadequate resources, political harassment. Even where pay is adequate, the deterioration of resources discourages. At the same time, the problems with which 'social' professionals deal are dreadfully complex. They involve a mix of subjective and objective features, of people and situations. They require an understanding, for instance, of how self-esteem and 'ability' interact, or how social pressure produces ill-health, knowledges still largely intuitive. People's problems far outstrip the hand–me–down diagnoses of political ideologies, whether 'standing on your own two feet' or 'deprivation' – the crass stress on autonomy, or the determinism of 'environment'. There *is* a sense in which people can only help themselves. But stretched to an alibi for systematic individualism this ignores the conditions for such self-determination: the social securities (in the true sense) which are needed.

In addition, professionals are asked to serve contradictory ends. They must help 'clients' yet stay within the social forms prescribed, which are often calculated to limit change and growth. I must educate students, but also assess and grade them. As an educator, I find pleasure and some success in keeping open and hopeful about students, conveying to them their capacity for movement; as assessor I have to label and grade the level achieved. Relationships of learning, which depend on indeterminacy, jolt to the finite close of examination scripts. An equivalent tension in public policy has been the battle over the different modes of assessment ('formative', 'diagnostic', 'evaluative', etc.) for the National Curriculum (e.g. National Curriculum, Task Group on Assessment; see Department of Education and Science and the Welsh Office, n.d. [1987]). Despite the rhetoric of enterprise, the government has sought to limit human capacities within the social horizons it knows, its own 'benchmarks'.

Finally, I am afraid that professional practice is often 'ideological' in the strongest sense. Along with much good sense and really useful knowledge, professional expertise contains some illusory expectations, peculiar investments, vast egocentricities, pleasures of power and control.

So I am suspicious of myself, or colleagues, when there is no irony in our practice, and we play it strictly by the rules. The rules so often depart from what I know that we (teachers and students) can achieve, given the proper conditions and support. I know I would feel angrier still if I had to negotiate the Conservative National Curriculum! But perhaps we all have to learn to work on hostile ground, seeking out the contradictions, concessions and other spaces in official requirements, fortunately far from seamless. Attention to detail in official documents is required as well as the resistant mentality!

More particularly I find attempts at 'appraisal' (of university lecturers and others) ironic, laughable, naive. There is a mighty gap between 'efficiency' and practical effectiveness. In this contradictory world, teaching is a difficult, free-wheeling, somewhat opportunistic practice. It depends on the flows of energy and idiosyncratic pleasures and commitments of all those involved. These do not conform to management criteria. Cost-effective isn't education-effective, anyway: the one points to large lectures, mass examinations, students grabbing grades and lecturers grinding on; the other to the transformations of self and society learning really involves.

In more 'objective' kinds of appraisal it only seems to matter if the indicators are right, never mind the social consequences: masses of books published, a fast 'through-put' of students. I suspect that appraisal is no more than a currency of competition between managers, useful for building empires and legitimating hierarchies of pay and status; useful for control. Accountability to those we work with – trustworthiness – is something else. It involves space for admitting vulnerability unheard of in self-promoting guff.

But the more 'subjective' kinds of appraisal, as advocated in my own institution, may be worse. We are invited to explore our personal aims, and how far we have achieved them, with someone (a head of department or school) with power over our future. How generous! I explore later the importance of developing common aims, but official appraisal can only conceive of such an aim hierarchically. It individualizes and evaluates us as persons, not our tasks or conditions. Such a practice is too skewed by power, anxiety and resistance to have much practical value, except where the informal values of the working group come through, where trust exists anyway.

Professional aims must be debated and negotiated, especially with 'client' groups. Alternative forms of accountability will involve far sharper questions from wider sources than the current mixture of managerial assessments and humanistic 'development'. Who should be accountable to whom, anyway?

3 Informality, group work and alliances

So I find I am forced to work with some distinctions between the formal and informal levels. Formality concerns the duties which management imposes on us. We need to know these rules and to share a knowledge of them with students, so they know where they stand. But informality is about creating spaces for other things to happen. It is uncomfortable, contradictory, to insist on both – good results and these 'other things', but essential.

For many teachers who understand the importance of informality the 'something else' is a decent informal equality of manners with students that dispenses (where possible) with the more authoritarian defences. (In universities a typical defence of the mainly male teachers is to withdraw as persons from their teaching – possible in a lecture hall. This produces a nasty 'objectivity' of style and manner, which is also boring.) The rewards of informality for the teacher, when carried off, can be immense; but, though I consciously use informality, I am rather suspicious of the impulse in myself. I think it is possible to seek emotional support from students, who can give you lots of recognition, without questioning the relations of power of teaching situations. Friendliness and informality make the teacher more vulnerable certainly, and provide negotiative spaces which students may use, but this isn't a substitute for hard thinking about educational arrangements. It is here that group work is an important resource.

The great advantage of working in small groups, with both first-degree and post-graduate students, is that it makes the relations of power which play across educational situations more visible and negotiable. These relations often focus on the teacher. I find I cannot work productively with others, unless my power is explicitly recognized. Then it can be worked on, modified, made productive, even transformed. It sometimes happens, especially in postgraduate groups, that my power to set the agenda or steer the work is completely taken away. Though this is deeply instructive for all concerned, it is not, I think, the only productive outcome. The problem, rather, is to ensure that my power and resources as a teacher can be made to work to the benefit of all involved and for whatever collective project emerges. Of course, these forms of power at which, for the moment, I am the centre, are intrinsically composite: I inhabit the teacher's role certainly, but as a white middle-class male 'old enough to be your father'. It is this combination of features (and many others untheorized) that makes me so powerful in so many situations, and invests the teaching transaction with its wider social significances. There is always a politics of gender, class, age and race (minimally), round the table, in the room. Being nice, having no more of a politics than this, may simply mystify the asymmetries, making them *harder* to turn to others' advantage.

Power networks in groups often condense in the person of the teacher/ leader. Group work is valuable because, with the right 'rules', contexts and levels of trust, it provides optimum conditions for the usual pedagogic relations to be disturbed. But this is only one side of the practice, often its starting-point merely. Group work also draws on primary or face-to-face solidarities to give a concrete form to wider social differences and antagon- isms. The play of relations between teacher and taught is always accom- panied by a play of divisions within the group itself. I have worked with groups which have allied to modify my power and install a new agenda; but with others that have split into warring camps, leaving me 'respon- sible', but not knowing what to do.

In groups constituted around learning (as opposed to 'therapy', say, or sociability) the form in which differences most relevantly appear is in social orientations to knowledge. In ordinary group transactions, like negotiating what to read next week, differences become manifest. Or should do. In practice, there is a prior struggle. Without some prior transformation which sets new rules, some orientations to knowledge will dominate, others be silenced altogether. The group may look to me to set the agenda. Or it may suggest an agenda its members think I will approve of (like plunging into a list of 'difficult' texts). Or the women in the group may defer to those masculine needs which are so confidently announced as knowledges. Or some exceptionally articulate and politically clued-up alliance may override legitimate but quieter needs. Or someone in the group will feel himself entirely different from the others and stop coming. Such interactions happen all at once and the most powerful parties in each case may well be unaware of them.

The process of making all orientations to knowledge speakable, already begins the interplay of power, alliance and learning. Both the more and the less powerful (in any particular set of relations) have key roles here: the less powerful must gain courage to articulate the unspeakable; the more powerful must learn to relativize the framework they feel most comfortable with, to accord legitimacy to alternatives, and eventually give up some power.

It is useful to distinguish between two levels on which such interactions occur. Formally, there is the setting of agenda in the group – agreements about 'curriculum' or 'method'. It is important that such rules are explicit. There is also the informal, intangible play of alliance in discussion and decision-making itself. As the most powerful source of social recognition in a group the alliances the teacher makes are crucial. He or she has to be available to all, but this does not mean neutrality or treating all students as though they occupied the same place in relation to knowledge. The problem, rather, is how to exercise a power in ways that are enabling and empowering for others, so, generally speaking, in ways that equalize. As some recognition of difference and some equalization begins, really useful learning may start for all, not just from 'texts' or authorities, but from each other.

These are 'starting-points' in more senses than one. Though I think I have a distinctive teaching practice, developed over twenty years, much of what I do, successfully or disastrously, remains quite implicit, especially for me. I have not written about it before, even for myself. I wonder if the account is at all recognizable elsewhere – for example, in a school?

4 On indoctrination and fixed minds

The charge of 'indoctrination' levelled at left teachers misses many points. It supposes an impossible cultural theory, interesting, however, for the light it throws on those who use it. According to this view, children or students (or feeble folk unlike the speaker?) can indeed be 'indoctrinated', force-fed with vile ideas. Actually, the 'indoctrinated' resist such power; they transform the meanings of the message. It is normal to refuse knowledge in this way when it is at odds with your own frameworks. The lesson that *is* learned is different from the one that parent, politician, or newspaper editor intends.

My aim in teaching is not to replace an opinion by my own. Part of the pleasure is to put last year's version to fresh tests of truth and relevance. It would be a deprivation to stop learning in this way. I fear absolutism on left and right for the refusal to learn. It isn't only stupidity – a stop in the mind; there's a moral or political angle too: a refusal to admit the points of view of others, not necessarily to agree, but 'to take them on board' in the popular phrase. But I don't want to 'relativize' in my teaching either. I distrust too easy a shifting of frameworks: for an easy life, to impress, for higher marks (though, experimentally, it is interesting!). I'd prefer students to reach a position for themselves, hold it ironically, express it with 'nuance', be open to challenges – all those liberal virtues, yes! But I also want them to *be* somewhere, in the ideas themselves – perhaps in several different places!

It is harder to see that this is my own ideal orientation to knowledge, and that this might be relativized too. 'Fixed minds' have a basis in interest and anxiety and not only among the powerful. Fixity of point of view may be an indispensable defence, yet truly limiting, conservative, self-denying too. It is worth persisting, on another tack, when you meet such resistances: you know you are on to something important after all. Hard to take on board, here, are the criticisms of myself implied by such resistance. I am immobilized by her rejection of my knowledge, her envy for my position, her recognition of my contradictions and my 'hypocrisy' as well. I crave a bit of fixity myself!

Roger Scruton calls his book on Conservatism, a work of 'dogmatics' (Scruton, 1980, p. 11). I have not read a less relativizing author, a student less likely to learn. He glories, in a way I find neurotic, in his own absolutes. Similarly, Mrs Thatcher habitually absolutizes her statements, permitting no space for another point of view. Her model of cultural change is also instructive:

> A culture of courtesy could be reintroduced, and it could begin in the homes and go through the schools and into university life and then business. It could become ingrained and there are still plenty of societies in the world where it was. And, she repeated, it was natural to the British. ('This Is My New Crusade', *Daily Mail*, 29 April 1988)

Hmm . . . who are the 'indoctrinators' now?

5 Open Day; closed careers

The commonest question on University Open Day (when campus seethes with sixth-formers and college-goers) is 'What kind of job can I get with it?' I have an answer, on behalf of cultural studies, I am increasingly unhappy with, not because it is untrue, but because it is so conforming.

What I say is: 'Well, graduates in cultural studies have the same opportunities as arts and social science graduates generally: most go into business, or administration, or teaching, or research. But because we work around the media, leisure and social issues a lot, people often think of careers in these areas.' I end with interesting-sounding achievements of recent graduates.

What I would like to say is: 'Yes, jobs matter, not least for material reasons. But what will you have won for yourself if you get into higher education? Space denied to most others? Space away from the immediate pressures of the career or the marriage, the inevitability of which may change, who knows? Time for a thoughtful critical look at these conformities, and your own place in them? I hope your education will affect the way you see yourself, your history, your society, your values, and how you relate to others, including your intimacies. Cultural studies takes these questions on. It gives you lots of skills, many not usually taught in universities. These may be appreciated by employers of the usual kind, and we need to work on representing them. But many employers just want amenable servants, enterprising in the acceptable ways. Besides, no qualification gives you a job: you have to face the power to hire and fire. You will have to make difficult choices within tight constraints – but don't stop hoping either!'

Hardly revolutionary stuff! But will I risk even this, next Open Day?

6 Painful education

As 'ethnography' and everyday experience show, there's lots of hurt and harm around current educational arrangements: humiliations of exclusion and failure; the pain of being 'treated as a child'; the screaming boredom of being talked at routinely; the feeling of being at a complete tangent to a teacher or a school. For teachers who daily risk something of themselves in their teaching, there is the pain of rejection or worse.

Educational oppressions produce defences even among 'the successful'. As a teacher of BAs and MAs and PhDs I am surprised at the pain and defences uncovered. Always there are consequences for attempts to change. Defences are the main reality, the immediate context of practice, the day-to-day tissue. In more theoretical terms, the resistances of agents, especially their 'common-senses', must be the first objects of effective cultural interventions.

It is hard to convince people that space can be created inside the formalities, defensively seen as unalterable. It takes time to see that a piece of work can concern something that matters to the writer personally or politically. A range of imaginary topics may have to be got through first, phantoms of what the student thinks the teacher thinks is a proper essay/ project/dissertation/thesis. Where a student has long fought for his or her own orientations to knowledge against the grain, the teacher may encounter a resistant fixity of interest: I will do this at all costs; it is at least my own. Rights of participation – limited, contradictory but real – are commonly refused (or hardly heard) because so contrary to expectations: a sensible limitation of personal investment in a process hitherto found disappointing. Faced with the chance of determining their own agenda of study, of negotiating their own questions, students often lose nerve and ask you to decide. Yet when a break is made, self-confidence increases, energies are released and you are challenged yourself to go further. Sometimes positions are reversed: it is your own compromises which are disorganized now; you who disappoints the others.

7 Strategies and alliances

Each day seems politically charged. By actions and reactions I help to change the immediate relations of power, or reproduce them, release learning or corral it in the usual enclosures. I often know when I am not going to have the energy to help things change, but I am sometimes surprised out of this by the daring of others. The evening mood is a barometer of these small successes and failures.

Making alliances means more work but is immensely important, adding a kind of social (because spoken, shared, recognized) reality to projects. I often assume that my most immediate friends and colleagues, especially those I've worked with for a long time, see everything the way I do. It is important to make time to talk about common purposes with people you take for granted as allies. The greatest need, given the conditions, is for mutual support, opportunities to grumble, and time to deal with the subtle (or not so subtle) competitions that creep in. But it is a pity if talk stops there, without attempting to achieve a longer view. Without a collective discourse of this kind, any group (even of two or three), will be tugged hither and thither by the academic routines and the force of government and managerial controls, and lose all sense of a purpose of its own. With common purposes and daily solidarity much can be achieved. But alliances should never be presumed, but have, rather, to be worked at.

How can we move from the more immediate home–and–work-related alliances, to forms that cut across these sites? Unions, school governors and the various professional organizations and networks are important here. Interesting spaces are opened up by the government's promotion of parental involvement in schools, especially where this goes beyond governing bodies to meetings and working parties for special purposes. My most interesting and enlivening political experiences over the last few months have been in an Equal Opportunities group, convened, on the initiative of black parents, at my son's and daughter's school.

The danger of such groups is that they conform to the usual social admixtures – even the same people! The best things about this Equal Opportunities group have been the participation of pupils and the critical perspectives of black parents. Though the group is still insufficiently representative, especially in class and race terms, the usual teacherly/parental perspectives have been disturbed, and there is hope for realistic policies as a result.

As an extension of this experience around a school, I would like to be involved in some form of political engagement that would link the different public professions and contrive a really popular dialogue with clients. Even to get different professionals in one room to compare political notes would be an initiative worth taking. At the same time, it would not be enough to rely on the fact that most professionals are also clients of other professionals and often experience their power. The point is not to construct a politics of professionalism alone, but to modify professional practices by taking account of users' points of view. Such a politics would have to be as attentive to the differences among users and among professionals as to the common elements in professional-client relations. The hope would be to shift the larger political relations of force, including the New Right's advantages, eventually.

8 Let's choose an education!

'You have a right to choose an education for your own children,' they say, by which they mean a school. The two teenagers in our household go to the local comprehensive. I don't 'own' them; they aren't 'children'. They pretty much chose the school themselves, in the limited Thatcherite sense of 'choice'. We found out and advised; they 'chose' between existing options. I'm glad they made the choice they did. They are more alive to difference and inequality than ever I was, perhaps more concretely, more intimately, than I am now. Still, the challenge is interesting: if we/they really could choose . . .?

One criterion might be something less childish. Like so many youthful interviewees in this book, they hate the childishness of school. 'School is for teachers' they say. This may be unfair to teachers, who deserve consideration, but also very shrewd. 'Schools are for adults' might be shrewder. It is important to recall that modern mass schooling was invented for the surveillance and control of juvenile populations, and arose from profound social transformations in the relations between the household and the place of waged work. Only later were attempts made by social radicals to adapt it to 'equal opportunities'. There's this tension still at the heart of modern schooling. Is it avoidable?

The difficulty is to work out alternatives. A more open, permissive, network-like system, as envisaged by de-schoolers in the 1970s, could increase unfairness still further. Some measures for de-institutionalizing education (reducing the compulsory schooling period, for example, and extending 'training') would be gifts to the right and would reproduce the whole historical legacy of anti-education. There would be marvellous opportunities for cutting public expenditure: not 'care in the community' only (without funds), but education on the cheap as well.

But the pro-state-schooling strategy is paradoxical too. On the whole I support the plan of expanding public education, into a 'comprehensive' tertiary stage, and especially expanding 'higher education'. But if compulsory schooling is extended without changes of its form, content, levels of popular control and social context, what is to prevent the same old forms of resistance emerging, the same unequal outcomes, the same disappointing results?

That's why there have to be other dimensions to the reform of public education and its associated structures and cultures. Some of the uncompleted stories of educational reform will have to be taken up again, but in the light of the new post-Thatcher conditions. Top-down institutional changes, by government or professionals, are distinctly limited here: the hope must be for new educational *movements*, not restricted this time to the professionals, or to the schools. We need to articulate alternatives to New Right pieties at every level – in philosophies of teaching and learning, alternative curricula and methods, ways of intervening in existing forms of school and college government, as well as ways of changing the institutional structures in the long term. One element in such a reform should be a rethinking of the institutional constraints of school, and the kind of assumptions about parenting and childhood which underpin them. Only with the kinds of re-orientations discussed in Chapter 10 will the 'expansions' of Chapter 11 yield the results sought. Mere organizational change without the energies that social and political movements bring, will allow the new structures to serve the old reproductive ends.

Our Equal Opportunities experience suggests that devolved school government is now a crucial site on which such a politics can be constructed, more important than or as important as the policies of LEAs. Though the scale of this seems microscopic, most major issues can be raised. In arguing about Equal Opportunities, for instance, groups are forced to face the complexity of relating the different social oppressions, actually constituting the alliances in their policies. Such groups are a key site for the formation of teachers as transformed professionals, where new negotiative skills and identities can be learned. It may even be possible to extend the limited province of such a politics, by linking with the policies of neighbouring schools, especially where 'consortia' of different kinds already exist.

So perhaps that's a major criterion of choice? Choose a school if possible with a staff committed to working with students and the parental community, not just on individual children's problems (though that too) but on the wider social and policy issues. Then get stuck in!

9 Education with everything?

Reform education, yes, not just in structures and access, but in content, context and control. A rather different strategic tack is to turn attention to other sites, but consider them educationally. How do they contribute to the possibilities of social change and human growth? It seems to me that educationists ought to be more confident, but also better informed, about the educational potential (or nullity) of other practices. If we are asked to 'train' (rather as one 'trains' dog, cats or horses?), it seems reasonable to have things to say about what pupils are being trained for, and why such skills, or their impoverishment, are necessary. It is not the case that the division of labour or the work processes themselves are simply determined by technology or even by the pursuit of profit. All kinds of judgements about social uses enter into the choice of technology, or the organization of production and services. Nor are these only about what consumers want. Employers may choose to go for routinization of labour and attempts at tight control, or give more or less real powers of initiative to workers. The hierarchical divisions of labour may be kept as they are, or modified in the direction of the self-determination of the workers.

In the education–labour relationship, the influences, disastrously, are currently flowing one way: from the more conservative models of management into educational practices. One consequence is the coinage of silly jargon with no grasp of the concrete process involved. The notion of 'delivering the curriculum' as though it were a commodity in a package, with a kind of postbox at the other end, is a case in point.

Much the same could be said of other social sites: leisure, the household, friendships and 'relationships'. Each could be given a more educational character, with more opportunities to develop and grow. This will always involve tackling the existing hierarchies, using educational forms to expose them. What would be needed, for example, to ensure the right and opportunity for educational activity to every woman worker at home? What claim to times of her own? What forms of personal network and support? What other kinds of resource? What changes in the social relations of 'home'? What real adjustments of power and of opportunity between 'partners'?

Could we say something similar about 'politics' in its usual narrower sense? In my experience the boredom of college or school is nothing compared with that of most Labour Party meetings. The inflexibility of the party, its inability to take on board new points of view, except pragmatically and therefore, currently, often from the right, rests on the educational atrophy of its everyday practices. Until mainstream left politics regains its sense of intellectual and moral discovery, and acquires an ability to take on unfamilar points of view, it will remain a shadow of its adversary, in or out of government.

Re-reading this I'm struck by the bid I make for the hegemony of education. Still I leave it, as a bid too seldom made.

10 Revolutions and Education Unlimited

Modern theories of revolution are very reasonable. Extraordinary patience is required in the modern 'war of position'. While still refreshed by the insights of Antonio Gramsci's *The Prison Notebooks*, I increasingly wonder if his conception of strategic advance depends on the interwar communist experience of defeat, and even upon the immobilizing conditions of his imprisonment. Where are the gratifications in the long haul, the hard road? What hope for Thatcher's children, or their middle-aged or older parents for that matter, still craving for something speedier?

I wonder if the conditions are not now changing so fast that the long march might become a plodding-along-behind? Yet the old Jacobin/ Bolshevik model – to the barricades, comrades! – hardly matches today's complexities. Perhaps we need a third model of change: with elements of romance or hope, possibilities for immediate action, but 'realist' too!

Often absent is the imagination to grasp the enormity of today's changes and the very different future they open up. As the Soviets and Eastern Europe and Southern Africa seethe, fixed minds in the west on right and 'left' fail to comprehend the collapse of certainties: east versus west; capitalism versus communism; us versus them. Tarnished old folk-tales of Nation and Greatness are polished up instead. New 'thems' are sought apace. How threatening it is to lose a principal 'enemy'! Meanwhile for many of us the political horizons shift in kaleidoscopic ways: nation to continent to globe to eco-sphere, and back not to a national identify but to a region, a community, a particular cultural space, an 'ethnicity'.

As I write, a group of Conservative historians can propose a 'new' history syllabus – 'The Making of the United Kingdom'. There's no irony in the proposal: about the difficulty of naming our society (has 'Britain' gone the way of Albion?); about calling it 'united' or indeed a kingdom; or about seeing it as the end-point of history.

Characteristically in Britain, the most radical edges of change are cultural not 'political'. Because they often do not show up on a formal political map, and indeed are vigorously erased from it, they are often disregarded, especially by the powerful, stuck in their cultural absolutisms. From this point of view cultural change and diversity can only be 'seen' as a problem – the denial of nationhood or identity itself.

Yet the situation is of immense cultural diversity, flux and fission and fusion: tremendous cultural productivity in fact. The cultures of more recently settled communities (the usual subject of 'multiculturalism') are one particularly creative part of this. Even so, cultural differences or 'ethnicities' if you must, do not only arise in relation to 'race'. We live in a continuing cultural tradition, in which social differences have always been strongly marked culturally, often with unusual richness and subtlety. The dominant ways of living have always been negotiated, resisted, trans-gressed, transformed, by groups including social majorities who precisely do not recognize themselves in the main narratives of Britishness: neither in 'the British Way of Life' nor in 'the Making of the United Kingdom'. These groups have had to make up their own identities, subcultures, alternative ways of life, allocating social recognition and approval in ways that differ from the dominant version. It has been very difficult to be Black and British certainly; but it has not been particularly easy to be British (in the approved ways) and self-consciously working-class, or a woman, or gay, or Geordie or Scouse, or socialist, or a dissident member of the middle class. Given the selective character of what counts as English or British (the very specific social and cultural character of the Royal Family, for instance) most of us are bound to occupy this identity with a certain ambiguity.

Today's more-than-usual cultural productivity owes much to the deep-ening of social difference and the acceleration of social change, both produced in part by New Right policies. There has also been an extraordi-nary extension of the sources and kinds of cultural signs and symbols on a world-historical scale. From a metropolitan point of view, whole new systems of belief and living, whole new cultural vocabularies, suddenly come to view. The extraordinary emergence into the western public media of so-called World Musics is a case in point. Contrary to the usual analysis, this shrinking of the world cultural system does not necessarily lead to cultural uniformity. Rather the range of ways of signifying social difference is massively extended, with all kinds of fusions and cross-overs across the cultural systems. We might think, for example, of the diversity in actually lived forms of household in Britain today (rather than the normative stereotype of 'the family'); or the extraordinarily different orientations to religious belief, not just between religious (and irreligious) communities, but also within them; differences of political value – about the kind of society we should have – are certainly as diverse.

The cultural policy of the right is to try to override this diversity and change by reinstalling mono-culture, actually by imaginarily reinventing it, since a uniform Britishness never did or can exist, only a *selective version*, only an *invented tradition*. This cultural policy is 'romantic' certainly but a romantic reaction: it seeks to repress the actual changes and differences, and shrink the cultural world back again to manageable, parochial size. Paradoxically the attempt to unify by refusing or misrecognizing real differences will only deepen the diversity – as it always has. It will force culturally conservative communities to dig in around existing identities. It will encourage more inventive or more secure groups to live out their own alternatives, with an increasing sense of solidarity and difference. The contradictions between 'the British Way of Life' (the official versions) and how we actually live today will become even more manifest, intolerable and absurd.

It is not so much the economy that runs ahead of politics in modern Britain, more the culture, more the ways of life. This opens up tremendous political opportunities. There is a strong possibility of major political transformations of a peculiarly rooted kind. The political frameworks no longer correspond to where the people are; they actually prevent the political recognition of all the diversity and change. In Britain, no less than in China or the Soviet Union, some major shift, some revolution is necessary in the political superstructures – in parties, in policies, but also in the political institutions themselves.

The great need is for forms of politics and of education organized around the negotiation (not the attempted repression) of all these differences. In envisaging this practice, I find it easiest to imagine it as an educational process. This may be because I am a professional educator, completing a book on education, with other teachers (hegemony of education again!); but it may also be that a particular version of educational activity really is the paradigm case for the New Politics, or that it has above all to be 'educational.'

From this point of view, transformative social practice begins with the concrete exploration of how we are differently positioned in society and culture. Any stance which denies this fact will unmindfully reproduce the differences in non-negotiable ways. What the New Right embargoes most – knowledges of society and culture – are indispensable here. As we talk or battle over some particular project, we uncover no cosy and enlightening diversity, but unequal, explosive powers. Collectively we can choose to move in the direction of equality, and into another stage.

Negotiation cannot stop at recognizing differences. Ways must be found to work through antagonisms too: careful, respectful struggles, moments of challenge, anger, real intransigence, but also acceptance, recognition, alliance. The consequences are personal and political. Members have to let go absolutist stances towards 'truth', or culture, or political rectitude. Some defences are dropped. Risks are taken. People change. Change is recognized in others. There is room for celebration. At this point powerful parties fear loss, failure, obliteration. They may get nasty! (As often occupying this position, I can speak from it, though change seems equally difficult from other positions.) If we are to continue with *political struggle*, not wage bloody civil war, the more powerful must make themselves vulnerable by taking on board the claims of others. For this to happen, everyone needs to be assured that some parts of their identity will remain intact, so that change can be risked elsewhere. A most creative move at this stage is to question what benefits accrue from the status quo anyway, even for powerful parties. With the problem of values and desires now squarely posed, it is harder to call out the tanks.

I think that these forms of Education Unlimited occur all the time in classrooms, meeting-rooms, bedrooms and other places. They occur on grander platforms – between movements, nations and 'blocs' – as well. Education Limited seems an attempt to contain them in an increasingly brittle shell. I doubt if it will last much longer.

Bibliography

Adam Smith Institute (1984), *Omega Report: Education Policy* (London: Adam Smith Institute).

AEB (1984), *Report of Examiners*.

AEB (1985), *Report of Examiners*.

Aggleton, P. (1987), *Rebels without a Cause* (London: Falmer).

Aldrich, R. (1988), 'The National Curriculum: an historical perspective', in Lawton and Chitty, op. cit., pp. 21–33.

Allum, C. and Quigley, J. (1983), 'Bricks in the wall: the Youth Training Scheme', *Capital and Class*, no. 21, pp. 5–17.

Althusser, L. (1969), *For Marx* (Harmondsworth: Penguin).

Althusser, L. (1971), 'Notes on ideology and ideological state apparatuses', in *Lenin and Philosophy and Other Essays* (London: New Left Books), pp. 123–73.

Althusser, L. (1972), 'Ideology and ideological state apparatuses', in B. R. Cosin (ed.), *Education: Structure and Society* (Harmondsworth: Penguin), pp. 242–80.

Althusser, L. and Balibar, E. (1974), *Reading Capital* (London: New Left Books).

Anderson, P. (1987), 'The figures of descent', *New Left Review*, no. 161, January–February, pp. 20–77.

Apple, M. (1982), 'Introduction', to M. Apple (ed.), *Cultural and Economic Reproduction in Education: Essays in Class, Ideology and the State* (London: Routledge & Kegan Paul).

Apple, M. (1985), *Education and Power* (Boston, Mass.: Ark).

Apple, M. (1986), 'National reports and the construction of inequality', *British Journal of Sociology of Education*, vol. 7, no. 2, pp. 171–90.

Apple, M. (1987), 'Mandating computers: the impact of the new technology on the labour process, students and teachers', in S. Walker and L. Barton (eds), *Changing Policies and Changing Teachers* (Milton Keynes/Philadelphia, Pa: Open University Press), pp. 75–95.

Archer, M. (1979), *The Social Origins of Education Systems* (London: Sage).

Aronowitz, S. and Giroux, H. A. (1985), *Education under Siege: the Conservative, Liberal and Radical Debate over Schooling* (London: Routledge & Kegan Paul).

Atkinson, P. (1985), *Language, Structure and Reproduction* (London: Methuen).

Avis, J. (1983), 'Curriculum innovation in FE: a case study', *Stencilled Occasional Paper* no. 73 (Department of Cultural Studies, University of Birmingham).

Avis, J. (1984), 'Strategies of survival: pre-vocational students in FE', *British Journal of Sociology of Education*, vol. 5, no. 2, pp. 129–51.

Avis, J. (1985), 'The ambiguities of conformism: academic students in FE', *Sociological Review*, vol. 33, no. 4, pp. 708–40.

Avis, J. (1988a), 'White ethnicity; white racism', *Journal of Moral Education*, vol. 17, no. 1, pp. 52–60.

Avis, J. (1988b), 'Further Education in Transition' (unpublished PhD thesis, Department of Cultural Studies, University of Birmingham).

Avis, J. (1989), 'Student responses to the curriculum: towards an alternative practice', in D. Gleeson (ed.), *Training and its Alternatives* (Milton Keynes: Open University Press).

Ball, S. (1981), 'The teaching nexus: a case of mixed ability', in L. Barton and S. Walker (eds), *Schools, Teachers and Teaching* (Lewis: Falmer), pp. 159–75.

Ball, S. J. (1981), *Beachside Comprehensive* (Cambridge: Cambridge University Press).

Ball, S. J. (1988), 'Staff relations during the teachers' industrial action: context, conflict and proletarianisation', *British Journal of Educational Sociology*, vol. 9, no. 3, pp. 289–306.

Barker, M. (1981), *The New Racism* (London: Junction Books).

Barrett, M. and McIntosh, M. (1982), *The Anti-Social Family* (London: Verso).

Barton, L. and Walker, S. (eds) (1983), *Race, Class and Education* (London: Croom Helm).

Bates, I. *et. al.* (1984), *Schooling for the Dole* (London: Macmillan).

Benn, C. and Fairley, J. (eds) (1986), *Challenging the MSC* (London: Pluto).

Benn, C. and Simon, B. (1972), *Half Way There* (Harmondsworth: Penguin).

Ben-Tovim, G. *et al.* (1986), *The Local Politics of Race* (London: Macmillan).

Bernstein, B. (1975), *Towards a Theory of Educational Transmission*, Vol. 3, *Class, Codes and Control* (2nd edn, London: Routledge & Kegan Paul).

Bernstein, B. (1977a), *Towards a Theory of Educational Transmission*, Vol. 3, *Class Codes and Control* (3rd edn, London: Routledge & Kegan Paul).

Bernstein, B. (1977b), 'Social class, language and socialisation', in Karabel and Halsey, op, cit., pp. 437–86.

Beyer, L. E. (1988), *Knowing and Acting* (Lewis: Falmer).

Bishop, A. S. (1971), *The Rise of Central Authority in English Education* (Cambridge: Cambridge University Press).

Bishop, R. (1984), 'The Management of Decision-Making in Selected County Upper Schools and Community Colleges' (unpublished PhD thesis, University of Birmingham).

Boffy, R. (1984), 'FE and the YTS core', *NATFHE Journal*, October, pp. 18–21.

Boffy, R. and Cave, P. (1982), 'The Youth Training Scheme: a cynical betrayal?, *NATFHE Journal*, December, pp. 25–9.

Bosanquet, N. (1983), *After the New Right* (London: Heinemann).

Boucher, L. (1982), *Tradition and Change in Swedish Education* (Oxford: Oxford University Press).

Boudon, R. (1974), *Education, Opportunity and Social Inequality* (New York: Wiley).

Bourdieu, P. (1973), 'Cultural reproduction and social reproduction', in R. Brown (ed.), *Knowledge, Education and Cultural Change* (London: Tavistock), pp. 71–112.

Bourdieu, P. (1984), *Distinction: a Social Critique of the Judgement of Taste*, trans. R. Nice (London: Routledge & Kegan Paul).

Bourdieu, P. (1986), 'The aristocracy of culture', in R. Collins *et al.*, (eds), *Media, Culture and Society: A Critical Reader* (London: Sage), pp. 164–93.

Bourdieu, P. and Passeron, J. C. (1977), *Reproduction in Education, Society and Culture* (London: Sage).

Bowles, S. and Gintis, H. (1976), *Schooling in Capitalist America* (London: Routledge & Kegan Paul).

Boyd, J. (1977), *Community Education and Urban Schools* (London: Longman).

Boyson, R. (1975), *The Crisis in Education* (London: Woburn Press).

Broadfoot, P. (1985), 'Towards conformity', in Lauglo and McLean, op. cit., pp. 105–19.

Broadfoot, P. (1986), 'Assessment policy and inequality', *British Journal of Sociology of Education*, vol. 7, no. 2, pp. 205–24.

Brunt, R. (1987), 'Thatcher uses her woman's touch', *Marxism Today*, June, pp. 22–4.

BTEC/CGLI (1985), *Certificate of Pre-Vocational Education* Part A, B, C.

Butler, E. (1983), *Hayek: His Contribution to the Political and Economic Thought of our Time* (London: Temple Smith).

Cantor, L. (1989), *Vocational Education and Training in the Developed World* (London: Routledge & Kegan Paul).

Carspecken, P. (1983), 'What kind of education?', *Schooling and Culture*, no. 13, Summer, pp. 15–22.

Carspecken, P. (1985), 'Community action and community schooling: the campaign to save Croxteth Comprehensive', in G. Walford (ed.), *Schooling in Turmoil* (London: Croom Helm), pp. 107–36.

Carspecken, P. (1989), *Community Schooling and the Nature of Power: An Analysis of the Battle for Croxteth Comprehensive* (London: Routledge).

Carspecken, P. and Miller, H. (1983), 'Parental choice and community control: the case of Croxteth Comprehensive', in Wolpe and Donald, op. cit., pp. 154–61.

Carspecken, P. and Miller, H. (1984a), 'Community education in Croxteth', *Forum*, vol. 27, no. 1, Autumn, pp. 8–11.

Carspecken, P. and Miller, H. (1984b), 'Croxteth Comprehensive: curriculum and social relationships in an occupied school', *Socialism and Education*, vol. 11, no. 1, pp. 5–8.

Castells, M. (1977), *The Urban Question* (London: Edward Arnold).

Castells, M. (1978), *City, Class and Power* (London: Macmillan).

CCCS, see Centre for Contemporary Cultural Studies.

Central Statistical Office (1987), *Social Trends* (London: HMSO).

Central Statistical Office (1988), *Social Trends* (London: HMSO).

Centre for Contemporary Cultural Studies Education Group (1981), *Unpopular Education: Schooling and Social Democracy in England since 1944* (London: Hutchinson).

Chitty, C. (1987), 'The comprehensive principle under threat', in C. Chitty (ed.), *Redefining the Comprehensive Principle* (London: University of London, Institute of Education, Bedford Way Papers, no. 32), pp. 6–27.

Chitty, C. (1988), 'Two models of a national curriculum', in D. Lawton and C. Chitty (eds), *The National Curriculum* (London: University of London, Institute of Education, Bedford Way Papers, no. 33), pp. 34–48.

Clarke, J. (1979), 'Capital and culture: the post-war working class revisited', in J. Clarke *et al.* (eds), *Working Class Culture* (London: Hutchinson).

Cockburn, C. (1977), *The Local State: Management of Cities and People* (London: Pluto).

Cockburn, C. (1983), *Brothers: Technology and Trade Unionism in Printing* (London: Pluto).

Cockburn, C. (1987), *Two-Track Training: Sex Inequalities and the YTS* (London: Macmillan).

Cohen, P. (1982), 'School for the dole', *New Socialist*, no. 3, pp. 43–7.

Cohen, P. (1983), 'Losing the generation game', *New Socialist*, no. 14, pp. 28–36.

Cohen, P. (1984), 'Against the new vocationalism', in I. Bates *et al.*, *Schooling for the Dole* (London: Macmillan), pp. 104–69.

Cohen, P. (1986), 'Rethinking the youth question', *Working Paper 3* (Post-16 Education Centre, University of London, Institute of Education).

COI (Central Office of Information) (1988), *Britain 1988: An Official Handbook* (London: HMSO).

Coles, B. (ed.) (1988), *Young Careers* (Milton Keynes: Open University Press).

Community and Youth Workers Union (CYWU), Leicester Branch (1987), 'YTS Revisited: Working Paper on YTS in Leicester'.

Connell, R. W., Ashenden, D. J., Kessler, S., Dowsett, G. W. (1982), *Making the Difference* (Sydney: Allen & Unwin).

Cowling, M. (ed.) (1978), *Conservative Essays* (London: Cassell).

Cox, C. B. and Boyson, R. (1977), *Black Paper, 1977* (London: Temple Smith).

Cox, C. B. and Dyson, A. E. (n.d. [1970]), *Black Paper Two* (London Critical Quarterly Society).

Cox, C., Jacka, K. and Marks, J. (1975), *The Rape of Reason* (London: Churchill).

Cox, C. and Scruton, R. (1984), *Peace Studies: A Critical Survey* (London: Institute for European Defence and Strategic Studies).

Crispin, A. (1985), 'Finance as a means of control in English education: recent trends towards centralisation', in Lauglo and McLean, op. cit., pp. 119–29.

Cuming, D. (1983), *School-leavers, Qualifications and Employment* (available from the author at 6 Holgate, Nottingham).

David, M. (1983), 'The New Right in USA and Britain: a new anti-feminist moral economy', *Critical Social Policy*, vol. 2, no. 2, Spring, pp. 31–46.

David, M. (1986), 'Moral and maternal: the family in the right', in R. Levitas (ed.), *The Ideology of the New Right* (Cambridge: Polity), pp. 136–68.

David, T. (1988), 'The funding of education', in Morris and Griggs op. cit., pp. 28–54.

Davies, B. (1979), 'In whose interest', *National Youth Bureaux Occasional Paper* no. 19.

Deem, R. (1978), *Women and Schooling* (London: Routledge).

Deem, R. (1981), 'State policy and ideology in the education of women, 1944–1980', *British Journal of Sociology of Education*, vol. 2, no. 2, pp. 131–43.

Delphy, C. (1977), *The Main Enemy: A Materialist Analysis of Women's Oppression* (London: Women's Research and Resources Centre Publication).

Demaine, J. (1988), 'Teacher's work, curriculum and the New Right', *British Journal of Sociology of Education*, vol. 9, no. 3, pp. 247–64.

Dennison, S. (1984), *Choice in Education* (London: Institute of Economic Affairs).

Department of Education and Science (1985), *Better Schools* (London: HMSO).

Department of Education and Science and the Welsh Office (1987), *The National Curriculum 5–16: A Consultative Document* (London: DES).

Department of Education and Science and the Welsh Office (1988), *Science for ages 5 to 16: Proposals of the Secretary of State for Education and Science and the Secretary of State for Wales* (London: DES).

Department of Education and Science and the Welsh Office (1988), *English for ages 5 to 11: Proposals of the Secretary of State for Education and Science and the Secretary of State for Wales* (London: DES).

Department of Education and Science and the Welsh Office (n.d. [1987]), *National Curriculum: Task Group on Assessment and Testing* (London: DES).

Department of Employment (1985), *Employment: A Challenge for the Nation* (London: HMSO).

DoE/DES (1986), *Working Together: Education and Training,* Cmnd 9823 (London: HMSO).

Downing, H. (1981), 'Developments in Secretarial Labour: Resistance, Office Automation and the Transformation of Patriarchal Relations of Control' (unpublished PhD thesis, Centre for Contemporary Cultural Studies, University of Birmingham).

Edgar, D. (1986), 'The free or the good', in R. Levitas (ed.), *The Ideology of the New Right* (Cambridge: Polity), pp. 55–79.
Edgar, D. (1988), *The Second Time as Farce* (London: Lawrence & Wishart).
Edwards, R. C. (1979), *Contested Terrain* (London: Heinemann).
Eurostats (1985), *Education and Training*.

Fawcett Society (1985), *The Class of '84: A Study of Girls on the First Year of the Youth Training Scheme* (London: Walworth Rd).
FEU (1979), *A Basis for Choice*.
FEU (1984a), *Competency in Teaching*.
FEU (1984b), *FEU Statement on the Provision of Education and Training for Adults*.
FEU (1984c), *Common Core Teaching and Learning*.
FEU (1984d), *Profiles in Action*.
FEU (1984e), *Towards a Competence Based System*.
FEU (1985a), *Changing the Focus: Women and FE*.
FEU (1985b), *Progressing to College: a 14–16 Core*.
FEU/SCDC (1985), *Supporting TVEI*.
Finn, D. (1982), 'Whose needs? Schooling and the "needs" of industry', in T. Rees and P. Atkinson (eds), *Youth Unemployment and State Intervention* (London: Routledge & Kegan Paul), pp. 41–55.
Finn, D. (1987), *Training without Jobs* (London: Macmillan).
Fitz, J., Edwards, A. and Whitty, G. (1986), 'Beneficiaries, benefits and costs: an investigation of the Assisted Places Scheme', *Research Papers in Education*, vol. 1, no. 3.
Flew, A. (1987), *Power to the Parents* (London: Sherwood).
Foucault, M. (1979), *Discipline and Punish* (Harmondsworth: Penguin).
Foucault, M. (1980), *Power/Knowledge: Selected Interviews and Other Writings*, ed. C. Gordon (New York: Pantheon).
Freire, P. (1972a), *Cultural Action for Freedom* (Harmondsworth: Penguin).
Freire, P. (1972b), *Pedagogy of the Oppressed* (Harmondsworth: Penguin).
Freire, P. (1985), *The Politics of Education* (London: Macmillan).
Friedman, A. L. (1977), *Industry and Labour* (London: Macmillan).
Friedman, M. and Friedman, R. (1980), *Free to Choose* (Harmondsworth: Penguin).
Friedman, M. and Friedman, R. (1985), *The Tyranny of the Status Quo* (Harmondsworth: Penguin).

Gamble, A. (1981), *Britain in Decline* (1st edn, London: Macmillan).
Gamble, A. (1985), *Britain in Decline* (2nd edn, London: Macmillan).
Gamble, A. (1988), *The Free Economy and the Strong State* (London: Macmillan).
Gibb, V. (1983) 'The re-creation and perpetuation of the secretarial myth', in Gleeson, op. cit., pp. 182–96.
Giddens, A. (1976), *New Rules of Sociological Method* (London: Hutchinson).
Giddens, A. (1977), *Studies in Social and Political Theory* (London: Macmillan).
Giddens, A. (1979), *Central Problems in Social Theory* (London: Macmillan).
Giddens, A. (1981), *A Contemporary Critique of Historical Materialism*, vol. 1, *Power, Property and the State* (London: Macmillan).
Giddens, A. (1982), *Profiles and Critiques in Social Theory* (London: Macmillan).
Giddens, A. (1984), *The Constitution of Society* (Cambridge: Polity).
Gilroy, P. (1986), *There Ain't No Black in the Union Jack* (London: Hutchinson).
Giroux, H. (1983), *Theory and Resistance in Education: A Pedagogy for the Opposition* (London: Heinemann).
Giroux, H. (1987), 'Citizenship, public philosophy and the struggle for democracy', *Educational Theory*, vol. 37. no. 2, pp. 103–22.

Gleeson, D. (ed.) (1983), *Youth Training and the Search for Work* (London: Routledge & Kegan Paul).

Gleeson, D. *et al.* (1980), *Further Education or Training* (London: Routledge & Kegan Paul).

Glennerster, H. (1987), 'Goodbye Mr Chips', *New Society,* 9 October, pp. 17–19.

Goldstein, N. (1984), 'The new training initiative: a great leap backwards', *Capital and Class,* no. 23, pp. 83–106.

Gordon, T. (1986), *Democracy in One School* (Lewis: Falmer).

Grace, G. (1987), 'Teachers and the state in Britain', in Lawn and Grace, op. cit., pp. 193–228.

Graham, D., and Clarke, P. (1986), *The New Enlightenment: The Rebirth of Liberalism* (London: Macmillan/Channel 4).

Gramsci, A. (1971), *Selections from the Prison Notebooks*, ed. and trans. Q. Hoare and P. Nowell-Smith (London: Lawrence & Wishart).

Gramsci, A. (1978), *Selections from the Prison Notebooks*, ed. and trans. Q. Hoare and P. Nowell-Smith (New York: International Press).

Gray, J. (1988), 'Hayek', in R. Scruton (ed.), *Conservative Thinkers* (London: Claridge).

Green, A. (1983), 'Education and training: under new masters', in Wolpe and Donald, op. cit., pp. 58–70.

Green, A. (1986), 'The MSC and the three-tier structure of FE', in Benn and Fairley, op. cit., pp. 99–122.

Green, A. (1988), 'Lessons in standards', *Marxism Today,* January, pp. 24–30.

Green, A. (1988), 'Education and State Formation: The Social Origins of National Educational Systems' (PhD thesis, Department of Cultural Studies, University of Birmingham; publication forthcoming, see below 1990).

Green, A. (1989), 'Comprehensive post compulsory education and training: policies and prospects', in C. Chitty (ed.), *Access and Achievement: Studies in Post-Sixteen Provision* (London: University of London, Institute of Education, Bedford Way Papers).

Green, A. (1990), *Education and State Formation: The Rise of Education Systems in England, France & The USA* (London: Macmillan).

Green, D. G. (1987), *The New Right: The Counter Revolution in Political Economic and Social Thought* (Brighton: Wheatsheaf/Harvester).

Griffin, C. (1985), *Typical Girls?* (London: Routledge & Kegan Paul).

Griggs, C. (1988), 'Fee-paying education: the favoured sector', in Morris and Griggs op. cit., pp. 181–202.

Grosch, P. (1987), 'The new sophists: the work and assumptions of the FEU', in Holt, op. cit., pp. 139–64.

Habermas, J. (1981), *The Theory of Communicative Action,* vol. 1, *Reason and the Rationalisation of Society* (Boston, Mass.: Beacon).

Haddon, L. (1983), 'The Social Relations of Youth: a case study of the use of a further education college' (unpublished MA thesis, Department of Cultural Studies, University of Birmingham).

Hall, J. (1985), 'The centralist tendency', *Forum*, Autumn, pp. 4–6.

Hall, S. (1981), 'Cultural studies: two paradigms', in T. Bennet *et al.* (eds), *Culture, Ideology and Social Process* (London: Batsford), pp. 19–37.

Hall, S. (1988), *The Hard Road to Renewal: Thatcherism and the Crisis of the Left* (London: Verso).

Hall, S. *et al.* (1978), *Policing the Crisis* (London: Macmillan).

Hall, S. and Jacques, M. (eds) (1983), *The Politics of Thatcherism* (London: Lawrence & Wishart).

328   *Education Limited*

Hall, S. and Jefferson, T. (eds) (1976), *Resistance through Rituals* (London: Hutchinson).

Halsey, A. H. Heath, A. F. and Ridge, J. M. (1980), *Origins and Destinations* (Oxford: Clarendon).

Hannan, A. (1978), 'Problems, Conflicts and School Policy: a case study of an innovative comprehensive school' (unpublished PhD thesis, University of Leicester; synopsis in (1980) *British Journal of Sociology of Education* vol. 1, no. 1, pp. 107–9).

Hargreaves, D. H. (1967), *Social Relations in a Secondary School* (London: Routledge & Kegan Paul).

Hargreaves, D. H. (1982), *The Challenge for the Comprehensive School, Culture Curriculum and Community* (London: Routledge & Kegan Paul).

Harris, R. and Seldon, A. (1963), *Choice in Welfare* (London: Institute of Economic Affairs).

Harris, R. and Seldon, A. (1987), *Welfare without the State* (London: Institute of Economic Affairs).

Haviland, J. (1988), *Take Care, Mr Baker!* (London: Fourth Estate).

Hayek, F. ([1942–4] 1952), *The Counter-Revolution of Science* (Illinois: Free Press).

Hayek, F. ([1944] 1976), *The Road to Serfdom* (London: Routledge & Kegan Paul).

Hayek, F. (1960), *The Constitution of Liberty* (London: Routledge & Kegan Paul).

Hayek, F. (1979), *Law, Legislation and Liberty*, Vol. III, *The Political Order of a Free People* (London: Routledge).

Hebdige, D. (1979), *Subculture: The Meaning of Style* (London: Methuen).

Hillgate Group (1986), *Whose Schools? A Radical Manifesto* (London: Hillgate Place).

Hillgate Group (1987), *The Reform of British Education* (London: Claridge).

Hindess, B. (1987), *Freedom. Equality and the Market: Arguments on Social Policy* (London: Tavistock).

HMI (1985), *The Curriculum from 5 to 16* (London: HMSO).

Hobsbawm, E. J. (1969), *Industry and Empire* (Harmondsworth: Penguin).

Hollands, R. (1985), 'It's your life! – male working-class youth's orientations towards educational comics', in C. Points (ed.), *Working Papers for 16+ Media Studies* (Clwyd: Clwyd Media Studies Unit), pp. 133–45.

Hollands, R. (1990), *The Long Transition: Class, Culture and Youth Training* (London: Macmillan).

Hollway, W. (1984) 'Gender difference and the production of subjectivity', in J. Henriques et al., *Changing the Subject: Psychology, Social Regulation and Subjectivity* (London: Methuen).

Hollway, W. (1989) *Subjectivity and Method in Psychology: Gender, Meaning and Science* (London: Sage).

Holt, M. (ed.) (1987), *Skills and Vocationalism: The Easy Answer* (Milton Keynes: Open University Press).

Hough, J. R. (ed.) (1984), *Educational Policy: An International Survey* (London: Croom Helm).

Humphries, S. (1981), *Hooligans or Rebels?* (Oxford: Blackwell).

Huws, U. (1982), *Your Job in the Eighties* (London: Pluto).

Illich, I. (1971), *Deschooling Society* (New York: Harper & Row).

Illich, I. (1973), *Deschooling Society)* (Harmondsworth: Penguin).

Institute for Manpower Studies (1984), *Competence and Competition* (London: MSC/NEDC).

Jaggar, A. (1983), *Feminist Politics and Human Nature* (Brighton: Harvester).

Jessop, B. et al. (1984), 'Authoritarian populism, two nations, and Thatcherism', *New Left Review*, no. 147, pp. 32–60.

Johnson, R. (1982), 'Reading for the best Marx', in R. Johnson *et al.* (eds), *Making Histories: Studies in History Writing and Politics* (London: Hutchinson), pp. 153–201.

Johnson, R. (1983), 'What is cultural studies anyway?', *Stencilled Occasional Paper* no. 74 (Department of Cultural Studies, University of Birmingham).

Johnson, R. (1988), '"Really useful knowledge" 1790–1850: memories for education in the 1980s', in T. Lovett (ed.), *Radical Approaches to Adult Education: A Reader* (London: Routledge & Kegan Paul), pp. 3–34.

Johnson, R. (1989), 'Thatcherism and English education: breaking the mould or confirming the pattern?', *History of Education,* vol. 18, no. 2, June, pp. 91–121.

Jones, K. (1983), *Beyond Progressive Education* (London: Macmillan).

Jones, S. (1988), *Black Culture, White Youth* (London: Macmillan).

Kaestle, K. F. (1983), *Pillars of the Republic: Common Schools and American Society, 1780–1860* (New York: Hill & Wang).

Karabel, J. and Halsey, A. H. (eds) (1977), *Power and Ideology in Education* (Oxford: Oxford University Press).

Katz, M. (1971), *Class, Bureaucracy and Schools: The Illusion of Educational Change in America* (New York: Praeger).

Keddie, N. (1971), 'Classroom knowledge', in M. F. D. Young (ed.), *Knowledge and Control* (London: Collier Macmillan), pp. 133–60.

King, R. (1976), *School and College* (London: Routledge & Kegan Paul).

Kogan, M. (1971), *The Politics of Education: Edward Boyle and Anthony Crosland* (Harmondsworth: Penguin).

Kogan, M. (1978), *The Politics of Educational Change* (Glasgow: Fontana).

Labour Party (1989a), *Passport to Success* (London: Labour Party).

Labour Party (1989b), *Meet the Challenge, Make the Change* (London: Labour Party).

Labour Research, (1983), Labour Research Department, December.

Lacey, C. (1974), *Hightown Grammar* (Manchester: Manchester University Press).

Larrain, J. (1979), *The Concept of Ideology* (London: Hutchinson).

Larrain, J. (1983), *Marxism and Ideology* (London: Macmillan).

Larson, M. S. (1977), *The Rise of Professionalism: A Sociological Analysis* (Berkeley, Calif.: University of California Press).

Lauglo, J. and McLean, M. (eds) (1985), *The Control of Education* (London: Heinemann).

Lawn, M. (1988), 'Skill in school work', in Ozga, op. cit., pp. 161–76.

Lawn, M. and Grace, G. (eds) (1987), *Teachers: the culture and politics of work* (Lewis: Falmer).

Lawn, M. and Ozga, J. (1981), 'The educational worker: a re-assessment of teachers', in L. Barton and S. Walker (eds), *Teachers: The Culture and Politics of Work* (Lewes: Falmer).

Lawton, D. and Chitty, C. (eds) (1988), *The National Curriculum* (London: University of London, Institute of Education, Bedford Way Papers, no. 33).

Lee, J. (1987), 'Pride and prejudice: teachers, class and an inner-city infants school', in Lawn and Grace, op. cit., pp. 90–116.

Leicester City Council, Employment and Economic Development Unit (1985), 'Youth Unemployment in Leicester'.

Leicester City Council, Leicestershire County Council (1983), 'Survey of Leicester; Initial Report of Survey'.

Leicestershire County Council (1987), 'Your Move: School Leavers Information Pack 1986/87'.

Levitas, R. (ed.) (1986), *The Ideology of the New Right* (Cambridge: Polity).

Lipset, S. M. and Bendix, R. (1967), *Social Mobility in Industrial Societies* (Berkeley, Calif.: University of California Press).

Livingstone, D. *et al.* (1987), *Critical Pedagogy and Cultural Power* (London: Macmillan).

Lodge, D. (1980), *How Far Can You Go?* (London: Secker & Warburg).

Low, G. (1988), 'The MSC: a failure of democracy', in Morris and Griggs, op. cit., pp. 215–28.

MacDonald, M. (1977), *The Curriculum and Cultural Reproduction*, Units 18 and 19, Schooling and Society Course (Milton Keynes: Open University Press).

MacDonald, M. (1981), 'Schooling and the reproduction of class and gender relations', in R. Dale *et al.* (eds), *Education and the State* (Sussex: Falmer), pp. 159–78.

MacKinnon, C. A. (1983), 'Feminism, Marxism, method and the state: an agenda for theory', *Signs*, vol. 7, no. 3, pp. 515–44.

Maclure, J. S. (1986), *Educational Documents, England and Wales, 1816 to the Present Day* (London: Methuen).

McRobbie, A. (1978), 'Working-class girls and the culture of femininity', in Centre for Contemporary Cultural Studies, *Women Take Issue* (London: Hutchinson), pp. 96–108.

Mager, R. F. (1962), *Preparing Instructional Objectives* (Belmont, Calif.: Fearon).

Marquand, D. (1988), *The Unprincipled Society* (London: Cape).

Marx, K. ([1852] 1973), 'The Eighteenth Brumaire of Louis Bonaparte', in K. Marx, *Surveys from Exile* (Harmondsworth: Penguin), pp. 143–249.

Marx, K. ([1857] 1973), *Grundrisse: Foundations of the Critique of Political Economy*, ed. and trans. Martin Nicolaus (Harmondsworth: Penguin).

Maw, J. (1988), 'National Curriculum: policy, coherence and progression', in Lawton and Chitty, op. cit., pp. 49–64.

Melton, J. van H. (1988), *Absolutism and the Eighteenth-Century Origins of Compulsory Schooling in Prussia and Austria* (Cambridge: Cambridge University Press).

Midwinter, E. (1972), *Priority Education* (Harmondsworth: Penguin).

Minns, H. and Dombey H. (n.d. [1988]), *National Curriculum in English for Ages 5 to 11* (Sheffield: National Association for the Teaching of English).

Moon, B. (ed.) (1983), *Comprehensive Schools: Challenge and Change* (Windsor: NFER-Nelson).

Morris, M. and Griggs, C. (eds) (1988), *Education – The Wasted Years? 1973–1986* (Lewis: Falmer).

MSC (1984a), *Core Skills in YTS*, Part 1 and 2.

MSC (1984b), *Competence and Competition* (London: NEDC).

MSC, Leicester (1986), 'YTS in Leicester'.

MSC (1987), 'Youth Training News', July.

Mulhall, M. (1884), *Dictionary of Statistics* (London).

Murphy, J. (1972), *The Education Act, 1870: Text and Commentary* (Newton Abbot: David & Charles).

Neave, G. (1975), 'The reform of secondary education in France', *Forum*, Spring, pp. 58–61.

No Turning Back Group of MPs (1986), *Save our Schools* (London: Conservative Political Centre).

OECD (1984), *Educational Trends in the 1970s* (Paris: OECD).

Offe, C. (1985), 'New social movements: challenging the boundaries of institutional politics', *Social Research*, vol. 52, no. 4, Winter, pp. 817–68.

Ozga, J. (ed.) (1988), *School Work* (Milton Keynes/Philadelphia, Pa: Open University Press).

Ozga, J. and Lawn, M. (1988), 'Schoolwork: interpreting the labour process of teaching', *British Journal of Sociology of Education*, vol. 9, no. 3, pp. 323–6.

Palmer, F. (1986), *Anti-Racism: An Assault on Education and Value* (London: Sherwood).

Peacock, A. and Wiseman, J. (1964), *Education for Democrats* (London: Institute of Economic Affairs).

Pickvance, C. (ed.) (1976), *Urban Sociology: Critical Essays* (London: Methuen).

Polanyi, K. (1946), *Origins of Our Times: The Great Transformation* (London: Gollancz).

Pollert, A. (1981), *Girls, Wives and Factory Lives* (London: Macmillan).

Pollert, A. (1985), *Unequal Opportunities* (Birmingham: TURC Publishing).

Popper, K. (1961), *The Poverty of Historicism* (London: Routledge & Kegan Paul).

Poulantzas, N. (1975), *Classes in Contemporary Capitalism* (London: New Left Books).

Prais, S. J. and Wagner, K. (1982), *Some Practical Aspects of Human Capital Investment: Training Standards in Five Occupations* (London: National Institute of Economic and Social Research).

Racial Equality in Training Schemes (REITS) (1985), 'YTS or White TS?: Racial Discrimination and Coventry's Youth Training Scheme'.

Ringer, F. K. (1979), *Education and Society in Modern Europe* (Bloomington, Ind.: Indiana University Press).

Roderick, G. and Stephens, M. (eds) (1981), *Where Did We Go Wrong?* (Lewes: Falmer).

Rogers, T. (ed.) (1971), *School for the Community: A Grammar School Reorganizes* (London: Routledge & Kegan Paul).

Rose, J. (1989), 'Mrs Thatcher and Ruth Ellis', *New Formations*, no. 6, Winter, pp. 3–29.

Salter, B. and Tapper, T. (1981), *Education, Politics and the State: The Theory and Practice of Educational Change* (London: Grant McIntyre).

Salter, B. and Tapper, T. (1985), *Power and Policy in Education: The Case of Independent Schooling* (Lewes: Falmer).

Sampson, A. (1962), *Anatomy of Britain* (London: Hodder & Stoughton).

Sampson, A. (1982), *The Changing Anatomy of Britain* (London: Hodder & Stoughton).

Saunders, P. (1983), *Urban Politics, a Sociological Interpretation* (London: Hutchinson).

Scofield, P. *et al.* (1983), *The Tories' Poisoned Apple* (Leeds: Independent Labour Publications).

Scruton, R. (1980), *The Meaning of Conservatism* (London: Macmillan).

Scruton, R. (1981), *The Politics of Culture and Other Essays* (Manchester: Carcanet).

Scruton, R. (ed.) (1988), *Conservative Thinkers: Essays from the Salisbury Review* (London: Claridge).

Scruton, R., Ellis-Jones, A. and O'Keefe, D. (1985), *Education and Indoctrination* (London: Education Research Centre).

Seidel, G. (1986), 'Culture, nation and "race" in the British and French New Right' in Levitas, op. cit., pp. 107–35.

Seldon, A. (1986), *The Riddle of the Voucher* (London: Institute of Economic Affairs).

Sexton, S. (1987), *Our Schools: A Radical Policy* (London: Institute of Economic Affairs).

Sharp, R. (1980), *Knowledge, Ideology and the Politics of Schooling* (London: Routledge & Kegan Paul).

Sharp, R. and Green, A. (1975), *Education and Social Control* (London: Routledge & Kegan Paul).

Simon, B. (1981a), *Education and the Labour Movement, 1870–1920* (London: Lawrence & Wishart).

Simon, B. (1981b), *The Two Nations and the Educational Structure, 1780–1870* (London: Lawrence & Wishart).

Simon, B. (1985), *Does Education Matter?* (London: Lawrence & Wishart).

Simon, B. (1987), 'Lessons in elitism', *Marxism Today*, September, pp. 12–17.

Simon, B. (1988), *Bending the Rules: The Baker 'Reform' of Education* (London: Lawrence & Wishart).

Smith, R. and Knight, J. (1982), 'Liberal ideology, radical critiques and change in education', *British Journal of Sociology of Education*, vol. 3, no. 3, pp. 217–34.

Social Trends (1987), *see* Central Statistical Office.

Social Trends (1988), *see* Central Statistical Office.

Spender, D. (1982), *Invisible Women* (London: Writers and Readers Co-operative Society).

Stafford, A. (1981), 'Learning not to labour', *Capital and Class*, no. 15, Autumn, pp. 55–78.

Stanton, G., 'A profile of personal qualities', in FEU (1984d).

Stanworth, M. (1981), *Gender and Schooling* (London: Women's Research and Resources Centre).

Stone, M. (1980), *The Education of the Black Child in Britain* (London: Fontana).

Storey, J. (1983), *Managerial Prerogative and the Question of Control* (London: Routledge & Kegan Paul).

Tapper, T. and Salter, B. (1978), *Education and the Political Order* (London: Macmillan).

Tawney, R. H. (1931), *Equality* (London: Unwin).

Taylor, W. (1981), 'Contraction in context', in B. Simon and W. Taylor (eds), *Education in the Eighties: The Central Issues* (London: Batsford), pp. 17–37.

Tilly, C., Tilly, L. and Tilly, R. (1975), *The Rebellious Century* (London: Dent).

Troyna, B. (1985), 'The great divide: policies and practices in multi-cultural education', *British Journal of Sociology of Education*, vol. 6, no. 2, pp. 209–24.

Troyna, B. (1986), '"Swann's Song": the origins, ideology and implications of education for all', *Journal of Educational Policy*, vol. 1, no. 2, pp. 171–81.

TUC (1987), 'The Education and Training of Girls'.

Unemployment Unit (1988), *Unemployment Bulletin*, no. 28, Autumn.

Venables, E. (1967), *The Young Worker at College* (London: Faber).

Walkerdine, V. (1984), 'Developmental psychology and child centred pedagogy', in J. Henriques *et al.*, *Changing the Subject* (London: Methuen).

Walker, P. (ed.) (1979), *Between Labour and Capital* (Boston, Mass.: South End).

Walkerdine, V. (1986a), 'Progressive pedagogy and political struggle', *Screen*, vol. 27, no. 5, September–October, pp. 54–60.

Walkerdine, V. (1986b), 'Post-structuralist theory and everyday social practices: the family and the school', in S. Wilkinson (ed.), *Feminist Social Psychology* (Milton Keynes: Open University Press).

Warner, R. (1945), *English Public Schools* (London: Collins).

West, E. G. (1965), *Education and the State* (London: Institute of Economic Affairs).

West, E. G. (1975), *Education and the Industrial Revolution* (London: Batsford).

Whitehead, J. and Aggleton, P. (1986), 'Participation and popular control on school governing bodies: the case of the Taylor Report and its aftermath', *British Journal of Sociology of Education*, vol. 7, no. 4, pp. 433–49.

Whitty, G. (1985), *Sociology and School Knowledge: Curriculum Theory, Research and Politics* (London: Methuen).

Whitty, G. and Young, M. (eds) (1976), *Explorations in the Politics of School Knowledge* (Driffield: Nafferton).

Williams, R. (1965), *The Long Revolution* (Harmondsworth: Penguin).

Williams, R. (1981), *Keywords* (London: Fontana).

Willis, P. (1975a), 'How working class kids get working class jobs', *Stencilled Occasional Paper* no. 43 (Department of Cultural Studies, University of Birmingham).

Willis, P. (1975b), 'The main reality: transition school/work: SSRC report', *Stencilled Occasional Paper* no. 3 (Department of Cultural Studies, University of Birmingham).

Willis, P. (1976), 'The class significance of the school counter-culture', in M. Hammersley and P. Woods (eds), *The Process of Schooling* (London: Open University/Routledge & Kegan Paul), pp. 188–200.

Willis, P. (1977), *Learning to Labour* (Farnborough: Saxon).

Willis, P. (1978), *Profane Culture* (London: Routledge & Kegan Paul).

Willis, P. (1979), 'Shop-floor culture, masculinity and the wage form', in J. Clarke *et al.* (eds), *Working Class Culture* (London: Hutchinson), pp. 185–98.

Willis, P. (1981), 'Cultural production is different from cultural reproduction is different from social reproduction is different from reproduction', *Interchange*, vol. 12, nos 2/3, pp. 48–67.

Willis, P. (1983), 'Cultural production and theories of reproduction', in Barton and Walker, op. cit., pp. 107–38.

Willis, P. (1985), *The Social Condition of Young People in Wolverhampton in 1984* (Wolverhampton: Wolverhampton Borough Council).

Wolpe, A-M. and Donald, J. (eds) (1983), *Is There Anyone Here From Education?* (London: Pluto).

Wolverhampton Borough Council, Education Department (1988), *Statement of the Curriculum*.

Woods, P. (1983), *Sociology and the School* (London: Routledge & Kegan Paul).

Young, M. (ed.) (1971), *Knowledge and Control: New Directions in the Sociology of Education* (London: Macmillan).

Youth Employment and Training Research Unit (YETRU) (1987), *Confidential: Racism* (Birmingham: Youth Employment and Training Research Unit).

Youth Training Scheme (YTS) Monitoring Unit (1985), *The Great Training Robbery Continues* (Birmingham: TURC Publishing).

Index